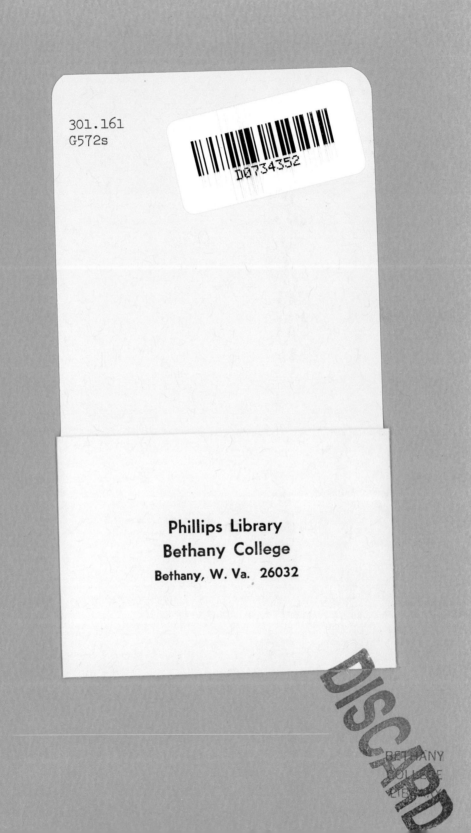

The Show and Tell Machine

The
Show
and
Tell
Machine

How Television Works and Works You Over

ROSE K. GOLDSEN

THE DIAL PRESS
New York

Published by The Dial Press
1 Dag Hammarskjold Plaza, New York, New York 10017

Manufactured in the United States of America

First printing

Library of Congress Cataloging in Publication Data

Goldsen, Rose Kohn.
The show and tell machine.

Includes bibliographical references and index.
1. Television broadcasting—Social aspects—
United States. I. Title.
HE8700.8.G64   301.16'1   77-22694
ISBN 0-8037-8614-X

To Imagination
To Authenticity
To Gabriela Samper

CONTENTS

FOREWORD

A generation ago, people in this country began to watch images of wrestlers, trained poodles, and pitchmen on television sets placed mainly in public places such as bars and store windows. Today the television set, standard equipment in the American home, so blurs the distinction between the public environment and the privacy of the family that it is ever present even as the tiniest babies are ushered into the social system. Human beings whose primal impressions come from a machine—it's the first time in history that this has occurred. What such an innovation might mean for the way human consciousness develops, quite apart from the content of materials the machine transmits, nobody yet knows.

"Call me at this number," says Joe Mannix, one of television's vast army of private detectives. The audience hears him repeat a seven-digit number beginning with 555, the exchange that connects a caller with Information. Any other seven-digit number is likely to be assigned to a subscriber. So many people in the coast-to-coast audience will dial a telephone number they hear over the air that giving Mannix a real number would amount to harassment of the person unlucky enough to possess it.

Rhoda marries Joe ("Rhoda"). Throughout the country people celebrate the event. Thousands of presents arrive at CBS headquarters on both coasts, at the local stations relaying the network feed, and at the offices of the MTM Company, the show's producers. The packages are addressed to Miss Rhoda Morganstern, the fictional lead.

Children in a sixth-grade class prepare their annual assembly entertainment for parents. They decide on a variety show featuring a chorus dressed as Mouseketeers, a skit poking fun at daytime serials, another starring a New York police lieutenant who is totally bald. An eleven-year-old baton twirler goes through her paces accompanied by an orchestral medley that includes the music of the McDonald's commercial, "We Do It All for You."

On July 28, 1976, New York Governor Hugh Carey signs a bill exempting the television set from being appropriated to satisfy money judgments. The set now joins all other "utensils necessary for the judgment debtor and family," immune from garnishment along with wearing apparel, household furniture, tableware, and cooking equipment.

Examples like these abound. They remind us that television surrounds us; that we are a suggestible lot; that, although individual behavior may be unpredictable, many aspects of mass behavior are quite easily manipulable through the power of suggestion. They should remind us, further, that at best only a blurry and highly permeable line separates what we think of as an objectively real world from a metaphoric one that arresting arrangements of images and sound can plunge us into. Finally, the examples illustrate how inescapable television is: whatever the set transmits now saturates the thought-environment in which everyone in the United States, as well as in countries that are our trading partners, lives and develops. What we can see, moreover, represents just the tip of an iceberg whose vastness cannot yet be gauged.

It is still possible to turn off the television set. It is no longer possible to turn off the television environment. I have observed the environmental takeover in my lifetime as the set opens the door of every home to images and sounds introducing and validating a total support system the broadcasting business nourishes and is, in turn, nourished by. Much of my career has been spent living and working in Latin America. There I have seen the same takeover by U.S.-based television, its imitators and its client industries. There is still a widespread fiction, however, that the overwhelming contribution of television to our climate of thought is a minor matter with only trivial effects. I believe it marks a cultural revolution, and this book attempts to point the direction in which I see it moving us.

I began research for the book sometime in 1972. I watched lots of television—a necessary but not a sufficient requirement for understanding the medium. To grasp the significance of what is visible on the screen it's essential to find out what goes on behind it. As an outsider to the business, I had to rely on sources in the public domain: books and newspapers; academic, professional, and trade journals; court decisions; congressional hearings; reports by government commissions, public-interest groups, and trade associations. Much essential information about broadcasting, however, has never been written down, and a great deal that has is not publicly available. I had to address many specific questions, therefore, to the people who command the information at the networks and production companies, as well as at the syndicating, advertising, and research firms. My preferred mode of doing this was by direct questioning, usually over the telephone. Writing letters of inquiry was much less satisfactory, since there was no opportunity to follow up the many nonresponsive answers I received.

I relied heavily on network sources of information. If my aim was to be sure that my recall of something I had seen on television was accurate, I usually queried network offices handling audience relations. If I needed the kind of detailed information that only a program handler could provide, my credentials as a broadcaster and columnist usually got me access to the offices handling press relations.

Information sources at the networks and stations that transmit the shows, however, often turned out to be as much in the dark as I was about the details I was seeking; so sometimes I queried the producers or syndicators directly.

My analysis of program content relies heavily on bookings during 1974 and 1975, since this was the period in which I was writing the manuscript. It was edited in 1976, and some new material was inserted at that time. Certain changes have occurred in the interim. Women and Blacks in strong-arm roles had only begun to make their entry into prime-time television; they now swell the ranks of police officers, government agents, and private eyes that television's good guys come from. We see them more often in bad-guy roles, too, hijacking planes, shooting hostages, leading revolutionary bomb crews, masterminding bank holdups, and so on. Black sitcom families and Blacks in commercials have become commonplace. Porn, which started out low key in prime-time 1973, has become increasingly evident: As of this writing network shows still stick to occasional soft-core, relying mainly on standard settings porno films have made familiar, but providing so far only the quick glimpses and titillating allusions television has always resorted to, stopping short of explicit sex acts.

These changes represent no real alteration in the general themes, program policies, and modes of decision making described in the book. Nor do I see any fundamental change possible within the present structure of the television business. The job of those who man the network bureaucracies, and the advertising and public-relations agencies feeding into them, is to attract attention and keep as many heads as possible turned toward the screen. If they were to abandon policies that effectively accomplish the task, even pursue them less than diligently, they would be remiss in their responsibility to the corporate enterprises whose executives make the policy decisions. These executives, in their turn, do what must be done if their companies are to fulfill obligations to stockholders who invest in businesses that are the more profitable the more human attention they manage to cultivate and harvest. It's the business of the midway, spruced up a bit and headquartered in fancy offices in New York and Hollywood.

The Federal Communications Commission, or any other regulatory body, for that matter, is not likely to be a source of change either, as I see it. The FCC has consistently interpreted its congressional mandate in the most limited sense. The commissioners are understandably reluctant to exercise government power over press content; and television—commercials, animated cartoons, game shows, and all—is still treated as our press, even if we have allowed it to be colonized by descendants of the brothers Ringling rather than of John Peter Zenger and Benjamin Franklin. There has been equal reluctance to bring pressure to bear on the way the business organizes itself economically.

The same hesitancy characterizes other regulatory bodies and overseeing committees. The upshot of it all is that executives at network headquarters have had pretty free rein to set most of the conditions determining the nature of virtually all television fare. For these reasons, the book pays attention principally to network programs and practices.

Among the many aspects of television this book does not go into is its takeover of popular sports, a serious omission that I must acknowledge. One reason is that I have not done the research on the structure of the sports business that would be essential to any explanation of how the television business has come to exercise control over this stockpile along with all the others.

I am aware, too, that the book passes over commercial television's occasional departures from the usual standardized formulas and serialized fare. Nor do I pay much attention to public television, not very different from network television, to be sure, but still—*vive la différence!* The airwaves offer us the modern equivalent of a vast public library, and my aim is to analyze an overall acquisitions policy. The occasional volume stuck on a remote shelf or a few fancy ones placed conspicuously in a display case to impress the trustees scarcely illuminate that policy.

Technology—cable, videodiscs, satellite transmissions, and the like—may well change the way we receive the images and sounds of television into our homes, may even involve more of our senses, not just sight and hearing. The power to determine acquisitions policy may pass from the networks we know to some other kind of interlocking arrangement. Neither technology nor a new table of organization in a new bureaucratic structure is likely to bring about major policy change in a business dedicated principally to the amassing of attention. Such an enterprise has few degrees of freedom. All it can do is to devise more and more arresting ways of convoking crowds, aiming at the same time for economies of scale. That adds up to massification, no matter what technology is employed, no matter who gets a key to the executive washroom, and even if a few avant-garde "boutiques" are allowed on the fringes of the blaring, glaring midway.

It seems a far cry from the wrestlers and the poodles to the introductory porno that now clamors for nationwide attention. We watch the one as we watched the other. We stay up later than ever watching old movies, talk shows, and rock concerts. There seems to be something downright irresistible for all of us, the world over, in the moving, talking image.

I'm not suggesting that this is something new, only that the

scale has changed. All known human groups have found fascina-
tion in moving, talking images, and incorporate them in drama
and dance, music and art, song and story, toys and games. If a
trait turned up with that much regularity among bees or herring
gulls, it would surely be classified as a species trait—whether
transmitted genetically or some other way. Why hesitate to call
it that when it turns up among us?

Like all primates, we are creatures in whom curiosity is easily
aroused. We overhear someone talking; it's a thoroughly human
reaction to want to listen. An uncurtained window offers a
glimpse of something that is none of our business; it's a
thoroughly human reaction to want to stay in the shadows and
watch.

But I'm convinced that there's more to it than curiosity. I
suspect that we human beings possess a drive to move out of
isolation in our own twenty-four-hour-a-day reality that's as
basic as the hunger drive, as compelling as the sex drive. Perhaps
if we could not escape from the confines of our own life experience with some reasonable and rhythmic frequency, we would all
go mad. If my hunch is anywhere near the mark, then drama and
dance, music, art, song, story, toys and games are our escape
hatches, our safety valves. I confess I find it frightening to see
control of access routes pass out of our own hands, out of the
hands of artists, craftsmen, and lovers of art whose primary
allegiance is to a work's authenticity, and into the hands of a
small group of anonymous men and women ill equipped to take
charge, unaware even of the extent of their responsibility.

I wrote the book with two classes of readers in mind. The
general reader who wants to know how the television business
works and what it is contributing to the thought environment
may wish to skip the footnotes and appendixes. There I include
documentation, details, and elaborations that are of interest principally to students and technical and professional colleagues,

especially those in communications, sociology, and methodology who may wish to use the book in their own research and teaching.

Many people have helped me think the book through from initial conception to final manuscript. Since I cannot name them all, I express a general *thank you* that is nonetheless heartfelt. Stations WHCU AM-FM and WVBR-FM in Ithaca, New York, deserve special mention for yielding up ten minutes each week for my radio series, "Blowing the Whistle on Broadcasting." The programs let the general public in on whatever my current research turns up that I think aids an understanding of how the social system works and how the institution of broadcasting fits into it. The university grants me the inestimable privilege of spending my time teaching and writing on any subject that interests me, and I am grateful. Since it is for the sake of freeing me to act in the long-range interests of the community, I figure that puts me in the role of community consultant. The broadcasts are my way of delivering progress reports.

My students, especially a small group here and abroad who work closely with me, have helped me more than they know. Our mutual struggle to create an authentic teaching and learning environment for each other, as we study communications systems together, sustains me and gives me daily joy. I include in that group my secretary, Margo Quinto, who stuck with the manuscript to the finish.

—Ithaca, New York
December 31, 1976

The Show and Tell Machine

1

The Television Environment: Stage Set for Desensitization

The television day in most of the United States begins between six and seven in the morning and ends an hour or two after midnight. Decisions on the material that will fill these hours are made by station managers, who command the nation's only licensed transmission facilities.[1]

Whatever they approve for broadcast is sure to gain access to the eyes and ears of a citizenry whose widespread custom is to set up a television receiver in the home's intimate environment and keep it activated an average of about seven hours a day. At virtually all commercial stations, the station managers choose to deliver the same programs and schedule them at the same times of day, with the result that at any given hour, virtually identical images and sounds issue from virtually all transmitters. It all coalesces into a kind of cloud that settles over the country from coast to coast, a cloud of visual and aural symbols creating the new kind of thought–environment in which Americans now live.

The general population does not usually recognize the airwaves as a coast-to-coast highway with direct access to seventy-
one million homes. Nor does the public usually notice how television's massive contribution to the environment we make and
share with each other drastically alters the public culture. It is,
however, quite customary to accept television as "the new member of the family."

Like any other family member, the television set becomes a
presence in the household. Sometimes it commands attention,
sometimes it yields the center of attention to others. Most of the
time the images coming through its screen and the sounds coming through its loudspeaker join the rest of the family—at mealtimes and bedtimes; at times for working and relaxing; when
visitors come or when the family is alone. Like any other new
family member, it alters traffic patterns, changes the rhythms of
the day, the very atmosphere of the homes it enters, introducing
its own views of the world, its own interpretations of reality, its
own images and symbolic forms.

Commercial stations account for all but about 15 percent of
total broadcast hours. These stations sell access to the homes
they penetrate to private interests eager to bring themselves and
their wares to the attention of the regional and national markets
that television instantly assembles for them. During certain periods of the day, about six hundred of these stations yield up their
transmitting facilities to three major broadcasting systems: The
American Broadcasting Companies, Inc., CBS Inc., and the National Broadcasting Company (ABC, CBS, and NBC). Each
owns five television stations—fifteen transmitters which provide
direct access to 33 percent of all television homes.[2] Their contracts with affiliated stations give them further direct and simultaneous access to virtually every home in the country, especially
during the hours of heaviest audience accumulation. In effect,
the networks rent from the local stations the right to use their

transmitting facilities for about twelve hours each day. Thus it happens that broadcast materials selected by executives at just these three centralized companies penetrate homes in all areas and regions, converting the country into a vast national neighborhood.

TELEVISION ORGANIZES TIME

In the physical universe, different species are segregated in space, organizing earth's surface into its distinct patterns. In the electronic universe of television, different broadcast materials are segregated in their own periods of time, patterning the flows and rhythms of the minutes and hours of the day, the days of the week, even of the seasons.

Broadcasters around the country program each day as almost identical "dayparts," filling each with programs of such familiar and repetitive content and scheduling them with such predictable regularity that they mark the ebb and flow of the twenty-four-hour cycle: prime time at night; the daytime TV of late morning and early afternoon; certain hours for morning news, evening news, and late shows. In just such a fashion did the medieval day ebb and flow with its dayparts, each of which also bore its special name: prime, terce, sext, none, and vespers.[3]

The rhythm is broken on weekends. Then daytime TV disappears, replaced by the only block of hours set aside for programs to attract children (Saturday mornings) and religious people (Sunday mornings). Both weekend afternoons go to big-league sports events. All are equally stylized. The rhythm of prime time (the evening hours of greatest audience concentration) is paced to the longer swells of a seasonal ebb and flow. The whole country stirs in September, as new series open and old ones begin new cycles for television's "first season." Families spend as much as three and four hours a night in front of the set, getting to know the new offerings and renewing acquaintance with the old ones.

The press is laden with review and comment, speculating about which shows will last and which will close. Then comes a period of reshufflings and reschedulings. Shows that fail to attract enough advertising revenue disappear from the airwaves, replaced by others that presumably may be more successful at amassing audiences. Sometimes a "weak" show may be given a reprieve—repositioned in a more favorable time slot or bulwarked by a stronger "lead-in" or set up against still weaker competing shows on the rival networks.

Series that survive this first culling run about thirteen original episodes, interspersed here and there by a few repeat performances. Then the "first season" comes to a close. Television's "second season" begins with the New Year. New series replace those that have been closed out and old series rerun episodes shown earlier. Summer-replacement season begins in April and lasts throughout the summer. This is the time for new tryouts and old reruns. Since pilots the networks have considered but rejected are also booked at this time, the season is also known in the business as "bombout season."

For years these seasons remained reassuringly constant until September 1974, when the A. C. Nielsen Company, whose business is to count the house, switched to computers. Since then, this rating company has delivered overnight reports on audience size and composition, enabling network executives to decide immediately after opening night whether to keep or cancel a series.[4] As a result, the customary seasonal rhythms are prefaced by a brief period of frenetic cancellations, reshufflings and reschedulings.

Pilots have traditionally been the single "made-for-TV" movies which the networks rely on as the major vehicle for testing the popularity of a series idea. With the opening of the 1976–77 season, the pilot movie was joined by the "pilot package," three to six episodes strung together and billed as a "mini-series." Like the pilot movie, those that attract and hold audiences of a certain size are reordered, while those that do not are kept on the shelf until it's time for the next "bombout season." If the pilot package idea catches on and expands, it could change the rhythm of the television seasons.

The television experience is so widely shared in this country and has gone on so consistently for so long, that the meaning of each daypart and each season is well known to virtually all Americans. Simply by scheduling a program or event in one daypart rather than another, one season rather than another, broadcasters indicate to the entire country how much importance it warrants.

Network time signifies more importance than local time and prime time more importance than daytime. Late-night hours are more important than early-morning hours: they attract bohemians and sophisticates, so almost anything goes and whatever appears has a chance of moving into prime time. Early morning, on the other hand, attracts working people and "straights." Unimportant.

On weekends, the one or two local studio talk shows scheduled for Sunday mornings often allow certain dissident groups to appear on a panel—perhaps a representative of the National Organization for Women, the Urban League, or a Native American group. Representatives of these groups take advantage of the occasion, whenever it is tendered, to voice complaints about what they see as a tendency for American society to shove square pegs into round holes. For them, all is not well. Scheduling something in this Sunday morning "for some all is not well" half-hour signals supreme unimportance.

COMMERCIALS: VISITATION OF AWARENESS

In every program, in every daypart, in every season, appear the ever-present product commercials—tiny vignettes, each little drama rarely lasting more than sixty seconds, often thirty seconds, sometimes twenty seconds, even ten. Commercials introduce every program, interrupt every program, and separate each program from the one that follows. Their rhythm sets up a more rapid counterpoint to the slower movement of the dayparts, short, staccato bursts subdividing each component half-hour, filling about 22 percent of all broadcast time.

To the audience, commercials and other promotional materials are interruptions to the program. To the broadcaster, the program is an envelope into which he can tuck commercials for delivery to the public. To the law, both programs and commercials are usually defined as press materials, protected by the First Amendment to the U.S. Constitution.

Like national parks, off-shore oil, and other public patrimonies, the airwaves belong to the people of the United States. This public grants their use to leaseholders who contract to transmit over them only materials which serve the interest, convenience, and necessity of the public. It is faithful fulfillment of this statutory obligation upon which the license to use the airwaves, in principle, depends. The supervisory agency is the Federal Communications Commission (FCC).[5]

Commercials that support the enterprise have become so much a part of American life that the public pays them only glancing attention, viewing them as sometimes amusing, sometimes offensive, often irritating, but on the whole tolerable interruptions to the programs they choose to watch. Through the casual, ubiquitous, and repeated exposure television bestows, commercials visit effortlessly upon the entire population—from the youngest child to the oldest graybeard—an awareness of companies, brand names, products, services, and selected attitudes and values to go with them, that in an earlier day would have required hours spent poring over images and text in disciplined and concentrated study of every mail-order catalogue in the country. In the same effortless way, families get to know the shows and stars the three networks regularly feature as well or better than they know their own cousins, aunts, grandparents, and godparents.

ASSEMBLING ATTENTION

Television programs are made and booked to capture attention and hold it until the commercial comes along. Although the broadcasting business likes to kid audiences into thinking they are the customers of television, they are in fact the product television offers for sale. The programs corral them so they can be counted off.

Sometimes television watchers are likened to voters, the audience presumably "voting" by changing channels or turning off the set. Such "voting" for programs, however, occurs in a system that disenfranchises minorities who have no way to place their own candidates on any ballot, no way to mobilize public support for converting themselves into majorities. Without such institutionalized procedures, even the most widespread discontent can find no orderly way to become an effective policy-making force. In their absence the main recourse is the negative power of boycott—in this case, simultaneous blackout of millions of television screens. In the political sphere such acts would be called plebiscite, general strike, or insurrection. A political system that offers only these alternatives for making the public will known is called totalitarian. We do not yet have a similarly familiar term for our television system.*

Television programs face a continuing dilemma. To hold an audience, they must evoke human feelings, stir human emotions,

---

*The term *oligopoly* has been suggested; and it is indeed suitable for the economic arrangements that exist in television. It is unpleasant to the ear, however, and not as widely understood as *totalitarian.* When this country was founded and none of these terms was in current use, the term *established*—as in *established* religion—was used to describe a system which offered the populace an officially approved ideology.

engage human passions. Yet as soon as viewers find their intellectual curiosity awakened, as soon as they allow themselves to be
gripped by fear or anxiety, love or hate, terror or revulsion or
rage, as soon as they are on the way to being overcome by
laughter or engulfed by tears, the program delivers them to the
commercials. Reactions that have been engaged are disengaged.
Under an avalanche of repetition and a constant barrage of
interruptions, emotions the programs might have called into
being simply have no chance to develop. All are aborted virtually
at the moment of conception.

Television programs resolve the dilemma quite simply: they
just give up any pretense of trying to awaken consuming interest
or achieve true, dramatic depths. Thus, most of the fare offered
on American television is the electronic equivalent of materials
appearing in the pulp magazines or near-pulps, in the mass-
produced paperbacks, comic books, and tabloids available at any
newsstand. Indeed, these are the sources from which many television programs were originally derived. Other programs reverse
the cycle, reappearing on newsstands in print versions sold by
syndicating companies or by the syndicating arm of the production company that initially turned them out. These syndication
companies circulate, recirculate, and recycle television shows.

People in the television business are quite explicit in admitting
that the programs aim principally to attract audience attention
without asking for the deep investment of self that drama which
takes itself seriously—or any serious discourse, for that matter
—demands. "We're a medicine show," they say, and indeed it
has become quite acceptable to treat the airwaves as if they were
an invisible midway. Even news programs deliberately avoid
providing the context that is needed to make sense out of the
events they report. Within the tight confines of the evening news,
about two dozen topics are touched upon in as many minutes so
that indiscriminately jostling up against each other are announcements of war efforts and peace efforts, famine and pesti-

lence, football scores and baseball scores, beauty pageants and moon landings, Dow-Jones closing stock-market averages and the weather. The stage is set in such a way that any interest or feeling which may have been aroused by one of these announcements is likely to be extinguished by the next following hard on its heels, or by the commercials.

Television watchers quickly learn to vary the amount of attention they pay to television, diminishing it when the commercials come on, increasing it for the program. No matter what the set is bringing into the home, however, it rarely gets full attention.* Television's images and sounds, designed for the mundane familiarity of the home environment, fit themselves in and around its daily routines, a pleasant and comfortable accompaniment to them. Daytime serials are made to accompany housewives as they iron or do household chores. Saturday-morning cartoons accompany children at play. A social group watches a news broadcast or a crime show and the programs weave themselves effortlessly around the conversation and the banter. If the doorbell buzzes or the telephone rings, it's the easiest thing in the world to withdraw attention from the set in favor of the visitor at the door or the caller on the line.

In about 40 percent of American homes there are two or more television sets, and frequently one of them is set up in the bedroom. Children climb into bed with their parents and all watch together in pleasant, cozy relaxation. When a child is ailing, the set keeps him company in the sickroom. The television set joins lovemaking as couples cuddle up together and watch the screen.

---

*Exceptions occur, usually historic on-camera firsts, such as assassinations and ensuing state funerals, good for several replays. The first moon landings—but not later ones. The first broadcasts or congressional hearings such as the Kefauver committee's hearings on crime, the Watergate panel of the House Judiciary Subcommittee, and the like. As these kinds of broadcasts become more routine, it is to be expected that they, too, will fade into the background.

Some people place a television set in the bathroom: it is relaxing to lie in the warm bathwater, letting muscle tension drain away, half watching the familiar images on the screen, half listening to the familiar sounds.

The standardized format of television demands divided attention: now the program, now the commercials. Viewers bestow divided attention: the set and the home, the home and the set. Even if someone watching alone should find something in the program more than mildly stirring, attention is distracted by familiar house noises as the furnace clicks on or off, an elevator groans to a stop, the dog whines fitfully in his sleep, the logs in the fireplace crackle and snap. And then the commercial comes along, the watcher turns away, gets a beer from the refrigerator, a sandwich, to return, refreshed and relaxed, to the sounds and the images appearing on the screen.

DESENSITIZATION AND BEHAVIOR MODIFICATION

Reciprocal inhibition is a technical term describing this way of reacting with divided attention. It is often deliberately taught in psychological laboratories and consulting rooms as a technique for bringing about *systematic desensitization.* It can be done with electric shock; it can be done with images. The procedure which uses images and fantasy materials to extinguish emotions and excise feelings is called *imaginal desensitization.* [6] This technique is effective in stripping people of their feelings, "whittling away"[7] at emotions until a person can remain relaxed, undisturbed, and unmoved even as he watches scenes that had originally occasioned his gravest concern, acutest distress, most painful anxiety. Those who practice this technique claim that the emotionless state it brings about becomes generalized so that when a person trained in imaginal desensitization comes upon scenes in real life that are the same or similar to those he has seen over and over again as imaginary dramas, he can even then continue to remain detached and unmoved by them.[8]

In the desensitization laboratory, as in home viewing, the atmosphere is pleasant, familiar, unthreatening, predictable, legitimate. There is no room here for passion and emotion, no room for panic, disgust, revulsion, horror. Desensitization sessions discourage such intense feelings in favor of the placid feelings of well-being that go with relaxation, unguarded acceptance, predictability, reassurance. Desensitization sessions chase away even quieter emotions: no room here for dislike, not even for mild rejection. As soon as any disturbing emotion begins to be felt, viewing is interrupted to allow relaxation and placidity to take over. The nice feelings replace the intense ones, extinguishing the old association and ushering in the new one. The technical term for this is *positive reinforcement*. Through desensitization and positive reinforcement, the viewer learns the new associations and unlearns the old, a systematic mode of emotional education and reeducation.[9]

Dramatizations are effective aides to emotional reeducation: psychodrama, sociodrama, role-taking, role-reversals. They provide opportunities for rehearsal and repetition, allowing new associations to entrench themselves more securely as old ones are shed. They are effective not only for those who take the roles, but also for those who watch. The social reinforcement brought about by group sharing validates the legitimacy of accepting the new associations. Such emotional reeducation in socially shared situations, particularly with dramatic aids, is called *consciousness raising*.

Systematic imaginal desensitization whittles away at feelings and emotions a person's past has taught him to attach to images, symbols, relationships, events. Repeated negative and positive reinforcement show him, as his old emotional ties are extinguished, how to reattach his feelings to new ones, while consciousness is raised through rehearsal in imagination of dramatic role playing socially shared. In the clinical situation, these procedures are called *behavior modification.* The parallel to the broadcast materials television brings into the home and the circumstances under which people admit them is exact.[10]

Therapists engaged in behavior modification claim that it takes between ten and thirty sessions to wipe out even the most deeply rooted associations.[11] They claim that imaginal desensitization breaks associative links as strong as those binding alcoholics to alcohol and homosexuals to same-sex partners. They claim rates of "cure" that exceed those reported for psychoanalysis, depth psychology, many group techniques, and many other procedures of psychological counseling. The cure rates reported for imaginal desensitization accompanied by consciousness raising are even more impressive since the images viewers are asked to watch are not impressive dramatic productions, skillfully mounted, embellished by experienced actors and actresses delivering clever dialogue aided by elaborate sound effects and rich orchestral music. Quite the contrary, the images viewed in imaginal desensitization sessions have been produced by amateurs, conjured up only in the subject's own imagination. They exist nowhere except in the mind's eye.[12]

Suppose these "subjects"—these *people,* as I prefer to call them—had been viewing real dramatic productions, skillfully mounted, enacted by experienced actors and actresses delivering clever dialogue, aided by elaborate sound effects and carefully orchestrated mood music. Would they have unlearned their deeply rooted emotional associations even more quickly? Would they have learned to reattach them elsewhere and then would that "deconditioning" and "reconditioning" have engaged even deeper levels of their personalities? Would the result have been even more lasting? And what if they had spent all their formative years viewing those scenes, not just ten to thirty brief sessions in a consulting room?

IMAGES AND IMAGINATION: ART, MIND, AND METAPHOR

The procedures and practices which modern behavior therapists and patients carry out in treatment sessions are private versions of those all cultures carry out publicly, particularly in socially shared spectacles. Such events are not designed deliberately to "cure" this or that individual's painful feelings and replace them with pleasanter ones; yet they do something essentially similar for the social group as a whole. Since human feelings have a certain promiscuous quality—they can attach themselves to virtually anything—every culture must cultivate the feelings of its own members, routing them frequently and periodically so that most people will be likely to make and maintain the proper attachments. Public spectacles signal to all which feelings are appropriate and which are inappropriate under given conditions —however the particular group defines "appropriate" and "inappropriate." Repetition and social sharing validate the definitions.

It is an ancient insight, not just a newly discovered principle of contemporary psychology, that access to human feelings is through human imaginations. Myth and story, drama and art, music and poetry, play and games and dance and ritual, all touch imaginations and form imaginations—the very terrain in which human minds develop. Socrates warned that stories shape the minds of children.[13] A contemporary philosopher, asking, "What is called thinking?" answers: Thinking is metaphor, minds are made by poesy.[14] *Mind: An Essay on Human Feeling* is the title of one of this century's seminal works on the nature of human thought.[15] At the beginning of the eighteenth century, Andrew Fletcher saw the potential political power residing in control of symbols that capture imaginations through song and story.[16]

Those who are unwilling to pay attention to history or acknowledge the enduring wisdom of the collective conscience can turn to literally tons of research reports in sociology and psychology that document how easy it is to get people to attach, detach, and reattach their feelings and emotions as a consequence of the associations that images dramatizations and films and even still photographs and passing discourse have released in the imagination.*

Some of this research is kept under lock and key, available only to those who have hired researchers to conduct the investigations on behalf of their companies, products and ideologies. Much of it, however, is available in professional journals serving the subfield of public opinion, spun off by the academic disciplines of sociology and psychology, then picked up by students of political science, child development, education, journalism, communications, and so on. To trace the intellectual origins of this kind of scholarship would lead us far back in time. A list of those who have written the classic works of the present century and have set its particular style would include Walter Lippmann and Harold D. Lasswell, as well as Harwood L. Childs, Carl Hovland, Robert K. Merton, Paul F. Lazarsfeld, and Samuel A. Stouffer.

The power to dominate a culture's symbol-producing apparatus is the power to create the ambience that forms consciousness itself.[17] It is a power we see exercised daily by the television business as it penetrates virtually every home with the most massive continuing spectacle human history has ever known. Wittingly and unwittingly this business and its client industries set the stage for a never ending performance stripping away emotional associations that centuries of cultural experience have linked to patterns of behavior, institutional forms, attitudes, and values that many cultures and subcultures revere and need to keep vigorous if they are to survive. The daily consciousness-

---

*The appendix to this chapter, on page 292, lists some of the relevant literature.

raising sessions transmitted by television demonstrate the narrow range of alternatives selected by a handful of people as eminently worthy of attention and collective celebration.

The unanticipated outcome of it all is that the United States of America enjoys the dubious distinction of having allowed the television business to score a first in human history: the first undertaking in mass behavior modification by coast-to-coast and intercontinental electronic hookup.

2

Desensitization
and
Resensitization:
Erosion of
Family Feelings

Daytime serials, prime-time series, and the block of weekend shows beamed at the nation's children, all signal to the watching nation that the emotions which bind people together in family units are trivial and transitory. Daytime serials repeatedly dramatize situations that reduce these emotions to one-dimensionality. Prime-time shows feature either "sitcoms" that ridicule them or crime shows that obliterate them from the nation's principal collective experience. Programs targeted especially to children recycle prime-time shows, following the same formats, featuring the same plots, the same stars, the same emotional level. Saturday morning becomes a training ground where beginners can easily pick up all the skills they need to become full-fledged television watchers.

Soap operas are daily consciousness-raising sessions which, since the days of radio, have become a part of the shared social experience of four generations of Americans. The television business calls these serials "family dramas," and the country has become accustomed to the term. This chapter, analyzing the manner in which soap operas treat family life, suggests that it might be more appropriate to call the soaps "antifamily anti-dramas."

As of this writing, forty-two and a half network broadcast hours are turned over every week to the stylized daily episodes of daytime serials. Along with the spliced-in commercials (about ten hours), they daily serve up the same caricatured images denigrating family life. The whole package is by now so embedded in our culture that no account of the American way of life can omit mention of its regular diet of soap operas.

TRIVIALIZING EMOTIONAL COMMITMENT

Soap operas talk family, but the daily role-playing sessions they target to every American home do violence to any reasonable conception of family commitment—not by decree, not by polemic, not by dramatic declamation, and very likely unwittingly. The episodes pick away at the notion that people in human families try to commit themselves to each other as deeply as their individual failings permit; and that it's the stuff of tragedy when a family can't hack it. They whittle away at the fundamental sense of trust every human family tries to imprint on its members. The job is subtle and effective, like water wearing away rock.

Soap-opera people live in a world of fly-apart marriages: throwaway husbands, throwaway wives, and—recently—throwaway lovers. Quite plausibly, the disposable marriage is a source of disposable children. Indeed, the most effective way the soaps do violence to images of family commitment is by a visual code that implicitly denies that children are important in family living. As the episodes spin out their daily show-and-tell, the country is scarcely permitted to see any children at all. This is in marked contrast to the commercials, in which children take principal roles—infants fighting wetness, youngsters eating candy, drinking pop, loving Ronald McDonald, flying over earth's surface in defiance of the laws of gravity, delivering disquisitions on PH in shampoo and fluoride in toothpaste, or singing and marching to the praises of Bumble Bee tuna fish.

During the first half of 1975, I counted 137 adults who were sexually active in the soaps, whether teenagers or grandparents, who had major or minor speaking parts. But only a half-dozen children had any speaking parts deserving of the name—under 5 percent of the total. (Twenty more children were either glimpsed or kept offstage while adults discussed or mentioned them.)

The audience does not have an opportunity to see children in soap operas partly because the serials picture conception, pregnancy, gestation, and birth as such chancy matters. Soap operas saturate the air with images showing these human developmental processes as troublesome, scary, fraught with danger, laden with unimaginable dread. Suppose a daytime-serial woman finds out she's pregnant. The chances are about seven to ten that she's not married to the father or that the pregnancy is unwelcome to one or both parents—the result of accident, thoughtlessness, deception, or rape. It's seven to ten again that the fetus won't make it through to term.

If a baby manages to beat the overwhelming odds the soaps stack up against him and survive the hazardous journey through the birth canal, the odds are heavy that the birth will take place at grave risk to the mother's life and that the baby will turn out to be weak and sickly. In short, the soap-opera formula presents the child as both threat and victim—themes that students of propaganda claim will undermine anyone's image.[1]

The few children the soap operas show the nation can't count on their own faulty, sclerotic, and unreliable bodies to see them through the week; neither can they count on their shaky social world to support them through childhood; it is a world stuck together with spit and Scotch tape. Every one of the children in the country's daily dosage of daytime serials—every single one —goes to bed unsure whether the woman called "mother" or the man called "father" will still be around for breakfast. Has one or the other taken off, checked out, flown the coop, split, disappeared? If the child isn't wondering about that, it's because he has already been left helpless—renounced, abandoned, snatched, stuck in an institution, or passed from one hand to another.

Saddest of all, nobody cares. Nobody really cares. There are lots of pious expressions of concern; but they fool nobody. The formula passes over the dependency of little children, dismisses their need for trust and stability and nurturance, with a slogan, a tear, a telephone call to the psychiatrist. The soaps are daily demonstration sessions of silly, trivial, false gestures to shelter, protect, and nurture children—gestures empty of passion.

These themes and the cavalier way the soaps deal with them so dominate all daytime serials that even a casual watcher cannot miss the point. For example, just during the first half of 1975, here is what the country was invited to see. (See also appendix, p. 297.)

Eleven pregnancies produced two miscarriages, two abortions under consideration, three births almost fatal to the mother, one of which took place during a blizzard without qualified medical assistance. Only one mother was lost in the year's first half: Addie Williams died just after being delivered of her baby, Hope, who survived. Addie died not of the terminal cancer she was suffering from, nor from the complications to be expected when a grandmother goes through pregnancy and parturition. She was killed in a car accident ("Days of Our Lives"). Of the eleven pregnancies, only one involved a woman and a man who were married to each other, living together in reasonable harmony, with some hope of welcoming the new baby into a home they were trying to make as pleasant, secure, and loving as their own resources and human limitations made possible.

The children who survive turn out to be in pretty bad shape. About half of those the nation was invited to see or glimpse or even hear mentioned were sick or abandoned children, victims of an accident or of genetic anomaly, or suffering serious physical and psychological damage at the abusive hands of someone near and dear to them. Jamie Coles barely survived abuse and battering by his own socialite mother, Stacy ("All My Children"). Freddie Bauer had only recently recovered from a series of harrowing experiences. He had been lost on a canoe trip, then suffered amnesia—a condition once endemic only to soap-opera adults but which has spread to the children ("Guiding Light"). Little Megan, born prematurely to her unmarried mother, Cathy Craig, turned out to have a congenitally deformed heart ("One Life to Live"). Little Phillip Tyler managed to pull through a splenectomy, the question of his paternity as well as his physical condition complicated by his rare blood type ("All My Children"). Samantha, daughter of unmarried Pam Chandler, was born with hyalene membrane disease, a congenital lung condition ("Guiding Light"). Motherless Skipper Mackenzie had a heart malfunction that kept him from playing with the other kids ("Somerset"). Tommy Hobart had to be protected from his stepfather who, when he was on the juice, abused the child ("General Hospital"). Erich Warner had been adopted by his own father and Father's new wife. Father's old wife, Erich's mother, had managed to forget completely about her own child. That was when Erich almost died in the plane accident that had brought about his mother's amnesia. She was kidnapping him when the accident happened ("The Doctors"). T. J.—another child who had been abandoned—suffered from malnutrition, ulcerated legs, and psychological damage, all requiring hospitalization ("The Guiding Light"). And so it goes—flush-away fetuses succeeded by defective children victimized by their own parents, betrayed by the very people children place their trust in—all presented with a degree of emotion appropriate to a case of acute hangnail.

Adults responsible for children in soap operas get up and walk away from them or just pass them on from hand to hand as if they were Easter chicks. Every one of the children in six months of these daily consciousness-raising sessions had gone through the trauma of separation from parents. Diana Lamont, having decided to live with her young lover and bear him a brand new child, turned her back on her husband and the not-so-new child they were raising, Johnny ("Love of Life"). Diana Taylor had only recently returned to her baby, Martha, having left her some time before to spend a term in jail ("General Hospital"). The case involving the Wilkins family and the Vincent family was more complicated. Wendy Wilkins, child of divorce, had to be prepared to accept her mother's intended as a new father. The bother of it all was that Wendy loved her own father, ne'er-do-well David Wilkins. Mother Stephanie, wondering how on earth she might get her daughter to accept a replacement, cooks up this idea. Ex-husband, David, is to tell Wendy that he is not her real father, pretending that her real father was mother's lover, Dr. Tony Vincent—a ruse designed to make Wendy feel fine about the reconstituted household and thus accept Dr. Tony as a replacement for dismissed ex-father, David. Tony Vincent, in his turn, has to agree to leave his own wife in order to carry out the ploy. The scheme backfires, though. Stephanie's ruse is aborted at the very last minute when ex-husband David chickens out and the matter becomes moot when Dr. Tony dies after a heart attack ("Search for Tomorrow").

Lori Kirby is the only child on the list who was not defective or sick or broken by accident, the only one living at home with her natural mother and father while they were joined in matrimony to each other. Even so, no dispassionate observer could very well call Lori's home life emotionally on the level. The family had just been put back together. Mother and Father, Chris and Larry Kirby, decided the very day their divorce decree was handed down that it had all been a slight mistake. So they remarried. Alas, any pleasure Lori may have expected when she found her family reunited was destined to be short-lived. No sooner had they remarried than Mother and Daddy were at it again, hammer and tongs. Larry claimed Chris was rejecting him sexually and there were those incessant arguments about whether Chris should use the pill or Larry should get a vasectomy. Any veteran student of soap operas would recognize this as a natural opening for Chris to become pregnant with yet another unwelcome child—except for one thing: NBC canceled the series. ("How to Survive a Marriage".)

THE NOT-SO-MEANINGFUL RELATIONSHIP

The children are passed along from hand to hand mainly because soap-opera people marry and remarry all the time. There's a steady stream of traffic in and out of marriages, in and out of beds. In the early seventies, directives from network executive suites lifted an old taboo in order to permit the frenetic couplings to take place outside of marriage. Not that it makes much difference. Since the early days of radio, soap operas have acted out unions that are casual, without solemnity, without commitment. The post-taboo "meaningful relationship" is about as meaningful as "Pebbles and Bamm Bamm"; but so was the pre-taboo legal marriage. Just as the country got used to the old product, it got used to the new, improved product. It will get used, as well, to whatever is in store next time around, whenever the executive suite yields to the ever mounting pressure to sprinkle new, improved ingredients into the formulas that keep those heads turned toward the screen, that titillate interest but smother feeling.

My half-year count yielded fifteen marriages, nineteen shackings-up, and another nineteen separations or divorces—final, pending, threatened, or under consideration. (Since the men and women of the soaps combine and separate and recombine with each other like so many volatile chemicals, a census must double-count couples who started out shacking up with each other and then married; or otherwise linked pairs who split off and recombined into new attachments.)

Eight of the fifteen marriages involved recidivists. The word with its suggestion of compulsive delinquency is more appropriate than its synonym, just plain "repeater." Most of the brides and grooms were marching down that aisle for the second or third or even for the fourth time—as when Rachel Davis Matthews Clark Frame became Rachel Davis Matthews Clark Frame Corey—only briefly, since that marriage began to founder within a matter of weeks ("Another World").

In an earlier day, bigamy was an approved way for a soap-opera husband or wife to couple with the next-in-line, second in popularity, perhaps, to amnesia. As soon as divorce was approved for inclusion in the formula, however, bigamy began to be phased out, although it has not yet been abandoned. Two of the marriages in the half-year count were bigamous. Tony Powers had married Dr. Alan Stewart, thinking her husband dead. He was not. Then there was the Ben Harper–Betsy Crawford marriage. Ben knew very well what he was doing. He had suggested to his wife, Arlene, that they get a temporary divorce so he could marry Betsy and collect the half million his mother, Meg, had promised as a wedding present when he did. He would then divorce Betsy, he told Arlene, and remarry her. Arlene said "nothing doing," dug in her heels and held out for bigamy ("Love of Life").

It's not exactly bigamy when a man hangs on to his mistress even though he marries another woman. So the Tiffany Whitney–Noel Douglas marriage was not included in the total for bigamous unions. Noel was still keeping Tracy Dallas and had no intention of unloading her ("Edge of Night").

From the beginning of the seventies, the count for pregnant

brides began to drop steadily year by year, mainly because the new, improved formula phased out the "unwed mother" and phased in the "single parent." No longer did the young woman "in trouble" have to die, miscarry, lead a life of shame, or marry. She could go it alone; which is what Cathy Craig did ("One Life to Live"). Pam Chandler, too ("Guiding Light"); and Augusta McCloud planned to take the same route ("General Hospital"). Diana Lamont, one of the many pregnant grandmothers in the soap-opera population, wondered whether she might find herself in the same boat if her lover's divorce did not come through in time for them to marry before the baby came. She need not have worried; she miscarried before year's end ("Love of Life").

The do-it-yourself marriage ceremony has been in vogue among daytime serial couples for quite a while. Maybe it began four or five years ago when Phillip and Tara Tyler declared their undying love for each other in a "meaningful relationship." They pledged themselves in a homemade ceremony which they claimed was as binding as any marriage. But then Phillip went off to war leaving Tara pregnant. So Tara married Chuck, his cousin, and never said a word about her child's paternity. Phillip, back from the war, got Erica Brent with child and married *her* ("Search for Tomorrow").

The trend, however, spread from one network to another. Over at CBS, Jill Foster was in love with Phillip Chancellor ("The Young and the Restless"), who was married to another woman. Phillip had given Jill a ring and said they'd make their engagement public as soon as he could bring himself to tell wife, Kay, he wanted a divorce. Even before Phillip said a word, Kay knew what was going on and tried to forestall the break-up of her home. She began to work subtly on Jill's insecurities, filling her with misgivings about her own working-class background, convincing her she could never make it in Phillip's high-class world because she lacked the social graces his wife would need. Jill wavered every time Kay pointed out that she was just a hairdresser who had never gone to college, while Phillip was so top drawer he ordered wine in French. At the right psychological moment, Kay called upon Brock Reynolds (her son by an earlier marriage) to close in for the kill, as it were. At his mother's instigation, he agreed to court Jill but then fell in love with her and proposed. Jill decided to visit her benevolence upon Phillip Chancellor by jilting him and marrying Brock. As things turned out, Brock and Jill did not, however, exactly get married. Brock read the Song of Solomon, they locked eyes, the camera closed in and—break for the commercial. Jill, always a loyal girl, never permitted Brock to consummate their "marriage." And so, when Phillip got around to divorcing Kay, Jill was ready to marry him—on his deathbed, alas! He was expiring as the aftermath of an accident his wife, Kay, had brought on. Oh yes—Jill was pregnant at the time with a child she claimed Phillip had sired.

Note that Brock replaced his own stepfather in Jill's bed. Such mildly incestuous overtones are very much in evidence throughout soap opera's daily consciousness-raising sessions. At least six pairings just in the half-year soap-opera census smacked of incest. The triangle made up of mother and daughter with the same man is not unusual. Julie Anderson revived an old affair with Doug Williams—the same Doug who had been Julie's stepfather by marriage to Addie, Julie's mother. Doug was free to resume the affair with Julie, Addie having cleared the decks for this replay by cashing in her chips in a car accident ("Days of Our Lives"). The mother doesn't have to die, though, in these Humbert-Humbert affairs. Scott Mackenzie vacillated between Jill Farmer and Ellen Grant (Ellen, the mother; Jill, the daughter; both widows—"Somerset"). Trish Clayton's stepfather had a habit of walking into Trish's room while she was dressing. Trish was apprehensive that the gleam in his eye boded no good ("Days of Our Lives"). Margo Flax and Paul Marten had just married and set up their new home. Claudette Montgomery, Margo's daughter by one of her former husbands, appeared unexpectedly (having left *her* husband) and moved in with them. As Claudette tried hard to replace her mother in Paul's bed, the whole country watched to an obbligato of detergent commercials ("All My Children").

The incident that was more than mildly suggestive of incest, though, occurred in NBC's "Somerset." Heather Lawrence's lover, Greg Mercer, turned out to be her half brother. They had shared a mutual father some time back. Greg found out about it just in time but he simply couldn't bring himself to tell Heather about the shamefulness of the bond between them. This case was a bit unusual for soap operas, but not just because of the real blood tie between the pair. The writers had tried, at least, to show Greg's desperation as he scurried this way and that in frantic but futile attempts to extricate himself and his sweetheart from their tragic situation.

Life has a way of playing these kinds of tricks on us poor mortals, and hosts of men and women have been caught before in the same tangled webs. Art and literature allow us to enter into their stories, inviting us to share the deep emotions of those trapped like Greg and Heather, even though their particular personal tragedies may be remote from our own lives. It's the human way to exercise our feelings and keep them in shape, just as jogging exercises the muscles and the heart. Claudette Montgomery is not the first woman to hanker after her mother's bed mate and Scott Mackenzie is not the first man to find a mother and her daughter equally exciting. Soap operas, however, remain deaf to the emotional overtones that reverberate through such relationships when they occur in our culture. Treating them as gimmicks to keep the plots moving, they reduce all passion to the level of the

cheery eulogies to Comet and big-machine Dash that interrupt incessantly.

Ignoring the tragic element in the human condition, just passing it by, anesthetizes emotions instead of quickening them: this
goes on every day in mass desensitization sessions which soap
operas target to the nation's homes.

3

The Family
in Prime Time

The television business calls "prime time" the block of approximately three hours every night when it is a widespread national custom to turn to the television set to watch network programs.[1] Whatever is scheduled for these evening hours has maximum opportunity to penetrate the greatest number of homes. Advertisers, therefore, are charged *prime* rates for commercials shown during these *prime* hours; hence the term.

Like the soaps, these prime-time programs also whittle away at the emotions developed in family life. Images of any emotionally meaningful life in an intact family are almost nonexistent. The few programs that feature people who live in complete families, in relationships that engage their deepest feelings, are typically historical dramas or "sitcoms."* The historical dramas

---

*This is television shoptalk for situation comedies, a comic-strip formula translated into television drama.

show an intact family as if it were a relic of this country's past. The sitcoms, complete with laugh track primed to go off every thirty seconds or so, play the family for laughs.

In the 1974–75 television year the television business offered sixty-nine series, featuring pretty much the same characters each week, in pretty much the same settings, getting into pretty much the same kinds of scrapes and resolving them in pretty much the same ways. In about two-thirds of these shows—reasonably typical of the season before and equally typical of the season which followed—the featured characters had no noticeable family relations at all, or, if a family tie was mentioned, it was an offstage one, relegated to an occasional glimpse here, a passing comment there. Most of these prime-time series, whose visual codes and story lines denied the family, were television's favorites: crime shows and "action-adventure" shows.[2]

Eight weekly series that year showed the nation protagonists with visible family ties, currently living in a family situation and emotionally anchored in it. Yet they represented a pretty narrow range of contemporary family images. Just two shows in the first season featured twentieth-century families in which a mother and father were raising their own children: a white family ("Apples Way") and a black family ("Good Times"). By the time the second season had rolled around, only one of them was left: "Apples Way" had been canceled, leaving "Good Times" standing alone.* It was joined by "We'll Get By," which survived for thirteen episodes. For the rest, parents raising their own children were played in period costume as if such families were relics of our past: "The Waltons" (the Depression years of the thirties), "Happy Days" (the Eisenhower years), "Little House on the Prairie" (the 1880s), and "The New Land" (1858).

Other prime-time series acknowledged that children exist and

---

*Even this family was deprived of the father when the new season rolled around—killed in an accident! (The appendix on p. 310 details family relationships.)

that they grow up in families, but featured families broken by divorce, desertion, or death. "Texas Wheelers" showed a family of five, the father a shiftless no 'count, *Tobacco Road* type whose three children were being raised by their eldest brother, a lad scarcely out of his teens. "Sunshine" featured an attractive young widower bringing up his five- or six-year-old daughter alone. "Sons and Daughters" featured teenage sweethearts. Anita lived with her father; her mother had deserted the family to live with another man. "Paper Moon" invited viewers to follow the adventures of Moze, raising his almost nubile daughter, Addie, who was motherless. Nobody ever came right out and said in so many words that Moze and Addie were father and daughter. According to the show's "handler" (the person who handles public relations for the program) at ABC, the relationship between Moze and Addie had deliberately been left unclear. "To stimulate viewer interest," was the way he put it.[3]

The kind of contemporary family the television business booked for the country's peak viewing periods that year was a family made up only of adults. Even then, the booking agents preferred broken families. Clifton Curtis was shown living with his mama ("That's My Mama"). Lamont Sanford was shown living with his papa ("Sanford and Son"). Barnaby Jones, a widower, was featured along with his widowed daughter-in-law, Betty ("Barnaby Jones").[4] Shortly after "Rhoda" opened, in September 1975, Rhoda and Joe married: her first, his second. The marriage barely lasted two seasons. "Maude" brought into millions of homes every week a household headed by Maude's fourth husband, Walter.

Childless couples were evident in prime-time television that season. The Hartley family ("The Bob Newhart Show") was one. Emily and Bob, married five years when the 1974–75 television year opened, were still childless when it closed. Petrocelli and wife opened in September 1975 and so did the Adamson couple—both pairs childless ("Petrocelli" and "Born

Free"). The most famous of all American families, the Bunker household, consisted of two adult couples living together, the Bunkers and the Stivics. (Gloria, the Bunkers' daughter, is married to Mike Stivic.)

Just in case the nation missed the point, one episode, "Gloria's Shock," (October 26, 1974, and repeated at least twice since then) was a consciousness-raising session on the desirability of childlessness. Mike Stivic insisted that he and wife, Gloria, should have no children, all for the sake of zero population growth and female self-determination. Gloria was at first furious; but by the time the most widely shared half-hour in the two-hundred-year history of this country had come to a close, Mike had won Gloria over to his way of thinking. It would have been childlessness for the Stivics except for one quirk of fate. During the summer of 1975, Sally Struthers—the actress who plays the Bunker daughter—refused to report for rehearsals without renegotiation of her contract on terms more favorable to her. The script writers were instructed to write her out of the show while negotiations were going on. Thus, the Stivics moved out of the Bunker house in September 1975 and Gloria was not seen for the first four episodes of the season. The excuse: pregnancy. The contract renegotiations were completed, Gloria turned up in the fifth episode, and some months later the whole nation was treated to another consciousness-raising session on the advantages of natural childbirth with the husband in attendance. The following year, Mike got a vasectomy.

Even the supporting cast in prime-time television series is locked into the same family patterns written for the stars: broken families, offstage children, if any. Maude's household included Carol, her daughter by Maude's husband number one. Carol, divorced and husbandless, was often seen; Phillip, the boy, was primarily kept offstage. The leading character in "Friends and Lovers" was fictional Robert Dreyfus, who often visited his brother and sister-in-law and their unseen baby. Mannix's secretary, Peggy, a widow, raises her eight- or nine-year-old child who is very rarely on camera ("Mannix"). In one episode the boy figured importantly in the plot. Even then he was seldom seen. The bad guys had kidnapped him and held him hostage—offstage. Rhoda and Joe met when Brenda, Rhoda's sister, was minding Joe's son by his first wife. The child appeared briefly in the show that launched the series, and has been glimpsed once or twice since. He lives with his mother where most television children belong—behind the scenes ("Rhoda").

Lou Grant, Mary's boss ("The Mary Tyler Moore Show"), started out with a wife and grown-up children living at home. Separation—divorce—and Lou Grant finished the season on the eligibles list. Murray Slaughter in the same show often referred to his wife and family—invisible throughout the season. Phyllis Lindstrom, Mary's neighbor, had an invisible subteen daughter, Beth. When Phyllis opened in her own show the following year ("Phyllis"), the writers killed off her husband, presented her as a widow, and allowed Beth, now visibly nubile, to appear on stage.[5]

It was the year that Howard Borden shacked up with Bob Hartley's sister ("The Bob Newhart Show"). He referred every now and then to his eight- or nine-year-old son, but the lad continued to live with Howard's divorced wife—offstage.

If television shows a contemporary family living together and caring deeply about each other, it is sure to be a setting for comedy. The 1974–75 television year opened with twenty-two weekly situation comedies. More than half of them chose a format that played the family for laughs. Eighteen new shows made their debut during the second season that television year: only six showed people who lived in families (one crime show and five "sitcoms").[6] Of these just two survived: "The Jeffersons"—a family consisting only of adults—and "Barney Miller." "Barney Miller" was not, properly speaking, a family sitcom, but a slap-

stick cop show.[7] Still, the protagonist, Barney Miller, was married and his wife and teenage daughter appeared onstage in that
first cycle with reasonable frequency. In subsequent cycles, they
disappeared.

MEN WITHOUT WOMEN

The fantasy the television business likes best to serve up as food
for the nation's imagination is men without women. It's a standard formula—a savior brings the bad guys to inexorable justice
meted out by the forces of the State. During the 1974–75 television year, saviors ran from Matt Dillon (at the same stand for
twenty years in "Gunsmoke") to Steve Austin, half man, half
robot ("Six Million Dollar Man").

Steve Austin, a cyborg, is to Superman what the Mazarati is
to the bicycle. An astronaut who had crashed when he was
test-flying a plane, Steve lost his own limbs and the sight of one
eye. He was fitted with atomically powered arms and legs and a
high powered bombsight replaced his eye. In January 1976 he
was joined by a lady Cyborg (Jaime), like him pieced together
and powered by atomic energy. In Jaime's case her hearing has
been atom powered as well as her limbs. Both Steve and Jaime
are shown as the new, improved version of the human species.
Azriel Bibliowicz has pointed out in an unpublished paper that
the symbolic meaning is the exact opposite of a story like *Pinocchio* and similar tales. In *Pinocchio,* a nonhuman creature
longs to reach a more enviable state by becoming human. "Six
Million Dollar Man" reverses the fable: it is the nonhuman
condition which is the enviable one.

Prime-time television gave the country male saviors in all
shapes and sizes and packagings: fat like Cannon, in a wheelchair
like Ironside, totally hairless like Kojak, suffering from a trick
back like Harry O, attractive ex-cons like Rockford ("The Rockford Files"). They were served up as young swingers like Man-

nix, and old and gamy like Barnaby Jones. No matter—their
common characteristic was that they all got along beautifully
without needing or being needed by a real live woman to whom
they committed their loyalty or their love, with whom they
shared any long-term responsibility for anything. For all these
television *machos,* it was a dead woman, a one-night stand, or
nothing. Ironside lives out his days with the memory of a lost
love. Barnaby Jones mourns a dead wife. Lucas Tanner's whole
family had been killed. Did Matt Dillon court Miss Kitty all
those years they were together in "Gunsmoke," or were they just
pals? Ben Cartwright lived without a woman for fourteen years
on network television before he rode off into the sunset of endless
reruns. His three single sons got involved with this girl and that
one, and even Ben, himself, fell in love in at least one episode of
one of television's longest running series, "Bonanza." Ben and
the lady said goodbye tearfully, knowing that it could never be.
As fate would have it, it had been Ben, himself, who had gunned
down the lady's husband. Self-defense.

The series, "Baretta," offers a nice illustration of television's
unmistakable preference for men without women. It opened in
1975, a recycled version of "Toma," a forerunner which had
closed the preceding season. Tony Musante, the star of "Toma,"
surprised everyone by quitting the leading role in the successful
series after just one season. Left with a profitable show but no
lead, the ABC network commissioned the rewrite job that turned
out "Baretta." Toma had been billed as a loving husband and
father, even occasionally seen tucking his children into bed and
kissing them goodnight on camera. Baretta's fiancée died in his
arms on opening night. Thenceforth, he appeared as a womanless
savior, dedicating tireless efforts to righting the wrong that made
him so by flushing out all wrongdoers. Another vow, another
knight; yet there he was, an attractive and vigorous young man,
available to come on strong whenever the writers got the cue that
it's time to move him into the swinging-singles set; which is

precisely what happened as the 1976–77 television season opened.

The television formula must hem in the lovelife of its saviors. Redressers of wrongs must be free to dedicate every ounce of attention and energy and pour all their emotions into solving the weekly problem and rescuing the weekly victim. There is no room for any long-term commitment to a woman and children under such circumstances. For many years, the same requirement ruled out any sexual involvement for these *machos*, as well. Those were the days of "twin-bed television," the long build-up period when executive suites at the networks declared that respectable people could never be divorced and nobody, not even married couples, could be shown sharing a bed. According to the old formula, sexual involvement without marriage was a punishable offense; such goings-on were rarely allowed onstage; and when they were shown, the affair could come to no good end. It was this "twin-bed ruling" that made television's heroes into knights-errant. They had to be mobile and freewheeling, romantic yet unconsummatable, monklike. Caine, the half-white, half-Oriental hero of "Kung Fu," was the ultimate embodiment of the symbol. The country saw this prototype of the unattainable, loveless-womanless-*macho*-knight-errant weekly wandering through the American frontier. Caine was literally a priest, "of the Shaolin variety," according to the ABC network's publicity releases for the show.

It was only with the demise of the twin-bed ruling that television heroes were permitted to begin to swing. One of the first was Kojak, a cop who had been divorced. Every now and then the audience was granted a glimpse of the lieutenant's private, off-duty life, suggesting that the makings of a middle-aged swinger had been built into the part. Writers for the show remained rather reticent about the matter, allowing just those brief glimpses, those unstated innuendos. By the time "Harry O" opened a year later, however, it looked as if the osteopath had prescribed bed exercise for this detective's weak back. "Ethnics" got their own swinger with Chico ("Chico and the Man"), the blacks got theirs with Clifton Curtis, sexy, black, bachelor barber. The woman Clifton loves, however, is his mama ("That's My Mama").

The whole country watched the antics of Hawkeye and Trapper, two drafted civilian doctors in the Korean War theater. They were swingers at the front and swingers whenever they were lucky enough to make it to R & R in Tokyo. Hotlips and Frank, of the same M*A*S*H unit, bedded down every time they could manage to sneak to the supply room. Bob Hartley's friends, coworkers, and even his patients—turned out upon occasion to be a rather swinging lot ("The Bob Newhart Show"). On "The Mary Tyler Moore Show," Ted Baxter rather fancied himself as a swinger, even if he was a little clumsy at it. He seemed to quiet down a bit after he and Georgette started living together that year. After his wife left him, Lou Grant, Mary's boss on the show, tried his hand at swinging. Even Doctor Joe Gannon ("Medical Center") began to move cautiously into the swinging-singles set.

In the same season the lady swingers began to appear in prime time. "Karen," a new series about an eligible bachelor girl with a social conscience, joined two series featuring lady cops. Christie Love was the black one ("Get Christie Love") and Pepper Anderson was the white one ("Police Woman"). Christie was provided with a man who was unmistakably sweet on her, but her fierce independence and professional zeal kept her wedded to the job. The case of Pepper Anderson left things a bit more ambiguous. In every episode it looked as if she might have something going with her superior officer, Bill Crowley; but Pepper had become a cop out of reverence for the memory of her own deceased husband, a police officer killed in the line of duty. The writers never made it clear whether the relationship with Crowley was a love affair or whether the audience was being shown the same kind of sexless devotion prime-time television likes so much to demonstrate between male couples on the force.

Male couples are popular on television, pals and buddies who would go to the stake for each other if necessary. Steve McGarrett and his young colleague, Dan Williams, repeatedly demonstrated their very special relationship; McGarrett even using a pet name for buddy Williams: "Dan-O" ("Hawaii Five-O"). Officers Reed and Malloy continued cruising together as they had been doing since 1967 ("Adam 12"). These cop pairs reach back into television's past, even to the days of radio, rivaling the story of Damon and Pythias as a symbolic tale of love between friends.

ON-THE-JOB FAMILIES

It's hard to determine where to classify Lieutenant Mike Stone, a widower, and his sidekick, young and single Officer Steve Keller ("Streets of San Francisco"). Should they go in the column for male couples or the column for on-the-job families? What about Dr. Marcus Welby and Dr. Stephen Kiley? Throughout 1974–75, as they had since 1969, they continued to share their practice and their living quarters ("Marcus Welby, M.D."). Were Peggy and Joe Mannix and Peggy's usually invisible child, Toby, an on-the-job family ("Mannix")? These relationships remained puzzlers, never clearly stated. What *is* clearly stated is prime-time television's preference for showing the country people who are coworkers on a job but who relate to each other as if they were a family. Ironside's "family" is probably the prototype: the three young people who worked for him often took their meals at his table, even cooked for him. They addressed him as "Chief," much the same way that some British families say "Governor" instead of "Father." The same pattern of familylike relationships turned up in the triumvirate of rookie cops under Lieutenant Ryker's fatherly supervision ("The Rookies") and the triumvirate of young informers under Captain

Greer's fatherly direction ("Mod Squad").[8] Weekly, the nation joined "the bunch" at WJM-TV's newsroom where Mary Richards worked ("The Mary Tyler Moore Show"); "the bunch" at the police precinct where Barney Miller worked ("Barney Miller"); "the bunch" at Open America where Karen worked ("Karen")—all metaphors for family relations. People who happen to find themselves on the payroll of the same bureaucratic outfits act not as if they belonged in the same labor union, but rather as if they were brothers and sisters, fathers and sons, husbands and wives. Boss and hired hand, supervisor and underling, superior officer and inferior—such power relationships are blurred as the television formula substitutes for them a watered-down family image.

The hotel setting of "Hot l Baltimore," a second-season opening that year, moved the family metaphor out of the work setting into a hotel setting. The switch in the formula provided a bit more flexibility since transients could file in and out of the story just as they filed in and out of the hotel lobby—satellites orbiting around the nuclear cast that was also the nuclear-family substitute.

Even though the familyless loner turns up with such inevitable consistency that the formula is recognizable by anyone, executives at network headquarters are reluctant to talk about the business's insistence on blue-penciling images of people who live together in family units in which a man and a woman seriously commit themselves, to each other, to their children, and thus to a long-term future. One producer, interviewed by a *New York Times* reporter, said he "hadn't given much thought to the phenomenon." He departed from protocol, however: at least he was willing to speculate about it. Showing people anchored by the commitment of marriage is—well—troublesome in a prime-time television series. Marriage and the family tie a character to domestic situations and "can mess up the pacing of a show," he said. "The FBI" was one series he cited as an example. In its initial cycle, one of the regulars was married. His home and family interfered with the story line, so the writers quietly, unobtrusively, dropped all references to a wife after just a few episodes.[9]

The entertainment business's trade press, however, is not at all shy about admitting that the vanishing family on prime-time television reflects deliberate program policy. The theory is that it encourages identification with the show, inviting the viewer to take part in the dramatic role-play. Here's the way the virtues of the television series, "Family Affair," were detailed in *Variety* by the syndicating company advertising it for sale:

A mother's other family.

When "Family Affair" brought an irresistible new family to network television, there was no mother. So women immediately adopted "Family Affair" as their favorite television sitcom . . .

Audience composition was beautifully balanced. Except for one pretty skew toward women 18–49. This group represented 70% of all daytime women viewers . . .

When a series of this high calibre comes along, a station has only one reasonable course of action: follow a woman's lead and adopt.

"Family Affair" from Viacom, naturally.[10]

"Women are selling 'Family Affair' for us," says Viacom's advertisement on the cover of *Broadcasting,* June 10, 1974. "It's the kind of family every woman wants to join," says another *Variety* advertisement on February 13, 1974.

It would have been pretty difficult for any American to miss the broken family featured in "Family Affair," since it ran through five prime-time seasons and two daytime seasons on CBS, and continuing sale in this country and abroad is assured. The series chronicles the adventures of three orphaned children adopted by their Uncle Bill, a bachelor architect living the life of a swinging single in a glamorous New York penthouse. The children are placed in the care of bowler-wearing Mr. French, a paragon who—as nanny-tutor-butler-chef—keeps the household running impeccably, and as an added bonus speaks with a British accent. The advertisement is not a bit reticent about acknowledging that the show's success depends on inviting women to weave their fantasies around repeated images of motherless children in the care of a man who lives without lasting commitment to a woman he loves, who in turn commits herself to him, to the children, and to the future. Family values? Desensitization coupled with negative reinforcement, the ad implies, is good for sales.

4

Assembling
the Child
Market

Children growing up in the United States today live in an atmosphere totally saturated by television. Daytime serials are targeted mainly to adult women, many of whom are housebound in the constant company of infants, preschoolers, and toddlers. The images and sounds of the programs envelop these children, awake or asleep, alert or drowsy. By the time they are of school age, they can watch the comfortably familiar shows on their own and talk over the stories and characters with each other. Even children whose families may insist on excluding soap operas from the home, cannot avoid getting to know about them anyway. Along with the rest of television, the soaps are embedded in the culture of childhood.

So are the prime-time serials and the programs made especially to attract children. They are aided further by a total marketing system which provides children with games and dolls, books, comic books, records, clothes, furniture, foods, candies, drugs, vitamins, pencils, crayons, notebooks—an almost endless list of items all bearing images of the shows and the stars. At play, the children imagine themselves as Kojak[1] or the Six Million Dollar Man, as Police Woman or Mary Tyler Moore. Imagining is what makes imaginations.

The television business sets aside a block of weekend hours for programs made specifically to attract children to the television screen. Sometimes called "the children's ghetto," these hours are filled with shows whose reiterated images and formulas do their own bit to discredit family life, substituting the gang of children and teenagers as a preferred social setting for meaningful emotional involvement.

On both network and most nonnetwork stations, preferred hours for amassing "the juvenile market" are from 8 A.M. to noon every Saturday. Programs, varying little from year to year, are principally animated cartoons provided by a handful of studios in Hollywood. An occasional variety show turns up, and from time to time an action-adventure series. About 16 percent of ghetto time goes to commercials and similar intrusions on the children's attention.[2] These programs make up only about 8 percent of the television diet consumed by children up to eleven years of age.[3] They are nevertheless much in demand by advertisers, who seek them as showcases for exhibiting wares they wish to impress upon the consciousness of children and of those who purchase things on behalf of children.

BLACKING OUT THE FAMILY

Let's take as an example the 1974–75 television offerings,[4] reasonably representative of the usual series networks book to attract children to the set. Not one series featured an intact, contemporary family, forging and reforging emotional bonds. Instead, the children were invited to see "The Addams Family," an animated series that featured a family of lovable monsters. "The Jetsons" dramatized family life in a push-button society of the future. "Valley of the Dinosaurs" and "Korg" showed Stone Age families. Note that these shows followed the lead of the prime-time selections, presenting intact families as if they were museum exhibits, either relics of a long lost past or an exhibit in the fanciful world of the future. The rest of the shows beamed at the children featured broken families, platoons, teams, and gangs.

Indeed, the broken family is more evident in programs scheduled for the children's ghetto than on daytime serials or prime-time shows. "The Partridge Family," a well-known broken family, has received a good deal of network exposure. It started out as a series in prime time featuring live actors, then was recycled as a cartoon version, "The Partridge Family, 2200 A.D." Both versions featured a mother raising her fatherless children with the aid of her agent, whose role in the family remained unstated. Mother and children were rock stars. The cartoon version moved the lot of them into the world of the future. "These Are the Days" showed a widow at the beginning of the century raising two children with the help of their grandfather—likewise widowed. "Land of the Lost" featured a motherless family (father and two children), transported back in time to the Paleolithic age, trying to find their way back to the present.

This count notes only the presence or absence of a formal structure of family life in the images beamed at children. Another investigator, analyzing programs booked to attract children in earlier seasons, noted not only presentations of formal family structure; he also counted incidents of what he called "nurturing behavior."[5] He was interested in images of an adult taking care of a baby or a sick child, comforting a hurt or unhappy child, serving food to a child or even just sitting down and having a real meal with a child—the mundane behavior that goes on when people care for children and care about them. Scenes showing someone bathing or helping a child dress or cleaning him up or picking him up or wiping his nose; scenes showing someone getting a child ready for bed, embracing or kissing him, tucking him in, telling him a story or singing a song to him. Scenes showing an adult playing a game with a child just for fun; these were the kinds of images he tallied. He reported exactly three instances of such nurturing behavior in fifty-eight half-hour episodes that he observed.* He went on to count the number of times these shows featured any kind of family ritual or reunion or celebration: a birth, christening, first communion, confirmation, or bar mitzvah; a family gathering to celebrate a birthday, anniversary, graduation, engagement, wedding, funeral; a family sitting down together for a holiday dinner. He found just one such scene in the whole batch: a pair of motor cars were joined in holy matrimony by a clergyman car![6]

He kept track of the use of family names on the shows he analyzed. "About 60 per cent of all the characters seen in the 58 episodes analyzed have no last names," he reported.[7] Only five among the thirty-three separate series he listed included family names in the title,[8] and *Mr., Mrs.,* or *Miss* are unheard of forms of address on these shows.

Those who book the shows into the children's weekend block like plots that delete mothers and fathers entirely. Twenty-five of the thirty-five series scheduled in the 1974–75 season blacked out parents (four kept some kind of family tie going among the featured players, but not parental ties.)[9] The rest showed mixed gangs of teenagers and children with no parents in evidence, or military and paramilitary units and teams.[10]

---

*Interesting to note: there were no instances of children playing unorganized games with each other, either.

Featuring the Gang

The social group television likes best to feature in the hours allotted to children is the gang. Sometimes it's a gang of animated human or humanoid figures; sometimes it's a gang of animated animals; sometimes it's a gang of animated motor cars. The audience is invited to like these gangs and identify with the children and adolescents in them, or with the anthropomorphic characters in the animations. Whether the gambit is successful or not depends, of course, on the child. Still, one thing is certain. The reiterated showing of this kind of social grouping, and the social support system that glamorizes it, legitimizes the teenage gang as a viable social structure; any child growing up in this country can scarcely miss the signals.

The chronicle for the 1974–75 season, which follows, begins with Yogi Bear since the title chosen for this ABC series makes the point in a nutshell: "Yogi's Gang".[11]

"Superfriends" featured Superman, Batman, Wonderwoman, and Aquaman—a whole hour of antics by this Nietzschean gang in body suits who zip around the universe zapping the bad guys. "Scooby Doo, Where Are You?" built each episode around the adventures of an animated dog and his gang. "Speed Buggy" featured an animated automobile and a pack of teenagers. In "Wheelie and the Chopper Bunch," an animated car is plagued by a gang of animated motorcycles. "Fat Albert and the Cosby Kids" followed a gang of black teenagers week by week. In "Lassie's Rescue Rangers," Lassie was the star, just as she had always been in the Lassie series featuring real people, real dog. In this cartoon version, she appeared with her own gang of animals—a mountain lion, a skunk, a raccoon, an owl, a rabbit, a raven, a turtle, and a porcupine (integrated, as it were). "Sigmund and the Sea Monsters" featured kids and puppets ganging up to keep the grownups in the dark about their adventures.

Action often took place in a clubhouse that only the gang might enter.

TEENAGE PAIRS

Along with teenage gangs, the television business repeatedly books shows featuring the teenage pair. "Jeanie" was about a teenage girl who used her magic powers either to embarrass or to rescue her teenage boyfriend. "Goober and the Ghost Chasers" featured a lovable dog with the talent of making himself invisible. His constant companions were two teenage reporters, one male, one female.

Goober borrowed the transformation trick from the Superman formula, which never dies. So did "Hong Kong Phooey"; in each episode a humanoid dog (Penrod Pooch), working as a janitor in a police station, pulled the old Clark Kent stunt to transform himself into Supersleuth, Hong Kong Phooey. "Shazam!" resuscitated Captain Marvel, who has been around about forty years, having moved to thwarting bad drug-pushers instead of the bad Axis menace. The lines of goodthink* dialogue remain unchanged, however. ("There are many ways to avoid responsibility, but there is only one way to face it," someone in Greek battle dress intones. "Holy Moley," ripostes Billy Batson.)

ADULTS IN PLATOONS AND TEAMS

Sometimes shows booked for the juvenile market feature adults. When this is the case, the adults are usually in tight, hierarchic formation. During the 1974–75 season, the children got an animated version of "Star Trek," featuring the captain and crew of a spacefleet in the world of the future. "Emergency Plus Four"

---

*The term was created by George Orwell, and used in his book *1984,* to refer to pious platitudes expressing unquestioning acceptance of officially approved attitudes, beliefs, and values.

(in animation) featured a paramilitary unit, firemen rescuing the victims of a weekly catastrophe. "The Harlem Globetrotters Popcorn Machine" glamorized a team of professional athletes. Even "The Adventures of Gilligan", an animated version of a show made originally for the adult market, featured a common sailor and his captain, who maintained that relationship even after being shipwrecked on a desert island.

From the point of view of public policy, it makes little difference whether these programing formulas are deliberate or accidental. What is clear is this: night after night and year after year prime-time television joins daytime television in doing violence to the emotional relations that bind people together in family units. Daytime shows do so by trivializing these relations. Prime-time shows do so by ridicule or—and this is the preferred mode —by obliterating from the nations's principal collective experience authentic images that arouse authentic feelings about authentic human relationships. In the parlance of behavior modification, this is *negative* reinforcement. Programs booked into the children's ghetto follow the lead of prime-time programs and add their own special fillip: dramatizations of the joys of gang life.

5

Keep the
Children
Coming Through
the Pipeline

Programing for children operates as if they were cub scouts training on Saturday mornings for the stronger stuff that comes up later. Series after series booked "for your children's viewing pleasure" recycle old scripts and plots, using the same characters, the same voices, the same formats and gimmicks borrowed from shows originally bought to attract general audiences. Spinoffs—a programing device that propagates television programs the way plants are cloned from slips and cuttings—are as evident in the children's ghetto as they are in the prime-time hours. A character who has proved to be an attention-getter on one show is promoted, so to speak, turning up as a "tentpole" character starring in his or her own show; or a format that has proved successful in one series is booked for children, with fanciful animals in the well-known roles originally played by real human actors.

CLONING PROGRAMS

Some examples. In September 1975, ABC raised the curtain on "The Oddball Couple," a "new" kids' show. It was an animated spinoff of "The Odd Couple," a show the same network had bought for prime-time showing in 1970 and had run for five consecutive years. They did the same thing with "Kung Fu": "Hong Kong Phooey" was the title of the animated series offered to children from 1974 to 1976: each animated episode was beamed to the children three times in 1974, then scheduled to run in triplicate again during the 1975–76 television year. This is standard practice for shows aiming to attract children. A series is ordered by cycles: usually thirteen to sixteen episodes in the first cycle are shown over a two-year period. Six airings per episode on network time is the usual quota. Then, if the series is not renewed, these episodes are turned over to a syndicating company which sells them to any and all takers here and abroad, for endless and repeated reruns.

"Hong Kong Phooey" 's animated hero, no less than his Oriental counterpart in the nighttime slot, glorified and advertised "the martial arts"—which is what ABC's releases call those karate chops, kicks to the kidneys and the groin, rabbit punches, eye gouges, and the like. The animated series targeted to children joined seventy-two episodes of the original "live on film" show for grownups already available for sale forevermore.[1]

Gilligan is an all-time favorite with the television bookers. ABC announced an animated version, "Adventures of Gilligan," for its 1974–75 Saturday line-up for children. The following year they scheduled "New Adventures of Gilligan"—more of the same. Sixteen animated episodes were manufactured, each scheduled for the usual six airings, joining ninety-eight episodes packaged from the original network series for grownups, which ran from 1965 to 1967.

"Planet of the Apes" was another recycled show beamed at the children. NBC had announced the animated version for the 1975–76 Saturday-morning lineup. The series continued the adventures of characters the whole country had seen in a CBS prime-time slot just the year before. Thirteen episodes and four repeats shown in grownup time were joined by seventeen animated episodes the network scheduled for six showings each.

"Emergency Plus Four," animated version, was booked to attract children in 1973, ran through two seasons (1973–75), and was scheduled for still another cycle in 1975–76. It followed the pattern of the original show which had premiered in grownup time in January 1973. NBC rebooked the original for the full season, 1973–74, and continued to rebook it 1974–76.* Its ninety episodes plus reruns were joined by the twenty-four animated episodes the same network had targeted for repeated showings to children on Saturday mornings.

"The Partridge Family 2200 A.D." was cloned for showing to children from the original series, which ran on the CBS network for four years. Ninety-six episodes are in cans and up for sale in syndication. The children were told that the animated version was new, just for them, when it opened in 1974 on CBS. Of course it was the same family of rock singers, going through the same paces—this time in the world of the future. Ninety-six original episodes plus repeats were shown on grownup time; sixteen original episodes were scheduled for six airings each in children's ghetto time.

"Lassie's Rescue Rangers," featuring animated Lassie and her gang, opened in 1973 and was rebooked in 1974, joining 521 episodes of the original Lassie series, which began in 1954 and is still up for sale in syndication.

"My Favorite Martian." The animated series targeted to children opened in September 1973 and ran for two television years, until 1975. Action in this animated series centered on the antics

---

*And again in 1977.

of an "uncle" from Mars and his nephew—same formula, same gimmicks that the whole country had gotten to know when CBS ran the original series: one hundred and seven episodes now join the twenty-four animated episodes.

"The Addams Family," in animated form, opened "good as new" for the children in 1973, and ran until 1975 just as they were when they appeared "live on film" in grownup time, 1964–66 on ABC. Sixty-four episodes join the animated episodes for sale here and all over the world.

"Star Trek," is a perennial favorite with television booking offices. In some areas of the country the original series has been repeated as many as a dozen times in a single listening area. College students can recite chunks of dialogue, word for word. The seventy-nine episodes of the original show, which opened on the NBC network in 1969, now join the set of animated episodes, each of which was beamed at the children at least twice over a two-year period. As of this writing, a full-length feature movie is in production[2] and this country's first space shuttle has been named, "The Enterprise." It was a last-minute change by Gerald Ford, then caretaker president filling out Richard Nixon's unfinished term of office. He preferred the name of "Star Trek" 's spaceship to the name originally selected for the real one: "The Constitution."

In "The Brady Kids," two families come together when a widowed mother marries a widower-father. She has three daughters; he has three sons; the reconstituted family adds up to nine —the ninth is the maid. The 52 animated episodes for children followed the same pattern the 117 episodes of the live-on-film version ("The Brady Bunch") had shown the whole country during 1969–74.

Maxwell Smart is a zany secret agent starring with his female companion, Ninety-nine, in "Get Smart." This series was shown on CBS 1965–69 in the live-on-film version and its 138 episodes are available for sale to any buyer. The children were treated to

the whole thing in an animated version, "Inch High Private Eye"
—13 episodes each repeated three times during the 1973–74 television season.

Pebbles, daughter of Fred and Wilma Flintstone, made a sudden transition from infant to teenager, and so did Bamm Bamm,
son of Barney and Betty Rubble. They appear together forever
in their own show, "Pebbles and Bamm Bamm," which opened
in 1971 on CBS and ran through the 1971–72 season there. The
following season they joined their parents in "The Flintstone
Comedy Hour" only to return to their own show for the 1975–76
season.

The recycling pattern for this series is somewhat special since
the progenitor that spawned the versions shown in the children's-
ghetto hours was one of a kind: "The Flintstones" was originally
an animation booked to attract general audiences, not just children, during the 1960–66 television years (166 episodes are
available for sale). It was successful in recruiting grownups to
watch, and the children who joined the general audience kept
watching too. Without waiting for the Flintstone series to run its
course, NBC signed on "The Jetsons," an animated family virtually indistinguishable from the Flintstone family. The gimmicks,
however, are switched by eons; the Flintstones live out their
suburban, detached-dwelling life in Paleolithic times; the Jetsons
do the same in the world of the future. "The Jetsons" played to
children in 1969, 1971, 1972, and 1973—24 original episodes each
unreeled six times for a total of 144 showings.

"All in the Family," top ratings-buster in the television business, appeals to the broadest range of taste among the current
crop of adult television watchers. Once today's children have
matured, will their tastes have diverged to the extent that the
Bunker family—by then canned and for sale in syndication like
all the rest—can no longer be expected to attract such widespread attention? Insurance against this possibility is built into
the recycling process. Pebbles's voice in "Pebbles and Bamm

Bamm" is the voice of Sally Struthers, the star who plays the Bunker daughter in "All in the Family." "The Barkelys" is a family of animated dogs, and the father is indistinguishable from Archie Bunker. This cartoon series opened in 1971—seventeen episodes each scheduled for six showings on network time alone.

BREAKING THEM IN ON TV FORMULAS

When little-league beginners in television watching are not being trained on animated versions of stars and shows made to attract general audiences, they are being trained on shows that teach them the formats and formulas television likes. "Lancelot Link, Secret Chimp," opened in 1970 and ran on ABC for two years. Fifty-two episodes are available in syndication. The formula: the usual cop-detective-crime show. "Houndcats" opened on NBC in 1972—twenty-six episodes in multiple repetitions. It starred a zany cat-and-dog detective team, just like any other cop-detective-crime show. "Run, Joe, Run" was shown on NBC beginning in 1974. It follows the formula of the prime-time series, "The Fugitive." "The Hudson Brothers Razzle Dazzle Comedy Show" which opened in 1974 (twenty-four episodes plus repeats) is just like any comedy-variety show on grownup time. "Runaround": NBC aired this game show for the 1972 semester—a give-away show no different from any give-away show in grownup time. "Funky Phantom" opened in 1971 on ABC and ran for four semesters. It often based its plots on well-known movie and television programs.

Such a programing policy trains children in their earliest years for the advanced television watching they are expected to graduate to. Its more immediate aim is to keep children of all ages lined up in front of the television set, minimizing the possibility that any of them—even the very youngest—will drop out. "We gear our Saturday schedule basically to an age group of from 3 to about 11," said Mr. Allan Ducovny, explaining the policy he followed when he was director of children's programing at CBS. And he went on to add that animations are especially useful since without them "the 3-to-5 year olds might drop out . . ."[3] This is a policy all three networks follow. None of them makes any distinction between imaginations ready for Mother Goose and imaginations ready for Washington Irving and Mark Twain.

All three networks muster their full battery of resources to keep audiences glued to the set, sprinkling exhortations to keep watching throughout any television day. Saturday morning is no exception. Here is a summary of notes taken shortly after the 1973–74 television season opened; they can be replicated almost any Saturday at any time of year.

> "Emergency Plus Four" is about to start at 9:30 A.M. on NBC. Mixed in among the usual clutch of commercials introducing it, I see a set of clips showing scenes from the episode of "Butch Cassidy" scheduled to go on a half-hour from now. A voice admonishes us to be sure not to miss it. "Stay tuned," says the voice, "for 'Butch Cassidy' right after 'Emergency Plus Four,' next on NBC." The show goes on. The usual interruptions advertising candy, toys, and soft drinks are joined by scenes from "Emergency" to be shown tonight in grownup time and the voice tells us all to be sure not to miss it at 8 P.M. on NBC.
>
> It's now 10 A.M. and "Butch Cassidy" is about to start. Tucked in among the back-to-back commercials introducing it are scenes from animated "Star Trek" and the voice orders us again to stay tuned, be sure not to miss "Star Trek" right after "Butch Cassidy," next on NBC.
>
> 10:30. "Star Trek" begins. Captain Kirk, Mr. Spock, Doc—the whole gang—reproduced feature for feature in animation. "Kirk to *Enterprise*. Beam us aboard, Mr. Scott." Same voices, same transporter room, same bridge. "Stay tuned," says the voice-over, "for 'Sigmund and the Sea Monsters,' next on NBC."

If the children in the audience obey that voice of authority, they will "stay tuned" clear through, from 8 A.M., when the ghetto hours begin, to at least 9 P.M., when the curtain drops on the last rescue the "Emergency" squad is to perform that night from 8 to 9 eastern time. That voice of authority has already taken its toll, as American children now substitute hours of television watching for hours they used to spend playing with each other. Any parent who does not wish his child to spend the day this way must countermand those repeated exhortations, continually pitting his own authority against the networks'.

It's already a lost cause. A colleague who wished to study children's spontaneous play and games in Ithaca, New York, time-sampling all the different elementary-school neighborhoods of the community during after-school hours on warm, fair-weather days, found that there were virtually no children in the public domain. He described the neighborhoods as "deserted villages."[4] Indeed, one of the most important accompaniments of the way American television is organized is the disappearance of spontaneous play and games among unsupervised groups of children.

MAGIC AND WITCHERY

The most casual television watching on Saturday morning reveals that problems are customarily solved by means that either use magic explicitly, or by means said to be scientific and technological, but which are actually more magical than anything else —such as the starship *Enterprise* transporter room, which moves people from the starship to faraway places and back again ("Star Trek"). The claim is that it's done by advanced technology, so it's hard to notice that at the present moment and until further notice it's a magic trick.

Magic performed by witches, and witchery, are popular on the programs network booking agents line up for children.[5] Jeannie —a genie, not strictly speaking a witch—was featured in animation during the 1973–74 and 1974–75 television seasons. Forty-eight episodes of the animated version now join the 139 episodes of "I Dream of Jeannie," which had appeared on network television from 1965 to 1970, now for sale in syndication.

Sabrina is another witch, one of the most popular characters among network buyers catering to "the child market." She was the lead in "Sabrina the Teenage Witch"—seventeen animated half-hours that ran through 1969–72, each in multiple showings. Meanwhile, even while teenage, animated Sabrina was on stage at CBS, the original show she was patterned after—"Bewitched" —was playing to children at the ABC network 1971–73. The public interest, convenience, and necessity, network executives had decided, would best be served by offering the children reruns of the identical show whose 252 episodes had been aired on the ABC network 1964–72, and were still around in syndication buys.

The image of young female witches will ever be entrenched in the culture of American childhood. Just during the first half of the decade, animated Sabrina, the young witch, live-on-film Samantha, in the original version, and Jeannie the Genie dominated the children's ghetto for about three hundred showings, as episode after episode starring these young ladies was repeated and repeated and repeated. As of this writing, these three series are still going strong in reruns through syndicated sale.

GALAXIES OF STARS

It is common practice for the animations to reproduce the likenesses of the original stars. This has been done in such series as "The Osmonds," "The Jackson Five," "The Partridge Family," "The Brady Kids," "Star Trek," "Emergency Plus Four," and "The Jerry Lewis Show." It is equally common practice for stars to visit back and forth on these programs and when they do, they, too, are reproduced feature for feature. The children get to know Raquel Welch, Elvis Presley, Sean Connery, the Rolling Stones,

Ed Sullivan, Marlo Thomas, Mama Cass, and Jonathan Winters —all these performers and others appear often, in animated form, as guest stars or visitors to programs the business urges the children to watch every weekend.[6]

During 1972 through 1974, "ABC Superstar Movies" filled over a hundred half-hours in the children's ghetto on Saturdays. The program spliced together animated clips based on a number of movies and television shows, the animations reproducing the likenesses of the stars.* "The New Scooby Doo Movies" (1972–74) used the same cut-and-paste formula. The children were urged to watch animations of none other than guest stars Phyllis Diller, Sandy Duncan, Davey Jones, the Harlem Globetrotters, Sonny and Cher, Carolyn Jones, and the whole cast of the Addams Family—to mention only a few.

The stars who took the original roles in series booked at first to recruit grown-up audiences often record the soundtracks accompanying the recycled animations the children get. The voices of Captain Kirk, Mr. Spock, and Doc in the animated "Star Trek" are the voices of William Shatner, Leonard Nimoy, and DeForest Kelley, actors still going strong elsewhere on television and in reruns of the original version of "Star Trek." Bill Cosby, the black television star, not only gets title billing in "Fat Albert and the Cosby Kids"; his voice also is heard on the soundtrack.** It is difficult to think of a child growing up in this cultural habitat who does not now, and will not in the future, register at least a flicker of warm recognition when he sees those well-loved profiles, hears those attention-getting voices, associated as they must be with the nostalgic memories of childhood days.

---

*Its opening show, September 16, 1972, showed clips from one of ABC's favorite series for grownups and children alike: "The Brady Bunch."

**Bill Cosby is also featured in the Children's Television Workshop program, "Electric Company," and in numerous commercials.

6

People
and Spaces,
People
in Spaces

The animated cartoons delivered to the children in such massive doses first by networks, and then by syndication companies selling network castoffs, join the rest of television in shaping the culture each new generation learns. Story and drama, music and dialogue help children learn to make sense out of the world; and in the learning they literally make their own senses. Language takes note of this: we say a child develops "an ear" and "a taste" for music or "an eye" for shapes and colors and fashions; and just as surely as the children store the food they eat—not *in* their bodies but *as* their bodies, they store the images of the television dramas not *in* their minds, but *as* their minds.

Can blue jiggle? What color is the letter *A*? Can I explore in a picture? When I look in the mirror, do I see myself or is it someone else? Why don't I see myself when I look into a daisy? How does light sound? Can a stone dance? When will the square be round? Where is the automobile's voice? What does it eat? If you fall, can you break to pieces? Where does the line go? When the fire goes out, where is it? Is the bubble thirsty?

These are the kinds of questions children ask every day. Poetry or naïveté? Ignorance or artistry? Sometimes it is wise to treat them soberly, taking advantage of the chance to expand the child's store of information—even if it means going to the encyclopedia to look up the hard ones. Sometimes it's a good idea to treat them playfully, exercising the imaginations of the child who asks and the adult who responds as they move each other back and forth between a world of fantasy and a world of reality.

Cartoon animations answer these and similar questions for children, quite literally. Blue jiggles, squares turn into circles, stones get up and dance, automobiles converse and sit down to meals, human figures shatter to pieces and are instantly reconstituted as the pieces pick themselves up to rejoin each other. Animated cartoons are said to be especially attractive to children, partly because of this very quality of versatility. Other charms, however, make them at least equally attractive to network executives, who book them consistently to convene "the weekend child market." (From 1970 through 1974, 77 percent of children's weekend shows were animations.[1]) These networks and a handful of agencies represent the interests of a handful of advertisers—corporations who are in no way publicly accountable and whose decision-making processes are closed to public scrutiny.

Indeed, it's not clear who finds the animations more attractive —the children who watch them or the network personnel who book them. Their advantages from the businessman's point of view are obvious: they can be produced by low-priced, programed industrial processes rather than by high-priced, thoughtful artistic processes.[2] They can employ a cast of thousands; and they can be hooked into lucrative syndication and endless franchising deals.

Limited Animation and Computer Techniques

Producing animations today is a vastly different process from the original mode of making animated cartoons. It used to be an art as well as a craft, requiring painstaking, lovingly made paintings and drawings—twenty-four for each frame—that were, in themselves, works of art; and, of course, very costly. Even then, however, the final product was standardized and frozen. Walt Disney, perhaps more than any other person, was influential in developing and popularizing the animation process that phased out dramatic improvisation, dramatic art, artists, and artistry. "Everything is preplanned," says an admirer of the Disney system. "Nothing is left to the temperament of the stars, to the day-to-day inspirations of director and cameraman, or to the vagaries of light and weather." Disney called animations "the most controlled form of film-making imaginable."[3] In his studios, animations were produced by processes at least as close to engineering as to art.

Mickey Mouse made his debut in 1928.[4] Since then, the animation process has been steadily industrialized. Like any other business, animation studios have tried to cut their costs by moving to areas of low labor costs[5] and by systematically transforming the craft into an assembly-line process. "Limited animation" uses only four to six drawings per frame instead of the original twenty-four. The frames, moreover, can be kept in stock and reused, drawings repeated not just within the same episode, not just within the same series, but also from one series to another. Stock shots from "The Flintstones" can do double duty in "Pebbles and Bamm Bamm." A new series can be pieced together from segments of old ones. A show that may once have taken months to produce by hand can now be turned out in four to six weeks. Savings that accrue for series that run in seemingly inexhaustible cycles such as "Pink Panther," "Bugs

Bunny," "Archie," and so on, are considerable.

The limited-animation process ensures uniformity and standardization from the outset. The cartoons are always the same kinds of simplified line drawings, the same backgrounds, the same jerky movements. When someone walks, his limbs move but his body does not. He addresses a group: his lips move, his eyes may blink, but his face remains expressionless. His listeners are frozen, equally expressionless, unresponsive. The soundtrack reproduces the same musical notes over and over again. The dialogue reproduces the same vocal styles, tones, modulations, phrasings. The laugh tracks reproduce the same bursts of laughter.

Now that computer techniques have been introduced into the animation studios, even cheaper productions are possible,[6] and standardization spreads to even smaller elements of the cartoon-making process. Artists and craftsmen can be entirely replaced by technicians, who break down a visual presentation into information bits. Stored in the computer's memory bank, each bit is retrievable on demand as electronic impulse, and can be reproduced endlessly by computer printout. This opens the possibility of standardizing even finer elements in any scene. Almost any feature can be used over and over again—these eyes, those lips, that nose—hands, arms, torsos, the same furniture, table service, vehicles, roadside scenes, flowers, trees, animals; even movements such as a stride or a dance step. Everything! At first glance the computerized result, translated into a picture, may seem new and different. But, just like the fourteen or so different auto models the Ford Motor Company unveils every season, when you examine them up close, you see they are all made of virtually the same components.

Walt Disney Studios now uses data processing to animate life-size three-dimensional figures in the performance of entire shows, complete with voice and music. The movements and the sounds are broken down into their component parts and stored as information bits in the memory banks of digital and analog computers. When a technician-programmer issues instructions, the computer operates the dummies accordingly, by electrical, pneumatic, and hydraulic hookup: always the same dummies, always the same movements, always the same sounds, combined and recombined over and over again. The process is called "audio animatronics," and the people at the Disney studios think of it as "animation in the round."[7]

A still more sophisticated technique produces images in color and in three dimensions by computer. No artwork other than the crude sketches of a story board is required. Each element in the sketches is described in computer language: dimensions, lighting, color, movement, and so on. The description is then relayed to corresponding codes in the machine's memory bank. The computer then dutifully generates the picture as per instructions. A motion-picture camera photographs and develops the picture and the final product is available in a day. "That's all there is to it."[8]

These computerized procedures guarantee that no materials produced in this fashion can ever break away from the margins rigidly built into the data bank: color values, lines, and outlines, lights and shadows, motion, motility, mobility, sound—all are permanently fixed; or at least until "central" sends a memorandum to "creative" with instructions to refurbish the data bank. To developing imaginations they offer a pool of imagery that becomes more and more homogeneous, more and more mechanical, less and less variegated, less and less artistic.

Uniforms and Career Apparel

The animation process, standardizing the fantasy environment that nourishes young imaginations, even makes it easy for the children to tell the good guys from the bad guys by putting everyone in easily recognizable uniforms. In the weekend shows television beams to children, about 27 percent of the characters with speaking parts typically wear military uniforms[9] like the crew of the *Enterprise* or team uniforms like the Harlem Globetrotters or magic-savior body-suit uniforms just like Superman. About 30 percent wear "career apparel,"[10] a euphemism for the word *uniform.*

Marketing as well as technical considerations make standardized costuming attractive to those who produce and book animations targeted to children. When the same characters turn up in the same costumes over and over again, their "recognition factor" is enhanced. The practice also makes it impossible for anyone in the so-called "creative" end of the business to show dramatically that, even if people in the same occupations often share the same social perspective, they do not all think and behave alike. Such a complex idea is the sort of thing that's usually relegated to goodthink one-liners on the soundtrack. Doctors wear a white coat and carry a stethoscope; scientists wear the same white coat but carry a clipboard instead.* Both are either very good or very bad. Whether good or bad, however, they are always very smart. Cab drivers wear visored caps and windbreakers, have the walk-on parts, and are not smart at all. Once a child learns the appropriate "career apparel," he knows exactly what kind of behavior and reactions go with it: uniform. That's what the word means, after all: uniform.

We say children watch television. And yet, of course, they do much more than watch the images television brings to them; they live the entire drama.[11] These are some of the pervasive experiences children draw on as they develop themselves—their characteristic ways of walking and running, moving and dancing, getting into and out of vehicles, sitting down and standing up, bowing and bending, jumping and skipping. Television initiates

---

*They often wear neat Vandykes that make them resemble the good colonel who advertises Kentucky Fried Chicken.

them into a whole world of body language—learning to increase or diminish the distance between themselves and others to signal intimacy or aloofness, acceptance or rejection, affection or hostility.[12] The animated cartoon dramas and their outline figures show and tell and show again the same standardized movements and relationships of people and spaces, people in spaces.

7

Two Laughs
a Minute

The laugh track is the evolutionary outgrowth of the studio audience. In the days of radio and early television, old-time performers such as Jack Benny, Fred Allen, Jackie Gleason, George Burns, Gracie Allen, and others whose comic styles depend heavily on timing and pacing, found that working in an empty recording studio was like playing to an empty house. Cutting themselves off from audience response deprived them of cues they needed to deliver the punchline. Bursts of laughter as members of the technical staff reacted to a gag or a piece of business were simply not enough.

It was to fill this void that audiences were first invited to attend the studio performances. Just as their laughter cued the actors, it cued home audiences as well, signaling the punchline, teaching the whole country not to miss the point, legitimizing gag-line humor for the country at large.

Audiences, however, are notoriously volatile. Sometimes they catch on, sometimes they do not. Producers, therefore, began to improve their reactions. They started by nudging studio audiences with cue cards; they ended by nudging the home audiences with laugh tracks.

The laugh track is now as essential to television comedies as the gags, the business, and the music. A burst of laughter every thirty seconds is a normal quota for network sitcoms such as "All in the Family" or "Barney Miller," as well as for "Pebbles and Bamm Bamm."

LAUGH AND THE WORLD LAUGHS WITH YOU[1]

The comedy shows that amass child audiences during Saturday morning hours are just as dependent on the validation of audience laughter as any other type of comedy show. The Harlem Globetrotters perform before a studio audience. Six men hold up white placards. H-E-A-L-T-H. "That's right, health!" they cry. Trumpets blare. Everybody laughs and applauds as the camera pans to show children in the studio audience having a good time, laughing, clapping, jumping up and down, as the Globetrotters assure them and the country that health is a very fine thing, indeed. One Globetrotter, dressed like a robber, accosts a victim.

ROBBER: Give me your money.
VICTIM: Say "Please."
   (Laughter as robber obliges)
VICTIM: You didn't say "thank you."
ROBBER: Thank you.
   (Laughter as victim turns over his money)
FIRST OBSERVER: This show is dopey, but it proves that it pays
     to be polite.
SECOND OBSERVER: Yeah, but how *much* does it pay?
   (Laughter)
FIRST OBSERVER: That depends on our sponsor. You see, he pays

us. Come in, sponsor.
    (Laughter. Blackout.)

The children in the studio audience and their enjoyment are an indispensable part of the show.

The laugh track is built into the factory-made animations no less than the shows performed by live-on-film actors performing before live-on-film audiences. Bugs Bunny engages in his usual antics with Elmer Fudd. (Laugh track.) An animated doctor car pours medicine into the carburetor of an animated car that is ill. (Laugh track.) A bumbling Great Dane is chased by a caveman. (Laugh track.) The Addams Family enters a baking contest and uses alligator eggs to make the batter. (Laugh track.) Pebbles and Bamm Bamm are chased by a weird-looking prehistoric creature. (Laugh track.)

A child who might not be quite attuned to these jokes or the gags of the Harlem Globetrotters, or any other gags on the shows beamed at children, learns an important lesson: that he or she has missed the point—whatever that point may be: Don Rickles insulting someone, Bugs Bunny imitating Don Rickles insulting someone, and so on down the line. Or the point could be what people in the business call "comedic violence": an animated creature is flattened by a steam roller (laugh track) or comes apart in a flurry of dismembered limbs (laugh track) which miraculously reassemble themselves into an intact body (laugh track). In any case, the laugh track is an unmistakable technique acting as positive reinforcement for this particular brand of standardized, sight-gag humor.

Children are sensitive to music and easily catch on to musical jokes. The bassoon, for example, frequently used in comic opera to underline a piece of buffoonery, can make some children laugh just at the sound of its *bla-a-at.* Not that the programs booked for Saturday mornings ever give their audiences a chance to learn or appreciate that sort of joke; the rock music they specialize in has no room for bassoons. Still, some children among the millions who make up the television audience surely discern musical jokes in the arrangements they hear. The child in the home audience who laughs, however, quickly learns something when the studio audience and the laugh track remain silent: negative reinforcement extinguishes the tendency to react.

Visual jokes, too, can strike the funnybone of children, especially those with a bent for art. A child looking intently at a familiar design might burst out laughing in delight when the eye plays a visual trick, jumping a background motif to the foreground and switching a foreground motif to the background. It's a visual pun—but any child who discerns one in the network fare quickly learns a lesson when his amusement is not echoed on the laugh track: negative reinforcement again.

Virtually all the cartoons aimed at children use a canned laugh track made up of laughs that have been pre-recorded and categorized into various reaction categories and various lengths. They are activated by an engineer in one of the dub-down processes of the production.[2] Among the scores of these cartoon shows that I have seen on television, I have never noted one that pumped up the laugh track for an artistic or musical joke of the kind I have described. These cartoons teach and legitimize only one kind of humor: drop-your-pants, pie-in-the-face, the big boff, and the one-liner.

LAUGHTER ENGINEERS

"I'd be willing to bet," a comedy writer told me, "that the laughter the kids are hearing this Saturday morning could be the same laughter you heard on one of the family sitcom shows I wrote in the sixties." The audiences that produced the roars, titters, and chuckles of the canned laugh tracks these shows splice into their tapes, the gags that set them off, the actors delivering the lines, the shows themselves—have all long since passed on, many of them dead and buried literally as well as figuratively. But the laughter they produced or elicited has been immortalized electronically and is used over and over in shows distributed throughout the nation, throughout the world.

The feat is accomplished by a firm which has cornered the laugh-track market: Northridge Electronics. Charlie Douglas, head of the firm, considers himself a virtuoso with the "laff-box" that produces the tracks he feels can make or break a show.

The laff-box is activated by a bank of thirty-six keys, much like typewriter keys. There's a foot pedal, too, so that the person who works the machine plays it something like an organ. Inside the box are lengths of audio tape—"loops." About ten different laughs are recorded on each loop; thirty-two loops in the box, three hundred and twenty laughs in all. These three hundred and twenty laughs can be combined in an almost infinite number of combinations of "uproarious" and "spontaneous" laughter. Each loop is activated by its own key. An extra key activates an applause loop.

Every conceivable kind of laugh has been preserved on these loops. Guffaws and belly laughs, hoots and hollers, giggles and chuckles and titters. Chortles. Whoopers. Screamies. A sobbing laugh that sounds like crying. Laughter that explodes only on sharp intakes of breath. Laughter that explodes only as breath is expelled. Charlie Douglas and his assistants (he calls them his "laff boys") mix them skillfully to produce the kind of laughter a producer or director orders, from "a big boff" here to "a long climax" there. He can serve up the laughter of men only, or just women laughers. There's a key for "sharpies": the term refers to the one or two "sharp" people in almost every audience who get the point of a joke a split second sooner than others. They begin to snort or titter or build up to a laugh just a bit before the whole audience bursts into an appreciative roar.

Mixing laughter to order is a high-level skill. The trick is in the timing. A virtuoso of the laff-box must not anticipate the joke too far in advance, or the cue telling the audience, "funny," will be lost. On the other hand, the main roar of laughter must be preceded by a few strategically placed bursts occurring just before the big one. That's called "giving it a little tickle" and it signals that a roar of appreciation is to follow.

The human laugh has its own cycle, beginning quietly, swelling to a climax, fading out. A chorus of human laughs fits the same bell-shaped curve. Orchestrating canned laughter to emulate these sounds is something like cueing the instruments in a symphony orchestra. The operator has to let the swell of laughter run its full course, then "tail it out" and "slide it under" the next line of straight dialogue—that is: no laugh may bury the gag line!

From a producer's point of view, canned laughter is preferable to real, live laughter. If the people in the studio audience were to laugh spontaneously any time the spirit moved them, they could use up valuable time. If the show isn't really funny, it could be disastrous to depend on live laughter. Imagine piping into twenty million homes a show billed as a comedy hour, with just a sprinkling of weak titters on the tape!

Deleting the laugh track entirely, however, would be an unacceptable solution. Producers do not like to release a comedy show without laughter on the tape. The home audience needs space for its own laughter and must not miss the next joke because they're still laughing at the last one. The laugh track synchronizes home laughter with the properly timed laughter of the tape.

Producers feel the canned laughter is more real than "unsweetened" laughter.[3] "Real audiences sound phonier than the laugh track." "They freeze up and act unnatural." "Live audiences in from the street are tense and nervous." "At times the live audiences yock it up *too* much." "Audiences just never laugh or respond on cue, they do the strangest things."[4]

One reason studio audiences cannot be counted on to laugh

properly is that they can hardly see the performers through the swarm of cameras and cameramen, announcers, lights, sound men, props, musicians, microphone booms, dancers, stagehands, and assorted production assistants. These mechanics of producing the show, moreover, can be as interesting to the audience as the show itself, so they often forget to laugh.

A producer tells the studio audience frankly, "You're here to work, to provide laughter . . ." and reminds them not to let the goings-on distract them. "If one of the cameras gets in the way, you can see everything on the monitors up there."[5]

It's easy to understand, then, why the laff-box has turned out to be such a handy gadget. The laughter specialists who run it work with the sound specialists to produce a "quality product." For example, a show like "Bewitched" is usually recorded on three separate reels of eight or nine minutes each. The sound is on one track, the music on another, sound effects on still another, and a special track is reserved for dialogue. The specialists have to "mix" the sounds—run them all together on a single track. It is at this point that the proper assortment of laughs can be selected, the sound of the laughter balanced to harmonize with the rest of the sound, and the timing perfected to correct any errors in the performance.

Mixing goes on much the same way in shows that claim to have been filmed before a live audience. The laughter broadcast to the nation in the final version has still been dubbed. "Sweetened" is the way they say it in the business. A show like "All in the Family" is taped before at least two live audiences. The final program is spliced together from the better parts of the taped final dress rehearsal and the taped final performance, just as the laugh track is put together from the better bursts of laughter, regardless of which gags occasioned them.* The mixing and the splicing reduces an hour and a half of takes before several audi-

---

*The term is "accumulated laugh track." The accumulated laughter of the studio audiences can still be sweetened by the addition of canned laughter as needed.

ences to the twenty-two minutes appropriate to a television half-hour.

In this fashion, a social policy has evolved for shaping the public's sense of humor. Now experts make sure that, if the show's producers in Television City think it's funny, the whole country will think it's funny. The laughter engineers make it possible to bypass the rank amateurs of laughter—the people who used to laugh heartily when they thought something funny and who refrained from laughing—even booed—when they did not.

8

Cooking up
Audiences

Producers of programs booked to assemble the child market rely heavily on laugh tracks that let the children at home hear how a properly appreciative audience behaves. Occasionally these shows use on-camera audiences that can be seen as well as heard; but studio audiences and audience "reaction shots," although increasingly noticeable on shows targeted to children, are more likely to turn up in shows targeted to adults, such as game shows, variety shows, rock spectacles, and sports events.

Audiences that whoop and holler, stamp and hoot, laugh, giggle, and guffaw spontaneously and on cue are recruited according to explicit specifications from the producer. There's a special art to cooking up audiences; it's come a long way from the early days when Dick Clark rigged studio audiences attending his broadcasts in order to avoid frightening the adults at home:

73

People didn't dress like that in the Fifties. We made them look
like that because that's what adults wanted them to look like and
it would not frighten them to the point where they'd take the
show off the air. If we let the kids come in off the street in black
leather jackets and dungarees and boots and studded jackets and
the greased-back hair and all of that, we wouldn't have lasted.[1]

Concocting the studio audiences goes beyond just filling up the
seats at the taping session—not hard to do since there are typically more requests for seats than seats available. The problem
is getting the *right kinds* of people. If television shows admitted
only those who have the time and inclination to go from studio
to studio and wait around for tickets to free television performances, audiences would be cluttered up with the wrong kinds
of people: too many old people, too many women past childbearing age, too many casually-employed and unemployed (which
includes unruly teenagers). Producers correct for this by calling
on the services of "audience recruitment specialists," agencies
that provide studio audiences to order.[2]

Different producers like different audience mixes. The producer of "The Carol Burnett Show" orders lots of bright, shiny
teens and twenties for those front-row seats. Dean Martin's producer wants college students and servicemen in the batches he
orders from his suppliers; but he also wants just a pinch of elderly
men and women, perhaps to add a soupçon of staidness. Blacks,
too, can be seen judiciously sprinkled through most studio audiences these days. They made the abrupt transition to television
visibility shortly after the passage of the Federal Civil Rights Act
of 1964.

Most producers cast the studio audience just as they cast any
other role in the show. They know that the spectacle to be
beamed into the nation's homes is not just, for instance, Carol
Burnett and gang doing their stuff. It is Carol-and-gang-doing-
their-stuff-and-being-appreciated-by-the-right-kind-of-audience-
as-they-do-it. The "right kind of audience" is the kind that lets
us envision ourselves as part of the spectacle. We're watching at

home; yet we join the vast audience lucky enough to have joined the show *in person*. Their obvious appreciation enhances our own and we lay ourselves open to the contagion of shared enthusiasm. If our reactions synchronize with those of the people on camera, it validates our own taste and reinforces it. If we happen to lag a bit behind them, feeling puzzled about what occasions a burst of applause or missing the point of a joke they laugh at, the on-camera audience provides us with plenty of signals that will help us pick up cues for more appropriate reactions next time around. It's a most effective way to convert disparate individual taste into cohesive mass fashions, and to do it fast.

People in the television business are well aware of their powers to create and mold public taste and they know that carefully selected studio audiences help the process. They prefer to keep a low profile on this sort of thing, though; so the public's attention is rarely called to the studio audience's role in manipulating taste for the show's stars, its style, and its values. Even a game show like "Let's Make a Deal," for which those who wish to attend are instructed to report in costume, downplays what is quite obvious to millions of viewers coast-to-coast: namely, that the audience has been selected by a casting office.

Rock shows are a special case. Fans turn up at rock concerts as much for the sake of meeting each other and just being together there, as for the music. Indeed, it's hard to say whether the rock spectacle's main attraction is the music and musicians, or whether it's the audience milling about, dancing in the aisles, singing and laughing and screaming, scuffling and fighting, smoking and drinking, making jokes, even making love. Thus, when the ABC network moved to adopt the rock scene for television, its promoters had to assure potential viewers in advance that "the right kind of audience" would appear on camera, properly cast to fulfill the expectations of the most exacting and sophisticated rock connoiseurs. Age, sex, clothing, life-styles— all would have to pass muster.

DO-IT-YOURSELF AUDIENCE CASTING

ABC's "In Concert" series features hard rock. In contrast to bubblegum rock and shlock rock, the niche for hard rock on television is its late-night slots. Constituency for these programs is still limited (the full harvest of youngsters raised on bubblegum rock has not yet been brought in); but they happen to attract the most significant packet the television business can deliver to its advertisers—an audience the market-research people label as "young spenders" and potential "new-family-formation agents." This is the audience that must be pleased, its ranks augmented.

Audiences suitable for rock concerts are mass audiences: not hundreds, not even thousands, but tens of thousands must be moved to the suitable level of frenzy. A rock concert without such an audience is as unthinkable as one without electric guitars. The usual audience-recruitment specialists are not geared to handle such a volume of traffic and the houses in which the concerts are taped for television do not seem to have whatever it takes to generate the proper electric atmosphere of a Woodstock.

Most late-night rock concerts on television muddle through, however, relying on trick camera work to paper over the audience gap. Shots into the pit are angled to pick up the light glancing off all those sequinned costumes, polished guitars, and chrome-decorated drums. The home screen, then, shows a few highlighted cheekbones, a few writhing bodies; but for the most part, halolike circles of light and glittering crosses hover over a sea of undifferentiated black which could be filled, for all we know, with thousands of enraptured fans instead of vacant seats.

Tricks like this are good enough to avoid public embarrassment at the sparse audiences; but unseen audiences do not do the job producers want done. They simply do not permit the needed "imaginal identification" between home audience and studio audience.

These considerations fed into ABC's decision to undertake its own do-it-yourself audience-recruitment effort. Their debut was "California Jam"—a live rock concert, an all-night marathon, an outdoor happening, a "TV Event"[3] booked, staged, and recorded on audio and video by ABC Entertainment. The two hundred thousand people ABC charged for the privilege of attending it paid for eighteen solid hours of rock performed by eight different groups.[4] They paid, as well, for the privilege of working for ABC, which billed "the excitement of the 200,000 rock fans who were there" as one of the principal attractions of the show the network urged the whole nation not to miss.[5] ABC Entertainment came away with a modest profit; ABC "In Concert" came away with four ninety-minute rock programs complete with proper atmosphere created by "the right audience."

IMAGES THAT COALESCE INTO MARKETS

It's not just rock fans who are gratified by seeing in well-chosen audiences and stars images of themselves as they are, as they might be, and as they would like to be. There is something about "seeing oneself in the picture" that is just plain rewarding to most human beings in our culture. It seems to be close to whatever it is that makes people in a street crowd wave at the newsman's camera as he films a public event, whether it's a coronation or a bomb scare; close to whatever it is that makes us look for our own faces in the front-page photograph of the crowd at the Fourth of July celebration we attended; close to whatever it is that makes it almost impossible to ignore your own voice when you hear it played back on a record or a tape. It's very similar to a biofeedback mechanism.[6]

Those who run the television business are no more specialists in biofeedback than dog breeders are geneticists. Their day-to-day experience with the process, however, gives them an empirical understanding of what is going on, if not a theoretical one,

and they turn it to their own advantage. They have seen the way
fashions burgeon and mass markets coalesce around people who
share identifiable images of themselves, who recognize themselves in each other. They use the mechanism to consolidate old
markets and create new ones. Since it works with the youngest
children as well as with the rest of us, the television business is
reaching down to younger and younger age groups, searching for
"subteen" stars who might create, attract, and hold a "child
market" focused on identification with the models of behavior
they exhibit. They started with "teeny boppers," then moved
down to "weeny boppers."

Weeny boppers are diligently sought after but not easy to come
by. *Variety* reports that searchers for "micropubescents" and
"weeny boppers" are finding it difficult to turn up eligibles and
that "none has yet made the quantum leap to Hitsville" to match
the standard set by the Osmonds, the Jackson Five, the Partridge
Family, and the Monkees.[7]
One reason the search is so intense and unrelenting is that the
half-life of a weeny bopper is ephemeral. The Osmonds, for
example, started out as a group of six. Merrill got married,
Donny's voice changed, and Marie flowered into an unmistakable teenager. Little Jimmy moved up to fill the spot his older
siblings had vacated, but he can't last long; he's already four feet
tall!
Lena Zavaroni looked like a likely prospect. For a while, every
subway station in New York was plastered with pictures of this
child who "belts out torch songs with a fervor that might make
Mae West blush."[8] Among her popular numbers was a song
entitled, "Help Me Make It Through the Night" and she sang
it with "an assortment of glottal show-biz squeaks and ornamen-
tal flourishes worthy of the aging Judy Garland."[9] The advertisement her recording company placed in *Variety* billed her as
"Lena Zavaroni: The Red Hot Mama That's Only Ten Years
Old."[10]

ABC's five owned-and-operated UHF television stations booked Tanya Tucker, "14-year-old country-and-western star" for guest appearance on their monthly "Rainbow Sundae" program.[11] Her repertoire featured a number entitled, "Would You Lay With Me (In a Field of Stone)?"

The search for weeny-bopper stars to attract and create weeny-bopper markets is no less intense when it comes to the unbilled stars of the commercials. It's a bit easier to turn up eligibles here; since the children acting in commercials are on camera briefly and do not have to sustain a dramatic role for any protracted period, almost any child will do. As one writer put it, "Real actors are rather hard to find in the under-10-year-old category, but 'real faces' [his quotation marks] are available in every shape, color and expression."[12] He goes on to admonish those aspiring to produce commercials to be sure to select appropriate "real faces"—those that provide an identifiable model which children in the audience can adopt and emulate.

> When you use a child, use one a little older than the age of the child to be sold [sic]. A 7-year-old demonstrating a product aimed at a 5-year-old is more effective than a 5-year-old would be. All children aspire to be older, more grown up.[13]

It is the emulation of the same admired images that coalesces the market, bundling the children into identifiable packets that can be sold to advertisers. It's as if the people running the television business, as well as those who run the client industries handling its market research and advertising, were taking literally Walt Whitman's poetic insight that all of us—but especially children—become what we behold.[14]

9

Saturating
the Sound
Environment

Just as they train beginners for more advanced television watching, the series booked into the children's ghetto hours are also vehicles for cultivating brownie and cub-scout consumers of marketable music. Show business uses the term "to showcase;" and that is precisely what these weekend children's series do: they showcase the television programs today's children will be urged to watch throughout their lives; and they showcase the musical styles, the musical instruments, the records, the tapes, even the very musical groups themselves, that are being marketed by broadcasting's client businesses, many of them outright subsidiaries of the networks' own parent companies.

The policy is to saturate the sound environment in which the children form musical tastes that will last them a lifetime. That's how it happens that programs targeted to children are loaded with the marketable "properties" the big record companies stock and with the stars the big talent agencies stockpile to fill the insatiable appetite for bookings that the broadcasting business demands.

There is nothing subtle about the procedure. NBC booked the Monkees, a rock group, during 1966–68. They turned up again as a children's-ghetto offering on CBS 1969–72. When the 1973–74 schedules were being drawn up, ABC picked up the same group for still another return engagement, sixth time around. Total: fifty-eight half hours of this show were shown by all three networks—not counting repeats; and they are still around, sold over and over again by Columbia Pictures Television, the syndicating company that markets them for endless rebookings.

"The Partridge Family," about a rock group consisting of the mother and five children, opened in 1970 on ABC—ninety-six episodes plus repeats. "The Jackson Five," about a rock group of black children, opened in animated form in 1971, returned in 1972. "The Osmonds," about their white counterparts, opened in 1972 and played their return engagement in 1973 (animations, too, of course). Then Donny and Marie Osmond, as young and attractive teenagers, reopened in prime time (November 1975) "live" on film.

Here's how "The Jackson Five" was advertised by the syndicating company that packaged it for sale and distribution after the series had completed its network run:[1]

TOPS WITH KIDS...

Fabulously successful during its network run, *The Jackson Five* animated series of 23 half hours is now available for local programming. The series follows the adventures of the world-famous young music group as they pursue their highly successful music career. In each show, the boys "perform" two musical numbers, including some of their best-selling record hits like "ABC," "Goin' Back to Indiana," and "The Love You Save."[2]

It is a point of interest that the television promos for "The Jackson Five" and "The Osmonds" (to mention just two) do not use the animated children but the real children.[3]

Even when network booking offices claim they are engaged in public-service programing for children, they plug rock music. The ABC network's "Schoolhouse Rock" series is a good example. It opened in January 1973, and the network's advance publicity releases hailed it as "ABC's answer, via arithmetic, to Sesame Street's animation of the alphabet."[4] The series began with "Multiplication Rock," featuring such titles as "Naughty Number Nine," "Zero My Hero," and "Three is a Magic Number." It was soon expanded by a set of companion spots entitled "Grammar Rock," focusing on the use of words and their meaning. In September 1974, still another series appeared, "America Rock," honoring the bicentennial with animated spots celebrating events in history.[5] Each spot features rock music and light shows along with the explicit lesson visualized by the animation. ABC's Advanced Program Schedules describe the segments as "a series of 4-minute animated films designed to teach through action and original music." (They are actually three minutes long.) The sentence does not specify precisely what it is that the films are designed to teach; but it is certain that, regardless of intent, they teach musical style, musical idiom, music appreciation, and they ease the children into rock culture as much as they instruct them in parts of speech, numbers, and history. "Multiplication Rock" has been issued as an album by Capitol Records and sales are said to be brisk.[6]

Whether or not the musical group is featured complete with title billing, many of the shows booked for the children's weekend block are saturated with rock music, complete with the light shows that are part of the rock scene: not only "The Monkees," "The Partridge Family," "The Osmonds," and "The Jackson Five," but most of the other children's-ghetto shows as well. Every episode of "Pebbles and Bamm Bamm" featured Pebbles's own rock group punctuating each program segment as a sort of musical curtain—usually four times per half-hour. "Josie and the Pussycats" pulled the same stunt. "The Brady Kids," likewise. "Charlie Chan and the Chan Clan" delivered rock with an Oriental flavor. "Butch Cassidy," "Fat Albert and the Cosby Kids," "Archie," "The Harlem Globetrotters"—rock, rock, and more rock.[7]

Add "American Bandstand" a program that has been pumping manufactured music into the country's airspace for more than two decades (it opened on the ABC network in August 1957), emceed by Dick Clark. Mr. Clark's brand of rock is called "schlock rock" in the business, sometimes "bubblegum rock." His show is produced by Dick Clark Enterprises, an umbrella corporation sheltering a number of related businesses, among them thirty-three different record firms. This reached national attention during the 1960s when the congressional hearings into payola in music and broadcasting took place.[8] These hearings revealed what virtually everyone in the business knew: that the common practice of paying off broadcasters to showcase music preferentially had been going on for decades. Mr. Clark told the committee that he not only paid off other disc jockeys to plug his company's music; he customarily plugged his own labels on his own shows. (Why not? The networks were doing the same with their labels. Companies in the business of producing television shows were doing the same with theirs. Mr. Clark merely followed suit.)

Since September 1963, "American Bandstand" has filled the ABC network slot that closes off the children's ghetto each Saturday morning. Before that it was broadcast daily in after-school time slots from August 1957 to September 1962—plus evening shows programed twice a week for the last quarter of 1957; plus evening programs every Saturday from February 1958 to September 1960. An ABC special on May 9, 1975 celebrated the twenty-third birthday of the program with an hour-long show originat-

ing from Dick Clark's "old bandstand home," (WFIL-TV, Phil-
adelphia) switching to Mr. Clark's "new bandstand home" in
Las Vegas. It capped two earlier specials in December 1959 and
January 1974.

Using one medium of entertainment as a conduit to deliver
consumers to a related medium is nothing new in the business.
It used to be done by back-and-forth channeling among motion
pictures, radio, and records. Up to the close of the decade of the
fifties, the procedure for merchandising songs, groups, and musical styles was to get them built into movies, Broadway shows,
live network radio programs (such as the Jack Benny programs,
for example), and recorded music programs (such as Martin
Block's WNEW "Makebelieve Ballroom"). Four large record
companies were in a position to use each of these media to their
own advantage, owing to their corporate links to radio and movie
firms. RCA Victor, linked with the NBC network and a number
of radio stations, was affiliated to the RKO Film Company.
Columbia Records had its own radio network—CBS. Decca,
affiliated with The Music Corporation of America, the powerful
Hollywood movie and radio talent agency, eventually came to
own Universal movie studios. Capitol Records was linked until
1950 to Paramount Pictures, which in turn was linked to ABC
and ABC Paramount—both branches of movie firms. ABC Paramount had the additional advantages of the tie to the ABC radio
network. (Its tie to the ABC television network did not become
important in this regard until the sixties, when television viewing
began to replace movie attendance and radio listening as the
national pastime.)[9]

WHAT KIND OF SOUND?

The bubblegum rock delivered to children during the weekend
all follows the same pattern—thirty-two bars in four-four time,
a limited range of instruments, and a chord structure that smacks

either of the ballad or the blues. Not the least of the advantages in booking this kind of assembly-line music is that it's easy to interrupt every thirty-two bars or multiple thereof to make way for the commercial; and the average duration of a complete number from beginning to end is about three to three-and-a-half minutes, allowing a goodly portion of commercials to be generously sprinkled into any stretch of time devoted to rock numbers.

The rock music featured on Saturday-morning television may be hyped up by strings added to the drums and bass section, perhaps an extra electronic instrument here and there. Still, the same canned music is spliced into all the shows so that there is little room for variation.[10]

The outstanding characteristic of the music aimed at the children is that it is loud and bouncy. With good reason. The transmission is monaural and the shabby speakers built into most television sets guarantee that the sound will be one-dimensional and tinny. Improving the receivers in television sets would not resolve the issue, either, since network programs are piped all over the country via AT&T telephone lines, which carry a single channel signal. It exaggerates the situation only slightly to say that even if the receiving equipment in the home were of high caliber, the sound still coming over the AT&T lines would approximate the sound of an AM car radio.

What is lacking in musical value is made up in decibels; the music broadcast to the children gets louder and bouncier every year, and youngsters raised on it get used to it. When the Rolling Stones performed at Madison Square Garden, the audio level in the front of the audience reached 136 decibels. The performance was amplified through 150 speakers delivering 16,000 audio watts of power.[11]

AT&T promises to provide a new "high quality audio channel" and possibly a second channel for stereo telecasts.[12] Alternative feeds are already possible—microwave and satellites are already on the scene and who knows what technological innova-

tions lie ahead? Meanwhile, however, a generation of children
has been formed in an environment saturated with the sounds
and rhythms of poorly transmitted rock music, produced to
order and on demand according to specifications having to do
more with market considerations than with musicianship. Television transmission, blurring the sounds and running them together, has reduced music to noise; razzle-dazzle electronics has
accustomed a whole generation to deafening sound levels.

Under such conditions, Beethoven doesn't stand a chance.
Neither the composer nor his music appears on network television. For example, during 1970, the year that marked the two-
hundredth anniversary of Beethoven's death, the networks dedicated no more than two or three slots to any commemoration of
his works or his passing. In 1973, ABC television offered him to
prime-time audiences once: an ABC special packaged Beethoven
along with Stevie Wonder, Gilbert O'Sullivan, and Bette Midler.
Snatches of melodies extracted from well-known Beethoven
compositions (da-da-da-*dum*) jostled against snatches of rock.
Peter Ustinov, who took the role of Beethoven, delivered gag
lines in a Henry Kissinger accent ("Yes, I often find myself, when
in my own presence, overcome by awe."), which occasioned
much hilarity—sweetened, of course, by a laugh track. This is
network television's customary approach to any kind of serious
music: if it appears at all, it's played for laughs. ABC advertised
the program as "a rock, pop, folk and fun-filled evening of music
and entertainment."[13]

THE SOUND ENVIRONMENT
IS NOT TRIVIAL

Some things we can tell each other better in the language of
music and song than in the language of words. For most people,
making music together—experiencing music together—is ex-
hilarating. We feel each other's presence in a special way. In this

sense, the sound environment we live in is certainly not trivial. Music forms consciousness and raises consciousness by binding people together. Music synchronizes groups. Each member of the group feels the same rhythms, the same beats, the same pulses, the same timings, and in this way the conditions for empathy and mutual awareness are created.

Oppressors seem always to have sensed this: in Nazi concentration camps, for example, singing was a punishable offense. During slavery in this country, South Carolina, Louisiana, and Virginia passed laws declaring it illegal for Blacks to beat out their musical rhythms on drums. What more eloquent testimony to some deep awareness that controlling the music of a people is a way of controlling a sense of social self, a sense of cultural identity?

Music reminds us that there are levels of experience whose existence our own culture officially takes no notice of. Awareness of experience denied surfaces in dreams and longings, feelings and flashes of insight. Music can convert such fleeting, individual experiences into more lasting, collective ones, which can then become a force for social awareness and cultural change. Music externalizes insights so that they can then be tied to stories—the dramas that release thought.[15]

Mass-produced and mass-distributed rock music does this now instantaneously, for uncounted numbers of young people worldwide. As rock culture develops further, the protopolitical feelings and leanings it cultivates and nurtures become increasingly clear. Even as Dick Clark Enterprises organizes a series of television programs designed to cash in on the nostalgia of the seemingly innocuous bubblegum rock he helped to popularize during the rock-and-roll years[16] (over a thousand programs), the music he championed more than two decades ago has continued to evolve. It moves, now, under our very eyes. Passing from the celebration of sensation that the Beatles advertised in the sixties to a new kind of celebration in the seventies, it is "shock rock," a shadow, an inkling, a dim suggestion of an outline of something not yet clear to us, waiting, waiting for the proper political moment.

SHOCK ROCK*

Shock rock goes on in concert halls, arenas, and open fields. Yes, and on television, where it is showcased in the late-hour slots in full view of the nation, yet is still almost an underground happening. A good example is the Alice Cooper show. Alice Cooper was one of the name rock stars ABC booked for its late-night "In Concert" series. Alice is a man—Vincent Furnier—and his act includes live chickens, snakes, headless dolls, a guillotine, and even a simulated hanging to keep the fans titillated. As part of his act, he dismembers a doll and tosses its limbs to the fans. Their clutching hands, reaching out in an attempt to grasp a limb or a body-part as a souvenir to commemorate the evening, become part of the show. Alice's customary clothing is a black leotard that looks like a frogman's wetsuit or Spider-man's attire, with the addition of white, jagged stripes simulating lightning flashes. His face is painted in a grotesque way, caricaturing even the caricature of clown makeup—white paint, heavily-styled eye make-up, exaggerated lashes in a webby design, curious patterns along the cheekbones, wild tousled hair. This act was broadly publicized when ABC booked it[17]—but other acts that customarily filled the slot were often much the same.

Squeals of delight, cries of fear, and shrieks of pain resemble each other acoustically, just as paroxysms of ecstasy and paroxysms of pain involve similar body movements. The Marquis de Sade knew about these similarities and found erotic pleasure in testing the margins where the distinctions blur. Shock rock does the same. The excesses become so apparent that people in the

---

*Sometimes called "punk rock."

business are beginning to wonder whether this is a marriage of music to show business, or something else. For example, the New York chapter of the National Academy of Recording Arts and Sciences convoked a panel to discuss the issue. *Variety* reported that the meeting was well attended and that "Drag and fire livened the season's first monthly meeting," as the discussion got underway. One participant remarked about the musical aspects of these spectacles, somewhat wistfully, perhaps: "Just playing guitar doesn't seem to be enough." Another characterized the combination of shocking spectacles, music, and show business as "extreme decadence"; but then he went on to praise it as a new form of rebellion, a new form of anti-establishment defiance. Another panel member felt it was all a tempest in a teapot.[18] After all, he said, "it's only rock and roll." The consensus was that there was no point in making a fuss; it's just theatrics, "and theatrics have been around a long time"[19]—a point of view that justifies simulated Roman circuses, gladiatorial games, hangings, and autos-da-fé.[20]

There is no doubt that crowds found "entertainment" in these earlier, ghoulish spectacles just as they find it today in Alice Cooper, Deep Purple, David Bowie, Lou Reed, or the Blue Oyster Cult. Deep Purple, booked by ABC for "California Jam," is one of those shock-rock groups whose act ends in an orgy of destruction—guitars are smashed, the stage is engulfed in staged flames that look as if they could burn everything to a cinder. Others in this vein are the Dictators, David Bowie, the New York Dolls, and Left End.

The Blue Oyster Cult uses a swastika as an emblem; advertisements promoting them are purposely ambiguous, hinting at Nazism and reminiscent of the sadistic excesses that went on in concentration camps and slave-labor camps. The Dictators is a similar group whose repertoire includes a song entitled "The Master Race." Sylvain Sylvain of the New York Dolls features an Iron Cross as part of his costume. Promotional material included in the first album produced by Left End, a rock quintet, boasts that the group has "beaten up members of audiences, set off smoke bombs in bars, and dragged a road manager . . . down a flight of stairs by his neck." The oddly-inverted boosterism of the record album continues to praise the group for having sent boxes of garbage to Cleveland radio-station program directors. "The device worked as the album got Cleveland airplay."[21] This group has been known to throw dead frogs into the audience. As the tiny green corpses hit home, the audience's squeals and screams mingle with the "music" and become part of it.[22]

Both the auto-da-fé and the kind of spectacle presented by Deep Purple cater to the basest in mankind rather than to the most sublime, to be sure; still, there is a vast difference in scale. The earlier spectacle did not enter the home and was not simultaneously advertised throughout the nation, indeed, throughout the then known world, ensuring the immediate legitimization that social sharing confers. Nor were the admittedly base emotions so aroused immediately deadened by being surrounded by nostrum-peddling.

It all seems a far cry from the bubblegum rock launched in a modest enough manner by Dick Clark in his days as a simple Philadelphia disc jockey. The sound and the props may be different, but the format and the philosophy remain virtually unchanged. It's still thirty-two bars in four-four time; it's still music from which everything has been stripped away but its attention-grabbing potential; it's still an assembly-line factory product packaged and sold as a purchasable commodity.[23] When Mr. Clark's alma mater, Syracuse University, invited him to receive an award for "Distinguished Service to Broadcasting," he reviewed his own career, characterizing himself as "a gentle Sammy Glick" and his motivation as "unadulterated greed." The practice of using "American Bandstand" 's access to children's homes as a way of forming their musical tastes for the profit and aggrandizement of his own companies seemed quite acceptable as Mr. Clark told the story to the members of Alpha Epsilon Rho, the national radio and television honorary fraternity that granted the award. "[It] takes being part prostitute to stay alive," he explained.[24]

THE NETWORKS ARE INVOLVED

Mr. Clark's interests in thirty-three record companies are trivial compared to the interests the three commercial networks have in manufactured music. All three are multinational conglomerates, with subsidiaries in the music and record business. At CBS, there is the CBS Records Group, well ahead of the equivalent enterprises at the other two networks. The CBS Records Group is the world's largest producer, manufacturer, and marketer of recorded music; and more than half of CBS Records' domestic sales are in contemporary rock. Here are some of the "names CBS Records owns"—as they say in the business: Janis Joplin. Bob Dylan. The Raiders. Blood, Sweat and Tears. Andy Williams. Johnny Mathis. Ray Conniff. Ten Years After. The New Riders of the Purple Sage.

Those are just the tame ones. Columbia Records owns the Blue Oyster Cult and has run advertisements for this group. The Dictators record on the Epic label, also owned by Columbia. Alice Cooper's records are produced by Warner Brothers Records, a subsidiary of Warner Brothers, Inc., in turn a subsidiary of Warner Communications.

There is also CBS Records International with twenty-five foreign subsidiaries. CBS owns record clubs and stereo clubs that are the largest organizations of their kind in the world. The Columbia Cassette Club is also a CBS enterprise.

There is the CBS Musical Instruments Division—a subsidiary that includes the Fender Guitar and Amplifier Companies, Electra Music, and Rogers Drums.[25] These companies are selling the kind of equipment that is indispensable for rock music, both

professional and amateur, cashing in on a newly emerging practice among teens and subteens who establish amateur rock
groups just like the ones that appear on the Saturday-morning
children's cartoon series.

NBC is a wholly owned subsidiary of RCA, one of the twenty
largest industrial corporations in the world. NBC owns RCA
Records; and they, too, are busy—like CBS—in related activities: tapes, cassettes, a record club, commercial record pressing,
tape-duplicating and recording services, licensing and franchising here and abroad.[26] RCA owns Camden, Red Seal, Victor, and
Victrola labels. They distribute Amsterdam, Blue Time, Bob
Thiel Music, Contact, Erato, Flying Dutchman, Grunt, Mid-
land, International, Reggae, Signature, Wooden, and Wind-
song.[27]

ABC Records, Inc., is a wholly owned subsidiary that manufactures and distributes canned music just as the other network
subsidiaries do—producing phonograph records, tapes, cassettes, music, and audio-visual products for the national and
international market. Like the others they, too, are linked to
music-publishing companies and distribution networks here and
abroad. Some of ABC's major labels are Dunhill, Impulse, Command, Probe, Bluesway, Dot, Westminster Gold—and, most
recently, Anchor Records, whose mission is twofold: "to dis-
cover and develop foreign talent with international sales potential and to market exclusively the ABC catalogue of records,
tapes and published music in the United Kingdon."[28]

This is corporate cronyism on the grand scale we seem to have
become accustomed to in the United States today, and it is by
no means unique to broadcasting. What is unique is that deci-
sion-makers in the business use their unprecedentedly privileged
position in controlling the new member of everybody's family to
do what family members have always done—which is to color
and shape the environment within which upcoming generations
are formed and form themselves. Whether responsibility for deci-

sions about the music that makes a whole country's sound environment—perhaps a whole world's—should be so distributed is a matter of serious public policy, and it deserves the spotlight of public attention and debate. Instead, it is left to rest, by default, in the hands of those whose top priorities are "will it sell?" Will it sell the music? Will it sell the children?

10

Forms
of Address

Words have power. Those who rule our symbols rule us. "Advertisers, newsmen, novelists, movie makers and others who create and manipulate our symbols are a ruling class, whether they know it or not," says an outstanding semanticist turned politician.[1]

Words can do violence. Distorting meanings, misusing language, "destroys our mooring posts and undercuts the forms of relationships we are used to."[2] The line that makes us fast to social relationships is the same fragile line that moors us to our social system and our culture. When that line begins to fray, we hardly notice. Then, all strands part. We are at sea, lost and rudderless. Only then do we see how linguistic territory that once belonged to everyone and to the future has been utterly taken over, thoroughly colonized.

The British television series, "Upstairs, Downstairs" (first shown on public television for thirteen weeks beginning January

6, 1974, then repeated several times), gave Americans a lesson in the way social structure is embodied in everyday language. Just one little gem of an exchange between Hudson and Hazel Forrest laid bare the rules of social relations that are welded to language and reinforced every time we talk to each other.

The series centered on the Bellamy household: Upstairs, Mr. Bellamy, a commoner but now a Member of Parliament; his wife, of the British nobility; their son, James. Downstairs, the servants. Mr. Bellamy had hired Hazel Forrest, who came to the house every day to work—upstairs—as his secretary. Hazel, a middle-class young lady earning her living, always addressed the butler as "Mr. Hudson"—the same way the downstairs staff, the servants, addressed him. To the upstairs family, the employers, he was always "Hudson"; while Hudson, of course, always said "Milady," "Mr. Bellamy," or "Mr. James." The first concession he ever made to Hazel, signaling his reconciliation to the idea that she might marry Mr. James, thus becoming the Bellamys' social equal, occurred when she addressed him in her usual way: "Mr. Hudson," she said. "Just 'Hudson,' Miss," he responded. He smiled, they exchanged glances, and in that instant both knew that their relationship had reached a new level. She was still *Miss* Forrest to him, but he was just plain *Hudson*.

That is just one little illustration of the heavy baggage of social structure carried by forms of address. We used to be able to pack an equivalent wealth of meaning in the thee/thou form of address. It's gone now, and we lost a rich set of linguistic signals along with it. We send out the same kinds of signals, though, with the same economy, when we use names, titles, and credentials in talking to each other. For example, if we overhear a conversation in which one person is saying, "Mr. So-and-So," but the other person doesn't use any corresponding title in return, it's a good guess that the people conversing do not consider themselves to be on the

same social plane.* That's what Hazel and Hudson were signaling to each other, after all: who gets the honorific and
who does not is a sort of linguistic flag.

That world of social meaning was easily compressed in the
brief interchange between Hazel and Hudson, who were speaking British English. Most of us who speak American English
would find it a bit awkward to say "Hudson" in direct conversation with the man. We'd probably need a bit of time to get used
to it before we could say it easily and naturally, without even
noticing it, the way the people in the Bellamy household did.
(The American television show, "Family Affair," provides an apt
illustration. The butler on that show is nearly always "Mr.
French," rarely "French.")

This last-name form of address has not entirely disappeared
from American English, though. It persists in certain institutional settings and in particular occupational groups. Hospital
staff, for example, often call each other by last name alone; not
the doctors, not the administrators at the top, and not the orderl-
ies and maintenance people, but the middle-range personnel such
as dietitians, nurses, therapists. Athletic coaches often address
members of their teams by last name alone.

In our American language there is just one institutional setting
in which the last-name form of address in face-to-face conversation is a matter of explicit protocol: the military.

There are exceptions, of course, and deviant forms of address
surely persist here and there. Some Quakers in our country still
use the thee/thou form of address. Yet I, for one, have never
heard just plain people talking to each other that way—only
clergymen, and then they were talking to God. Certain very
old-fashioned husbands and wives refer to each other as "Mr.

---

*The same asymmetric use of a title could occur when a younger person talks to an
older one, or a student to a professor, or a professor talks to the president of the
university or to someone on the board of trustees.

Bennett," "Mrs. Bennett." Such eccentric speech patterns do not have much of a chance to spread outward from the cultural pockets that maintain them unless they are socially shared. We would all have to have repeated opportunities to experience the hows and the whys of these special forms of address before they could possibly infiltrate our own vocabularies. Widespread social sharing does not guarantee adoption, but it certainly is a prerequisite for adoption.

In this, as in so many other spheres, television is the trendsetter. Whatever linguistic forms are employed on prime-time television will immediately and simultaneously be shared on a scale unprecedented in human history.

The 1974–75 television year opened with "Kodiak," "Kojak," "Kolchak," "Khan!," "Cannon," "Mannix," "McCloud," "Columbo," "Petrocelli," "Baretta," "Ironside," "Archer," "Nakia." The 1975–76 television season brought along "Bronk," "McCoy," "Starsky and Hutch." In 1973–74 the country was offered "Griff," "Shaft," "Hawkins," "Chase," "Banacek," "Tenafly," "Toma"—shown weekly and widely advertised before they closed; "Banyon," "Madigan," "Alias Smith and Jones"—shown weekly and widely advertised the season before that (1972–73). Twenty-six prime-time show titles, twenty-eight crisp, barked last names. This is the form of address appropriate in American English for military people talking to each other in military settings. The consistent use of the clicking sounds in these names is the vocal equivalent of a snap of the fingers—a peremptory way of attracting attention. That's how doormen used to attract the attention of taxi drivers before the din of the city made it impossible. It's how a maître d'hôtel summons a waiter.

The titles of these shows do not even indicate the full extent of nightly television's predilection for the military form of address. In dialogue, too, there is a constant barking of these last names. In most of the shows that feature redressers of wrongs,

it is the preferred way in which the fictional characters identify
themselves and address each other. Top man in "Hawaii Five-
O," Steve McGarrett, is usually just plain "McGarrett" to most
of his staff. He refers to himself that way, too, answering the
telephone with a clipped "McGarrett." When he shows his badge
as official identification, he announces laconically, "McGarrett,
Five-O."

Sitcoms and Variety Shows Signal Respect for Stars...

Our language uses first name and last name together as a way of
reducing social distance, moving out of an arm's-length relationship but not all the way.* Show business resorts to first name and
last name mainly for show titles—a practice which reflects more
concern about billing and less concern about social relationships.
But that does not mean that the rules of social relations embedded in our naming patterns are thereby repealed. Many of the
rules that govern our speech have been learned unwittingly. They
are so internalized, so much a part of our ways of thinking, that
to speak the way we do seems "natural," almost inborn; our
conscious attention is scarcely involved. In internalizing the
rules of speech and language, we also internalize the social grammar that goes along with them. There they all remain, equally
beyond our conscious attention, equally "natural."

Television business people are not linguists—they are in show

---

*For example, I often receive letters from former students, now professors themselves,
beginning, "Dear Rose Goldsen." That's not usual in American English. Still, the more
formal, "Dear Professor Goldsen," seems less appropriate to someone on a professional
level on a par with my own. I suppose they feel they are no longer youngsters, either.
Even so, after many years of "Professor Goldsen," "Dear Rose" doesn't come quite so
trippingly to tongue or pen.

Since 1974 or so even this is changing. In my introductory lectures I now admonish
students not to call me by my first name until I give the signal. The same treatment is
not accorded to my male peers.

business. They understand what they call the "marquee value" of a name. The stars hire agents who fight hard for top billing —which is represented by having the star's full name in the title. Contracts specify details about billing: is it to be last name alone, first name *and* last name? One last name? Two last names? What about initials? What about first name alone? How long will the name appear on the screen? How often will it be shown and mentioned on the show? In advertising? What about the size of the letters, the layout of the billboards and their positioning in the show's "intro" and "outro"? No detail involving names and naming is too trivial to be the object of meticulous attention, the subject of wrangling negotiations.

So it's no accident that the 1974–75 television season gave us "The Mary Tyler Moore Show," "The Bob Newhart Show," "The Bob Crane Show," "The Carol Burnett Show," "Tony Orlando and Dawn," "The Mac Davis Variety Hour," and the "Dean Martin Roasts".* All were comedy-variety shows or situation comedies; all cashed in on the marquee value of the star's full name, even while enhancing it further. The previous year we had "The Flip Wilson Show," "The Doris Day Show," "The New Bill Cosby Show," "The Sandy Duncan Show," "The Paul Lynde Show," "The Julie Andrews Show," "The New Dick Van Dyke Show," and "Rod Serling's Night Gallery"; plus four others that continued on into 1974–75. The linguistic payoff of these kinds of billings is the signal to the country that "name stars" deserve respect.*

---

*The tradition of the "name" show is not a new one. It stems from radio days ("The Jack Benny Show," "George Burns and Gracie Allen," and so on), and was cemented for television when "Toast of the Town" was renamed "The Ed Sullivan Show" in September 1955.

*Shows that feature redressers of wrongs occasionally depart from their customary titles that bark the last name of the cop-detective-agent-lawman-hero. When they do, they accord the fictional hero the dignity of his or her full name: "Barnaby Jones," "Get Christie Love," "Hec Ramsey," "Dan August," "Matt Helm," send out the signal that a respectful social distance is to be maintained.

...And Credential Bearers
Deserve Respect

We use a person's credential along with his name to signal social distance. When we say "Doctor" So-and-So, or "Reverend" or "Counselor" or "Professor", we acknowledge social superiority or an arm's-length relationship. This form of address is quite common on prime-time television. We find it in both the titles of the shows and in dialogue. Everybody in the country must know Marcus Welby, M.D., by now. Who ever thinks of good Doctor Welby as just plain Marcus or Marc? Virtually nobody on the show calls him that, either; it's "Dr. Welby." In 1973–74 we had not only the good doctor, but also "Owen Marshall, Counselor at Law." Even when the credential is not included in the show's billing, it still gets heavy play in the dialogue. On "Medical Center," it's almost always "Dr. Gannon," occasionally, "Dr. Joe," very rarely just plain "Joe," and even more rarely an unadorned "Gannon." "The Bob Crane Show" gave the country lessons in academic etiquette. A short-lived second-semester offering (1974–75 season), this show adopted the formula of the Archie comics, switching it from adolescents in high school to adults in medical school. The students always used first names among themselves; but you can bet your sweet life they said *"Dean* Ingersoll" and *"Dean* Hartigan" when they talked to the top brass; even when they just talked about them. On television, the professionals with credentials are pretty much the only people who get the unmodified linguistic sign of superiority or social distance.

Television Denies Social
Distance Among Laymen

The equivalent linguistic forms for those who lack professional credentials would be Mr., Mrs., or Miss. We couple them with last names to indicate social distance, formality, respect. Hudson sent out the cue to *Miss* Forrest that she was on a superior level and he on an inferior one. When he went downstairs, however, and he and the cook called each other *Mr.* Hudson and *Mrs.* Bridges, the signal was: respect, social equality, yes; intimacy, no —this was to remain an arm's-length relationship. (At least, publicly. Sometimes in private they reverted to the first-name form of address, appropriate to their long-standing private relationship—an intimate one, it turned out. They had been engaged for years!)

But Mr., Mrs. and Miss* have disappeared from the show-and-tell of television titles. "Our Miss Brooks" may have been the last of them; and that was a holdover from radio days. Indeed, these forms of respectful address are virtually disappearing from dialogue in the shows, as well. We had *Miss* Kitty for nineteen years of "Gunsmoke," but then she disappeared—written out of the show when it embarked on its twentieth. That's an old-fashioned form of address signaling more warmth than *Miss* Russell, while still maintaining respectful social distance. (The black Mammy who always said *Miss* Scarlett loved Scarlett O'Hara, but she never forgot her place.)

Keeping the star's full name in titles reminds us not to forget completely about the distance between a television star and the rest of us. Still, it's just a reminder: dialogue on these shows goes all the way and everyone gets the intimate, family form of address—just first name alone. "Miss Burnett" on the show? Hardly! It's "Carol" of course. And who would ever call Dean Martin "Mr. Martin," unless they were reaching for one more laugh? Thus do we inform each other that—yes, we are all equals, whether we live in Television City or in Peoria.

---

*Ms., a deliberately manufactured form of address, does not deserve discussion here. It belongs with other examples of imposed linguistic forms such as *gay*, meaning homosexual; *bathroom bowl*, meaning toilet; *wetness*, meaning sweat or urine; just one more example of papering over social conflict by inventing new words that attempt to correct social injustice by stripping away its history.

The format of the situation comedies, combined with show business's own custom of calling everyone by first name, provides extra opportunities for all parties concerned to cash in on the marquee value of the star's name: often the fictional character of the sitcom maintains the star's own first name, and the dialogue repeats it over and over again. If the name of the leading character on a hit show is fictional, however, the marquee value of that name brushes off on the star, and vice versa. Remembering Hawkeye paves the way to remembering Alan Alda. Alan Alda on talk shows and quiz shows helps us all remember Hawkeye and "M*A*S*H." It's just that much easier to reinforce the association by keeping the first names identical. Thus, Mary Tyler Moore appears as Mary Richards on her weekly show, where everyone calls her Mary. Bob Newhart plays Bob Hartley and everyone calls him Bob—even the secretary-receptionist who works for him. But wait a minute—he's a doctor even if his degree is the Ph.D. and not the M.D. Thus, we all have plenty of opportunity to observe him answering his telephone, "Dr. Hartley." He introduces himself as Dr. Hartley. When his clients are on camera, they call him Dr. Hartley. On prime-time television, even the sitcom, nonphysician doctor gets his due!

While in the past the show-business practice of forgetting last names and thereby denying social distance was usually confined to the in-group at the performing end of the business, now it is moving out into the public and begins to take over even star billing. It starts out—appropriately enough—with younger stars, not older ones. Sonny Bono and ex-wife, Cher (not yet thirty, they say), have always billed themselves just that way. Their first prime-time series was "The Sonny and Cher Comedy Hour." Then divorce split them as if by binary fission into "The Sonny Comedy Revue" (1974–75, first semester) and just plain "Cher" (1974–75, second semester.)

WOMEN, BLACKS, AND
"ETHNICS" FIRST

Sitcoms have been using just first names as their titles for a long time. Perhaps it started way back with all those Lucy shows. Before Lucille Ball took to doing specials, three generations of her series had run since the first one opened in 1953: "I Love Lucy," "The Lucy Show," and "Here's Lucy." Since Lucy, we have had lots of similar show titles: "Maude," "Diana," "Dirty Sally," "Karen," "Rhoda," "Cher," "Fay," "Phyllis," "Bridget Loves Bernie," "Chico and the Man." That is just a partial listing. Counting from the 1972–73 season onward, there have been twenty-five bookings into prime time of sitcoms and comedy-variety shows that used a person's first name alone as title. Sixteen of them announced the names of women; four announced the names of "ethnics."

"Ethnic shows" is what the television business calls shows about Blacks, Jews, Italians, and anyone who speaks with an accent. "Chico and the Man" is an "ethnic" show. The term is ambiguous—by design. It allows Chico's origins as a Puerto Rican, Mexican, Cuban, or whatever to remain unclear. Thus, no specific group is offended and Chico invites nationals of twenty-two Latin American republics, plus Spain and several Caribbean islands, to identify with him.

"Ethnics" and Blacks who live in families "jes lak" white folks are new to prime-time television. They made their debut in 1972,* the year "Sanford and Son" opened. Also opening in 1972 was "Bridget Loves Bernie"—a series featuring an intermarriage that joined the Steinberg family, who sold salami, with the Fitzgerald family, whose son was a priest. Lots of yuk-yuks in that cross-cultural setup, even though it turned out to be short-lived. In

---

*Television—like the rest of show business—has never been reluctant to show Blacks tap dancing and singing and playing the banjo. It's a heritage of minstrel-show days, and quite different from starring black people in dramatic or pseudodramatic presentations.

1975, "Joe and Sons" opened—about an Italian-American motherless family named Vitale. Even in show-business circles, where
the last name has been *de trop* since early Hollywood days, when
a language of public announcement is adopted that reduces social
distance, it's women, Blacks, and "ethnics" first.

SHOW-BUSINESS CULTURE BEGINS TO MOVE OUTWARD

Show-business people are no different from the rest of us. Their
tribal practices may seem exotic to those of us who live in another world and speak a different language, but to them all this
seems normal and natural. These particular practices, however,
spread fast from in-group circles at the performing end of the
business into much wider circles. Children, for example, learn
show-business forms of address and adopt them, substituting
them for patterns of speech their own families may prefer. You
can see them following television's linguistic leads as they incorporate the television characters in their play: pretending to be
McGarrett, Kojak, Ironside, or the Chief—no first names, no
titles, no Mr. The girls play at being Cher, Carol, Mary—no last
names, no titles. The same show-business practice is affected in
"Sesame Street" and "Electric Company." These shows star
people with no last names—Susan, Gordon, Bob, Luis, Maria.
(Only Mr. Hooper, the elderly storekeeper, is honored with a last
name and a "Mr.") The children seen on these shows have no
names at all—it is only the grownups, the animated figures, and
the puppets who are rescued from anonymity.

Treating everyone on a first-name basis, and dispensing with
any honorific such as Mr., Miss, or Mrs. is not exactly a practice
unquestioningly accepted throughout the country—to say nothing of the entire English-speaking world. Family names are not
to be lightly discarded, and names have more than marquee
value. Names, particularly last names, are an inescapable and

public reminder that the present moment both embodies and creates history. The family name puts the present in its place, so to speak, by forbidding us to forget that time flows. Many families seek to preserve the last name as a source of identification for their children, worthy of their pride and respect.[3]

Calling someone Mr., Miss, or Mrs. So-and-So, moreover, announces that some relationships must remain at arm's length, that not all are necessarily intimate—an idea that many families like to pass on to their children. Television's massive denial of these forms—by obliterating them—now puts on the defensive the many families that would prefer their children to accept and internalize their own speech styles and the values implicit in them—not television's.[4] The situation is compounded as export versions of these linguistic styles are dubbed into the soundtracks of programs now being sold all over the world.

Television's show-and-tell spreads its own practices fast. I note that last names have begun to disappear even among those who work at the business end of the media bureaucracies and satellite industries. This is brought home to me every time I call the various sources I have to get in touch with to corroborate the materials I manage to dig up about the television business. As my calls get switched from one receptionist to another, one secretary to another, one girl Friday to another, I get to talk to quite a lot of people on the lower levels of these bureaucracies. "May I have your name?" I ask this routinely. The answer usually comes back, "Janie," "Toni," "Sherry." "Don't you have a last name?" is my customary follow-up. It's fifty-fifty whether the young lady will answer, "Just Janie," or whether she'll relent and tell me her last name.

It works in reverse, too. When I finally get to the public-relations person or the press representative at the network or the account executive at the advertising agency or the vice president of some media-buying service or trade association he's very likely to call me by my first name. Of course, these people are likely to be men and, even if I'm just as much a "doctor" as Bob Hartley, I'm still a woman. It's mainly women who man the telephones down there at the network offices and on Madison Avenue, and they don't use my first name the way the men do. It's reminiscent of the way Mary Richards calls her boss Mr. Grant while he calls her Mary. (It's not necessary to be paranoiac to grasp what's going on in television, but I sometimes think it helps.)

Things are changing before our very eyes. An interesting case is a show that opened in September 1974: "Harry O." According to television's linguistic rules for cop and detective shows, the title ought to be "Orwell" or "Harry Orwell." But language is organic: it makes social change and registers social change. As first-name forms of address sweep first show business and then move outward to take over the rest of the country, as last names begin to disappear, this show illustrates the flexibility of language. The rules bow and bend but do not break when the winds of change buffet them: the vestigial initial of the disappearing last name remains, sort of like the vermiform appendix.

And what is the lesson the business beams into our air every weekend in the programs it directs to the nation's children? Since "Mr. Wizard" disappeared from network television at the close of the 1971–72 season, not one of the titles booked into the weekend children's ghetto has adorned someone's last name with a Mr., Mrs., or Miss. Week after week, I listened in vain for a snatch of dialogue in which any child or any animated figure with a speaking part addresses an adult quite naturally as Mr., Mrs., or Miss So-and-So.* If one of them did so, it slipped past my ears; I see not one hatch mark under this heading in my notebook.

These incessant demonstration sessions are beamed at children

---

*Mr. Spock in "Star Trek" is not a real exception. He has no first name: moreover, the *Mr.* conforms not to civilian etiquette, but to naval protocol for addressing a first officer.

who have internalized neither the nuances of the English language nor the nuances of the social structures they are learning and relearning with it. In the face of such an ideological onslaught, Mr., Mrs., and Miss can scarcely escape the fate of the good, English word, *Madam,* which used to be a perfectly respectable way of indicating respect—indeed, extreme respect—for any lady so addressed. Today it's the word for someone who makes a living managing a house of prostitution.

CONTROL OF LANGUAGE MEANS CONTROL OF CULTURE

Night after night, prime-time television bombards us with linguistic cues that signal specific information about social structure. We hardly notice how crime shows repeatedly use language that makes the way military people relate to each other seem perfectly "normal." It seems equally "normal" that credential beareres are the only ones who consistently merit signs of respect and deference, while television's lay population—the men and women who populate situation comedies and variety shows—are our peers, almost like members of our own families, even if the stars deserve just a trace of extra respect and deference.

Do these modes of address actually mirror a social-linguistic reality "out there in the real world," with television acting mainly as a faithful recorder of the kinds of organic changes that normally occur as language and social structure evolve together? The question poses false alternatives. Television dialogue must be effortlessly understood by mass audiences; thus it simply cannot rely heavily on pure invention of linguistic forms that would not be widely recognizable.

No—television's power to change our language rests not so much in invention. It resides much more in being able to pick up, propagate, and legitimize for all America linguistic styles that would otherwise not have the same chance of emerging from the subcultures that originated them.

This is not to say that the social-linguistic changes discussed here are deliberate. "The heart has reasons which reason knows not of." In much the same way, unrelated, individual decisions arrived at independently by persons separated in time and space —who may not know each other but who belong to the same subculture and thus "speak the same language"—have a cumulative impact on American English that goes beyond the reasoned intention of any person or group of persons.

The power to change the structure of language is the power to change thought, and through it, to change the structure of society without a vote being cast!

11

Words Are
a Clumsy
Way of
Talking

Sometime around World War II the country switched from "chopped meat" to "hamburger." The demise of chopped meat in America was accompanied shortly thereafter by the demise of the armpit. No more armpits—only underarms where consumers are urged to spray, smear, and roll on products the television voice calls "antiperspirants," a word which did not exist a generation ago. This new term is still being worked over, and the next step already on the horizon is "antiwetness spray product."[1]

The wetness in question should not be mistaken for the same wetness that certain brands of nonfabric diapers are said to keep away from baby's skin. It is to be hoped that the next generation will not confuse urine with sweat any more than the present generation confuses a "body bar" or "beauty cleanser" with a cake of soap. The word "diaper," by the way, is fast becoming "diper"—resulting in a gross national saving of an incalculable number of syllables, as millions of us follow the lead of all those television voices reducing the original three-syllable word to two.

"Wetness" is quite different from moisture and from moisturizing, which is what a lady washing her face does as she rinses away some kind of cream or the lather from one of those "beauty cleansers." The process will leave her complexion clean and fresh, whereupon she is urged not to remain content but to cover it immediately with a flesh-colored cosmetic the television voice is very likely to call "hypo-allergenic."

That television voice is informed by a pharmacopia which lists depressant drugs as "calmatives" and analgesics as "pain relievers." It urges everyone to buy products that relieve "fullness" or "gasid indigestion." The terms could be some new-fangled way of talking about old-fashioned indigestion and bellyache; but then again, they may belong in an array of new miseries listed in advertising's *materia medica,* which the television voice depends on. Among them are "the frizzies"—an ailment that splits the ends of the hair shaft; "trouble-falling-asleep"; and "chewing problems"—a difficulty some people experience when their chewing gum sticks to their fillings instead of wadding itself into the nicely masticatable cud the people selling Freedent urge all America to chew.

The television voice talks about dentures, dentifrice, and tooth polish. (Who on television ever refers to false teeth, toothpaste, or toothpowder?) Women with big busts ("full-figured" women, says the voice) are ordered to buy a special "bra" available in any store that sells what the voice calls "quality lanjeray."

"Being that Kitty couldn't go, I rejected the invitation," says the scion of an upper-class soap-opera family. When his snobbish mother objects that the fiancée of his choice is their social inferior, he says he refuses to "pamper to" his mother's wishes[2] —he will not give up his intended! It's a strange way of talking for a man who has received "the best education money can buy."[3]

In one of my radio broadcasts I was describing the level of

taste among those who are privileged to enter every home in the country without knocking, trying to attract attention to

> . . . products to kill the smell of sweat and remove armpit stain; sanitary napkins, toilet paper, medications to move your bowels, remedies for piles, poison to kill roaches, shoe insoles that "eat" foot-odor—all clamoring insistently and publicly for attention.

I was alone in the studio, but a friend who was with the rest of the staff on the other side of the glass described to me later what had happened.

During most of the broadcast, he said, they were all talking among themselves, paying no attention to my voice in the background. At these words, however, everyone fell suddenly silent. One of the station managers clapped her hand to her forehead and exclaimed. "She *did* it! She went and *did* it!"

No sooner had I signed off than her voice entered my studio. "Can you come to my office and bring your script?" It was not really a question.

I stood in front of her desk as she read it. "Toilet paper," she said. "Sanitary napkins. Piles. You can't say those things on the air. You just can't!"

"Why not?" I asked. "Commercials for these products are targeted to seventy million American homes every day. What's the difference if they say 'bathroom tissue' and I say 'toilet paper'? Everyone knows we're talking about the same thing."

She looked puzzled—honestly puzzled.

I continued. "I thought you might be bothered by this broadcast, so for your sake I skipped the line in my copy that mentioned 'products claiming to kill crotch-odor,' even though vaginal suppositories and deodorant sprays are advertised publicly on radio and television every day."

"It's different," she said. "It's not the same thing."

Of course she was quite right. It's not the same thing. Advertising language does something more fundamental than simply applying a phony silken sheen to what is still discernible as the ear of the sow.

Language describes existing realities, to be sure; but it does more than *just* describe; and the reality it describes is not immutable. Language guides our vision, making it easier for us to look here and avoid looking there. If we do not look, we do not see —which is how it happens that language can even change the way we experience reality, almost without anyone noticing.

"Hamburger" angles vision away from something that women of an earlier generation looked at very closely when they shopped for meat in the butcher shop; what kind of meat is the butcher feeding through the grinder? They kept an eye on the meat and called it by its name; chopped steak, chopped brisket, chopped chuck—chopped *meat.* "Antiperspirant" distracts attention from what these products may be doing to human sweat glands. All the made-up words of medical advertising jargon divert attention from the nature of real illness, the sources of real pain, and the drugs that go into the advertised remedies. Paradoxically, the invented illnesses for which we are urged to buy remedies encourage us to entrust still more responsibility for our own well-being to credential-bearing experts, who deliver advice for "problems" that have no business being dignified by that term in the first place.

Advertisers are keenly aware of the paradox. The case of "hypo-allergenic" makeup is illustrative. About thirty-five years ago, the use of the term *nonallergenic* was prohibited by the Food and Drug Administration, based on the fact that every ingredient in make-up has a potential for producing an allergic reaction in someone. Only recently, however, have the cosmetic companies become aware of "a remarkable interest exhibited by consumers" in the allergy-arousing potential of makeup on the market. "We were faced with a dilemma," said Dr. Earle W. Brauer, Revlon's vice president of medical affairs, explaining the company's decision to market Etherea, its "hypo-allergenic" line. "When we reached the position where hypo-allergenic was of interest to Mrs. Average Consumer," he explained, "Revlon resisted because it would mean that all products made prior to this date were allergic [*sic*] and that made no sense . . . we'd been making hypo-allergenic cosmetics and not calling them that. We had to do something that would make them even more hypo-allergenic." He says that this was accomplished by removing offending ingredients from the basic formula. Since the difference between products labeled "hypo-allergenic" and others is thus a matter of subtraction, it posed a problem in the advertising campaign: how to reassure those who might find it alarming if they became aware that the original product Revlon had been selling had been de-fanged, so to speak. The dilemma was resolved by stressing that Etherea was *more hypo-allergenic* than Revlon's earlier products.[4] Thus, by endowing it with a greater negative quantity, the advertisers blessed the product with *more* of *less.*

A television voice tells us to buy beer and soft drinks in the new "convenience packages"—a term that glosses over any inconvenience such packaging visits upon an overburdened ecological system that can never dispose of the aluminum cans and the bottles the same voice calls "disposable." Our automobiles are advertised in three sizes: "standard" (or "full size"), "compact," and "sub-compact"—terms that remind us of "normal," "borderline," and "subnormal." Thus do the very words channel our attention away from what we all find it easy to forget: that the "standard" cars, now providing a baseline against which the normality of all other vehicles is to be evaluated, are gluttonous gas-consumers whose production requires unceasing rape of the planet's nonrenewable mineral deposits and energy sources.

The language of advertising and the language of bureaucracy borrow from each other. Just as the television voice says "bathroom bowl," meaning toilet, the bureaucrat says "to select out," meaning to dismiss someone from his job. At the Nixon White House people "misspoke themselves," they never said foolish or deceptive things or lied. A mistake in planning or prediction by top executives at our great oil and energy conglomerates is a "shortfall." Erroneous, even deceptive estimates submitted to the Pentagon by its suppliers are "cost overruns." Statisticians at our best universities calculate "acceptable rates" of crime, unemployment, war, highway killings, and nuclear destruction, just as our social scientists discuss the proper formulas for computing "kill ratios" in television dramas. As Richard Gambimo points out, information "is developed" as in a darkroom or laboratory; this saves the speaker from any obligation to explain whether he means compiled, sought, filed, pursued, fabricated, altered, concealed, or revealed, at the same time that it skirts the fundamental matter of who "developed" it anyway.[5]

During World War II, the term *national security* was invoked as nations were trying to secure their territories against physical invasion and as constitutional systems were trying to secure themselves against takeover by fascist, totalitarian ones. Three decades later, quite different meanings have become attached to the term. "Freedom of the President to pursue his planned course was the ultimate national security objective." This was Egil Krogh's definition when he was assistant to John D. Ehrlichman in the Nixon White House. He explained it all to the judge who was sentencing him for his part in the illegal activities that have come to be known as *Watergate*. (Thus has history attached a wealth of meaning to a word that used to designate simply a posh Washington residential and office building.) Mr. Krogh said his experience had made him painfully aware that euphemisms—devious ways of saying things—had channeled his own attention away from what used to be a quite different sense of morality. "I see now," he said, "that the key is the effect that the term, 'national security,' had on my judgment. The very words served to block critical analysis."[6] It's the same trick the television voice relies on, diverting attention, angling vision toward deliberately highlighted aspects of reality.[7]

DRAMATIC LANGUAGE: HIGHLIGHTS AND LOWLIGHTS

Words point to more than they specifically say; what counts is the afterglow, the meaning rippling outward. Meanings in human speech have fuzzy edges, wavy margins—more like a beam of natural light than a laser beam.

We speak to each other in a complex language that goes well beyond words—a language that packages our words with movement, intonation, expression, stance, timing, pacing, cadence, associations. Dramatic presentations do the same in show-and-tell for the audiences. Television commercials are tight dramatic presentations that use all our languages to angle our vision their way.

> We asked people if they would stop and help if you had tire trouble. Here's what they said:
> "No, I keep my nose out of other people's business."
> "No, because I'm afraid . . ."
> "No, why should I?"
> "No, I just don't . . ."
> "I would not stop for anyone, period."
> "No, I might cause an accident."
> "No, I used to stop, but not any more."
> "No, I don't really want to get involved."

Each of these remarks is made by a driver who speeds past a motorist waving frantically from the side of the road. The camera's eye sees the scene for you from a vantage point behind the wheel of each car. It's as if you were in the driver's seat; as if it were you refusing to slow down, refusing to come to the aid of the man signaling desperately for help. Then comes the punchline of this commercial: "That's why Firestone puts a belt of steel between you and tire trouble."

This little drama, played scores of times, showed the country alienated and fearful drivers refusing to aid a fellow human being in trouble. That stranded man—why does he feel so helpless? Why is he so frantic? Is something more dire, perhaps, going on there, at the side of the road? There are many dramas in the drama—yet the words, images, sounds, music, all ask us to focus on the flat tire, as the only problem worthy of notice. The rest is treated as if it were so utterly normal for people to behave in this fashion that it's not worth our attention.

The Kellogg Company pays for a television advertisement they define as a public service they perform on behalf of the nation's children. Nationwide advertising in other media calls the country's attention to their own beneficence. "Thirty two million children will be seeing this 'Good Breakfast' message," says one advertisement about the other. The text explains that "it's no easy job to convince people, especially children, of the importance of good nutrition." Still, "Kellogg's believes it's worth the doing."

The television advertisement shows an athletic coach with his team of children—all black.

> COACH: I want to show you kids what can happen if you don't eat a good breakfast. OK, now, pretend you're a car. OK? Come on!
>
> KID: Can I be a bus?
>
> COACH: OK, you're a bus. Now you're all driving down the street, just so cool . . . then all of a sudden, wham! Bip! You run out of gas! Well, you know what? That's just what can happen to you in the morning if you don't eat a good breakfast. You can start slowing down and getting droopy. Look—it's dumb to run out of gas. Just fill your tank up with good things like these. . . . Fruits like grapefruit . . . a peach . . . or juice. And then have some other good things like waffles, bacon and

eggs, or cereal with milk, a sliced banana . . . some toast. Y'know, a good breakfast can help you drive through the whole morning. So always fill 'er up right. 'Cause running outa gas gets you nowhere fast.[8]

This advertisement, given nationwide exposure in print as well as on television, attempted to teach every child in the country that his body was an automobile—quite different from the body image ancient Greek culture tried to teach its children, that the body was a temple![9]

A commercial for the movie *Death Wish* was broadcast repeatedly on network television. We learned that the film was about a man whose wife and daughter had been mugged and raped. Consumed by a desire for vengeance, he dedicates himself to tracking down and murdering the criminals. We see the star, Charles Bronson, as a voice-over says: "He's out to get the mothers. Every mother is afraid of this vigilante."

The whole commercial lasted about thirty seconds. Yet, millions of us who attended to it understood the feelings of anger and hate, despair, repugnance, disgust, and desire for vengeance that such harrowing experiences must have evoked in the man. Charles Bronson, even in the brief shots the commercial allowed us to see, managed to suggest them all. In just those thirty seconds, the little drama collected and concentrated these emotions—and then the whole vignette was summarized in this special way of pronouncing a single word, "mother."

In that context the word no longer means "mother". It is shorthand for an obscenity, one of the most devastating insults in the English language, "motherfucker." Among the millions of people whose homes the commercial entered, some surely knew the derivation of the now tainted word. Others, who may not have been aware of this particular bit of social and linguistic history, were left with no doubt in their minds that "mother" can be an insult, a fightin' word, an epithet—even a word a man might hesitate to use in front of his own mother! The thirty-second drama succeeded in turning a word's meaning *for the whole country* into its own opposite.

Aldous Huxley, describing a fictional totalitarian society of the future, anticipated that the word "mother" would become an obscenity under such social conditions. He did not trace the source to obscene language commonly used in the submerged parts of society we normally do not look at, but rather to the scientific procedure of producing embryos *ex utero*. [10]

ATTACHMENT AND PACKAGING OF MEANINGS

All dramatic staging is a deliberately contrived package of concocted meanings. Since the job of the advertiser is to package specific meanings and call them to the attention of the public,[11] the dramatic-staging opportunity television offers, plus its widespread coverage, has given an unprecedented boost to the business.

"I believe I can package Hitler right now." The remark is attributed to Jerry Della Femina,[12] owner of an advertising agency with a reputation for extreme skillfulness in concocting, controlling, and disseminating the meanings his clients pay him for attaching to their products. Mr. Della Femina explains quite clearly how it's done:[13] The advertising specialist collects symbols whose social history is such that they typically evoke positive feelings of approval and affection. He concentrates them in a "package"—a drama, a slogan, an image, a story, a song, a ballad. Set Hitler in the same package and—given mass exposure and frequent repetition in well-chosen contexts—it would be quite reasonable to anticipate a large-scale reversal of the feelings many Americans have learned to attach to the man and the social system he represented.

Mr. Della Femina summarized a principle that guides all advertising. Meanings must be *attached;* packaging does the job; and it can work with Hitler just as it works with Alka Seltzer. Social experience endows symbols with an emotional charge that behaves very much like an electric charge. (Not by accident do we say "charged with meaning.") A Hitler symbol, given the chance to rub up against the rest of the symbols Mr. Della Femina would package with it, can attract their positive charge to itself in the same way that the power of a magnet "rubs off" on iron filings entering its field. Since experience can be vicarious (one doesn't have to know Hitler to have an emotional reaction to him) dramatizations, which provide vicarious experience in concentrated form, are powerfully effective packages. On television, they are immediately guaranteed widespread coverage—a social sharing that converts private experience into inescapable social experience.

A dean of the advertising business tells the story of his first insight into the process and its workings:

> Zalmon Simmons, the original head of the Simmons [mattress] Co., told me years ago that George Dyer had done more for his business than any other one man.
> "What did he do?" I asked.
> "He taught me what business I was in," said Mr. Simmons.
> "How do you mean that?" I asked again.
> "When Dyer called on me for the first time, he asked me what business I was in. I thought it was a foolish question, but I answered, 'Making and selling beds.'
> " 'Wrong,' said Mr. Dyer. 'You are really in the business of selling sleep—good, refreshing, sound sleep.' " [14]

What Mr. Dyer knew was that attaching the positive charge of "good, refreshing, sound sleep" to just plain, ordinary "bed" enhances its meaning and makes "bed" a more desirable symbol. That was way back in the 1920s, though. Today's advertising agency attaches the positive charge that goes with Joey Heatherton, the sex symbol, as she writhes on a Serta mattress, huskily singing its praises.

It works both ways, of course. As the positive charge rubs off on the recipient symbol it leaves the "voltage" of the donor symbol somewhat diminished. Purina Dog Chow shows us a drama in which several dog species—dachshunds, terriers, spaniels, bulldogs—tell the audience in appropriate accents how much they like this dog food. The English Bull, with a thick British accent, says, "This is Dog Chow's finest hour." Another commercial reassures the audience that it's safe to eat potatoes without fearing excessive weight-gain, and closes with the phrase, "There is nothing to fear but fear itself." The quotations are allusions to remarks made by Winston Churchill and Franklin Delano Roosevelt talking about what they considered national survival. A *Variety* commentator finds the juxtapositions with dog food and potatoes offensive—which is, after all, a matter of his taste. The observation that such associations cheapen the historic figures and events whose charge they borrow, however, is right on the mark.[15]

Patriotic symbols pack a strong emotional charge—which explains why so many advertising agencies like to stuff a client's product into a package containing lots of folk customs and references to easily recognized historic occurrences. In this, the soft-drink companies are outstanding. A Coca-Cola advertising campaign bears a patriotic title: "Look Up America." The agency launched it with a press conference called for July 3, 1974 (regrettably, July 4 was a holiday).[16] A sister product, Pepsi Cola, sticks with the slogan, "Pepsi people, feelin' free," and their "packages" are chock full of the same symbols of Americana—the marchers and the bands, hayrides, ballgames, picnics, and scenes reminiscent of an America Tom Sawyer and Huck Finn grew up in.

Ancient and revered religious symbols pack a hefty positive charge too. Cameras shoot into the light, wreathing Coca-Cola and Pepsi Cola bottles in heavenly halos. The agency handling the Datsun account shows Noah, at the first sign of the deluge, leading the animals, two by two, into his Datsun pickup truck. Their current slogan is "Datsun saves." In a commercial for a department store, a minister performing a marriage ceremony interrupts to admire the groom's clothing, asking the price of each item, giving the groom a chance to tell where it was bought.[17]

Diminishing the "charge" of revered symbols by these kinds of juxtapositions cheapens a value that is not a market value, and so complaints about the practice are not taken seriously. Moreover, symbols like these are in the public domain—priceless and thus worthless; nobody has "standing" to prove loss or theft, Noah cannot file for accrued back royalties and Winston Churchill's estate cannot sue for "defamation of symbol." The cost of ravages visited in the present on what belongs to everyone collectively, now and in the future, is left for succeeding generations to tot up.

Advertisers promoting prophylactic sheaths worn by the male during sexual intercourse have not hesitated to use the Bible as packaging for their product. In July 1975, television advertisements for Trojan condoms appeared on the air for the first time when KNTV, San Jose, California, agreed to run two thirty-second spots. One showed young, strong hands, just a man's hands, carefully, competently fashioning a baby's cradle. The other showed a pair of young honeymooners, a beach scene, waves ebbing and surging as they embrace. The television voice admonished the audience that parenthood should be responsibly undertaken intentionally, and intoned, "To everything there is a season and a time to every purpose under heaven." (Ecclesiastes 3:1).

As of this writing, television commercials promoting condoms are still not accepted nationally. The KNTV broadcasts were part of a three-month test run arranged by the Poppe Tyson agency, which handles the Trojan account for Young Drug Products Company. Mr. Poppe, however, believes that it's just a matter of time before these commercials join all the rest in America's living rooms. His agency uses the same strategy that has succeeded in gaining the necessary approval for all the other "personal products" whose promotion was once considered inappropriate for unannounced entry into the home, but which are now very much in evidence.

Decisions about this sort of thing rest with fifteen men and women who call themselves the Television Board of Directors of the NAB's Code Authority.* These people are not accountable to the public (most television listeners don't even know the code exists, much less the board). They hold office by authority of those members of the National Association of Broadcasters who voluntarily join the Code Authority. Commercials for what the business calls "personal products" are submitted to this board, whose members then decide whether they are tasteful enough for repeated entry into seventy-one million homes. This board's accumulated decisions over the years, ratified by the membership, have converted every living room in the country into a midway, opening them all to the hawkers who enter and exit ten to twenty times an hour without bothering to knock.

Over one hundred stations do not even sign up for the NAB code, so the Poppe Tyson agency's representatives began their campaign to get condom ads on the air by approaching the first dozen or so stations on the list of nonsubscribers. KNTV was the first to agree to take the test commercials. When viewers first telephoned irate complaints and wrote indignant letters, the station manager immediately withdrew the spots. But then, when a counter-campaign of calling and writing made it clear that ratings would not suffer, the commercials were reinstated.

---

*A similar board passes on radio commercials, supposedly independently of decisions taken by the Television Board.

This is what the broadcasters call an editorial decision, and in the name of press freedom they claim that theirs is the sole right to make such decisions. Their shelter is the First Amendment to the Constitution—an amendment written by men who assumed that such decisions would be guided by conscience, not by audience ratings, made by people who look their customers in the eye every day and knock before entering their premises, without a troupe of barkers in tow. The courts have still not caught on to the difference.[18]

The Television Board seeks public reactions to the Trojan request, as it has to others of a similar nature. No effort is made to determine the public's reaction to yet another uninvited pitchman in the home. Instead, the board invites comments from experts in population problems, psychology, sociology, and religion, soliciting their opinions about the advisability of public information about condoms and their use in family planning! The assumption that commercials are the only way or the most advisable way to get out the word remains unquestioned, excluded from the agenda, out of order for the debate.

Even as this book goes to press, the Television Board is again considering the Trojan case. The decision could go either way this time around; but I haven't the slightest doubt that sooner or later little dramas about condoms will be acted out in American homes along with all the others. They will join the disembodied nose that sneezes a fine spray as a voice praises Allerest; the naked toes that giggle at the delights of Desenex; the man who asks, "Do you mind if I talk about diarrhea?" and then proceeds to do precisely that; the wife who proves she loves her husband by taking Geritol; the husband who refuses to kiss his wife until she dispels her foul mouth odor by using "his" mouthwash; the father who won't get dressed until someone hands him an aerosol can with "his" deodorant; the girl who stretches the crotch of her pantyhose on camera and invites the nation to admire it, and so on. The men and women of the Television Board of Authority and their constituency have had no difficulty reconciling these unannounced commercials with their own standards of taste, which then, through the power of television, mold standards of taste for the country as a whole.

When stars and "personalities" agree to appear in commercials, they insist on immediate and substantial compensation to make up for any possible diminution of their own market value. It is rumored in the business that Sir Lawrence Olivier was paid a quarter of a million dollars for a thirty-second drama that packaged Polaroid cameras with him. It sounds like a huge sum until one realizes, as Sir Lawrence's agent undoubtedly did, that this theatrical artist of extraordinary dramatic talent agreed to yield the star role to a Polaroid camera, contenting himself with the supporting part. He agreed to be booked into a house which assured him only the most glancing attention by the audience. He agreed to settle for no billing, the performance yielded him no critical acclaim and—to cap it all—when the show closed, nobody even bothered to remark its passing.

COATTAILS AND FLY-BYS

Advertisers paying the bill like to package their products in or near popular shows even when the image or reference is so fleeting that it seems barely worth the trouble. Many people in the business claim, however, that such "fly-by's" and "coattail plugs" are among television's most effective sales pitches since they partake of the show's aura of glamor and acceptability and register on consciousness when people are inattentive, their guards lowered. The montage introducing "Hawaii Five-O" at one time included a clip showing a United Airlines plane—a "fly-by" paid for by the company. A "coattail plug" for the same airline appeared at the end of every ABC sports event—a rapid voice accompaniment to the "crawl" listing credits at the end of each show:

Travel arrangements made through a promotional fee paid by United Airlines, flying roomy DC-10 and 747 Friend Ships to eighteen U.S. Cities, United Airlines, the friendly skies of your land.

Continental Airlines, too, likes the coattail plug. For the privilege of being packaged just ten seconds with Johnny Carson in NBC's "Tonight Show," the company has paid a hundred dollars a second.

Sometimes these rapid packagings are bartered. Morgan Limousine Service, in return for just a mention in the Carson package, has picked up and delivered many of the show's guests without submitting a bill. The Sheraton hotel chain has put them up free in return for a mention here, a mention there. When on camera, Johnny Carson, the show's host, always wears clothes available for purchase from the company he owns, Johnny Carson Apparel. Game show host Bill Cullen, on the other hand, always wears clothes provided by Barney's Men's Store on his "Winning Streak" and "$25,000 Pyramid."

The game shows, which dominate daytime television and the "access hour" (the hour preceding the first network hour) are, in fact, total commercial packages made to display the merchandise they give away to winners. Even so, coattail plugs are still delivered by a pitchman. "It's a microwave oven! From the famous Tappan full line of kitchen appliances, the new countertop microwave oven, today's convenient way to cook food in minutes, not hours. Plugs into standard home electrical outlets. From Tappan—since 1881." That sort of spiel is called a description, and is not counted in the NAB's self-imposed code specifying limits to the number of commercial minutes subscribing stations really ought to stick to.[19]

These game shows are packages for the software of television itself: the stars and the shows that feature them. Many nighttime stars reappear on these daytime shows. Those who do not, themselves, appear on camera as daytime regulars in shows such as "Hollywood Squares" and "Celebrity Sweepstakes," are promoted over and over again anyway in the very content of the questions. (How many sons does Bing Crosby have? Name three stars who have won Emmies. "The Odd Couple" appeared on what television network? Is the family featured in "Happy Days" named the Cunninghams, the Bunkers, or the Jeffersons?) Thus are the packagers themselves packaged in this total support system the business has created. It's a way of making sure they never lose their "charge."

ADVERTISER VIGILANCE TO KEEP THE PRODUCT FROM LOSING ITS CHARGE

Advertisers try to make sure their product runs no risk of ending up in a package that jostles it against symbols that could diminish its value by draining off some of its charge.

Instructions for a show sponsored by Camel cigarettes admonished the writers:

> Do not have the heavy or any disreputable person smoking a cigarette. Do not associate the smoking of cigarettes with undesirable scenes or situations plot-wise. [sic][20]

Cigarettes had to be smoked gracefully, never puffed nervously. A cigarette was never given to a character to "calm his nerves," since this might suggest a narcotic effect. Arson was excluded from the numerous violent crimes the writers were instructed to feature because arson might remind the audience of fires caused by cigarettes. No one could cough on the show. Sensitivity to symbol jostling at work.

Since those days, an act of Congress has excluded cigarette commercials from the airwaves. The surgeon general of the United States announced in 1964 that he and his advisers were convinced that cigarettes are to lung cancer what coal dust is to black lung disease. This opinion persuaded a congressional majority that the practice of using the public airways to urge the use of cigarettes might be construed as inconsistent with the franchise-holders' statutory obligations to program "in the public interest, convenience, and necessity." The tobacco business joined the television and advertising business in lobbying against the legislation when it was proposed. Now that it is in effect, they lobby equally valiantly for its removal, citing as evidence of broadcast advertising's minor role in popularizing smoking the fact that, after all, cigarette sales have not declined—indeed, they have increased.[21] Ah! But as long as Dean Martin continues to allow his charm, skill, and reputation for glamor to brush off on the cigarettes he chain-smokes on the air, television continues to do its bit to legitimize the smoking habit in our culture—perhaps even more than those paid commercials ever did!

In 1974 the American Society of Travel Agents filed a formal complaint with the agency handling the Alka Seltzer account. They said a commercial packaging Alka Seltzer in a drama ridiculing travel agents diminished their value. The drama opened with a husband and wife sitting near a construction site, bulldozers leveling everything in sight. The husband shouts to be heard above the din: "I asked the travel agent where we can go for a little peace and quiet." "He said, 'Mr. Fields, I know just the place for you.'" And then the punch line—"I need an Alka Seltzer!" The director of public relations for Miles Laboratories understood the complaint and obligingly ordered the writer to switch from "travel agent" to "brother-in-law" or even just "the man."

An advertising executive for a theater chain said he was "shocked" at a McDonald's commercial calling attention to the high price and low digestibility of current cinema fare, and immediately alerted the National Association of Theater Owners in New York and Washington to persuade the McDonald Corporation's agency to withdraw the spot.[22] It was done forthwith, and without any need for further discussion on the part of the business people involved about their initial assumption that public attitudes would "catch" some of the negative charge in those comments criticizing movies, once they received widespread exposure; and that this would operate to the detriment of the movie business.

Food companies insist that their ads be positioned at a safe distance from commercials for products claiming to ease "stomach distress." The agencies handling accounts for sandwich spreads specify that their commercials must be safely distanced from any ad for toilet cleaners, deodorants, or pet foods. This sort of protection is guaranteed by the television networks through what they call "pod" protection; and time-buyers negotiate "the protection situation" along with the price. The issue is to group adjacent commercials in their own little package or "pod," which insulates them against contamination from any leakage of charges borne by symbols in a competitor's package or "pod." It's done by "positioning" each at a safe distance from the other—safety defined as something from a ten- to a thirty-minute separation for a sixty-second spot. (A thirty-second spot is guaranteed only against a competitor's intrusion into the one-minute or two-minute commercial break it appears in.) No doubt is left about the seriousness of this matter: if the advertiser finds out his commercial has not been properly insulated, he may demand a "make good"—that is, a rerun of the spot at no additional charge.[23]

The "protection situation" is negotiated just as sharply to neutralize undesirable charges that might contaminate the advertised product by leaking over from the show, itself. Automobile advertisements must be safely distanced from any drama that involves car accidents. On the CBS show "Mannix," the hero drove a Chevrolet Camaro. General Motors donated seven of its cars to the show, with the stipulation that the bad guys must never be seen driving a Chevrolet and any time there is a car crash the car that gets totaled must not be a Chevrolet.[24]

Beer and wine advertisers demand insulation for their commercials from shows whose action involves drunks or excessive drinking. A cold-pill commercial was removed unhesitatingly from its initially unsafe position near the film *Valley of the Dolls*. The network immediately acknowledged in this manner the reasonableness of the claim that the drug commercial could easily have picked up a negative charge from the film's indictment of drug use.[25] Leakages from news reports are just as deadly, and advertisers demand protection against them, as well. "If there is a plane crash in the news, we are not allowed to run this commercial," was accidentally appended to a Sperry Rand commercial scheduled to be broadcast during NBC football in the 1973–74 season.[26]

An executive at one of our largest advertising agencies, Benton and Bowles, declares that "the advertiser has the right to determine whether the *program environment* in which his commercial is placed is compatible with his message and in keeping with the standards of taste of his corporation," and goes on to say that the advertiser must give careful thought to the question whether "the impact of his investment will be diminished by the program content . . ."[27]

To people in the business, it all seems eminently reasonable. "After all, if a guy spends $40,000 for a minute of prime time, he wants to make sure the damn thing runs properly." The remark is attributed to the president of a firm that is in the "broadcasting service" business. These firms employ screeners who check that the commercials paid for by their clients have been run, run with the proper frequency and for the proper product.[28] They also exercise all due vigilance to make sure that program content adjacent to the commercials under review has been selected with an eye to the advertiser's "right" to a proper context for his ad.[29]

There are about two dozen firms specializing in this type of screening. The best known are Agency Services Corporation and the Leslie Harris Company. It is of interest that the screeners are given access to the programs in advance of their actual airing—a privilege which until recently had been denied to newspaper and magazine television critics and columnists on the grounds that it could be viewed as an infraction of freedom of the press.

Some of the tales about advertisers exercising this "right" have found their way into the general lore of the business, so that almost everyone in it knows the one about the gas-company sponsor that insisted upon having the writers remove from a show about Nazi Germany any reference to *gas* chambers. In the production of a drama about the Andersonville trial, the sponsor, an automobile concern, instructed that President Lincoln not be mentioned by name, since the "Lincoln" was a competing automobile, and, to avoid possible offense to Southern viewers, that the title be changed to "The Trial of Captain Wirtz," to disguise the fact that the story concerned events in a Confederate stockade for Union prisoners of war.[30]

Of course the same process works in reverse and the meaning of the program content—drama or news—is diminished and distorted as a result of *its* appearance surrounded by banal commercials. Television viewers do not normally complain about this —or if they do, the networks rarely oblige with "make-goods," and their complaints rarely get wide circulation. Airing of public complaints about commercials on the Royal Shakespeare Company's production of *Antony and Cleopatra* is one notable exception.

The ABC network had dedicated an entire Saturday of prime time to a broadcast of this play. The *New York Times* television critic had given it a favorable review. Irate readers, who had followed his advice not to miss it, rebuked him soundly for a thoroughly misleading review: his review had not even mentioned the commercials! Yet their presence had completely changed the dramatic experience for many who had seen the play. "At the end of the play," wrote one man, "the split-second cut from the dead Queen of Egypt in robes of state to a middle-aged man in pyjamas, announcing 'that's my last cough,' would have been incredible, except by then, after three hours of similarly ludicrous high-jinks, not even a plug for an asp antidote would have been surprising." Others said they tuned out after a half-hour.[31]

Some of these examples may verge on the ludicrous; but they are not to be taken lightly as indicators of the value of "charges" packed into symbols, the volatility of those charges, and the way context determines and distorts meanings for us all. Edward R. Murrow knew about it back in 1958 when he said, "The sponsor of an hour's television program is not buying merely the six minutes devoted to his commercial message. He is determining, within broad limits, the sum total of the impact of the entire hour."[32]

12

Involuntary
Servitude*

There's an insightful expression in American English that is passing out of fashion: "to put someone in mind of something." The phrase refers to finding similarities. ("He puts me in mind of his father—they have the same expression about the eyes.") Its broad, generic meaning is to call up a memory, often an elusive one, through association. ("Hearing just a few bars of the melody put me in mind of the day we first met.")

Packaging symbols the way advertising does is a way of rigging the odds that Polaroid cameras will *put us in mind of* some of the charm, glamor, and talent of Sir Lawrence Olivier whether or not we remember *him.* Calling headache remedies "pain relievers" makes it less likely that constant repetition of the ads will

*Although it is pervasive throughout this book, this seems an appropriate place to acknowledge my intellectual debt to Marshall McLuhan. See especially his *The Mechanical Bride* (Boston: A Beacon Book, 1951) and *Understanding Media: The Extensions of Man* (New York: A Mentor Book, 1964).

put us in mind of a current social policy that daily urges a whole country—a whole civilization—to take drugs and to take them lightly. Chevrolet wants to be sure that its Camaro will not *put us in mind of* epidemic accidents; and so on.

I like the expression since it reminds us that if something is put into the mind, someone or something must have helped to put it there. Advertising jargon abounds with metaphors acknowledging that the task of the business is to do precisely that. "Promotions Vie for Share of Mind" is the title of an article in *Advertising Age*.[1] The author of "24 Questions to Help You Evaluate Your Commercials" asks, "Is your 'share of mind' as good as your 'share of market?'" and he discusses the need to forge "a favorable mental link" to his product.[2] Another specialist tells how "to map the mind of the sophisticated candy buyer, the 10-year-old . . ." in order to get him to want a candy bar called Milk Duds.[3]

What advertising puts into the mind is not the product, of course, but some kind of associative link to it. The agency for Milk Duds could not literally place a single candy bar in the mind of even one of those sophisticated ten-year-old candy buyers; but their advertisement—at the same time that it called attention to the product—now called up experiences that had already been registered in the child's mind and linked them *to* the product.

"Mapping the mind" means only doing the necessary anthropological field work to find out what kinds of experiences are widespread among the ten-year-old set, available to be called up and put to work in the service of Milk Duds.[4] The commercial is a subtle way of impressing the children who happen to become exposed to it into a kind of involuntary servitude never envisioned by the framers of the Thirteenth Amendment to the Constitution. The viewers have to do the work of *calling to mind* what the commercial *put them in mind of.*

SOCIAL SHARING—EXTENSIONAL THRUST

"Come to where the flavor is," says a famous cigarette advertisement. It shows a man's hand holding a cigarette, a bridle, and a bit, and just enough of his red-shirted torso to reveal the slight bulge of a cigarette pack in his shirt pocket. Barely discernible through the fabric is the lettering on the package: *Marlboro.* It's not necessary to notice the brand name, though, since the slogan and the suggestion of a cowboy-outdoorsman is enough to get the audience to do the rest of the work, completing the association and re-creating the full story the advertisement calls to mind. We must *make sense out of it,* or else the whole image makes no sense. Saturation advertising over the past decade has virtually guaranteed that all of us have learned how to make the designated association—inescapable, now, because of widespread social sharing.

Even if the commercial is in a foreign tongue you are not excused from your allotted task. In Colombia I saw television commercials for the same product, Marlboro. The little drama was acted in Spanish, of course. It showed emerald prospectors making camp in the rugged mountain country where the mines are; where men as rough and tough as any old Alaskan claim jumper brave the wrath of Federal troops trying to protect government-owned mines from just such raiders. The same music, the tattoo on the arm, the outdoor camping scene, forced any members of the audience, whether or not they understood Spanish, to perform the job of calling that brand of cigarettes to mind.

Social sharing does more than guarantee that the lesson of the ads will be widely learned. Shared awareness provides what economists call "a multiplier effect," what advertisers call "extensional thrust." It's another way of saying that something extra happens as we communicate with each other about experiences we share, especially public ones. Once they enter the public domain, then we, ourselves, fix them, so to speak, in the cultural habitat. Television—commercials and all—now provides the single most widely shared public experience. We hum the tunes of the ads, make jokes about them. Children pick them up and weave them into their games and stories. Their symbols appear in the very household objects we surround ourselves with, and in the clothing we wear. They turn up again in the television programs we watch—as questions on quiz shows, satire in variety shows, one-liners in comedy shows. We join the laugh track's guffaws when two young men about to go out on the town say, "Let's get the girls to flic our Bics," and we even bombard the comedians with suggestions for such gags, hoping to be paid for our contributions but equally delighted if they simply honor us by using them.[5] The advertisements are assimilated into the art environment, worked into collages, montages, assemblages, representing us around the world and in history. We all join in to do the work of the advertisers. We *put each other in mind of* their products, we *call them to mind,* ourselves—the greatest force of unpaid labor since the pyramids were built.[6]

If enough of us do enough of this work, the product reaches the pinnacle most advertisers aim for: converting the product name or the "hook" that brings it to mind into a household word. A soft drink is advertised as a "quench thirster." The commercial for Cheer detergent stresses its effectiveness in hot, cold, or warm water and the same voice tells the country about *tempacheer.* The actress moonlighting in a commercial for paper towels says her brand is "the quicker picker upper." The voice in the commercial that advertises prepared meats insists on saying *bolona,* while another voice plugging a cake mix insists on saying *stroosel.* An advertising campaign for Old Forester bourbon creates a word, "Forestering, which to them and, they hope, eventually to you will mean drinking . . ."[7] "Admiral has become a household word," says the television voice plugging that brand of household appliances.

A successful example of this creation of household words is the word *coke* for Coca-Cola. "Gimme a coke" gets most people a Coca-Cola. It's the rare clerk alert enough to ask "Coke or Pepsi?" The chances are very remote indeed that he'll ask "Coca-Cola, Pepsi Cola, Royal Crown Cola, or some other brand?"

Occasionally the "household word" strategy backfires. The case of *Xerox* is a good example. Xerox is a trademarked name that has become a synonym for making dry copies and for the copy itself. Yet, during the Senate Watergate hearings, when Senator Sam Ervin, Jr., looked over his glasses at a witness and repeatedly said on national television, "Suh, we'll Xerox a copy for you," the company's counsel for copyrights and trademarks, Robert L. Shafter, took exception. In a letter to the North Carolina Democrat he admonished the senator, who had held the whole country enthralled, that Xerox is a trademark and "as such, use of Xerox as a verb is improper."[8] Senator Ervin said he would try to oblige, but continued to make the same slip on the air. Next appeared national advertisements: "Please Don't Use Our Name in Vain," was the presumptuous headline. "There is no such thing as a Xerox. You can't make a Xerox. You can't go to the Xerox. And you can't Xerox anything. Ever."[9]

The apparent paradox is easily explained. Mr. Shafter's letter to Senator Ervin included the remark, ". . . misuse of Xerox on national television can be potentially damaging to us." The advertisement quoted above closed this way: "We're happy to have you use our name. All we ask is that you use it the way the good law intended." At the time in question, an antitrust suit was pending against the Xerox Corporation, the Justice Department alleging that, through systematic exercise of monopolistic power, this company had made it impossible for any similar business to compete and survive. In an economic system that claims to be based on the principle of fair competition, locking up the necessary technology in a single corporate compound in this manner is serious antisocial behavior, subject to prosecution like any other racket to ensure monopoly. Who knows to what extent the Senator's unwitting cooperation with the Justice Department in acknowledging a Xerox monopoly in the popular mind was instrumental in the company's decision in November 1974 to file a consent agreement?[10] At any rate, no similar campaign was ever launched in South America, urging our neighbors south of the border to cease and desist from saying "The Xerox Program," when they mean "Plaza Sesamo." That is the Spanish language version of "Sesame Street," sponsored throughout the continent by the Xerox Corporation in the interest of promoting good corporate relations and a favorable image of the company, according to one of their top executives.

LEARNING WITHOUT INFORMED CONSENT

Johnny Carson chats with a guest about a motion picture, *Shampoo.* The film's leading character is a hairdresser who uses his position as a springboard for sexual encounters with his women customers—not a bit difficult, since in the film his clients proposition him with dreary frequency. One of the guests says, "It figures. A woman comes in for a shampoo, the hairdresser massages her scalp, rubs her shoulders, her neck—no wonder the girls 'get off' on that." They go on to remark that the film showed hairdressers as real he-men, not necessarily homosexuals—a discussion which prompts one of the guests to talk about his recent "coming-out party."

The people on "The Tonight Show" did not invent these vernacular expressions. They were simply employing a kind of private language people in show business are comfortable with and take for granted. Those in the audience already familiar with the terms did not need the lesson. Others learned their meaning from this show, picking up their general sense from the context: "reading the context." Still others missed the point entirely, perhaps even thinking they heard wrong. That's how it is with any lesson —always a few slow learners.

Pepper Anderson ("Police Woman"), posing as a prostitute to catch illicit gun runners, says of a friend, "Yes, Charlene *tricks* for Jerry." Pepper's colleague on the force, Bill Crowley, must divert Charlene's attention as part of their plan to entrap the villains. "Call her up, Pepper," says Bill, "and tell her you have this tall, attractive *john* who's heard a lot about her." McGarrett on "Hawaii Five-O" orders his assistant to *get a make* on a suspect and determine his *MO*. Then they *put out an APB*. Not everyone understood before the show that Charlene's pimp was named Jerry, that Bill Crowley was about to present himself to a prostitute as a potential customer, that McGarrett wanted the suspect's file to look up his usual methods of work, and had ordered an "all points bulletin" issued to alert all police sources to pick up the suspect on sight. Most, however, were sure to have learned these meanings after having seen the broadcast.

Television commentators discussing this country's space shots, particularly in the simulated intimacy of panel discussion, often referred to the number of *Ks* it cost the country to launch them. The country quickly learned that this was a way of referring to thousands of dollars. The term, originally shoptalk among scientists and engineers, began to move outward, receiving additional "extensional thrust" as the social experience of space shots was shared nationwide—worldwide—through television.

As the guest on the Johnny Carson show said, "It figures." Scientists and engineers develop their own shoptalk just as do people sharing any occupation, any style of life: the police and the underworld develop theirs; show business people theirs, homosexuals theirs, and so on. Jehovah's Witnesses, tinkers, artists, and high-rise steel workers have their private ways of speaking, too. Television, however, beams out to the whole country only its selected and limited vocabulary and no other.

Television allows advertisers to attach meaning to gestures that then need no words to make the audience do its job of learning the proper associations and calling them up, on command. Children, for example, often make a popping sound by sticking a finger inside the cheek and flicking it out suddenly, pushing out a column of air. Most children pick up the trick on their own—to the annoyance of adults who have to live with them. If a child in the Denver, Colorado, area does this, however, it could be his way of commenting on a soft drink called Red Baby. At breakfast, a man makes a twisting gesture with his right hand. It could be his way of commenting on frozen orange juice. Only those who have shared the social experience which exposed the children to an advertising campaign for Red Baby that featured the trick;[11] or to the television commercial for frozen orange juice in which a man expresses astonishment that the drink his wife has served is not really "fresh squeezed"* can understand these gestures. As enough of us learn the gestures, however, they become the equivalent of the household word.

There is the musical equivalent of the household word, too. Certain commercials featuring music have been repeated so often and have received such widespread coverage that by now many Americans can substitute a snatch of melody for the name of the product associated with it and be well understood by their contemporaries. We hear the tune of "It's the Real Thing"; it *means* Coca-Cola. We hear someone singing, "Schaeffer Is the One Beer to Have," and it *means* Shaeffer beer.[12] The melody of "We Do It All for You" *means* the McDonald's Corporation and its products. Advertisers know about the calling-to-mind power of music and stress the usefulness to them of "haunting musical

---

*The twisting gesture suggests an old-fashioned orange squeezer. Apparently the director of the drama was unable to find an appropriate gesture to call up the image of an electric juice extractor.

presentation of the brand name for strong identification."[13] Increasingly they "believe that music will become an even more important selling tool."[14] Some advertisers buy the rights to an established hit song that is already widely known and "already has a built-in mood"[15] attached to it. Coca-Cola, for example, bought the song, "Country Sunshine," which it stuffed into their advertising package right along with the Americana and the halos. The tune Uncle Ned in the Sominex commercial picks out on the piano is "And the Band Played On." In this way, the songs all America sings become attached to the products a few Americans sell.

Such music often goes through a reverse cycle. Constant repetition of the catchy tunes fastens them in the mind and we find ourselves humming and whistling them unwittingly. For recalcitrants, slow learners, and those with a tin ear, the lesson is made explicit. Thus, a United Airlines Commercial shows a busload of people singing together lustily and *con brio,* "Fly The Friendly Skies of United," and a McDonald's commercial shows a whole town marching and singing the song their advertising agency commissioned.

Other advertisers prefer to custom-order the kind of music that can conjure up the moods they would like to associate with their products. "We'd like to show you what music can do. . . . A few notes can create a mood, give the listeners' mind a chance to work, to develop mental pictures." This is part of the text recited on a sound sheet—a 33 1/3 rpm record pressed on special material suitable for binding in a pamphlet or magazine, appropriate for insertion in a folder, leaflet, or newspaper. The voice continues, "You can create in your special audience the feelings designed to get the reactions you need." As the voice dies away, music swells up—a full orchestral medley that gives way to bouncy Dixieland selections, among which I recognize only "Toot, Toot, Tootsie, Goodbye." The voice closes the side: "It's easy to get people to listen. . . . Sound sheets can create a receptive mood, a mood that opens people's minds to what you have to say."[16]

Music ordered originally to adorn commercials is offered again for sale to the public that massive television coverage taught it to. A medley of familiar commercials is available on a long-playing record by Arthur Fiedler and the Boston Pops.[17] A more recent example is the song made for the Pathmark commercial (they call it "The N-R-G Song"). It has been recorded by Avco Records and has been offered for sale at Pathmark stores: seventy-nine cents a record, thirty cents off to customers who bring in the coupon from the corresponding newspaper advertisement.[18] Far exceeding any monetary profits resulting from this gimmick is the profit derived from "extensional thrust" as the record in the home teaches and reteaches the lesson learned by so many without any exercise of conscious will.

Advertisers, like other trade groups, like to decorate each other with special awards for outstanding achievement. Awards go to the commercials of the year that display various kinds of excellence. Musical excellence is evaluated according to the degree to which the music sticks in the mind. Musical value has nothing to do with the case. It's the catchiness of the tune that counts, its usefulness as a "hook."

MNEMONIC LANGUAGE

There's nothing new about argot, made-up words, meaningful gestures, and catchy melodies. What is new is the widespread and simultaneous social sharing through television which guarantees that meanings known to the few and deliberately invested by the few, will be adopted by the many. In the past, these devices have been used more to *limit* the number privy to special meanings. Prisoners, for example, have used them to prevent guards from understanding their conversation. Jargon and special gestures permit them to converse within the hearing of guards who ostensibly speak the same language yet who have been excluded from understanding as effectively as if they spoke a different tongue.

Both exclusion and social sharing can be very effectively accomplished not only by attaching new meanings to old words and inventing new ones but by attaching new meanings to well-known tunes or commonplace gestures. In any case, the meanings are readily learned by "reading the context." As of this writing an increase has been noted in the use of citizen-band radio. Drivers communicate with each other as they travel along highways, and a special vocabulary has grown up among them. They identify themselves by code names: in my area, there is "Ice Cube," "Papa Joe," "Hickory Nut," "Honeywagon," "The Black Knight," and so on. "Break ten for Honeywagon," means "Please clear channel ten so I can locate Honeywagon." (Channel 10 is reserved for searching out people rather than for conversation.) "Give me a copy," means state your location, or identify yourself. "Smokey" means the police. Drivers use citizen-band communication to advise each other about speed traps. ("Smokey going north near Exit Ten.") It is possible for the uninitiated to listen to these conversations without understanding a word. It is also possible for someone who pays attention to learn the code by reading the context. Highway patrols, for example, quickly learn it and answer in kind. So far, these exchanges remain good-natured and help to alleviate boredom on long drives. Their potential for something beyond that remains untapped.

If exclusion is the objective, the context can also be rendered less readable by changing the language's rhythms and pacings, its intonations and pauses—the sort of thing that makes it difficult for speakers of American English, for example, to follow those who speak West Indian English. It's not the words that trick the ear, it's the music.

In a field in which time is money, a master craftsman of the little dramas we call commercials has found a way to utilize these insights as a means of saving both. Clipping syllables is one way of saving time: for example, the word *automo . . .* is as understandable as the word *automobile.* Or it can be done by superimposing one sound over another. The human ear is quite capable of selecting the sounds that are meaningful to it, relegating to the background the sounds that "make no sense." It's the way we speak and listen to each other in a noisy room. We can do the same thing listening to a recording that has superimposed competing sounds on the same tape. Tony Schwartz calls this "mnemonic speech" and has employed it to make commercials which publicly broadcast sounds, words, and names heard by everyone, yet understood only by the particular groups in the audience who are "in the know."

> For example, in a commercial for the movie *Woodstock,* I designed the names of the rock groups in the movie into mnemonic speech. For many adults, the names were imperceptible, because the full names were not sufficiently isolated for them to hear and learn. For teen-agers, or those who knew the rock groups' names, the design was both pleasant to the ear and clearly perceptible. They recognized the names of their favorite groups and tuned in the names they wanted to hear. Another commercial, for a bank, produced exactly the opposite result. Here, a list of bank services was compressed even more than the rock groups' names (the bank spot compressed forty seconds into ten, while the rock spot compressed twenty-four seconds into eight). Adults had no difficulty perceiving all the services mentioned, but teen-agers, who have less familiarity with banking, could perceive only some of the items mentioned. Teen-agers who heard both spots felt certain that the banking spot was more compressed. Adults judged the relative compression of the two spots exactly opposite.[19]

By not "fully isolating" the names of the rock groups in his *Woodstock* commercial, Schwartz's technique prevented the outgroup from learning their names: background noise simply made it too difficult for naïve members of the audience to read the context; those "in the know" were reached without difficulty.

In the television business, "reach" means "teach," and the lesson goes well beyond vocabulary improvement. Talk-show hosts are not the only ones among us who demonstrate a casual approach to public discussions of sex and sexual deviance. The voice on the *Death Wish* commercial is not the only one in the country that utters "mother" as an epithet. Crime shows are not the only teachers of underworld jargon. Coca-Cola and the Xerox Corporation are not the only sources of newly emerging household words. Neither the customs and manners of those who produce this stuff, nor their intentions are the issue.

It is their power that deserves public attention and debate. Access to television gives those who have it and those who buy it unprecedented power and privilege to show and tell all of us over and over again their own views of propriety and impropriety, to express their own attitudes and modes of speech, beaming out lessons in their own customs, their own values, their own life-styles, their own slants on reality. The rest of us have no equivalent opportunity to show and tell ours.

The result is domination of socially shared experience that is unique in history for its vast and simultaneous penetration and coverage. In such a medium, word wedded to image and music behaves like a virus, casting off its disguise as a simple "cell" and burrowing its way into the body social, changing the nature of the culture that breathes life into human minds.

13

**One Size
Fits All:
Ratings Stack
the Harvest**

The United States of America has developed a culture industry[1] that contracts employees to mass-produce metaphors. The materials that enter the home through the television set—the dramas and music, singing and dancing, the images in news, documentaries, soap operas, quiz shows, crime shows, and cartoons—act as a sort of benign cattle prod. They gently and pleasantly nudge us until we amass ourselves in front of the screen; and just as cattle allow themselves to be herded into cattle runs, we respond by herding ourselves nicely together, scarcely noticing that we offer up our attention to the harvesters.

The research arm of the television business is essential to this industrial process. Its "formative research" tests in advance whether the programs are likely to be effective prods. Its "summative research" sorts viewers into bundles of a thousand each and sells them to the highest bidders. Counter-research called for by public advocates and regulatory bodies tries to establish scientifically whether the prods have damaged the product.

The A.C. Nielsen Co. provides the principal service which makes possible the pricing system that holds this whole structure together.* Nielsen computers keep track of television sets in use and log each program—even segments of programs—entering specially selected homes. Information on size and quality of the crop is then sold to advertisers and network salespersons, who pore over the charts as they dicker about the prices each grade of audience should bring.

"Day by day, hour by hour, minute by minute, we monitor America," a Nielsen executive told me. "Our computers are always on the job, keeping track of what the nation watches."[2] This is a matter of pride at Nielsen headquarters, where the audience-counting business is viewed as an important research operation.

Two basic figures issued by the A. C. Nielsen computers make it possible to price the product: the rating and the share. Both depend on a single key figure: the number of television homes in the country—as of this writing more than seventy million.[3] The all-important "rating" is simply the proportion of these seventy million television sets that tune in a given program. If a program gets a rating of thirty, say, a simple calculation—30 percent of seventy million—yields the first figure needed for bargaining about price: twenty-one million homes penetrated by the program.[4]

A second Nielsen figure is necessary before anyone can talk dollars and cents: the share. Not all television screens are bringing in programs at any given television moment. Since some households allow themselves the privilege of not watching, the share figure is essential in distinguishing the winner in a three-way competition: it tells what share of active television screens

---

*Other rating systems—Arbitron, BAR, TvQ—are summarized in the appendix on page 327.

each network was lucky enough to harvest for itself. Suppose a high-rated program such as "All in the Family" got a fifty share one night. The figure explains that while half of all television homes on the job were doing their bit for the sales department of the CBS television network, which fed the show to its affiliates, most of the remaining sets in use were working for the sales departments at ABC or NBC.[5]

With these two figures—rating and share—buyers and sellers can begin to negotiate price. The bottom line, the point of the whole procedure, is CPMPCM—cost per thousand per commercial minute—usually abbreviated as simply CPM. CPM tells the asking and bidding prices for the salable commodity created by television programs: audiences. The rating system stacks them neatly into bundles of a thousand for easier "sale and delivery to the advertiser."

Since people in the business say they buy and sell time, it is easy to overlook the fact that it is actually batches of people that are being bought and sold. Buyers pay for people by the minute just as they pay for rented premises by the month. The commodity is people in the first instance, just as it is premises in the second.

Industry shoptalk recognizes this quite clearly: Dan Carswell, an NBC vice president, is quoted as saying: "Remember, we're not selling the program; we're selling the *audience* for the program," pointing out that "television networks gather audiences and then 'sell' that audience to advertisers." The executive producer of Columbia Pictures Television's "Police Story," says, "We're basically bound, our hands are tied, by the fact that we're a medicine show. We're here to deliver the audience to the next commercial. The entire night's programming is a lift-off to the highest corporate profits."[6] "The children we have available to sell would be fewer," says a researcher discussing the disadvantages of certain rating procedures.[7]

The commodity must still be graded. As in any other market,

some audiences are quality goods, some are bargain-basement junk; and not all bundles command the same price. Women between the ages of eighteen and forty-nine are television's "quality product." Since they are the country's heavy-duty buyers, they command good prices from advertisers eager to win their attention in order to teach the advertiser's curriculum: how to feel a need for something, how to recognize a product that claims to satisfy that need, and how to value the attributes that allegedly do the job. Men eighteen to forty-nine, the nation's buyers of certain heavy goods, are another "quality product," sought after by advertisers of automobiles, for example. Then there are advertisers who wish to call attention to wares like credit cards, wines, and similar luxury products. They seek consumers in the proper income groups and buy audiences that include a respectable number of bundles in the higher brackets. Advertisers of bubblegum, soft drinks, fast foods, candy, breakfast foods, and toys buy audiences that include the proper number of child-bundles. And so it goes: advertisers negotiating to buy their people in properly labeled bundles, not grab bags.

The special word for the labels stuck on the bundles is *demos* —short for *demographic composition.* Advertisers search the Nielsen printouts detailing characteristics of audiences to each program, to be sure they include so-and-so-many women eighteen to forty-nine whose family income puts them in a particular income group; so-and-so many heads of households in upper level occupations; so-and-so many children aged three to eleven; and so on: different CPMs for different demos.*

The Nielsen rating system has all the fanfare and all the hardware of the scientific laboratory: mathematical formulas for sampling; computer programs, computer language, printouts, feedback, bevies of statistical and sociological consultants producing

---

*See pages 330–336 for tabulations that list demographic breakdowns the rating systems customarily provide.

and evaluating formulas, and the like. And yet "the big board" of the rating system operates like a gigantic Ouija board.

THE NIELSEN DATA BASE

The Nielsen system relies essentially on two national samples. Sample one provides the NTI (The National Television Index), which tells how many television sets are turned on and which programs they are bringing into the home—the base for estimating those all-important figures: the rating and the share. Almost twelve hundred people in the NTI sample agree to permit the A. C. Nielsen Company to place a special gadget inside their television sets.[8] The "little black box"—an "electronic miracle" the Nielsen people call it—records, thirty seconds by thirty seconds, whether the set is turned on and what channel it brings in. This information is relayed directly to a central computer which stores the information, processes it, and within forty-eight hours gets the printouts back to subscribers—principally networks, advertising agencies, and the advertising arms of major national corporations.[9]

The second Nielsen sample—about two thousand homes—is the NAC (National Audience Composition) sample.[10] Someone in each participating household agrees to keep a detailed diary reporting which programs are watched and attended to by each member of the family quarter hour by quarter hour. The diary keeper is supposed to note program and channel each set in the home is tuned to, entering the name of the program, the number of persons viewing each, age and sex of each viewer. General background information about the household and its members is entered into the computer as soon as the household joins the NAC sample; so diary data can easily be correlated with number of people in the household, income, age, occupation of head of household, and so on, to yield the demos. People agreeing to participate in the NAC diary-keeping sample admit a second bug to the television set along with the "black box"—a gadget that buzzes three times every thirty minutes, accompanied by a flashing light, to remind the diary-keeper to make the proper entries in the diary. It's called a recordimeter. Diary keepers are paid fifty cents per week per receiver plus a proportion of any repairs their set may need during their period of service: 10 percent for color sets and 50 percent for black-and-white. They choose, in addition, a "premium," whose value I was unable to determine. "I can't tell you," said one of the Nielsen executives I talked to. "That's proprietary information." He said the gifts were chosen from a book like those that show merchandise exchanged for trading stamps. To avoid what the A. C. Nielsen Company calls "diary fatigue," each person in the diary-keeping sample is on duty one week out of every four. Thus, 550 diaries are analyzed the first week of every month, 550 each succeeding week, and so on.

Both samples are chosen at random, which means that the behavior of the people and families so selected is reasonably likely to mirror in microcosm what the rest of the country is probably doing at the same time. This is not the place to discuss the details of probability theory that have given rise to these and other sampling procedures. Still, it is appropriate to remark that, however many "errors" may creep in (and many do)[11] such procedures serve to arrive at fairly reliable *estimates of trends in aggregate audience size and composition over given periods of time and within certain specified margins of error.* Yet, when it comes to dickering over the price of audiences, people in the business treat the data as if these crude techniques of information-gathering worked moment to moment with absolute precision. The game is carried to such lengths that in 1970, for example, a drop of a fraction of a point in a network's average rating meant a loss of almost two million dollars in revenue.[12] In 1974, the word was that a drop of a single percentage point could have meant a twenty-million-dol-

lar loss in advertising income to the unfortunate network registering it.[13]

To determine with any accuracy how much networks charge
for their product is almost impossible. Their sales departments
issue rate cards listing CPMs, but everybody in the business
knows that the cards are as inauthentic as the commercials themselves. Commercial minutes are sold as packages, pieced together
according to dayparts. Until the bill comes in, the buyer is at a
loss to know how much he is being charged, and even then he
may be unable to unravel the cost of a given commercial, show
by show and time slot by time slot, since he pays for the total
package as a job lot.[14]

The biggest television advertisers are the "up-front buyers"—
companies that spend so much money on bulk purchases of
television commercials that the networks are willing to shave the
per-unit cost for them. Because of the extra bargaining power
this gives certain big companies, their time-buyers can commit
themselves to a contract under favorable terms much earlier than
companies with more modest television budgets. For years, the
number-one spender on television advertising has been Procter &
Gamble. They sign their network contracts early, well in advance
of other buyers. Procter & Gamble committed $145,740,000
to network television commercials for just the fourth quarter of
1974—the opening months of the "new" 1975–76 television season—signing well in advance of smaller buyers. Those with less
money to spend on advertising hold back, hoping there will be
enough unbought commercial minutes left just before September
openings to force the networks to lower their quotations. They
are "like youngsters standing around a pool, waiting for the first
guy to stick his toe in . . . to take advantage of some of the
bargaining after the big hitters are through."[15]

Package deals and last minute "adjustments" in rates introduce further confusion in efforts to estimate what the going
prices for audiences may be. Still, network time salesmen bandy

figures about; advertising agencies, media buying services, advertising reporters, and so on, make educated guesses on the basis of scattered bits of information that leak through, gossip and seat-of-the-pants intuition. The word for the fourth quarter of 1974 was $2.40 to $2.80 CPM on the average—up about 5 per cent over the comparable period of the year before. CBS and NBC were said to be charging an average of $70,000 to $80,000 per minute, while ABC's average rates were said to be somewhat lower.[16] Quoted prices for audiences delivered by the top hits in 1974 were: $125,000 per commercial minute for "All in the Family"; $100,000 for runners up, "Sanford and Son" and "Monday Night Football."[17] By the time the next season rolled around, prices were again up, with an average prime-time fourth quarter minute going for $90,000, and ABC in the lead.[18] Blockbuster shows have been known to sell at a quarter of a million dollars per minute. Among these are football spectaculars such as NBC's "Super Bowl XI," as well as *Gone With The Wind* and *The Godfather,* said to have brought in $234,000 and $225,000 per minute, respectively. Advertisers lucky enough to be showcased in any of the big hits paid well over the previous season's high and consider themselves lucky, at that. Only those who buy early and in large lots and who are known to be old and reliable customers have any chance at all of seeing their commercials appear in top-rated shows or even adjacent to them. Those that hang back are least likely to secure such placement for theirs.

It is increases and decreases in advertising revenues, based on fractional points this crude rating system chalks up, that determine whether the people who control the electronic press of television will permit a program to survive, or whether they will cut it off the air. It's like using a meat axe to perform brain surgery. People in the business often complain about the system; still, there is a sort of tacit agreement among them not to probe too deeply into the arcane basis of making the CPM calculations, for fear the whole flimsy structure might collapse. The Broadcasting Rating Council is a trade organization that keeps track of rating systems. Its executive director, Hugh Beville, Jr., is an expert in sampling statistics and the mathematics of probability. He has often pointed out that the initial sampling error increases almost exponentially each time the original sample is cut and recut to yield the demographic breakdowns examined so minutely when CPMs are negotiated. Quite aside from human error in recording and reporting, the augmented sampling errors are so substantial that subgroup extrapolations can be misleading to the point of fantasy. To correct the error, the BRC, in its wisdom, has ruled that beginning in Fall 1974, the A. C. Nielsen Company and the American Research Bureau (which issues Arbitron ratings) should "flag" various subgroup figures to call the attention of those using the ratings to the fact that the figures are too unreliable to be usable.[19] It's reminiscent of the old joke about the man who kept pieces of string in a box labelled, "string too short to be of any use."

THE "DEMOCRACY" OF THE RATINGS

The claim is often made that the rating system is democratic since it allows audiences to "vote" for programs they like, and by that vote ensure those programs' survival. The "votes," however, are by proxy; they are cast by audiences who are granted no privileges of citizenship in the networks that do the decision-making for them. The "voters" have no opportunity to define issues, draw up platforms, choose candidates, organize opposition, persuade others to adopt a new viewpoint or discard an old one, or to go out and stump among any constituency. Moreover, only programs that can act as a vehicle for commercials have a chance to "stand for election," as it were.[20] Finally, even by this limited definition of "voting," the few chosen ones who are allowed to cast a ballot are counted preferentially. Programs with identical rating and share figures meet quite different fates; one may be retained while the other is canceled.[21]

According to the logic of the rating systems, not all viewers are created equal. To an untutored eye a program may look like a winner, yet, if its support comes from people who are old, poor, rural, ghetto dwellers, black, Latin American, or from certain other racial or ethnic minorities, the lead is canceled along with the contract to renew. "Gunsmoke" was canceled after twenty years not because its ratings were low—it remained in the top twenty-five most widely viewed programs—but because it tended to appeal to rural audiences and older people. "We're talking about money. Audiences for Westerns are generally quite rural and generally older. You don't want 80 per cent of your audience over 50."[22]

Sue Cameron, writing in *Hollywood Reporter,* August 6, 1975, comments on ABC's shows, "Baretta" and "S.W.A.T." "Each show delivers at least as many 18–49 viewers per minute as the CBS and NBC shows combined," she writes. " 'Baretta' is No. 1 among both men and women 18–49, with a 15.6 young adult rating, compared to CBS' 'Mannix,' running opposite 'Baretta' this summer earning a 5.9 young adult rating . . ." She is quoting figures from the Nielsen NTI Report, which chronicles the breakdowns for various demos.

Popular programs that accumulate high proportions of the "votes" even of the "young adult market," may be canceled for reasons having to do with economic conditions in the syndication market. If selling the series in syndication looks more profitable than the network deal, the show may be withdrawn from network showing in favor of syndicated sales by its own production and syndication company. This was done in the case of "Mission: Impossible," to mention only one example.

A "democracy" that allows only "quality consumers" the privilege of having their "votes" count discounts minorities twice. Not only are their "votes" absent at the time of counting; in addition, throughout most of the time the business has been

using rating systems, minorities were excluded from the samples
privileged to "vote" at all. Until 1976, householders invited to
participate in the samples drawn up by the two principal rating
companies were picked at random from lists of telephone subscribers. Families without telephones had no chance, therefore,
to be represented in the sample, a practice that deprived them,
from the outset, of any chance to have even a stand-in cast a vote.
Since it is mainly the poor and old, members of minority groups,
and rural dwellers who do without the amenity of the telephone,
they are the ones who must do, as well, without the amenity of
even having someone in the sample "vote" on their behalf.[23]

Quality of programs has as little to do with the numbers game
that rating systems play as democracy has to do with decisions
to retain or cancel the shows. In any three-way contest, one
contender is bound to win, another is bound to place, and the
third is bound to end up in last position.[24] Television watching
is an entrenched national custom, moreover, and people turn *to*
the set as often as they turn *on* a specific program. Even those
who make a deliberate selection often keep the set activated when
the final curtain drops. That's why one of the most sensitive
predicters of a successful program is its "lead-in"—the program
immediately preceding it. One research report I have seen
claimed that more than two-thirds of brand new series garnered
ratings that were the same as their lead-ins or sometimes higher.

Ratings or no ratings, Americans can be counted on to go
daily to the available well of imagery and fantasy, no matter what
is offered. An audience measurement expert has named the principle that guides program choices *the LOP principle:*[25] audiences
scanning available offerings are willing to settle for the *least
objectionable program.* A corollary is the principle of familiarity:
the more familiar, the less objectionable.

Network executives are quite open about admitting that the
LOP principle guides their programing decisions, with the result
that all three networks stick to the same narrow range of stand-

ardized, imitative program fare. One size fits all. A network's
function is "to make as much money as it can in the time available to it. And that means that every segment of prime-time
. . . must be devoted to those shows that will reach the widest,
most desirable audiences. It is the ultimate ironic rule: the business is so good that it literally cannot afford to be different."[26]
"The price of failure," says an NBC executive in charge of programing, "looms too large for us not to make the pragmatic
decisions that are necessary."[27]

HYPING THE RATINGS

Since most people choose to watch television, and thus select one
or another available offering, it's easy enough to rig the ratings
by rigging the schedules. The trick is particularly apparent during four weeks occurring in November, February or March,
May, and July. Suddenly network fare seems to sparkle. Repeats
are unheard of. Whole slates of ordinary programs and series are
wiped clean, replaced by star-studded specials and blockbuster
movies (for example, *The Godfather, The French Connection, Dr.
Zhivago, Walking Tall*). These are "sweep weeks," television's
festival time. Networks exhibit their finery during these special
weeks, the only periods of the year when rating services measure
local audiences, market by market. The harvest of listeners each
station brings in for the "sweep reports" determines the size of
its take when the networks divide up revenues paid in by national
advertisers. A network that does not break out its best and
fanciest programing for the locals during "sweep weeks" may
lose its affiliates. Since millions of dollars are at stake, programing glamour during sweep weeks is done with painstaking care.
Even the White House staff respects sweep weeks, making sure
to schedule presidential appearances in such a way that they will
not adulterate program ratings.[28]

The opposite of sweep weeks are "black weeks"—four weeks

during the year (five every fifth year)[29] when the Nielsen rating system slows down. During black weeks, only *Fast Weekly Household Reports* go to subscribers. No demos. Without demos, low audience counts cannot substantially injure a network's competitive standing and thus lower its CPM rates; television programers, therefore, schedule programs fished up from the bottom of the barrel. "We're interested in audience size," explains a network executive, "and therefore we'll throw programs that achieve low audience levels into black weeks."[30] The result is that black weeks are devoted to reruns and occasional "cultural programs" that network vice presidents think will not attract large audiences.

They are often wrong. Ingmar Bergman's drama, "The Lie," produced originally for Swedish television, was slotted by CBS into a black week in 1973, on the assumption that American audiences are more lowbrow than Swedish audiences. CBS estimated, however, that thirty million viewers tuned in—more viewers than "Marcus Welby," competing against it, harvested.[31] One reason programs like this do not normally appear on American television is that they are not tailored to fit its procrustean bed. "The Lie," for example, ran about an hour and forty-five minutes, without nicely timed breaks for the commercials.

During Christmas week, 1975, every original program the three commercial networks beamed out was offset by more than twice as many repeats. The practice is by now a Christmas custom the networks have visited upon the country, since December 25 usually falls in a black week. Counting from Monday, December 22, through Sunday, December 28, ABC led with a ratio of almost three to one (sixteen and a half hours of repeats, six originals). CBS was next: a little more than two repeats for every original (fifteen against seven). NBC was the hero of the week: twelve and a half hours of repeats, ten hours of originals.

The terms of sale for program series specify a certain number of repeats per cycle. In the past, contracts used to call for thirty-nine originals and thirteen repeats. Sometime in the late fifties or early sixties, the networks began to alter the rates of repeated episodes. My informant at the FCC network office reports that there is no way of locating a record of how and when it began but he said "there was a gradual erosion." No action was taken by the FCC other than "jawboning." In 1972, a petition for rule-making was filed by Bernard Velmuth, a Hollywood writer, requesting the commission to adopt a rule requiring a 25 percent limit for permissible repeat episodes in a prime-time series in any given year. As of this writing, no action has been taken. The current ratio of originals to repeats for most series is fifty-fifty. It is not unheard of for a network to program more repeats than originals in a popular series targeted to adults. It is standard operating practice for programs beamed to children.

THE RATINGS KILL CULTURAL PLURALISM

Rating systems continue to dictate programing decisions in the culture industry only because mass audiences must be broken up into negotiable economic units. No matter how the glaring inadequacies of their techniques may be corrected or their procedures refined, they still have nothing to do with democracy in decision making. Decisions informed by the ratings guarantee pervasive sharing and support to whatever tastes of the moment happen to be widespread, easily disseminated, or not downright repugnant. Deleted from the public curriculum, under this system, are the materials minorities need to pass on to emerging generations if they are not to go into cultural oblivion.

Nor do decisions informed by ratings have anything to do with respect for popular culture and its preservation. These materials produced on order, to attract the attention of mass audiences who have had no hand in producing them, are the culture of the midway, not the culture of the folk.

In the long run, no single generation has the right or the wisdom to make final pronouncements on cultural worthwhileness. Such standards must boil up from the crucible of a whole people's collective and authentic experience, extending over some reasonable span of time. The judgment of a single cohort in history is always a minority judgment when cast up against the total of all generations that have a stake in the culture. For anyone's "vote" to be meaningful, more than one group or generation must be allowed to cast theirs "in the parliament of history."[32]

The handful of network decision makers who are guided by the silly numbers game of the ratings ruthlessly tyrannize a whole culture's future, enshrining the CPM as the principal value determining which strands shall be woven into the cultural fabric and which shall be plucked out forever.

14

Buying, Selling, and Engineering Software in the Culture Industry

To call the content of television "popular culture"[1] is as misleading as calling tonsilectomies "popular surgery" or automobiles "popular engineering."[1] Product specifications, understood by all parties to the contract, are dictated not by the populace but by the three commercial networks; ABC, CBS, and NBC. Just as small and not-so-small machine shops come and go, vying among each other to supply screws, say, to the Chrysler Corporation, television production companies come and go, vying with each other to supply programs to the networks. These three networks—like Detroit's big four, integral parts of huge international conglomerates—command powerful financial resources that permit them to cannibalize their suppliers or to dominate them.

Where else can a buyer be found if ABC, CBS, and NBC refuse to buy the programs? "We have only three customers —ABC, CBS, and NBC, and they have the ability to determine the purchasing price . . . and control . . . our program investments," says a vice president of a production company.[2] "It's not a free market. The market is the networks," says a television writer.[3]

Even though as early as 1957 about two-thirds of all programs booked for evening showings were produced or controlled by the networks—a proportion which by 1968 had risen to 96.8 percent —the Federal Communications Commission had nevertheless managed to overlook network domination of the market. Finally, in 1970, the commission took official notice of what was going on: "The three national television networks," declared the FCC, "for all practical purposes control the entire television production process from idea through exhibition."[4]

This state of affairs was scarcely surprising. It was inherent in the process of making and distributing television programs that by 1970 was well entrenched throughout the business: the networks themselves owned the companies that produced and distributed most of the programs they bought. Even where the networks did not own the companies outright, they often held financial interest in ostensibly independent companies.[5] The system allowed them to work both sides of the street. Through ownership and control of production companies, they could act as their own suppliers. Through ownership and control of syndication companies, they could sell and resell the very programs that repeated showings on their own network stations had made popular.

The order the FCC issued in 1970 required the networks to halt the practice of selling and reselling programs in which they had such financial interest. This order was vigorously protested on the grounds that it violated the First Amendment rights of the several corporations involved. The Supreme Court, however, decided otherwise.[6]

The FCC went no further, but the Department of Justice

moved in. The department filed a cluster of antitrust suits against the three networks in 1972, withdrew them, then reinstated them in 1974.[7] As this book goes to press, it looks as if the networks may begin to make some concessions in order to maintain the preferential market position they have so long enjoyed. NBC, whose parent company, RCA, is sensitive about the spotlight of official antitrust charges, has been the first to signal readiness to loosen its hold on the market for broadcast properties. ABC and CBS, however, are attempting to stand pat.

On November 17, 1976, the Department of Justice filed a proposed consent agreement that may terminate one of these suits. Its provisions would allow NBC to retain the right to produce its own shows, thus still acting as its own supplier—but only twenty-one and a half hours a week (two and a half hours in prime time, eight hours in daytime, and eleven hours in fringe time).[8] In accepting this position, the government has moved away from its original claims that such vertical economic arrangements in a single industry are illegal and make a mockery of any semblance of what broadcasters still call the "free market."

Independent producers wishing to supply programs to NBC have often been asked to sign contracts stipulating that they must rent the network's own production studios as a condition of the sale. ABC and CBS have done the same. The practice effectively locks the producer out of the rental market, depriving him of his "freedom to bargain" for more favorable terms elsewhere. The consent agreement says NBC will give up this practice—but again, only a little bit. In the future, the network will present its producers with contracts locking them out of the rental market for no more than a year at a time.

Network executives have always felt free to negotiate exclusive options for programs they wish to consider but are not quite prepared to sign. It's a practice that keeps such programs out of the "free market" and thus insulated from its alleged "natural

workings" until these executives make up their minds.* NBC
now indicates its readiness to require such exclusive options for
no more than 35 percent of programs it would otherwise have to
bargain competitively for against the other two networks. The
practice undoubtedly has implications that go beyond antitrust.
It may well be an offense to the First Amendment to the Constitution,[9] designed to protect a "free market of ideas" from ideological domination, as well as an offense to the Sherman Antitrust Act, designed to protect a "free market of buyers and
sellers" from economic domination.

NBC's lawyers have specified that the network is willing to
abide by these interpretations of antitrust requirements if and
only if their competitors, ABC and CBS, agree to do likewise.
(It's sort of like Al Capone agreeing to go to the pen if and only
if he is accompanied by colleagues in competing protection enterprises.)[10]

The proposed consent agreement lists other concessions NBC
is prepared to make without setting the prior condition that the
other two networks must follow suit. For example, NBC promises to limit its practice of writing an "exclusive" clause in its
contracts for feature films. From now on, the network agrees to
keep these films off the "free market," insulated from its so-called
natural workings, for a period not to exceed four years—
renegotiable under certain conditions to five.

Finally, NBC promises to cease and desist from long-standing
network practice of writing into contracts with producers a
clause giving the network the right to resell the program—in

---

*It is not at all certain that the metaphor of "the market," in which co-equal producers,
sellers and buyers look each other in the eye as they bargain from equivalent power bases,
ever was an apt way to describe economic relations under capitalism. Even assuming that
it once may have been so, however, it has long been outdated. In modern, post-industrial
society, mass-marketing techniques, including saturation advertising and public relations, have transformed any semblance of "the market" into "the midway"—a more
appropriate metaphor for the modern modes of producing, buying and selling. Economists, however, no less than their peers on the bench, do not seem to have taken notice.

other words, to cash in on profits from syndication. All three networks have followed this business practice for years, thus effectively barring entry into the syndication business of other entrepreneurs who may have wished to engage in it. This particular "concession" by NBC only underlines the ludicrousness of the entire affair, since the FCC's 1970 Order that already prohibited this practice antedates the proposed consent agreement by more than six years.*

Producers haven't liked the vertical economic arrangements that prevailed and still prevail in the industry. "Why can't there be open competition in TV . . . ? Why must all quality be forced through the bottleneck of three networks—and be at the mercy, at the bottom line, of three individuals? I do not think that's how free enterprise works." These remarks are attributed to Norman Lear, head of the production company that turned out "All in the Family," among other hit shows. It was occasioned at a meeting he called to bring together executives of twenty-three independent television-station groups, to whom he wished to sell "Mary Hartman, Mary Hartman," a daytime serial the networks had rejected. Mr. Lear went on to offer an easy solution: "a fourth marketplace, a fourth arena, if you will."[11] Mr. Lear recognizes that four is more than three, but the issue which refuses to go away is that oligopoly is still oligopoly.

Mr. Lear's sense of the kind of television software that is marketable evidently exceeds that of network executives. The first cycle of "Mary Hartman, Mary Hartman" opened in September 1975, booked for about ninety independent stations. The series was an instant success, warranting newspaper headlines, feature-magazine stories, even a cover story in *Newsweek* (May

---

*Turnover of personnel at the FCC is high and as national administrations change, any given decision may be rescinded or reversed by new commissioners who see things differently. Justice's decision to prohibit a practice the FCC had already prohibited is probably an attempt to ensure through such redundancy that the order stands regardless of changes in the make-up of the people serving on the FCC.

3, 1976). It has been lampooned in prime-time comedy shows and talked about on late-night talk shows. Even the New York Financial Writers Association wove their annual comedy show around it at the close of 1976. The series is discussed soberly in university circles and at psychiatrists' conventions. The National Academy of Television Arts and Science established a special category for the special award it wished to bestow upon the series: "Distinguished Achievements in Television."

The distinguished achievement of "Mary Hartman, Mary Hartman" is its broad caricature of television soap operas. The tentpole character is Mary Hartman, a suburban housewife beset by problems she seems to be unable to arrange in any reasonable priority. Wax build-up on the kitchen floor or a daughter who has been kidnapped—both are equally soul-wrenching to Mary. No matter what the problem, it's dealt with in the same flat, emotionless manner. Adultery or instant coffee, training bras or guns, orgasms, murder, or shopping lists—all get the same treatment. A police sergeant calls Mary to say her father is being held for exposing himself. "Can't talk to you now," says Mary, "I'm on the phone." At the station house the sergeant explains, "I don't know how to put this, but he exposed just what you think he exposed. What do you take in your coffee?" "Black, with cream," says Mary. The leveling of emotional pitch is supposed to be funny; surrealist humor, say some commentators, black comedy.

Sometimes the action turns on situations that are outrageously far-fetched. Mary is held hostage at gunpoint in a Chinese laundry. The local high-school coach dies by drowning in a bowl of chicken soup. A mass murderer dispatches a family of five and with equal deliberateness slaughters their goats and chickens. Here the emotional leveling is the result of treating horror as if it were just another banality, more surrealist humor, supposedly.

Mary is convinced that her problems can be solved if only she is clever enough to hit upon the right solution. She turns to television shows and commercials, to syndicated columnists and the *Reader's Digest*. Diligently she tries to put into practice their psychological counsel about how to raise the daughter she seems really to dislike, as well as how to behave in bed. Her hope is that her impotent husband will respond to the sexual advances these same sources tell her liberated women do not hesitate to make. That she takes these inauthentic sources seriously and keeps trying their simplistic solutions to complex problems is another source of the series' humor.

Some commentators have claimed that "Mary Hartman, Mary Hartman" will succeed in doing for daytime serials what *Uncle Tom's Cabin* did for slavery. Others have said that Lear has produced true satire, in a class with the dramas of an Aeschylus or a Shaw. My own opinion is that this series, like the rest of the Lear productions, is neither satire nor social criticism, but more of the same old stuff in a gaudier, more attractive, more sophisticated package.

"Mary Hartman, Mary Hartman" is based almost entirely on ridicule. We laugh at this show the way we laugh at a comic Valentine: the caricature is so broadly drawn and the traits it mocks are sketched in such familiar outline, that it can get away with very little art. It feeds us cues we know very well; they can always be counted on to trigger a guffaw.

Satire makes us laugh in a different way. Satire illuminates incongruities in customs and behavior that normally we do not even notice, or if we do, we politely overlook them. Satiric humor casts a different light on them; awareness breaks upon us, and, as it does, it wrests from us a burst of laughter. It's almost involuntary, like the gasp that frequently accompanies sudden insight. Through humor, the "hah-hah" of human laughter blends with the "a-hah!" of sudden understanding. The two go together.

"Mary Hartman, Mary Hartman," however, grants no such insight. It ridicules mass-produced entertainment, especially soap operas and the people who pay attention to them; but by now they are standard butts of ridicule. "Mary Hartman, Mary Hartman" mocks advertising, especially the commercials that support the television business; but then, they, too, are stand-bys for generating skits and gag lines. There is no illumination of the machinery that accounts for it all. It's the sort of thing that at best is caricature; it's certainly not satire.

For example, like the other soaps, this one, too, is a pieced-together set of dramatized segments that must fit themselves around successive bursts of commercials that interrupt every few lines of dialogue. This, the deep structure of soap operas, is what accounts for the emotional leveling the series tries to lampoon. Yet Lear ignores this structure entirely. Advertising, especially those commercials, is subjected to good-natured kidding in dialogue internal to the show, and the absurd dream world that soap operas project is reduced to even greater absurdity. Yet, like the other soaps, each episode of "Mary Hartman, Mary Hartman" remains its own package for the very real commercials that surround *it*, and they are played quite straight. Their presence still sets the pace of *its* dramatic action and still renders *its* character and plot development impossible. Indeed, by contrast with the deadpan acting and the flat delivery of lines in the show itself, the real commercials appear even more sprightly, more amusing, more deserving of attention. All this, Lear passes over.

The five-minute segments that make up each episode of "Mary Hartman, Mary Hartman" are still written by white-collar employees ("dialoguists") skilled at filling in the blanks to meet the requirements of the formula and the weekly production quota. Neither they nor the cast has the remotest chance to explore the funny side of the human failings we all share, the real workings of the social system we all live in. Instead, the writers can only hone to a fine point their skills in turning out one-liners; the actors, theirs in deadpan delivery.

Ridiculing soaps, commercials, and the people who take them

seriously, but leaving the structure that accounts for it all un-
scathed, is closer to college humor and skits at office parties than
to true satire. People laugh, enjoying the digs and jibes that are
funny only to those who happen to have shared a very special set
of social experiences that provide the context that lends the
humor; the skits themselves can only skirt sensitive terrain. This
is what "Mary Hartman, Mary Hartman" does, too. Only those
who know that television soap operas level emotional experience
(and not everyone does) can catch on that when Mary Hartman
does it so outrageously, it's caricature. Only those who know that
the advice in the *Reader's Digest* is inauthentic (and not everyone does) can get the point that when Mary Hartman takes it
seriously, it's worth a guffaw. The show itself provides not
a clue.

"Mary Hartman, Mary Hartman" is scarcely what public-
relations people call "a good press" for soap operas. Still, it's not
a bad press, either. The caricatures, lampoonings, and funning
are nothing more than feather punches. The genre itself gets off
scot-free. Lear never lays a hand on it.*

FORMATIVE RESEARCH: THE NEW SHOW-DOCTOR

To sell a program to a network, a producer must be able to
convince the buyer that his program will do the job it is meant
to do;[12] that it will get those audiences to array themselves in
front of the television screen in sufficient numbers to be sold
profitably to advertisers. As soon as a program has been bought
and launched, the network sales division needs the detailed ac-
counting sheets that tally the number of audience bundles produced, their special characteristics, and the time and place of

---

*The Lear organization decided to cancel further production after two years, the final
episodes scheduled for June 1977.

delivery—essential data in pricing the product of the television business and offering it for sale to the appropriate buyers.

Market research plays the key role in testing a program's potential popularity before it has been booked, as well as in tallying up the audiences it cultivates after it has been booked. The staffs that do this work may operate as independent firms or as divisions within the corporate structure of the network, the production company, or even the advertising agency.

The idea of testing shows before they open is not particularly novel. That's what openings in Boston and Philadelphia were all about in the old days when people used to go to the theater. Out-of-town openings gave producers a chance to observe the way real audiences reacted to the show. The parts that didn't quite come off could be beefed up, borrowing from the parts that got a big hand. If a show were judged beyond repair, a producer could cut his losses by scrapping the whole thing before, rather than after, he had incurred the expense of leasing a Broadway theater and launching the publicity. "It just didn't play in Peoria" is still very much a part of show-business vocabulary. The "formative research" of today is the evolutionary next step—the new form of pretesting a show, more appropriate to the electronic massification of audiences and the escalation of the amount of investment capital needed to mount it.

The director and show doctor, pooling their judgment as they sit together in the darkened house at the out-of-town theater opening, have now been replaced by program engineers—expert consultants with Ph.D.s in psychology, sociology, and marketing, and interviewers with questionnaires and clipboards, tape recorders and electronic gadgetry. Nobody can prove that the experts and the gadgetry are more effective in turning out a hit, but the "formative research" goes on anyway. Why not? The decision to book a series involves such astronomical sums of

money that the harassed executives who have to make the programing decisions are desperate for something—anything—that
will reduce the risk in that final judgment.[13] The research gob-
bledygook provides some of that confidence and is more respectable than a crystal ball.

The people who decide on the program are, after all, bureau-
crats slotted into hierarchic organizations in which other bureau-
crats can make or break their careers. That's another reason this
formative research is salable; it's a way of passing the buck. If
the program should "fail"—which means only that it does not
yield the bumper crop of audience bundles planned for—the
onus is on the research, and the bureaucrat who decided to book
the show or the series can present himself as blameless. One
long-suffering television writer made it very clear: "If they used
their own judgment and if there was a failure, they'd be responsible. They'd be canned. This way, they can blame it on the
tests."[14] Another television writer reports friendly advice his own
agent passed on to him. "The tester—I assume he's at least a
Ph.D.—said, 'You could have picked up half a million homes if
[the leading character] had just had a dog.' " The agent then
added, "When I heard it I could have killed myself. Why hadn't
I thought of that?"[15]

Up to now, program engineering through "formative research" has not been burdened by excessively heavy demands
since the television business, more like Volkswagen than
Chrysler, has contented itself with the same sturdy, reliable,
tried-and-true models each year. A program that turns out to be
a success one season is followed by scores of imitators hard on
its heels. The same blueprint is used season after season with
changes so slight they may go unnoticed by an untutored eye. "If
you go in with a new idea, really new, they get frightened. They
ask: 'What's it like? Is it a *Marcus Welby?* Is it a *Mannix?*'
They're always talking about their successes, all of which are
imitative. They want to imitate their imitations."[16] This has been
the state of affairs for most of television's history.

MAGOO HOUSE

Prebroadcast testing of shows and pilots is still the preferred technique of engineering shows, and all the networks resort to it. A special theater in Hollywood has been set up just for this purpose. Its official name is Audience Study Institute, but it is usually referred to as Preview House. (Some producers call it "Magoo House" because it uses a twenty-year-old Magoo cartoon to establish a benchmark audience response.)

The head of ABC's Audience Research Division describes the way the network tests its programs there:

> The use we make of Preview Theatre is for what is normally called program testing, and this includes pilots . . . it includes episodes of programs before they go on the air, and basically what we're trying to determine is viewer reaction to these shows . . . the techniques we use involve both what we call instantaneous reactions, which consists of viewers manipulating a dial as they watch the program to indicate how much they like or dislike certain parts of the show . . . the other information we get is from questionnaires which they fill out on what they like about the program, what they dislike, how they rate various characters in the show, their interest in seeing future episodes . . . their interest in the program as a potential series.[17]

Another ABC executive tells about testing the pilot for the series, "Paper Moon." "The actors came over well. . . . They related well together, and people reacted favorably to the show on film, in a test situation. . . . Hence, the program went on the air."[18] This was the series about Moze and Addie that aroused viewer interest by leaving it ambiguous whether the thirty- or forty-year-old man and the prepubescent girl he was traveling with were father and daughter or something else.

The ABC executives describing audience testing at Preview House were downplaying the drama of the testing procedures now in use. The dials they first mentioned, which allow a subject to register his "like" or "dislike" reactions instantaneously, are but a minor element in the arsenal of gadgetry now in use for engineering programs and commercials. Test subjects are wired up with finger sensors that pick up galvanic skin emissions (the human body's self-produced electrical impulses) and feed the readings into a machine that records them on a moving tape. The gadgetry includes laboratories with one-way mirrors that permit test subjects to be watched, often unknowingly, as they push the buttons, engage in role-playing, or allow their behavior to be observed, recorded, and analyzed. They respond to projective tests such as Rorschachs and TATs (Thematic Aperception Tests), answer semantic-differential scales—all crude but effective ways in the hands of experienced analysts to get a glimpse of deep-seated feelings and deep-programed responses that may be inaccessible to a person's own conscious awareness.

The electro-polygraph, familiarly known as the lie-detector, has been impressed into the service of the testers. Body processes such as galvanic skin reflex, blood pressure, and pulse rate are the physiological accompaniments of human emotions. They fluctuate as emotions are aroused—whether it's a suspect fearful that his lying response will be found out or a test subject excited or titillated by something in a television program. The electro-polygraph's sensors pick up the fluctuations and transmit them to special pens that jiggle with each measurable shift in the subject's bodily state. The jiggles are recorded on a moving tape that provides a visual record of the subject's emotional reactions at each moment during the show. The program to be tested has been broken down in advance into its component elements; so it's a simple matter to synchronize the jiggles on the tape with any particular event or occurrence in the program. Interviewers use the read-out as a point of departure for interviewing the test subjects, asking them to recall what went through their minds at each point in the program that produced any interesting jiggles.

The trick is really in the interviewing;[19] the machine tape is mainly a mnemonic device that permits reactions to be linked back to finely detailed program elements that simple recall would probably not be able to retrieve.[20]

OLD TABOOS AND NEW MARKETS

Pretesting programs allows the producers and bookers to make an educated guess about how far they can go in patching in lines and characters that depart from earlier guidelines. Programing decisions have moved out of the hands of a retiring generation of executives whose tastes were developed well before World War II. As younger men and women move into these positions, many of the old industry taboos that used to be taken for granted are falling by the wayside. The changes reflect the newcomers' taste, their sense of the tolerable margins of attention-getting behavior, and their cultivation of new markets. "It's the 'Hee Haw' generation passing on and the *Playboy* generation coming up," is the current slogan.

Programs associated with the name of Norman Lear have been the first to break the new ground. Mr. Lear and his production companies have successfully revised and refurbished television's old formulas for the entertainment comedies they specialize in, patching in characters and situations that the business had formerly declared taboo. In "All in the Family," a lovable bigot parries with his liberal daughter and son-in-law about topics that television had formerly remanded to the segregated compound of news and an occasional documentary. Now Archie Bunker and his "liberal" daughter and son-in-law tangle with each other over race prejudice, labor unions, contraception and family planning, breast biopsies, the role of women, mental retardation, intermarriage, homosexuality, and transvestism. Each episode is worked out as if it were a twenty-four-minute commercial on a particular subject.

It took a long struggle and much dedication on the part of Norman Lear and his associates to get the series accepted on their terms. They had to fight stubbornly against the conventional wisdom of network executives who were all for adulterating the new ingredients this series had sprinkled into the old formula. Formative research both helped and hindered Lear's crusade. ABC, the first network to consider the new model embodied in "All in the Family," kept the show on ice for three years and rejected two separate pilots for it because "it tested poorly." CBS then picked it up; its market-research people reported that "it tested well,"[21] and they booked it for January 1971 opening. The Lear-Yorkin stubborness paid off—as everyone in the business now belatedly recognizes, since "All in the Family" has turned out to be a top-rated show.

As soon as the Neilsen ratings corroborated the popularity of the new model, it began to spawn its own imitators:[22] "Maude," "The Jeffersons," and "Good Times," all Norman Lear shows, all variations of television's first ground-breaker. Bigotry is subjected to ridicule instead of sententious moralizing ("All in the Family"). A rich black family lives on New York's posh East Side, while an interracial marriage is shown for the first time on television—and shown in such a way that its critics are on the defensive rather than the other way around ("The Jeffersons"). A poor black family turns out to be just plain folks ("Good Times"). A thrice-divorced woman has a successful fourth marriage, and she and her bosom pal are allowed to speculate, at least, on whether to embark on an extramarital adventure ("Maude").

The shows sired by "All in the Family," granddaddy of them all, had been pretested on the hoof. Routine audience tests had revealed the special pulling power that certain supporting characters seemed to have: Maude when she visited the Bunkers; Florida ("Good Times") when she was Maude's maid; the Jeffersons when they were Archie's and Edith's neighbors. Other production companies quickly caught on to the attractiveness of these kinds of characters, as well as to the new and cheaper way of doing formative research: "Rhoda" (September 1974) and "Phyllis" (September 1975), produced by the MTM Production Company, are two good examples.* Rhoda started out as a bit of a swinger and married a divorced man. Phyllis became a swinging widow. Both were originally supporting characters in "The Mary Tyler Moore Show." Ratings indicated that the new ingredients the two ladies added seemed to be effective in attracting to the screen audiences which television had previously alienated—younger people, those with more schooling rather than less, and those at the liberal rather than the conservative end of attitude-rating scales. Such audiences are eminently salable and more than make up for any losses incurred if some of the fans of "Beverly Hillbillies" or Andy Griffith are turned away by the new ingredients; the latter are now past fifty-five and no longer the country's major purchasers.

NBC quickly got the point and "Police Story" led to "Police Woman," "Joe Forrester," and "Medical Story"; "Sanford and Son" led to "Grady." ABC entered the game with "S.W.A.T.," budding off from "The Rookies"; "Laverne & Shirley" out of "Happy Days"; and "The Bionic Woman," who, killed off on one episode of "Six Million Dollar Man," rose from the dead to appear in her own show. In this fashion, where seven shows once stood now stand nineteen, each virtually indistinguishable from its progenitor, entrenching the spinoff as a programing device just as "the son of . . ." was entrenched as a movie-making device.

---

*MTM is co-owned by Mary Tyler Moore and her husband. As the procedure entrenches itself further, joining the recycling process that converts prime-time shows into children's-ghetto programs, we can expect to see tribalization succeed simple imitation of earlier successful programs—clones replaced by speciation, so to speak.

BUILDING UP NEW MARKETS

The television business is engaged in never ending vigilance to maintain existing markets, never ending searches for new ones. It was an outstanding innovation in 1964 when television created "the child market" (ages three to about eleven) and "the youth market" (about twelve to seventeen).[23] The business keeps an eye on the market of "home formation agents"—young people who are setting up their own quarters alone or in tandem, just-marrieds and just-remarrieds. There are also: the market of "family formation agents" (women in the childbearing years); the market of ailing middle-aged and elderly (those who buy laxatives, remedies to relieve indigestion, insomnia, corns, loose false teeth, and so on); and the market of middle-aged and elderly in reasonably good health (those who need only hangover remedies and remedies for overeating, plus credit cards, travel agents, automobiles, home-improvement loans, and the like).

In addition, there are other newly emerging markets that television has only recently begun to adopt and adapt. Markets of "swingers-male" and "swingers-female," coalescing around images manufactured originally by *Playboy* and its imitators, have recently begun to be cultivated by television. Women suddenly aware of sex-role stereotyping, grabbed first as a market by organs such as *Ms.* and its imitators, are now attended to by television. Gourmet markets, homosexual markets, porno markets, formerly the preserve of special-interest magazines, pulps, and tabloids, are now being expanded and turned into mass markets by television or considered for development in the near future.

Recently, the homosexual market has begun to be cultivated by the television business in a rather gingerly manner. Here, again, Norman Lear's production company, now TAT Communications,[24] broke first ground with the series "Hot 1 Baltimore."

"Hot l Baltimore" did more than refurbish the now acceptable model Lear had introduced with "All in the Family." In the new show, each week's episode revolved about a bunch of bizarre, even raunchy transients. The scene was set in a seedy, rundown, eighth-rate hotel. Even the neon sign worked only fitfully, if at all; the *e* often did not light up—hence the title "Hot l Baltimore." Types never before seen on prime-time television comedies filed in and out of the story just as they filed in and out of the hotel lobby. The topics and character types the series featured went beyond even the revised specifications the television business had so recently made known: two prostitutes, a homosexual couple claiming to be married to each other, an offstage weirdo said to wear diapers and parade around with a cherry in his navel proclaiming he was a bun. One of the prostitutes—salt-of-the-earth type—had a best friend, a lady so naïve that she never caught on to the hooker's way of earning a living. The hotel's owner was a mother insanely devoted to her twenty-six-year-old son and obsessed by a compulsive need to protect the young man's honor. All these raunchy set-ups triggered the laugh track for boffolas every thirty seconds.

One episode of "Hot l Baltimore" even featured the "marital" difficulties of the homosexual couple. Unheard of! Homosexuality was a topic the television business had always shrouded in a deafening silence that did its bit to impede sympathetic understanding of a sexual deviation the human species is heir to.

The decision to treat homosexuality on a par with heterosexuality reflects newly emerging conventional wisdom that views homosexual intercourse as if "sexual preference" had no more psychosexual charge for the individual, no more sociological import for the social fabric,[25] than any other preference—olives in the martini versus onions, for example. It passes over the vast difference between acknowledging—indeed, vigorously defending—the private rights of individuals to their own bed habits, and publicly legitimizing an antiheterosexual role as co-equal with a heterosexual one in this society. Anthropologically speaking, the newly emerging conventional wisdom that declares homosexuality to be a sex preference[26] is equivalent to viewing anthropophagy as a nutritional preference or incest as an agreement among consenting adults who wish to engage in an affair.

TAT Communications, however, no less than the American Psychiatric Association, easily adopted this view of homosexuality and decided to weave it as a recurring theme into "Hot l Baltimore." ABC, its corporate face still red as a result of its classic boo-boo in rejecting "All in the Family" when it was theirs, decided to play along with Lear's judgment about "Hot l Baltimore." He had done it before, maybe he would do it again; maybe history would repeat itself with another hit show.

It did not. The series opened on January 24, 1975, and closed June 6, 1975. "The ratings just did not warrant continuing it," said one of Mr. Lear's assistants. "The show was just ahead of its time." I had learned that the episode of "Hot l Baltimore" dealing with homosexual "marriage" had been pretested to determine the adequacy of its treatment. The broadcast of February 21, 1975, had starred Gordon and George, the middle-aged homosexuals who lived in the hotel in what appeared to be a stable "marriage." They had been seen from time to time in the first episodes of the series, mainly in walk-on parts. The particular episode had moved them stage front and center, featuring the near break-up of their "marriage," retrieved at the last minute by the good offices of their friends and neighbors, the rest of the "gang" in the hotel.

By the time the curtain fell, the relationship had been reestablished and the moral proclaimed, "What's there to understand? Love is love—any kind of love, no matter where you find it!"

It's possible, of course, that this sort of syncretic approach to sex and love hit the country a bit prematurely, before the station managers who had the option of rejecting the network feed were

quite ready to refrain from closing it off for a program that
played homosexual "marriage" as not substantially different
from heterosexual marriage.[27] That's certainly in part, at least,
what the assistant must have meant by saying the show was
ahead of its time. Still, TAT Communication's decision to try it
out was neither whimsical nor accidental. Including homosexuality among the controversial issues that TAT Communications
wishes to call to public attention happens to converge with the
historic circumstances of the 1974–75 television year, in which
"Hot l Baltimore" was produced, tested, and launched. In the
two or three years preceding the debut of the series, the country
had seen homosexual organizations begin to go national and
public and engage in aggressive lobbying and a public-relations
campaign that presented the homosexual way of life as normal,
even desirable. The Mattachine Society, for years known to a
small in-group only, had "come out of the closet." Now people
from coast to coast were learning who they were and what they
believed about themselves. Newcomers such as Gay Liberation
and National Gay Task Force held marches that made the evening news broadcasts; they sent representatives to appear in
documentaries and on talk shows. Show-business people, always
more tolerant than others of alternative life-styles, found no
difficulty in welcoming them into the studios, and giving national
coverage to their claims that homosexuality is as acceptable as
motherhood, as lovable as apple pie.[28] New top brass at network
headquarters, socialized in show-business culture in a way that
old network brass had never been, were more easily persuaded
that, after all, it's a matter of taste.

It's possible that the people at TAT Communications believed
all these claims. It's certain that television's collaboration in
maintaining a national policy of shameful silence about homosexuality had done its bit to produce a generation of gullible
innocents, so there is no reason to believe that the TAT people
were any better equipped than the rest of the country to separate

the kernels of truth from the chaff of image-burnishing at the core of the homosexuals' public-relations campaigns.

It's also possible that TAT Communications and the ABC network that had bought the show believed that there was gold in them thar hills. A congeries of businesses has always clustered around the homosexual trade and cultivated that clientele. As the numbers of homosexuals have expanded at least with population growth, these businesses have become more and more profitable. Magazines that cater to homosexual readers now blitz the Madison Avenue space-buyers and time-buyers with their computer printouts showing how affluent the homosexual market is and what expensive tastes they indulge. To use the jargon of the business, there are good "demos" waiting to be exploited. *After Dark*, a magazine catering to the homosexual market, claims its readers have a median income of eighteen thousand dollars a year, 50 percent have valid passports, 80 percent buy one or more records a month, and adds other similar, delightfully titillating statistics. Another magazine, *The Advocate*, reports that 59 percent of its readers own stocks or bonds, 90 percent own stereo equipment, and 10 percent own their own businesses.[29] These demos would make any advertising department sit up and take notice. Wouldn't the television business, no less than any other business, be remiss in meeting its obligations to stockholders if it were to pass this market by?[30] After all, times and tastes change. Accelerated raunchiness is being successfully marketed in films, magazines, comic books—indeed, in all organs of communications, including billboards and similar graffiti. It's an everyday observation as well as a principle of behavior modification that an aggregate assault dulls the palate and that what was shocking to the generation that came to maturity ten years ago is not so shocking to the generation following on their heels and entering a different thought environment. Like every other production company, TAT is aware of the television business's insatiable appetite for software to keep those heads turned toward the screen and countable. The more television's product specifications can be loosened to permit variations without changing the blueprints, the easier it is to provide the business with the shows it needs. ABC knows it and TAT Communications knows it. If their effort had worked this first time around, they would have been the fustest with the mostest.

Just in case these claims seem excessive, according to an article in the *Wall Street Journal* on May 13, 1975, some of the other businesses engaged in marketing efforts to take advantage of the homosexual trade include Columbia Pictures; Falstaff Brewing Corporation; Acme Brewing Company; Metro-Goldwyn-Mayer; RCA Records—a division of RCA Corporation; Gulf & Western Industries, the parent company of Paramount; Twentieth Century Fox; Warner Brothers; and Bloomingdale's.

It is against this background that the decision to launch "Hot l Baltimore" must be viewed. Even so, the show probably would never have seen the light of day without the "formative research" that justified TAT's claim it would "play in Peoria." The Lear organization used its own modest testing department—just one intelligent and sensitive young woman with a sharp eye and ear and a tape recorder. She conducted the pretest for the show that starred the homosexual couple, just as she had pretested other episodes and segments of TAT Communications's other controversial shows. She told me that she had set up special screenings in New York and Los Angeles, and had invited the various homosexual organizations to send their own representatives. Following the prebroadcast showings, she invited these specialists to discuss their reactions to the program, to comment on its authenticity, to explain what elements of the characterizations they looked upon as accurate or inaccurate and why, where they thought improvements might be made, and so on.

Some of the test subjects liked the show and approved of its approach to George's and Gordon's marital problems. Others disapproved of the treatment, calling it stereotyped and moralistic. Most of them, however, had no difficulty accepting the show's pop psychology—neither did most of its eventual audience of twenty to thirty million people. All the comments the test session had elicited were recorded and sent on tape to TAT's permanent files. There they remain, to be consulted as source materials by producers and writers who wish to "authenticate" anything about homosexuality in new shows still in the pipeline and for years to come. The results of the test sessions were summarized and the resumes circulated to the producers and writers at TAT Communications. "This is interesting feedback and it's essential," I was told, ". . . for the purpose of consciousness raising among them." My informant added that the same homosexual organizations had been invited to send representatives to preview the episode in "Maude" presenting the same approach to homosexuality. Members of the American Cancer Society were invited to preview the episode of "All in the Family" in which Edith has a biopsy for a lump in her breast. Members of organizations active in the women's liberation movement were invited to the episode of "All in the Family" that centered on the appropriateness of the female initiating lovemaking ("Gloria Mixes it Up"), and members of Alcoholics Anonymous had been invited to the episode of "Maude" about Walter's alcoholism. "Did you invite anyone from the WCTU?" I asked. "What's that?" was the response. I said the initials stood for Woman's Christian Temperance Union. "Oh yes," she remarked, adding: "No, I did not invite them. I never thought of it!" Nor did she take the trouble to invite any Moslems or members of the many other religious groups that reject alcoholic beverages on religious grounds. So much for this method of achieving fairness and balance!

LOBBYING BY SPECIAL-INTEREST
GROUPS MARKETING IDEAS

And so it goes. Producers are now not only besieged by pluggers and advance men seeking showcases for consumer products but they are under pressure as well from pluggers of various ideologies. The Population Institute, for example, ran a series of conferences in New York and Los Angeles, to which writers, producers, directors, and key network officials were invited. The assembled multitude was made aware that television's show-and-tell for years had been pronatalist, glorifying families with more than two children ("My Three Sons," "The Brady Bunch," "The Partridge Family," "Family Affair," and others). The soap operas' penchant for solving old plot problems and launching new ones by having the woman become pregnant also came in for censure. These sessions raised the consciousness of the image makers, who in turn proceeded to raise the consciousness of the rest of the nation, as per instructions. Since then, several characters on "The Mary Tyler Moore Show" have casually discussed the pill on prime time, and soap-opera women mention it with dreary frequency. Walter has had a vasectomy ("Maude") and Mike and Gloria settled a bitter argument by first deciding not to have children then deciding on a vasectomy for Mike after little Joey was born ("All in the Family").

The National Association for Retarded Children has lobbied successfully to get television shows to showcase this organization's view of mental retardation—etiology, diagnosis, treatment, prognosis, and social policy. The American Cancer Society lobbies to influence writers and producers to showcase stories with happy endings about mastectomies and similar operations; to publicize detection centers and Pap tests; and to engage in debate about the cancer-producing effects of tobacco by inserting one-liners on the evils of smoking. Two decades of good-news medicine is now to be counteracted by Ralph Nader's public-interest raiders, who make themselves available to writers who feel they can sell shows highlighting malpractice, inequality in access to medical care, and inefficiencies in current medical-care delivery systems. National Gay Task Force, male and female chapters, make their Media Alert Network available for consultation. The monthly newsletter of the Writers' Guild routinely publishes a list of organizations willing to provide information and assistance to writers developing scripts on this or that subject.[32]

This all adds up to an efficient way of saving writers and dramatists the trouble of doing their own research on either the scientific aspects of these problems, their human aspects, or both. At the same time it avoids the unpleasantnesses that so often crop up when writers and dramatists creatively explore the complexities of these and other human and social-policy problems in ways that poke around the sore spots conventional debate prefers to bypass. Such potentially disturbing exploration does not "test well" and is censored before it ever hits the screen. Engineering programs is safer than writing, directing, and producing authentic artistic creations that explore authentic human problems in ways the nonspecialist can grasp on an emotional as well as a cognitive level.

15

Research With
and Without
Informed Consent

Research to test the attention-getting power of commercials is a specialized field of formative research. Human "subjects" or "respondents" are recruited and delivered to testers who employ all the gadgetry of the social-psychology laboratory to aid the producers' judgment about the best way to promote an about-to-be-launched breakfast food, vaginal spray, or household cleaning product. Marketing firms that need respondents detail their product specifications to agencies specializing in recruiting for them: "Eleven women, currently married and living with husband and one school-age child, family income at least $10,000 a year. Must serve snack foods." Successful recruiters are those who maintain what the trade refers to as "a stable"—a large, active card file of people from widely varied backgrounds who make themselves available on short notice.

Recruiters work either as employees of the research firms or as entrepreneurs running their own outfits. Such "respondent recruiters" deliver subjects for research much as "audience recruitment specialists" deliver audiences for producers.

A firm of typical recruiters works from a master file of perhaps ten thousand men, women, and children, about whom information has been previously collected in marketing surveys. The information compiled includes routine census data such as age, sex, occupation, and family composition. It also includes a host of details such as sleeping and eating habits, smoking and drinking habits, and even more intimate details of family life.

As of this writing, an energetic "subject" in the stable of a cooperative recruiter can earn as much as five dollars an hour. Thus, many who present themselves as "subjects" are in fact part-time workers in fairly regular, pleasant jobs that require no special training and yield incomes they have come to count on. It's a change from an earlier day when respondents were attracted as much by the glamor as by the stipend, when just being interviewed seemed appealing to people and the chance of being on camera—however briefly and even for limited, closed-circuit viewing—packed even stronger appeal. "People used to think that being interviewed was a great experience. They don't think that way anymore."[1] Now they do it for the money—and the attendant headaches are a source of concern in the business. Articles in advertising and marketing trade journals deplore the deteriorating quality of the product and the shoddiness of quality-control measures on the part of the recruiting agencies that supply it.[2]

OVER THE CABLE: TESTING WITHOUT INFORMED CONSENT

Now that some ten million television homes are hooked into cable systems (CATV), testers are relying more and more on them rather than on the warm bodies of "subjects," with all the attendant headaches they entail.

The cable makes it possible to test commercials and programs by scheduling "split runs." The term describes a standard procedure long used by those who advertise in newspapers, magazines, and via direct mail. Varying only the advertisement in question, otherwise identical versions of the issue go to matched groups in pinpointed regions. One issue of *Redbook,* say, goes to the area with version A of a cosmetic ad; the same issue goes to a matched area with version B of the same ad. Subsequent interviews with known recipients reveal what kinds of people recall which elements of the ad, and whether they bought the product. The interviews supplement inventory data at "points of purchase" (statistical information registering fluctuations in product sales in the test areas)—useful, but insufficient to provide real insights into the "motivational structure" leading from particular elements in the ad to "felt need" to actual purchase.

Split-run tests can be built into magazines, newspapers, and other printed materials since they meet two requirements. Each version of the advertisement being tested appears in otherwise identical environments. (It's the same magazine, after all, that goes to all regions and all subscribers; only the ad is changed.) Moreover, large numbers of recipients are identifiable through subscription lists and thus available for follow-up probes through interviews, questionnaires, and diaries. Materials going over the airwaves were never able to fulfill these two important conditions —until cable television came along.

About 15 percent of all television households in the country depend upon cable service. The cable company erects and maintains a special community antenna that relays the television signal to a central receiving station.

The antenna picks up the off-the-air signal direct from the broadcasting source or from more distant stations by microwave. (CATV stands for "community antenna television.") The improved signal is wired into subscribers' sets through coaxial cable entering their homes just as a telephone cable does.

Most systems charge about five to six dollars a month for the service but the fee may go as high as ten dollars in some areas. Subscribers pay a one-time installation charge at the outset, too —usually around twenty-five to thirty-five dollars.

Like the telephone company, the cable company is licensed and supervised (franchised) by the city whose streets must be dug up for the lines to be laid, then restored to their original condition. Moreover, in some areas where direct reception is so muddled by interference that virtually every home subscribes, cable service takes on the character of a public utility. Whether cable companies should be regulated by an independent commission, as public utilities are, is a matter of social policy under discussion.[3]

The cable company's central receiving station has the capacity of originating programs,[4] and it is this capacity that has proved a bonanza for the testers. The big-time operator in the testing field is AdTel, a subsidiary of Booz Allen & Hamilton, management consultants. AdTel operates split-run tests using cable systems in several cities. Subscribers to the cable service are hooked to alternative feeds and the client's "cut-ins" to be tested are piped to their sets along with the programs they turn to in the normal course of their television watching. In AdTel's case, "cut-ins" are usually paired versions of commercials whose pulling power the client wishes to test.[5] Cable subscribers whose sets are wired into pattern A of the system might see "The CBS Evening News with Walter Cronkite" interrupted by version A of a Sominex commercial; those whose sets are wired into pattern B of the system might see the same program interrupted by version B of a commercial for the same drug. "Of course, [sic] the corporate client must 'own' the time—either network or spot —on which the test commercial is cut-in."[6]

In order to pull off this stunt, the cable company serving the area must wire its subscribers into two separate systems that can provide two separate feeds. In one of the cities AdTel works in (they call it AdTel City) the cable company wired its entire system to AdTel's specifications.[7] The second cable system placing itself and its subscribers at the disposal of AdTel had installed a dual wiring pattern from the outset. AdTel, quick to see the advantages this system offered, promptly took it over and "physically combined the two cable systems into one dual-cable system for advertising testing purposes."[8]

AdTel supplements the statistical data gathered in this fashion by relating it to a variety of details, including those provided by a panel of diary-keeping families. The panels are said to consist of a thousand families on each cable who "record all their food, drug, and other purchases in a weekly diary. Each family is personally recruited and trained."[9] Their recompense is premiums whose value does not exceed $80 a year.[10] In 1973 the charge to their clients was $65,000 for split-run tests using just one of their dual cable systems with a modest saving for bulk buys— $130,000 for clients who buy into two systems. There are small add-on costs for additional data and special runs.[11] The firm, which began in a single city in 1967, now operates through cable systems in Charleston, West Virginia; Bakersfield, California; Davenport, Iowa; Moline and Rock Island, Illinois.

AdTel was not the first marketing company to get the point that subscribers to cable service could be used as captive "subjects" for tests of this sort. The earliest case I have been able to uncover was the Port Jervis Video CATV system which began to rent their subscribers to the market testers and their clients in 1964.[12] The Milwaukee system followed close on Port Jervis's heels, as did cable systems in Akron, Ohio; San Francisco, California; Wilmington, Delaware; and Grand Junction, Colorado.[13] The Cox Cable system rents its subscribers to the market testers.[14] TelePrompter Corporation set up a subsidiary, Television Testing Company, for the purpose of renting to testers subscribers to all cable systems owned by the parent company.[15]

The testers say they are convinced that the system works

mainly because the captive subjects are innocent of the fact that they are being used in a test. The firms take every precaution, therefore, to keep the subjects and the general public in the dark about their procedures. For example, when I wrote to AdTel's president, John Adler, asking for the names of the test cities his firm uses, he respectfully demurred, explaining that it would destroy the "research factor" in the markets in question if the people there knew that the tests were being run. The company's promotional booklet assures prospective clients that the people in the markets "operate under a real-life situation and are not aware of the relationship."[16]

Mr. Adler had every reason to take my discretion for granted since reporters—even top reporters with by-lines—have consistently played along with the marketing people, keeping the full story from general public knowledge. When the business was just getting under way, the reporter specializing in advertising news for *The New York Times* interviewed Mr. Adler, who consented to go on record "only with the understanding that the identity of his laboratory city would be kept secret." The reporter added a touch of sympathetic understanding. "Can't blame him, really, since it's so important for him to keep the reactions of the panelists as natural as possible. A lot of time, trouble and money went into finding this town . . ."[17] None of the reporters I interviewed in an effort to find out the names of the test cities was willing to reveal them, explaining as usual that it was "proprietary information." I found them out by taking a leaf from the testers' book: I hired a consultant who worked on Madison Avenue for many years and had good personal connections in the business. A few discreet inquiries turned up the names of the cities, but I do not have the names of whoever it was that blew the whistle. My consultant wrote that "like a reporter, I must keep my sources secret."

Keeping the secret of split-cable testing or revealing it has little to do with ensuring the "natural" behavior of subjects. AdTel admits a more compelling consideration for the maintenance of secrecy: competitors who might be tempted to "jam tests with unusual bursts of advertising and/or promotion."[18] A still more important reason for secrecy is that publicity could open the possibility of public scandal if subscribers were made aware that while they pay the cable company for services rendered by it, the cable company does not pay subscribers for services they unwittingly render to it. It is even possible that the city fathers might be persuaded to renegotiate those franchises that hand out unquestioned access to every home—an access then converted by the cable companies into a rental business.

Market testers did not invent this practice of using human "subjects" in tests, keeping them in the dark about it, and not telling them the results or the uses to which the results are being put. Psychologists and sociologists often use "naïve subjects," as they are called, and their professional associations write a lot of papers specifying the conditions under which this may be done and the canons of ethics that must guide the people who do it. Researchers in biology, medicine, and drugs do the same. All these fields have found themselves under fire from time to time for the carelessness some of their practitioners exhibit, bypassing ethical principles for the sake of quick results or easy access to test populations.[19]

The U.S. Department of Health, Education and Welfare requires any study seeking support from that department to prove that human subjects involved have given informed consent. This is defined as "knowing consent of an individual or his legally authorized representative, so situated as to be able to exercise free power of choice without undue inducement or any element of force, fraud, deceit, duress, or other form of constraint or coercion." A subject must be informed of his right to withdraw from the research "without prejudice to the subject," meaning prejudice to future care, reimbursement, compensation, employment, or any other condition. Subjects must be informed of any risk involved—defined as "possibility of injury, including physical, psychological or social injury, as a consequence of participation as a subject in any research, development, or related activity . . ."

According to the Nuremberg Code, established in war-crimes trials at the end of World War II, the voluntary consent of human subjects used in experiments is essential; experiments should yield results for the good of society; should be conducted by scientifically qualified personnel, and the experimental subject must be able to stop an experiment any time he or she feels it is undesirable to continue. None of these conditions characterizes split-cable testing.

The advertising fraternity, in contrast, endorses a principle that would avoid such troublesome guidelines by resorting to deception from the very outset. "Expose the individual to the commercial or print advertising in his home so that he has no idea that his viewing is part of a test."[20] The guiding belief here is that behavior of the many can and should be manipulated by a few acting principally in their own interests, which they define as coterminous with the public interest. Cable testing, now, raises this philosophy to a power. For the privilege of being used as "naïve subjects" in tests they know nothing about, whose results will yield them no reward, whose patrons want mainly to manipulate them further, the human guinea pigs involved pay a down payment and a monthly charge!

16

**Engineering
the Appeals
to the Child
Market**

Formative research that tries to find out what attracts the attention of children and keeps them glued to the television screen is a specialty in its own right. Since children rely less on language to convey their feelings and reactions than grownups do, those who analyze "the child market" have been particularly inventive in finding ways to enter a child's mind without depending heavily on verbal exchanges. One-way mirrors, hidden tape recorders, video recorders, finger-sensors, and the rest of the gadgetry are all standard equipment in many of the research labs that test children, as well as adults. It's the child's own imaginative play, however, his "pretend" life, his drawings and dancing and body rhythms and singing and shouting and leaping and jumping, that testers have turned into probes they depend on to penetrate what goes on in a child's mind as he watches television. The most elaborate techniques are employed to test the way children respond to commercials. When it comes to determining how they react to programs, the television business resorts to the word of academic consultants to justify the finished product, plus occasional cursory viewing sessions that yield materials useful for public-relations releases.

A number of market-research firms conduct research for clients who wish to develop commercials to attract children to their products. Among the best known of these firms is the Gene Reilly Group, an outfit catapulted into national prominence when it received about sixty seconds of national coverage in a network documentary. The documentary, "You and the Commercial," was produced by CBS News, and broadcast April 27, 1973, a "black week" free of listener ratings. This was the first and last time a national television audience was shown a glimpse of this essential component of the television business.

The Gene Reilly firm's advertising brochure says it is in "the people business" and that it serves its clients with "accurate, unbiased and continuing study of the U.S. child as consumer." It points out that "there are 37 million children in the 6 to 14 age group," and they "consume billions of dollars worth of goods and services every year. In terms of their direct consumption and their influence on purchase, they constitute a sovereign and enormously important market."[1]

In addition to the usual investigations custom-designed to answer a client's particular questions, the Gene Reilly Group provides a special syndicated service clients can subscribe to: four encyclopedic volumes filled with information detailing special characteristics of the six-to-fourteen-year-old "market," how to appeal to that "market," and what special needs can be developed there: volume 1: *The Assumption by the Child of the Role of Consumer,* (July 1973); volume 2: *The Child and What He Eats* (December 1973), volume 3: *The Child, The Media and the Message* (September 1974); volume 4: *The Child's Private World of Leisure* (April 1975).[2] In these volumes the subscriber can look up answers to questions of the following kind: What do children do in their spare time? What do they spend their money on? What products are children most anxious to acquire? What products do they talk about when they talk among themselves? What commercials did they talk about this month? Last month? Who are the most beloved heroes of today's children? What's their staying power—that is, did the children have different heroes last month? The month before? How may these heroes be transformed into role models?[3] (Translated, this means how can children be influenced to adopt prefabricated heroes as patterns for their own self-concepts now and in the future?)

The Gene Reilly Group is one among scores of research firms providing information to clients eager to aggregate children into markets. These firms claim that they can "unlock kids,"[4] that is, elicit from the children information about how they think and feel, in order to associate such thoughts and feelings with the client's marketing aims. It's not easy, since the "child is a moving target"[5] and cannot always be pinned down to concise and clear expression of feelings or state clearly what is on his or her mind.

Some firms—the Gene Reilly Group is one—are eclectic in their methods, employing intensive interviews, play groups, projective tests, one-way screens plus whatever other gadgetry seems indicated; but also resorting to mass surveys of children and their parents, frequently buying into nationwide polls such as those run by the Gallup organization.[6]

Others specialize in projective techniques. Among these is Child Research Service, a firm which claims it addresses itself to "virtually any marketing problem in which the child influences the purchase or is the ultimate consumer,"[7] and which reaches down into the four-year-old set. They "psych out" the children by examining their drawings and dramatic play for useful hints.[8]

Drawing—Children cannot always tell the group leader or write down in words the things they buy, the things for which they recall advertising, etc., but they can draw it. *Secret votes*—Children whisper their answers to the group leader or directly to the court stenographer. This privacy permits the shy or hesitant child to express his true feelings. . . . *Play Acting*—Children act out the things they can't write or say. They might "show" how they buy certain articles, where, when, etc. *Role-playing*—Children may pretend to be their mothers in vignettes in which they act out how they think other children feel about different consumer issues and problems . . .[9]

The children work in specially equipped playrooms strewn with attractive toys, crayons, finger paints, and other gear children like to play with. Sometimes the room is specially set up to simulate a particular environment—a kitchen, a supermarket, or even (in the case of a client who wanted advice on how to sell a hair lotion to children) a dressing room.

> . . . a variety of personal care products that children might like to use were arranged on the dressing tables. Children were asked to role-play a sleep-over visit, getting ready for a party, getting ready to go to bed, and getting ready for school in the morning. Throughout these games the girls' interest in and ability to use the client's product was observed.[10]

A one-way mirror, which permits an observer to watch the proceedings without being observed, is ubiquitous in such testing rooms. Clients paying for the research are often invited to join the research staff to see for themselves how the children react. "It's a good way . . . to develop a first-hand feel for the strengths and weaknesses of [the] product."[11]

> Observers can sit comfortably around the conference table to see and hear the sessions through one-way glass and, if you wish, closed circuit television while maintaining simultaneous communication with the moderator. You are there . . . yet you remain invisible, unseen by the participants . . .[12]

If the aim is to test a commercial or a television program, furnishings include a projector or television monitor, used sometimes in tandem with a "distractor." The program to be tested is shown on the television monitor set up in one corner of the room. In an opposite corner is a screen on which a slide projector concurrently projects stills of attractive scenes—landscapes, animals, children playing. An observer notes each time the children turn their eyes away from the test program in favor of the "distracting" scenes on the other screen—the distractor. The information is relayed to the writers and producer, who then doctor the material accordingly.[13]

Some firms like to emphasize their use of sophisticated gadgetry.

> Two instaneous measurements are available to the client to determine whether a commercial has the power to . . . hold the viewer's attention and to involve them in the film. The first of these is derived from responses given via ASI Recorder dial. This is a small rheostat dial attached by cable to the seats of a sample of 175 viewers . . . This provides a conscious interest dimension. A second sample of 115 viewers is equipped with a set of finger sensors . . . This automatic measure relates to the degree of subconscious involvement with the perceived stimulus. Both . . . responses are recorded by computer and presented graphically as continuous line charts . . .[14]

Still others stress their access to relatively large samples of children for tests that can claim greater statistical reliability for their results. In such mass testing, the children work in auditoriums with or without the gadgetry. Questionnaires are frequently used, and these testers like what they call "smiley scales"—a five-point or seven-point scale of moon-faces ranging from downturned mouth at one extreme to broadly upturned mouth at the other. The child checks the one that comes closest to his own feelings of like or dislike, approval or disapproval.

SCHOOLS ARE COOPTED

Large-scale tests of this sort often rely on the cooperation of local schools. "Educators are not in the business of promoting a particular manufacturer's product. But they are alive to the objectives of the commercial world, and with ever-tightening school budgets, willing to cooperate more and more."[15] As a result, the research firms "can get into schools and test our ideas with hundreds of kids."[16] This makes it possible to test the appeal of commercials, for example, using "a sample of 150 children in the target sex or age range appropriate to the product . . . The tests are conducted in schools in Northern New Jersey. Other test locations can be arranged . . ."[17]

The spokesman for this service goes on to explain how the school auditorium is converted into a mock supermarket for the purpose. Children file in as if for the usual school entertainment program. Before going to their seats they pass a simulated supermarket shelf bearing a variety of packages, and are told to pick up any package that appeals to them, as a gift. The entertainment is usually a movie or cartoon, the same sort of thing they might see on television. The difference, however, is that the client's commercials to be tested are spliced into the film or tape for these special schoolhouse tests.[18]

Supermarkets and schools chum up quite a bit these days. As the schools turn themselves into supermarkets, the supermarkets convert themselves into schools. One enterprising supermarket in Teaneck, New Jersey, recently set aside a whole section of the store for a second-grade classroom, complete with chairs, tables, and blackboards. The teacher conducted the lessons for her second-graders in full view of the shoppers.[19] The children, in their turn, could look up from their work at any time and see some of the nation's consumers wheeling their carts up and down the aisles, picking products off the shelves, out of bins, freezers, refrigerator compartments, deliberating about this "new improved product" or that one—educational in every sense of the word.

RECRUITERS

The children who file in and out of the testing and research laboratories, in and out of the special auditoriums, are recruited by the same kinds of agencies that funnel warm bodies to testers looking for adult "subjects." Requests come in for a half dozen boys and girls, say, ages six to nine, articulate, willing and able to talk about their feelings and accustomed to conversing with adults. "Any children with speech impediments, language problems, or other psychological or motor impairments are identified and if necessary isolated."[20]

Recruiters often operate through local PTAs, public and parochial schools, cub scouts, hospital auxiliaries, women's clubs, Rotary, B'nai B'rith, and so on. In this manner they can ensure delivery of batches of children if large samples are required. Since fees are paid ranging usually from one to three dollars per hour per child, the organizations welcome the additional funds for their treasuries. Children who participate in small groups and who are interviewed in detail, submitting to projective tests and psychodrama, are paid directly and may earn more—even up to thirty-five dollars a day; but such fees are the exception.

IT'S A BUSINESS...THAT'S NOBODY'S BUSINESS

To call this sort of data-collection "research" dignifies the process. No hypotheses are stated, no alternative hypotheses ruled out, no cumulative body of knowledge is enriched, and results are not subjected to public scrutiny by qualified peers applying agreed upon standards of evidence and subscribing to evolved canons of ethics. Typical problems the market-research firms investigate are: Why do children rip off the heads of Barbie dolls?

What kinds of premiums included in breakfast-food boxes will attract children to the product? Do children find bubblegum cards attractive enough to want to buy the product? How do they like powdered soft drinks? What about packaging medicines and cosmetics in containers that look like toys? Do children react more favorably to packages in primary colors or in pastels? What kinds of purchases do children influence? What kinds do they, themselves, make? The formative research of the program-tests determines whether the children caught the goodthink.

Research it is not; it's a business despite its name—*market research.* It has cashed in on a battery of elaborate procedures for soliciting ideas useful in advertising, product development, and pricing strategy. Nor does this business have anything to do with democracy,—despite its stated *raison d'être* of finding out "what the public really wants." Such a "democracy" asks people to open themselves to probes and questions, calls the answers a "vote," lies about issues, doesn't name candidates, and never announces results. Indeed, all "votes" remain "proprietary," owned by the client who pays for the job, to use as he sees fit, for his own advantage.

The whole procedure is an open secret—open in the sense that it's no news to anyone; secret in the sense that it is shrouded in a silence which insulates it from public discussion. The only way the public is involved is in offering up itself and its children as the prime material the testers process. Information thus provided is then duly locked away, closed to public inspection, debate, or review.

PROSOCIAL MESSAGES AND OTHER GOODTHINK

Television production companies call upon the trappings of academic research too, to justify programs made to convoke the "child market." Here academic consultants are used to aid the process. "Fat Albert and the Cosby Kids" is a prime example of the practice.

CBS booked "Fat Albert and the Cosby Kids" into the 1972–73 Saturday morning children's ghetto, with no more and no less fanfare than for the other programs signed that season. Although the network had not called much attention to it initially, they had employed an advisory panel of educators, psychologists, and sociologists to work on each episode of the series' first cycle, from proposed story outline to completed scripts. The panel was headed by Dr. Gordon L. Berry, assistant dean of the Graduate School of Education at UCLA. It included nine other members of the UCLA faculty as well as two deans: Dr. Dwight Allen, of the School of Education at the University of Massachusetts, and Dr. Nathan Cohen, of UCLA's School of Social Welfare. This advisory panel, meeting in solemn session, determined that the series should deal in real-life situations with emphasis on those in which young persons would have an opportunity to make value judgments and in which solutions would be realistically in their power. Dr. Berry stated the objective: "The key idea is to be entertaining and, at the same time, teach values . . . We're trying to get a message across, but not in a preachy fashion."[21] He couldn't have said it better if he had been talking about making a commercial for Barbie dolls!

After the series had run for two seasons and had proved to be one of the Saturday morning block's top-rated shows, CBS launched a nationwide campaign calling attention to the practice of bringing in credential-bearing academics as consultants to help engineer programs beamed at the nation's children. One ad, headlined "Laugh all you want, but this guy's a teacher," described the program as ". . . an extraordinary experiment in television education, created under the direct, detailed supervision of a panel of noted scholars and educators."[22] The purpose of "Fat Albert," indeed of all CBS programs, said the ad, was "to expand the child's understanding of self and the world, through the imaginative, unorthodox use of television." But then, the text gave the game away by making the criterion explicit: "Fat Albert delivers its message so effectively" that "nine out of ten (89.3%, to be exact) of 711 children interviewed received one or more pro-social messages,"—just as all those educators and social workers had planned.

The count was made by the Gene Reilly Group, which submitted to its client, the CBS network, a report entitled, *A Study of Messages Received by Children Who Viewed an Episode of Fat Albert and the Cosby Kids.*[23] The title is a misnomer. Nobody studied the messages! The so-called researchers counted the number of children who passed a sort of multiple-choice test after they saw the program. Some of the "messages" the academic consultants had ordered built into the program, which were "tested" by the Gene Reilly staff, were: Lying is bad. Work is important. Do the best you can. Work and school are equivalent. Do not be any of the following: rude, jealous, nasty, mean. Do be all or most of the following: friendly, obedient, considerate of others, tolerant of Indians, understanding of divorce. Do not engage in any of the following practices: writing on walls, destroying signs, teasing others.[24]

CBS distributed the *Study of Messages* free to anyone requesting it. The timing of the Gene Reilly study (February 1974) and the advertisement with its accompanying public-relations releases (week of April 1, 1974) is of interest. Network executives were to testify during the first week in April, 1974, before Senator John O. Pastore's Subcommittee on Communications, to report what they had done in response to the findings a blue-ribbon panel had reported to the surgeon general of the United States, to the effect that television programs featuring violence were a public-health menace, especially harmful to children.

It deserves mention that CBS has never funded a study or publicized research conducted by others that shows the number of *anti*social messages children also grasp as they watch routinely scheduled television programs. No other network has done so either; nor, for that matter, has anyone else in the television business, not even the numerous independent consultants attached to it one way or another. Whenever similar statistics are cited, moreover, to support claims that the usual television programs we see are loaded with "messages" about murder, mayhem, sexual foreplay, intercourse, rape, prostitution, pandering, drug addiction, and the like—badthink "messages" just as easily grasped by children and others as the goodthink messages in "Fat Albert and the Cosby Kids"—CBS research people join all the rest of the media-research fraternity in vociferously denouncing such evidence as totally inadmissible.

I have no wish to engage in this debate—it is my claim that television's effects are much more systemic, the effects of its explicitly intended "messages" the least of it. I only wish to highlight the double standard that underlies the whole fatuous exercise of this sort of media research.

It seems to be the prevailing view in network circles that the use of consultants pays off either in ratings, in Congress, or both. In any case, five of the six series CBS booked as newcomers to the 1974–75 Saturday-morning block credited academic consultants along with the producers, writers, directors, artists, musicians, unit managers, sound technicians, light technicians, and computer technicians and others who helped engineer the shows.[25] NBC adopted the practice, hiring a linguist to invent a special language—Paku—spoken by the Neanderthal family in "Land of the Lost," a show that premiered in the September 1974 ghetto. ABC hired academic consultants to "authenticate" their Stone Age series that season, too: "Korg: 70,000 B.C." Dr. Nathan Cohen moved from CBS to ABC as consultant for their series, "New Adventures of Gilligan," which opened in September 1975. The Bank Street College of Education signed with ABC to provide consultation on "Devlin," scheduled for the same opening date.

It is an aberration of our own culture, peculiar to this historic moment, that most of the art and drama our children see is produced and marketed like a pair of shoes. The writers, artists, and dramatists who cooperate in the enterprise are asked to pledge allegiance to the findings of "scientific research," allowing their own imaginations, their own vision, to be constrained by its presumably higher authority. Materials produced in this manner may sometimes serve as useful instructional tools; but I am convinced that they are not likely to be the best even for such a purpose. It is clear to me that they enrich their producers more than they enrich the children; how much they impoverish the culture, we cannot yet know.

The notion that academic credentials are evidence of a special pipeline to wisdom or creativity is a myth. That academic consultants agree to help engineer programs designed to amass children into audiences, attests to the pervasiveness of the myth at the same time that the practice perpetuates it. It is a myth that assumptions and procedures which have helped the networks and their clients create and expand markets, have something important to contribute to art, music, dance, drama, and creative play—especially to their role in ushering the young of the human species into their humanity. It is a myth that drama is understandable as messages; viewing *King Lear* as a series of information bits about filial loyalty misses the point.

In the long run, what is "good for children" can only be authentic art and literature and all the other expressive materials children need. They can thrive only on art that captures them without holding them captive, that helps them stretch and reach and grow as they exercise imagination, feeling joy and a sense of accomplishment in the doing of it. Then, no matter how much a child succeeds in grasping, no matter how much a child takes away, there is always more that beckons, spurring him on to reach and stretch and reach again.[26]

The social policy we have allowed to evolve in this country is based on the supposition that characteristics of artistic materials that are "good for children" can be looked up in a textbook or a book of formulas. Not so. Wise social policy can only provide the best possible supports for the best possible conditions that encourage authentic artists to develop themselves to the best of their ability as they do their best to make authentic art. Even though it is no easy task to decide what such social conditions may be, some things we already know. Neither authentic art nor authentic science is produced by committees and boards of experts. Certainly, authentic drama will not be produced by splicing together what "engineers of imagination" call "prosocial messages," what George Orwell called "goodthink."

VIOLENCE INDEX

The tallies accumulate, the statistics proliferate, the method-
ological debates grow denser and more obtuse. Researchers at
the University of Pennsylvania's Graduate School of Communication, under the direction of Professor George Gerbner, began
in 1968 to record the fine points of the violence in network
television programs, developing a summary statistic that con-
denses the elaborate tallies of the body counts and "kill ratios"
into a single figure—a "violence index" for television "drama."
This index keeps track of the ups and downs of television mayhem the way the Dow-Jones index keeps track of the ups and
downs in stock-market trading.

Senator Pastore, then chairman of the Subcommittee on Communications of the Senate Commerce Committee, thought it
would be a good idea for such a violence index to be published
and publicized. It could, he thought, alert the nation to fluctuations in the aggregate outpourings of violent imagery entering
the pool of symbols available to it.

Senator Pastore's suggestion, however, never got off the
ground. Although the nation is lulled nightly as newscasters
recite the litany of the Dow-Jones averages, an equivalent litany
reciting television's own "violence average" has been withheld
while methodologists debate the components of the index.[3]

The networks and the National Association of Broadcasters—
the trade association of the broadcasting business—continue to
claim (as they have since radio days) that there is no conclusive
evidence that their policy of programing violent television shows
is necessarily antisocial. Isn't *Hamlet* violent? *Macbeth? Oedipus?* the Bible? If our greatest literary and dramatic works do not
draw the line at violence, where is the justification for claims that
television dramas should do so?[4]

Some say it may even be a good idea to show violence on
television. Such dramatic actings-out could, after all, provide a

sort of cathartic outlet, allowing those among us who are be-deviled by antisocial impulses to discharge them vicariously, instead of engaging in real violence against persons or property.[5] Far from being antisocial, then, persistent showing of violence on television could be "prosocial" and network television policy a boon to the nation.

The discussions go on and on, while at television booking offices it's business as usual. The rate of violence per dramatic program or cartoon play has remained stable throughout the years the Gerbner project has been reporting body counts,[6] and the blueprints used by those who construct the shows remain unchanged. Only the styles of violence they demonstrate have altered. The manly cowboy who used to dispatch the bad guy with a right to the "button," never fought with his feet, never hit below the belt. In those days, good guys "fought clean"; even bad guys "fought dirty" only occasionally—and were hissed for it. Today's television features the kung fu and karate expert who thinks nothing of jumping a man from behind and dispatching him before he can turn around. Indeed, in the name of the liberation of women, "he" can now be transformed into a "she." The chase on horseback through scrubby brush and rocky can-yons has been replaced by the automobile chase, ending as the bad guy's car hurtles over an embankment or comes a cropper against a concrete piling, incinerating all parties concerned in time for the commercial break.

Many people of good will find it hard to believe that a national menu specializing in shows centered on killing has no ill effects. Since the television audience is now virtually the whole popula-tion of this country, plus vast overseas populations in countries that import our programs, it's a worrisome thought. Congressio-nal efforts to "do something about it" surface from time to time, but they have been sporadic, feeble, and impotent.

The Senate Subcommittee to Investigate Juvenile Delinquency was one of the earliest Senate bodies to inquire into the possibility that the television industry may be antisocial, inciting others to criminal behavior. Senator Estes Kefauver, a key member of the subcommittee, suspected that the continuous offerings of violent television fare were an important factor in rising rates of juvenile delinquency. The industry, called on the carpet to account for itself, denied that the programs booked into television were really "violent," and at the same time trotted out experts who pointed out that whatever violence there was really didn't do a thing anyway. Delinquency, they said, like any other kind of adolescent, preadolescent, or postadolescent behavior, was an outcome of an individual's entire life history. All of us, delinquents and nondelinquents alike, are affected by everything in our total environment. Since television programs are clearly not the total environment, it was not only unfair to make the industry take the rap for delinquency, but unscientific. Other experts countered that, nevertheless, television violence played a contributory role since it was part of the barrage of all "stimuli" that motivate delinquents to do the things they do.

The overall conclusion of the juvenile delinquency subcommittee was that such programs, at least in large doses, could be "potentially harmful" to young viewers. Industry spokesmen disagreed, but said they would reduce the dosage of violence anyway.[7]

Senator Thomas Dodd next picked up the gauntlet when he took over as chairman of the subcommittee. The senator ordered new body counts and found that violence on television had not abated one whit. Indeed, he declared in 1961 and again in 1964 that it "remains greater than it was a decade ago."[8]

In 1963, President John F. Kennedy's assassination appeared on camera, along with on-camera civil-rights demonstrations, followed a few years later by on-camera antiwar turmoil and on-camera student protest that looked like a revolution. In 1968, two months after the student takeover at Columbia University, a month after student and worker uprisings in France, five days after the murder of Robert F. Kennedy, President Lyndon B. Johnson established The National Commission on the Causes and Prevention of Violence. Its findings, released more than a year later, included a monumental staff report, *Violence and the Media*, more than a thousand pages chronicling the materials the nation's media empires produce and reporting the testimony of experts on the probable contribution of such stuff to violent, aggressive, and criminal behavior. The committee examined television, but did not slight mass-produced and mass-distributed print and radio fare as well. Their conclusion: "the probability [is] that mass media portrayals of violence are one major contributory factor which *must* be considered in attempts to explain the many forms of violent behavior that mark American society today."[9]

Industry spokesmen continued to demur, again promising that, nevertheless, in the future they would be more restrained in ordering and buying from their suppliers programs whose formulas starred violence.

Initiative in the Senate now passed from the Subcommittee on Juvenile Delinquency to the Subcommittee on Communications of the Senate Commerce Committee. The chairman, Senator Pastore, hit upon a new approach that might, he thought, get the television business to settle for somewhat lower body counts: public health. Even if it could not be proved to the satisfaction of the television business that their programs were causing violence in the streets, maybe it could be proved that there was a link between television-portrayed violence and disturbances in mental health. Senator Pastore had in mind a model similar to U.S. government efforts that had successfully resulted in official acceptance of research results claiming a causal link between tobacco and cancer. So in March 1969, he sent a letter to the newly appointed secretary of Health, Education and Welfare, Robert Finch, suggesting a similar procedure in the case of television programs. Senator Pastore's letter asked the nation's chief medical officer to set up a scientific advisory committee that would stimulate definitive research and then evaluate in a truly dispassionate way the evidence for and against claims that television violence was inciting behavior inimical to mental health, particularly (but not exclusively) in the case of children.[10]

This, too, came to pass. The Surgeon General's Scientific Advisory Committee on Television and Social Behavior was called into being, and began work on June 16, 1969. In the two years of its existence, the ten men and two women serving on it were asked to read, digest, and evaluate several tons of research reports churned out by social scientists to whom HEW had granted about two million dollars. The absurdity of most of the research[11] was compounded by the opaque and obscure language in which it was reported—five volumes loaded with technicalities and verbs in the passive voice. A summary volume managed nevertheless to convey the information that the evidence justified the conclusion that there is "a preliminary and tentative indication of a causal relation between viewing violence on television and aggressive behavior." The same sentence delivering this punchline, however, was burdened by the companion observation that the "causal relation operates only on some children . . . and only in some environmental contexts."[12] Thus did the twelve scientific men and women on the Surgeon General's Scientific Advisory Committee resoundingly refute anyone brash enough to argue that the observed causal effect operates on all children and in every environmental context.

Quite apart from the patent absurdity of citing a finding that would apply to "all children" as a standard of reference, the participants set the rules of the game from the outset in such a manner as to make sure that no finding could be extrapolated to "all children." For example, the populations in whom the hypothesized effects could be examined were to exclude "deviant children." The reasoning seems to have been that if violent television could be shown to produce or exacerbate mental or other kinds of disturbance in children who were institutionalized, mentally defective, deaf, hyperactive, brain-damaged, or operating under a variety of other kinds of handicaps, it would be unfair to include such findings in the report to the nation or to the scientific community. "The real issue is quantitative,"[13] the report "explained."

Senator Pastore, accepting the scientists' claims that they had isolated the effect of television violence on "aggressive behavior" the way virologists might isolate the virus producing warts, called it "a scientific and cultural breakthrough."[14] The surgeon general, in an article entitled, "TV Violence *Is* Harmful" declared, "we can no longer tolerate the present high level of televised violence that is put before children in American homes."[15]

But tolerate it we did. The University of Pennsylvania's continuing research found that in 1974 "the prevalence of violence declined only from 8 out of every 10 programs to 7 out of 10," while "the rates of violent episodes changed little in seven years . . . the prevalence, rate and saturation of violence in crime programs were up . . . Cartoon programming increased in the rate of violence per program . . ." and so on.[16]

Even after two decades of living with this sort of impasse, Senator Pastore still did not give up. He turned his attention to the Federal Communications Commission. The FCC is the modern form of the watchdog agency Congress established when it passed the Communications Act of 1934—the federal statute that launched the broadcasting business. The agency is charged to require broadcasters to correct any discrepancies between their legal obligation to program "in the public interest, convenience and necessity" and their actual programing practices. The Senate delinquency subcommittee's judgment that television programs consistently featuring violence incited antisocial behavior somehow had never moved the FCC to action. But now, the franchise holders operating television stations were persisting in broadcasting programs whose ingredients included a "scientifically proven" public-health menace. Senator Pastore reasoned that perhaps the FCC, this time, might interpret such policy as a discrepancy between promise and performance.

The chairman of the FCC, Richard E. Wiley, met with representatives of the broadcasting industry, and together they hammered out what they felt was a mutually acceptable solution, ratified forthwith by the National Association of Broadcasters meeting in national convention in April 1975. The solution was so-called "family viewing time." Broadcasters agreed that as of September 1975 they would serve the public interest, convenience, and necessity by establishing separate traffic lanes, one for programs with the virus, the other for programs without it. The infectious traffic lane is to remain closed in the early evening hours reserved for programs "suitable for family viewing." By this measure the nation's children, presumably more susceptible than adults to infection by violent programs, will be protected from catching mental disturbance by the simplest of all expedients—being sent to bed! Mr. Wiley hailed the NAB's vote: "What you have done is real self-regulation," he declared, "a landmark in the development of industry self-regulation."[17]

The "landmark" ruling sets up the separate traffic lane in prime time for the rough stuff, opening the gate at nine o'clock in eastern and Pacific time zones, eight o'clock in central and most of the mountain time zones. In some areas of the mountain zone the barrier goes down even earlier—seven o'clock.[18] The assumption that children are in bed at these times and thus protected against infection, is, of course, supported by no evidence.[19]

Over a hundred stations were exempt for two years from the family-viewing-time restrictions, leaving independent stations— those which do not rent the use of their facilities to any of the three commercial networks, free to schedule at any time the stuff that several congressional committees and a presidential commission have labeled a cause of delinquency and crime, that the surgeon general has labeled a public-health menace. After that date they are instructed to set up separate traffic lanes, channeling the rough and raunchy stuff into the later hours—nine o'clock, eight, or seven, depending on their time zones.

Stations violating the family-viewing-time provision incur no penalties other than possible citation by the Television Code Review Board. If they accumulate an "excessive number of citations," revocation of their membership in the Code Authority could be recommended—not a very threatening possibility, since to date no subscribing station has ever been asked by the authority to withdraw from membership because of such code violations.

Still another turn of the screw must be reported. On November 3, 1976, Judge Warren Ferguson of the Federal District Court in Los Angeles handed down a decision claiming that the family viewing hour violates the First Amendment rights of individual franchise-holders. The judge's decision ignored all that stuff about television violence constituting a public-health menace and leading to delinquency and crime in favor of the issues which impress him: government influence over program content and network influence over station licensees.[20]

The provisions of the family viewing hour were hammered out in private meetings between the chairman of the FCC and network executives. Thus did a federal official exercise government power to dictate program content, "lawless conduct," in the opinion of Judge Ferguson. Joining the commissioner as villain of the scenario are the network officials who, offering no more resistance than a wet noodle, succumbed to the jawboning.

That the membership of the NAB Code Authority subsequently voted to go along with the family viewing hour was self-regulation in name only, according to this decision. Broadcasters who voted for the family viewing hour are, like all other licensees,[21] required by law to abide by the provisions of the

Communications Act, which assumes (writes the judge) decentralized decision-making by those holding franchises. The power of networks to influence the vote, in contrast, indicates that centralized decision-making is the order of the day. In point of fact, the vote only imposed the will of a small group of people: the chairman of the FCC wielding government power, the network executives wielding monopolistic private power, and a few members of the NAB Code Authority, beholden to both.

For all these reasons, the "vote" makes a mockery of the intent of the law governing broadcasting, as well as the First Amendment to the U. S. Constitution, which not only enjoins government from dictating program content, but also places an obligation on broadcasters to withstand any such unlawful demands. So ruled the judge.

The decision opens a hornet's nest since it queries whether the one-man-one-vote axiom on which our theory of democracy is based makes any sense when voters have such vastly different degrees of lobbying power with government, such different degrees of economic power over each other.

Meanwhile, the broadcasters make it clear that nobody in the business really takes this sort of "solution" any more seriously than I do. In spite of the *cordon sanitaire* of "family viewing time," networks continue urging audiences throughout the broadcast day to be sure not to miss the evening programs still to come. Thus, tapes for daytime serials broadcast during lunchtime, when just as many children as grownups watch, routinely splice in promos urging the luncheon audience not to miss "Streets of San Francisco," "Kojak," "Police Story," etc., as well as crime movies such as *Death Scream, The French Connection,* and *Dirty Harry.* Network shows quarantined to the hours reserved for infectious materials are nevertheless a prime source of "action figures," toys, games, and even total play environments all children are urged to acquire, play with, and admire; and the urgings include television commercials usually clustered on Saturday mornings, during so-called after-school hours, and in the early evening hours, when millions of children watch. Shows like "Kung Fu" and "Ironside," zoned out of the family hour on network stations, are used for in-school instruction (see appendix on page 344).

The conclusion of the surgeon general and his scientific advisers might be presumed to warrant intensive news coverage and public discussion. Yet network news departments have never granted any more than the most cursory passing comment to the story, if they deigned to mention it at all! (No more did they bother to alert the nation to the earlier rendered opinions that violent television incites to delinquency and crime.) Industry representatives have consistently refused to participate in public conferences called by scientists wishing to discuss social-policy implications growing out of the research the surgeon general called into existence.[22] And yet, this is the very kind of research their spokesmen have been calling for, for over two decades, as a necessary prelude to any change in their program policies.

In 1954, Harold Fellows, then chairman of the board of NAB, was chided at hearings of the Senate Subcommittee to Investigate Juvenile Delinquency, since the industry had never followed through on the promise of launching research into the impact of television programs on children. Mr. Fellows responded that NAB would delay no longer. James T. Aubrey, then president of CBS, told the same subcommittee that a CBS study was, in fact, in progress and that it would reveal "the definitive story." The study Mr. Fellows promised was never made; the study to which Mr. Aubrey referred was not published until 1963. It turned out to be a routine report on the opinions, attitudes, beliefs, and alleged behavior of children as reported by their parents.

In 1961, a NAB spokesman, Mr. Leroy Collins, told the same

subcommittee that NAB desired to "join with others in underwriting the cost of a comprehensive study." A year later, the industry cosponsored a committee—the Joint Committee for Research on Television and Children. It was this committee that was going to stimulate the needed research and evaluate it, applying the most rigorous canons of science in a way that would certainly satisfy all parties to any dispute.

In 1964, Senator Dodd inquired about the research the joint committee was to have undertaken. Upon questioning, Walter D. Scott, then executive vice president of NBC, turned out to be rather vague about what had happened to that committee and its research. "I think that all of us are looking forward to the work of the Joint Committee," he said, "and counting heavily upon having some definitive work come out of that committee. I believe either five or six specific projects . . ."

His vagueness was understandable. By 1964, the joint committee had neither undertaken nor caused to be undertaken any research, definitive or otherwise, on television's effects on anything. (In seven years, only one report was ever published by the joint committee, a paper that analyzed what were claimed to be inadequacies in research performed by others.) Two years later, however, one piece of research was commissioned. Dr. Seymour Feshback tested his favorite hypothesis—that violence on television programs reduces aggression.[23] By 1968, Dr. Frank Stanton, then president of CBS, said that the committee, which he characterized as "a dormant organization," simply "fell apart."[24]

Since that time, the three networks have funded more or less elaborate studies designed to determine whether the straw that obviously did not break the camel's back may be exonerated of any contribution to its spinal collapse.[25] In spite of their acquiescence to family viewing time, network spokesmen continue to claim that it's all a tempest in a teapot. There's not so much violence on television, after all, they say; neither is there evidence of public displeasure.

Public displeasure is mentioned neither in the First Amendment, which broadcasters cite as justification for their insistence that they, and only they, establish rules about what goes over the air; nor in the Communications Act of 1934. Nonetheless, in spite of broadcasters' disclaimers, public displeasure has been very much in evidence. The FCC reports two thousand complaints received in 1972 compared with almost twenty-five thousand in 1974.[26] The increase continued in 1975.

Viewers claim networks and individual broadcasters do not respond to complaints.[27] Broadcasters claim that the absence of complaints indicates public acceptance. "In all of 1974," a CBS vice president says, "we got no more than 2000 letters about sex and obscenity and maybe 200 complaining about violence. That's really a pretty infinitesimal protest, considering our total audience."[28]

Television people no longer use the word "violence" if they can help it. "Conflict" is their preferred term these days. Nevertheless, networks and stations introduce warnings or "advisories" alerting the public to the raunchiness of some of their programs. An incomplete list of programs that bore such warnings during the first quarter of 1975 follows: First two episodes of "Hot 1 Baltimore"; *The Heartbreak Kid; Lizzie Borden; Frenzy; The Summer of '42; Electra Glide in Blue; Walking Tall; Crazy Joe; What's New Pussycat?;* "A Case of Rape" (rerun); *Death Stalk;* two husky doses of the two-part documentary, "Of Women and Men," ran repeated warning banners throughout the programs.

THE PUBLIC AND THE PUBLIC INTEREST

All the media research, the experiments, the statistics and "hard data" pass over the most obvious facts about television drama. The messages in these stories about good guys and bad guys go far beyond any "messages" about violence and crime that writers and producers engineer into them. They are more than demonstration lessons in mayhem, more than sources of contagion that could infect susceptible viewers with an acute case of aggressiveness.

The repeated acting out of television's crime show formulas in the context commercial television weaves around them, trivializes the death and destruction they feature and strips them of horror. After the hundredth viewing, after the hundredth commercial interruption, there is no more sting left in the stuff. The shows blend together in a single massive desensitization session conducted daily and nightly via coast-to-coast hookup.

Many are vociferous critics of this program policy. Many others feel vaguely uneasy about it. Few, even in broadcasting circles, are complacent. And yet, the public policy issue is rarely stated clearly and unambiguously: do the programs broadcasters consistently deliver to American homes indicate compliance with the spirit and letter of the law that set them up in business?

Broadcasters have no legal obligation to lower the incidence of aggressiveness among the nation's children, nor is it clear that this single industry's contribution to personality development can be isolated and measured. Yet, enormous investments of time, energy, money, and talent go into efforts to explain "scientifically" the role television plays in creating and cultivating such traits. Broadcasters do have a legal obligation to deliver programs that serve the public interest, convenience, and necessity. Not much effort goes to find out who among us believe their current practices and procedures indicate a good-faith effort to meet this obligation. Still less effort goes to calling the obligation to public attention or advising the citizenry of its policy implications.

The terms, "public interest, convenience and necessity," can scarcely be defined to everyone's satisfaction, for the criteria of judgment are to be found not in the scientific laboratory, but in the wisdom of collective conscience. Is the public served by providing a stream of programs that, routinizing murder, rape and violent assault, de-emotionalize their impact? Only conscience can say. Is the public's convenience fairly considered when almost all broadcasting hours go to entertainment—and of the most trivial kind? Is it a public necessity to treat children as markets, catering to their unformed tastes and thus shaping them? Does television's virtual elimination of the many kinds of music and art the country used to enjoy impoverish the public culture? Even if these programing practices conform to the ways broadcasters and their clients define the public interest, what about the rest of the country?

Legislators, who are the people's chosen representatives, and members of administrative bodies charged by law to guard the public interest, are expected to consult the public conscience as a way of informing their own. Instead, they have sought the advice of an elite group of experts who deliver their opinions as if they were based on the kind of evidence physicists cite when they explain the structure of matter.

We, the people, are used repeatedly as passive subjects whose behavior must be observed, analyzed, and interpreted by such experts. We, the people, have never been asked to provide the guidance that only an informed and enlightened citizenry can provide once the facts have been exposed and their implications openly debated. Do specific program practices such as the ones discussed in this book, strike the public as evidence that broadcasters consistently exercise good-faith efforts to serve the public interest? Do they lead the public to conclude that private interests are consistently favored over and above the well-being of the public body, now and in the future?

Meanwhile we continue, as we always have, to dip up our daily portion of imagery and fantasy from communally available sources. Only a "statistically insignificant" proportion of us keel over with lethal stomach cramps after taking a sip. But this is hardly proof that the supply is free of contamination. Millions of us continue to return for more. This is hardly a vote in favor of the proposition that the present generation and others yet to come deserve nothing better.

18

The State
Is the
Good Guy

The crime-show formula has become so predictable that all the different series merge into a single dramaturgy, a continuing morality play. These shows flood the country's cultural habitat with images of "violence raised to assembly-line efficiency."[1] Routinizing violence in dramas that pass over the human suffering it occasions is a way of numbing feelings of horror, grief, and revulsion. What emerges is "an organic pattern of explanatory violence"[2]—glorifying the state as protector of helpless victims in nightly desensitization sessions the populace has learned to take for granted.

Wrongs are righted, victims avenged, and victimizers awarded their just deserts. The timing is the same, the rhythm, the choreography, the cast, the denouements—everyone has learned just what to expect. On the top of the heap are television's Good Guys, for years mainly mature white males. On the bottom of the heap lie the Victims—piled up bodies of children, old people, poor people, nonwhites, young people, lone women—all done in by Bad Guys recruited principally from the lower social strata many of the so-called victims come from.[3]

THE STARS WEAR CIVVIES

Although the country is inundated on the nightly news with images of cops in action, complete with police cars, sirens, turret lights, helicopters, artillery vans, and uniformed men aiming guns at quivering flesh, it is really quite remarkable that the crime-show formula has featured uniformed cops relatively rarely. The heavy troops of highly organized, mechanized urban warfare in the service of the state are usually relegated to the bit parts. They wait in the wings until the star of the show gets the job done with simpler tools: his own cunning, a handgun, maybe a karate chop. Television good guys are still old-fashioned artisans, skilled craftsmen in the law-and-order game, scorning uniforms and preferring civvies. The uniformed forces appear just for the mop-up job at the end; they snap on the handcuffs and walk the bad guys off the set or load the ambulance that hauls away the corpses mowed down on camera by good guys provoked to take life in order to preserve life.

The 1974–75 television year provides good examples. My count for prime-time shows during that season showed thirty-four hour-long series that the business classifies as "action-adventure" or "crime shows." They all featured good guys who were cops or lawmen, secret agents or private detectives. They all acted out the usual ritual showing law defied, public safety endangered, peace and tranquility threatened, only to be restored by the time the commercial drops the final curtain. Yet only three of these shows featured cops in uniform. "The Rookies" starred three raw recruits, beginners, men who haven't yet learned to be real cops. "Adam 12" featured Officers Reed and Malloy, cruising around Los Angeles; but beneath the buttons and the brass the two men were civilians at heart. "Police Story," an anthology whose cast of characters changes weekly, usually featured a uniformed lead, sometimes did not.

Weekly shows that feature uniformed troops are more likely to be about medics than about cops. The men of "M*A*S*H" wore uniforms, but they're unmistakably civilian doctors who have been drafted. We see them at the job of saving life, not threatening it. The doctors on "Medical Center" wore hospital whites or surgical greens—not uniforms but "career apparel." "Emergency" featured a squad of uniformed men, paramedics on a rescue team. "Sierra," lasting for one brief semester, starred a uniformed rescue squad too—rangers in the National Parks Service.

Television's predilection for these kinds of saviors—cops, detectives, doctors, rescue teams—has an unanticipated consequence. The watching nation is nightly asked to share vicariously the attitudes toward death and suffering characteristic of professionals who deal with them daily. Professionals must learn to distance their own feelings from sympathy and empathy with the agonies endured by sufferers. It's a way of insulating themselves from what would otherwise be unbearable emotion if they allowed themselves to feel in an "unprofessional" way. The watching nation, now, is invited to pick up the same attitudes of distanced uninvolvement.

The rest of the good guys in my prime-time count for 1974–75 —thirty of them—always appeared in civilian dress. Whether employed by the state or in business for themselves, they all summoned the forces of the state when needed. Here are some notes I jotted down as I watched an episode of "Barnaby Jones" on February 4, 1975.

> The fugitive is holed up in the empty warehouse. Police cars close in, scream to a halt. Sirens wail—wah-wah-wah. Turret lights flash, casting an infernal glow over the scene. Now the warehouse

is surrounded, the area cordoned off. From his command position behind one of the cars, the lieutenant deploys the troops. The lone man inside peers through a slit in the blind, sees he's pinned down. The lieutenant (or is he a captain?) raises the bull horn. "You're surrounded," he bellows. "You don't stand a chance. Throw out your weapon and come out with your hands clasped behind your head." Two uniformed and booted men are on the roof of one of the sheds, two more on a nearby rooftop. Two others secure grappling hooks and climb up. All carry weapons. Rifles? Tommy guns? M-16s? The cops scramble around for more strategic positions, hold their guns at the ready, draw a bead on the hiding, sweating, panting, terrified, living target. The angle of vision lengthens the booted legs, foreshortens the torsos. Like ominously misshapen monsters, the uniformed men are silhouetted against a livid sky. Below are deployed the artillery, the heavy equipment, the ladders, grappling hooks, canisters of tear gas, ammunition. Cut again to the terrified man peering through the blind, trembling, naked of arms, alone.

That scene is reasonably typical of the images that these prime-time shows blanket the country with every night. My notes go on to say,

> The scene blends in my mind's eye with the scenes of *Fahrenheit 451*, firemen swooping out in force, barreling down the road in their clanging fire engines, called out to burn the books that a few nonconforming die-hards have tried to hide away in the totalitarian society Ray Bradbury imagined for a future whose seeds are always right here in the present. I find this all very scary.

Small Business in the Private Sector

Barnaby Jones is one of television's many ex-cops turned private detective. Barnaby is old but not a bit old-fashioned. He's clever and modern—with a scientific laboratory in his office. He's agile and a keen shot, outsmarting many a man younger than himself as he saves the victim and solves the crime. The arsenal of the state swings into action when Barnaby gives the signal. The uniformed men, minions of the law, break out the police cars and the helicopters, barrel down to the empty warehouse with the sirens, the turret lights, the radio systems, the guns, the grapples and tear gas and bull horns just for the finale. Then Barnaby turns away with a smile, an aphorism, a wise saying; he and his daughter-in-law link arms and follow the bad guys off the stage set into the sunset.

The final scene as they march off the bad guys always makes me smile. I sometimes keep three television sets going at once so I can see what the three commercial networks are targeting at our homes simultaneously. When the end of the television hour approaches, it's not unusual for my three screens to show the same scene—bad guys, hands manacled behind the back, herded off the set by underlings in uniform while the good guy—it could be Kojak or Cannon or Barnaby or Harry O—winds it all up with a one-liner that establishes his character, his trademark. Kojak's curtain line is a New York–style wisecrack: "OK, sweetheart, haul your tushie out of here." That sort of thing. Cannon reveals something about his gourmet taste. Chief Ironside parries a sentimental ploy with a coolly logical statement of just plain unadorned fact.

The television formula puts lawmen in the private sector to work as small businessmen in a one-man operation with perhaps a family member around to help out. The 1974–75 television season, for example, starred nine private eyes all working in this kind of set-up. Whenever Barnaby Jones was off on the trail of a malefactor, and Betty, his girl Friday, had to go downtown to look at mug shots in the police-department files, the office had to be closed down. (Did Betty pin a hand-lettered sign to the door saying, "Back at 4:30. Slip message through mail slot?") Mannix and his secretary, Peggy, and the Petrocelli couple were all in the same boat. Khan, an inscrutable Oriental, ran a detective business with just his son and daughter as his aides. Rockford worked alone with an occasional assist from his father. Cannon worked without even a part-time secretary or relative on the payroll. Harry O and Dave Barrett ("Manhunter")—loners.

These independents in the law-and-order game operate on a shoestring: small businessmen, but not small-time. They have good connections "downtown"—which is how it happens that an independent operator like Barnaby Jones can mobilize Interpol or get a call through to "Washington," hooking into the vast international network of instantaneous computer information which yields "a make" on anybody. That's how it happens that the state's official troops and heavy artillery turn up in time for the final action just before the last commercial reduces the whole episode to the level of bothersome household germs.

THE CIVIL-SERVICE BUREAUCRACY REPLACES THE FRONTIER SHERIFF

The rest of the lawmen on 1974–75 prime-time television worked for the government directly: city government, like Kojak; state government, like McGarrett ("Hawaii Five-O"); national government, like Lewis Erskine of "The FBI." They were still artisans, though. It was still their own brains, their own brawn, their own highly developed deductive skills that got the job done. The uniformed corps of professionals who unleashed the firepower at the end were supernumeraries summoned by the artisan-craftsman who's just a big old civilian at heart. Sure, he's high enough in the civil-service hierarchy to call the commissioner or the governor by his first name; but he stays a simple fellow, close to the common folk. We heard him worry out loud about his civil-service rating, his cost-of-living bonus, his retirement, reminiscent of the old frontier sheriff who used to be hired, sometimes right on camera, for "thirty a month and food."

The big-city detective has now replaced his brother-in-arms, the sheriff, at stage front and center. Frontier sheriffs used to be the favorites of television's booking agents; but this was the season that the era came to a close, when Matt Dillon quit the job he had begun twenty years earlier and moved over to prepare for syndicated sales, the equivalent of stock-company runs in the boondocks. At the end as in the beginning, Matt was the same country fellow in bluejeans. The only visible sign of office he ever wore was the federal star pinned to his beat-up leather vest; and he always broke the case himself while Chester or Festus minded the store. If a posse rolled up to help Matt out of a tight spot, it always arrived at the last minute, too—just the way the trucks and the police cars and the artillery vans of urban peacekeeping barrel up these days just before the curtain.

When the big-city detective took over as chief exemplar of law and order, even the external symbol of the sheriff's badge disappeared. The police lieutenant or the federal agent in civilian clothes carries his identification as a lawman in his wallet—one more plastic card along with the credit cards and driver's license —and it's all tucked in an inside jacket pocket. Styles range from Lieutenant Kojak, a natty dresser who likes high style; to Lieutenant Columbo, who looks like an unmade bed. Two beautiful women joined up for the first time in September 1974 (Pepper Anderson in "Police Woman" and Christie Love in "Get Christie Love"). Neither would be caught dead in a uniform! A shoulder bag is about as far as either of them would go. Lawmen yes, uniforms no—it's the soft sell and that's the way they book them.*

In February 1975, however, some new ingredients began to

---

*The appendix on p. 341 lists 1974-75 crime and action-adventure shows, specifying whether the protagonist is uniformed or in civilian clothes, and whether he or she works in the public or private sector.

crop up in the crime-show formula. That was when the new series, "S.W.A.T.," spun off from an old series, "The Rookies," made its debut. On the new show, the uniformed men and heavy artillery and precision equipment and firepower were no longer content to stay in the wings, no longer satisfied with the walk-on parts, no longer willing to wait around for the final wrap-up. With "S.W.A.T.", the heavy artillery moved stage front and center. S.W.A.T. is a five-man squad, a precision war-engine. One signal and they're on their feet. Five separate individuals are transformed into the single, synchronized fighting machine that is the elite police unit called S.W.A.T. Five graceful young men run past the gun rack. Each seizes his weapon, dips and swoops, bends and sways; not one breaks step. It's a ballet of uniformed, booted, gauntleted, helmeted young athletes, not a crew of simple civilians at heart who happen to put on uniforms when they go to work just like any gas-station attendant.

S.W.A.T. stands for Special Weapons and Tactics. The men in this elite corps are killer commandos, deploying an arsenal of heavy artillery, precision equipment, and firepower. The real S.W.A.T. team this program celebrates is the special unit in the Los Angeles Police Department which made its own television debut on May 17, 1974. That was when they shot down a band of urban guerrillas who called themselves the Symbionese Liberation Army while the television news cameras rolled, and the whole country watched the spectacle that night on the evening news broadcasts. The entertainment program called "S.W.A.T." yields top billing to the men and materiel of urban warfare. With "S.W.A.T." 's new, stepped-up version of television's ritual crime-show formula, the individual craftsmen of crime move slowly back into the wings to join the frontier sheriffs. With "S.W.A.T." the era of the soft sell has begun to draw to a close.

Television people have a word to describe a scene like the "S.W.A.T." ballet; they call it a "cameo," in appreciation of the craftmanship that permits a world of meaning to be compressed

into the most fleeting image, the tiniest lapse of time. The
"S.W.A.T." cameo of the synchronized, graceful men in the war
ballet appeared every week as the show's signature behind the
title and announcements that introduced each episode. The show
turned out to be ABC's top-rated offering, collecting an average
of thirty-three million people who admitted this show into the
home each week. It was booked for a return engagement in the
1975–76 television year, and maintained, even increased, its coverage. The S.W.A.T. team appeared as dolls for children to play
with and as board games, both nationally advertised along with
toy versions of the S.W.A.T. gear and equipment. There was no
way for this country's population to avoid learning who and
what S.W.A.T. is, what the team does, how it works. The whole
country began to recognize the cast. Many learned to like those
attractive young men; but even those who did not were unable
to avoid learning their slant on the world. After all, that is the
"lesson" in drama—any drama, good or bad. It makes consciousness, heightens awareness. There is no way to say "no" to
an angle of vision.

Congressman Torbert H. Macdonald (D.-Mass.), chairman of
the House Subcommittee on Communications, called
"S.W.A.T." "the worst thing to hit the United States since the
plague." Television critics have written about it as the "blood-
bucket sweepstakes . . . a paramilitary assassination squad that
literally blows people's brains out for an hour a week, in living
crimson." The ominous black uniforms the S.W.A.T. men wear
are "reminiscent of storm troopers."[4]

The show's producers went on record defending it: The uniforms the men wear are actually blue, they just photograph
black, they said. The repeated images glorifying commando tactics and urban warfare are neutralized by lines written into the
script for corrective purposes. Here's a line that says it's too bad
we have to call up so much firepower, but what are we to do since
the bad buys have the same equipment or better and don't hesi-

tate to use it? Here's another line saying that the men of
S.W.A.T. never make judgments themselves, but leave all that to
the state's judicial process—remember, we're a society of laws,
not men.[5] Still another line says S.W.A.T. men never shoot first,
always try to take the suspect alive, follow the commander's
orders.

Aaron Spelling and Leonard Goldberg, executive producers of
the series, were wounded, even puzzled, by the criticisms leveled
against "S.W.A.T." Spelling told *TV Guide* reporter Bill Davidson that he, himself, is a very warm person, called himself "a
bleeding heart liberal," and cited four NAACP awards to prove
it. Mr. Spelling said some of the violent action in the show had
been deleted. He said his staff was prepared to do even more of
the same kind of show-doctoring whenever unorganized television viewers generate enough pressure.*

Predictably, the watching nation tuned in; its best recourse
was to settle back and learn to appreciate unruffled yet another
variation of the ritual of violence perpetrated in uniform by
minions of an ever just, ever vigilant state.

Morality Plays and the Metaphor of Violence

Television's crime-show formula has been around long enough
and has been reiterated often enough to have become institutionalized as a nationwide curriculum. It teaches everyone the proper
type-casting for victims, victimizers, and defenders, always the
essential motif in the "organic pattern of explanatory symbolism."

In real life, these matters are likely to be bafflingly ambiguous.
It's not always easy to tell the good guys from the bad guys and

---

*The series, which ran on ABC from February 24, 1975 to June 29, 1976, includes
thirty-five shows, available now in syndicated sales worldwide.

most people, however admirable or despicable, turn out to be a complex admixture. Violence, itself, like pornography or crime, is not easy to define. The violence an established order exercises in maintaining itself is more easily condoned—even approved— than the same or lesser degree of violence unleashed by those who threaten authority. Most societies—ours is no exception— even define violence and crime one way for the powerful, another way for the powerless. That the "perpetrators" of each kind of violence run different social risks, and are assured different social fates, depends on where they stand in the social stratification system—the society's pecking order.

Such unequal definitions can be maintained as legitimate only as long as there are strong social supports assuring and reassuring the public that the necessarily selective angle of vision is "normal." Essential to this are socially shared, reiterated reminders that after all, this *is* the right way to look at things.

Television provides these reminders repeatedly. The same cloud of images blankets the country every night. As political power shifts, the demographic composition of television's fictional victims changes accordingly, albeit more slowly. One theme, however, remains constant. Against the ever-present danger that continually threatens ever-beleaguered victims, stand the forces of the State. "The State is your Protector, America," is the implicit subtitle appropriate for domestic showings of every one of television's crime shows. Abroad, the wording may change slightly: "The American State is your Protector, world." How right the victims are to acquiesce—even to welcome with open arms—the ultimate authority that unsheaths the most virulent forms of social control as protection!

This is not a matter of anyone's conscious will; it is an organic result of the social conditions that produce and distribute television fare for the purpose of engineering human attention. No matter how stirring the dramatic elements may seem to be at the outset, reducing them to a predictable formula acted out in continuous showings tends to produce placid acceptance, even boredom, in the audience. The easiest solution is to stir them up with attention-getting tricks. For years, violence has done the job, aided by sexual imagery and symbolism that in the seventies become increasingly more explicit, less metaphoric. Neither theme is explored in any serious way, however, with the result (sometimes intentional, sometimes not) that the status quo of existing power relationships ends up getting top billing every time.

The standardization and predictability of it all have so reduced the intensity of our feelings about what we see, and have relegated the social definitions of "good" and "bad" to so constant a background, that in the end, the resolution of the continuing dilemma of stylized victim, victimizer, and protector through state-condoned violence seems perfectly normal, perfectly natural, hardly worthy of serious concern, "just entertainment."

In an earlier day, we called such ritualized dramatizations *morality plays* since they signaled to the community where threat and evil lurked and how to recognize agents wielding legitimate power to suppress them. They provided a way of legitimizing moral authority in entertaining dramatizations rather than dull debates. Such lessons in moral philosophy were entirely accessible to common folk, leaving the disquisitions of theology, philosophy, and law to specialists with the right credentials.

Our modern morality plays, transmitted by machine, are no different. They, too, point the finger at the social strata from which evil emanates and signal the conditions that make it quite proper to shoot, kill, maim, hurt, rip, smash, slash, crush, tear, burn, bury, excise. What starts out as shocking becomes routine then is converted into ritual. Audiences become expert at appraising the virtuosity with which the formula has been worked out yet another time, watching with the detached appreciation of the connoisseur while emotions remain untouched.

If the familiar formula occasionally triggers a few "kooks and deviants" endowed with constitutions so weak that they tend to become infected with aggressive behavior or mental disorder from these shows, the country is reassured that it's really nothing to worry about: "The real issue is how often . . . the real issue is quantitative." If these shows occasionally trigger a few so misguided as to take them as a course of study in literal mayhem, it's a "trade-off." Like bombing your own troops in wartime, it's regrettable, yet worth the attendant benefits—at least in the eyes of those who call the shots.

19

Literacy
Without Books:
Sesame Street*

"Sesame Street" is a quality product turned out with care, fore-thought, and impressive investments of money, time, talent, and good will. Rejected by the commercial networks,[1] the program is as different from materials they broadcast to children as a Mercedes-Benz is from a Volkswagen. In contrast to commercial television's aim to amass as many children as possible into the vastest markets conceivable, "Sesame Street" tries to gather as many preschool children as possible into the vastest nursery school conceivable. Still, while commercial producers may in-clude in their program-specifications virtually any "message" that "works" to attract children to the set, "Sesame Street" may not. Specifications drawn up by the Children's Television Work-shop, insist on only "prosocial" messages, even if it means losing viewers.[2]

---

*Research for this chapter was carried out with the assistance of Azriel Bibliowicz.

"Sesame Street" is produced and distributed by Children's Television Workshop (CTW), which also franchises the sale of Sesame Street products. The first cycle of Sesame Street programs made its debut in November 1969 in this country and the series has been going strong ever since. Nineteen seventy-six marked the eighth cycle in the domestic series: which means that hundreds of these charming programs will have been broadcast and repeated, broadcast and repeated, coast to coast. At least fifteen million U.S. children have seen numerous episodes of "Sesame Street" during their preschool years.[3] The few who may not have seen the shows know about them anyway, having picked up the information from their peers and their general surroundings. One result is that "Sesame Street" characters and the "Sesame Street" slant on learning and on childhood are now entrenched in this country's thought-environment. The program has penetrated the culture of childhood so that three-year-olds who may never have heard of Paul Bunyan, Johnny Appleseed, or Brer Rabbit are almost certain to know Big Bird, Kermit the Frog, and the Cookie Monster.

In these respects, of course, "Sesame Street" is no more and no less educational than any other kind of television program the children watch. The difference is that educators and governments define the series as curricular materials, while the rest of television has not yet been officially approved on so widespread a scale by the educational establishment.[4]

THE CONTENT AND FORMAT

> Sunny day, keeping the clouds away
> On my way to where the air is sweet,
> Can you tell me how to get
> How to get to Sesame Street?

That's the signature song. When that tune comes over the speaker, preschool children within earshot run toward the television screen. They bounce with the bounciness of the tune, hum the melody, sing the words; they rock back and forth, jump or skip in time to the familiar beat. The song tells them the show is about to start.

Each program follows essentially the same format. About forty segments are spliced together to fill fifty-four minutes of broadcast time. About eight of the segments are live dramatic action that takes place on Sesame Street. The rest of the segments are animations, puppet sequences, and film clips that make up the CTW library, now available for worldwide sale and distribution.[5]

The show opens with a street scene. Number 123 Sesame Street is the house in which Gordon and Susan, a black couple, live. Bob, a white man, lives there, too. They are all great friends with each other and with all the people and creatures who live in the neighborhood or pass through it. That includes Maria—a beautiful chocolate-colored teenager said to be Puerto Rican (she speaks perfect unaccented English), Luis—a young Chicano, and muppets and puppets in assorted shapes and sizes. The cast of Sesame Street is integrated in every sense, not only by race, but by species, as it were, with regulars like Kermit the Frog, Ernie, Bert, Little Bird, and Big Bird (who is as tall as Wilt Chamberlain but clumsy and slow-witted).

Oscar the Grouch ("the only grouch on Sesame Street") lives in a garbage can. He is another regularly appearing muppet—a word which collapses "monster" and "puppet" into a single portmanteau word. The charming and fanciful creatures it refers to were created and copyrighted by Muppets, Inc., and belong to that company. The word *muppet,* however, has found its way into the English language and belongs to all English speakers forevermore.

Another regular on the show is Mr. Hooper, the elderly, white owner of a combination general store and candystore. He is kindly, understanding, warm, generous, hardworking, honest, friendly, and helpful to everyone. His store is a sort of central gathering place for the people and creatures of the neighborhood. He is the only character consistently addressed and referred to as "Mr."

Children are seen in some of the segments during each program. Their voices and laughter and shouts are frequently heard off-camera. They are not, however, cast as regulars on the show, and are rarely addressed by name. So far, on "Sesame Street" only the adults, muppets, and puppets have emerged from anonymity.

Each show tells a story about an event which is dramatized on the street. Gordon may star one day, Bob another; or it might be Mr. Hooper or Susan in the leading role. Sometimes there's a guest star like Jose Feliciano or Bill Cosby, Julie Andrews, Judy Collins. The drama of the day is divided into separate segments that are spotted throughout the fifty-four minutes the program lasts. Whatever the problem is that troubles Gordon or Bob or Susan or Mr. Hooper or Big Bird, the conflict is stated, faced, and ultimately resolved to everyone's satisfaction before the fifty-four-minute hour comes to a close. It's the same format the children get used to as they watch "Get Smart" or "Bonanza" or "Gilligan's Island" or "Bewitched"—or any other show on commercial television, for that matter.

What follows is a composite summary of the shows in the original cycles of "Sesame Street."

The scene opens with Gordon sitting on the stoop at 123 Sesame Street. He looks up. "Oh, hi!" he says. "Today the entire hour of 'Sesame Street' is brought to you through the courtesy of the Letter L, the Letter U, and the numbers 4 and 5. But most especially by this letter . . ." Gordon holds up a plastic letter Y and the camera homes in on it. This is what the television business calls a billboard. Since each fifty-four-minute hour of "Sesame Street" is sponsored by the letters and numbers the children are to learn that day, each program begins with the appropriate billboard plug, and ends the same way as the credits roll across the screen in what the business irreverently refers to as "the crawl."

The screen goes blank for an instant—then lights up again and we see an animated yellow bird which flies about, then comes to rest on a tree shaped just like the letter *Y*. "This is the Yellow Yahoo Bird," says an off-camera narrator whose delivery is reminiscent of Marlin Perkins introducing "Mutual of Omaha's Wild Kingdom." "When you ask the Yellow Yahoo if he enjoyed his lunch," the announcer continues, "he answers, 'Yes, quite Yummy; and then he Yawns.'" At each appropriate point, the screen shows the letter *Y*. It grows tall and short, fat and thin, changes its position, its shape, its color. That's television show-and-tell, the special advantage of the medium. Indeed, "Sesame Street" came into being precisely because the founders of Children's Television Workshop had the insight and imagination to exploit this technique to the benefit of culturally deprived children in inner-city slums, particularly the many Blacks and Puerto Ricans who watch lots of television but lack the infrastructure children need if they are ever to learn to read. The sponsor-letter of the day—in this case, the letter *Y*—always gets star billing, dominating stage front and center. Its attractive qualities are detailed, its praises are sung, just as in any real commercial the children see on television shows the major networks broadcast to them daily.

This Yellow Yahoo sequence takes about as long as a sixty-second commercial, a timing and resemblance which is not accidental. CTW started out with the idea of employing the same technique and approach that American television commercials have developed so effectively. According to CTW spokesmen, this approach was in fact "blatantly burgled from the advertising methods of Madison Avenue." The same gentlemen clarified CTW's philosophy of education: ". . . we are selling some basic skills in early education instead of cereal, toys or tooth-paste."[6]

Another founder of CTW, Joan Ganz Cooney, concurred:

An early conclusion of parents and experts who observed chil-dren's watching habits was the fact that the children responded most positively to commercials. They learned to recognize words and phrases long before they actually learned to read because of the simple, direct methods of rhetoric employed in the one minute product commercial. Pace, style, jingles, and repetition are key elements. At the Workshop we intend to employ these same elements to "sell"—if you will—the letters of the alphabet and numbers . . .[7]

It is not surprising to hear CTW staff members refer to "com-mercials" in their on-the-job vocabulary: "Let's plug in the com-mercial for the letter *Y* here and follow it with the spot for the number *4.*"

The next sequence features Kermit the Frog, who says, "We are fortunate today to have with us Professor Hastings, who will deliver a lecture on the letter *Y.* Professor . . ."

The professor turns out to be one of the absentminded variety television programs like so much to show children.[8] "Young man, what am I supposed to talk about?" he asks Kermit. "*Y,*" says the frog. "Because I forgot," says the professor, grossly misinterpreting Kermit's answer. People in the television busi-ness call this a "yuk-yuk" or one-liner, and "Sesame Street" sequences are replete with such gag lines—just like the ones Ted Baxter delivers on "The Mary Tyler Moore Show."

Now comes a brief film clip showing a lumberjack driving a twelve-ton truck into what seems to be a virgin forest. He sizes up one of the giant pines, explores the terrain, sets up his power equipment, and goes to work. The huge pine quakes and trembles as the saw bites through the base of its trunk. There's a groaning, a cracking, a roar; then, "Look out below!" shouts the man as the tree crashes to the ground.

This lesson in directional relations is followed by "Beat the Time." "We present your host, Guy Smiley," says an off-camera voice. (Drum roll, fanfare, and offstage applause.) Guy Smiley, a muppet, strides onstage, grasps the microphone, and gestures to the backdrop behind him, where we see a clock face marked off in sixty intervals, its single hand pointing to the twelve-o'clock position. "You know the rules," says Guy Smiley. "The contestant must answer the question before the hand on this clock makes a complete sweep. And here's our first contestant." (Fanfare and applause as the Cookie Monster shuffles up to the microphone.) "Can you name three things that rhyme with the word, 'rain,' and do so before the hand reaches zero?" asks Guy. "What's the prize?" Cookie Monster wants to know. "The prize is a . . . a cookie!" "Cookie, cookie, me love cookie," says Cookie Monster, loudly smacking his lips. (Laughter and applause.) His first answer is "cane." (Applause.) Now the second answer, "chain." (Applause.) The hand on the clock face is approaching the sixty-second mark. Ten seconds to go. Nine. Eight—but Cookie Monster has not yet hit upon the third answer. (Offstage gasping, muttering, shuffling sounds.) The host is agitated almost to the point of hysteria. "Will he make it? Will he make it before the hand reaches the time limit?" In the nick of time, Cookie Monster turns up with the right answer. It's "train." There he is at the throttle of a train that crashes through the wall of the studio as the offstage audience bursts into loud applause, cheers, and laughter. Fanfare as Cookie Monster demands his prize. Just like "Beat the Clock" or almost any other television game show.

The scene now returns to Sesame Street. Mr. Hooper is explaining to Susan that his sister is ill. Susan (who is a public-health nurse) offers to help. Mr. Hooper says thanks, but he can handle it, he'll call on Susan if he needs her. This lesson in neighborly cooperation is interrupted by a commercial for the number *4*. Again it's television show-and-tell at its best, as we see a variety of different kinds of objects in sets of four. The clincher is a chef carrying four cream pies. He slips, ending up in a pratfall with pie all over his face—just like one of the skits on "The Carol Burnett Show" or on "Tony Orlando and Dawn" or "The Hudson Brothers Razzle Dazzle Comedy Hour."

Now a sequence features Batman and Robin. "Holy vocabulary, Batman!" exclaims Robin admiringly as Batman catches the bad guy and trusses him up for delivery to the forces of law and order. In case there's a preschool child in the crowd who still does not recognize this as a curtain line when he hears it, the curtain is definitively rung down by still another commercial, the by now famous "Sesame Street" counting sequence: one, two, three, four, five, six, seven, eight, *nine,* ten—complete with rock music and light show. Ten spies wearing trench coats and pulled-down slouch hats (like Humphrey Bogart on "The Late Late Show" or Elliot Ness of "The Untouchables"), ten racing cars, ten animated dots, more rock, more light show. Again, television show-and-tell at its best.

And so the show progresses. The drama about Mr. Hooper and his ailing sister builds to its climax and reaches its final resolution just in time for the final curtain of the closing commercial. It's the Yellow Yahoo bird again, again perching on the tree he loves so well because it looks like a *Y.* Again the animated letters, and then the final billboard . . . the crawl . . . the music . . . and the program is over as the off-camera voice announces, "Sesame Street is a production of Children's Television Workshop" and the screen reports that "production funding for Sesame Street has been provided by the U.S. Office of Education, the U.S. Department of Health, Education and Welfare, public television stations, the Corporation for Public Broadcasting, the Ford Foundation, and the Carnegie Corporation of New York. Sesame Street and the Sesame Street sign are trademarks and service marks of Children's Television Workshop."[9] Virtually all the programs in the eight cycles of the series follow the same format.

LEARNING THE LESSON

It should surprise no one to learn that test results from this country and from almost every country in which evaluation studies have been made consistently show that the children who watch the program learn to recognize the letters and numbers and concepts "Sesame Street" tries to convey.[10] After all, it is a common enough observation that even the dullest preschoolers recognize the characters' television features. Children throughout the country know the Jolly Green Giant and associate him with the Niblets he symbolizes for LeSueur industries. They incorporate commercials in their play ("How'd you like a nice Hawaiian punch?"). They recognize Mother Nature and Ronald McDonald and Fred Flintstone and Mr. Clean and Mr. Coffee and Rosie the waitress and Madge the manicurist and Cora the country storekeeper and Mr. Whipple and Mr. Goodwin, and easily associate them with the products they stand for: margarine, hamburgers and fast foods, vitamins, cleaning liquid, filters, paper towels, dish-washing detergent, coffee, toilet paper, and toothpaste. In the same way, of course, they come to recognize the letter Y, just as they recognize the letter S that Superman wears emblazoned on his super-manly chest. They learn the concept *below*, associating it with the tree falling in the forest just as they learn that slow means fast when Steve Austin, the bionic man,[11] races to someone's rescue at eight frames per minute, but slow means slow in the Burger King commercial when the waitress for a rival hamburger chain fills a special order in the same slow motion.

It's just as easy to interest the children in the little dramas enacted by Susan and Mr. Hooper as it is to interest them in the

dramas enacted on the same television screens by the Cart-
wrights of "Bonanza," or Gilligan and his friends, or Louis
Erskine of "The FBI," or anyone else in the long array of
glamorous and attractive stars that enter their lives so frequently.

While it remains to be seen whether "Sesame Street" actually
provides preschool children with the fundamental skills they will
need later to explore the world books and literature can open to
them, it is clear that the series teaches them to read not books,
but television. They learn, for example, to piece together the
day's drama, unifying it into a continuous story in spite of all the
interruptions. This skill will stand them in good stead, helping
them to "read" the commercial television programs "Sesame
Street" in all its versions imitates. The offstage laughter of the
behind-the-scene audience teaches them to "read" the laugh
track that now defines humor all over the world. They learn to
"read" drum rolls and fanfares, voice-overs and pixillations.*
They even learn to "read" what in other contexts would be
puzzling statements directly contrary to lived experience, accepting them as television's acceptable constructions of false experience. Although there are frequent references to colors seen on
the screen, the many children watching black-and-white sets see
no colors. After their first puzzlement wears off, these children
learn to live quite comfortably with the contradiction, just as
they learn to live with television's constant claims that good guys
always thwart bad guys, the law is always on the side of justice,
action is the same as drama, and using this or that brand of
toothpaste guarantees love.

This is a kind of hyperbole that audiences raised on television
have learned to take for granted. It is quite different from fantasy's playful weaving back and forth between a world of imagination and a world of daily experience, thus extending the hori-

---

*"Pixillation" refers to speeded up, jerky movements reminiscent of the silent movies
unreeled just a bit too fast.

zons of each. Television's hyperbole constructs irreality as reality. Behavior that would call down punishment and censure if anyone were to engage in it is demonstrated as perfectly normal and acceptable. Examples: walking into someone's house unannounced; commenting about the odors or dinginess of the wash; frying a loaf of bread in deep fat; discussing publicly discharges from the body's nether regions; exclaiming rhapsodically about the color of the water in the toilet bowl; wolfing down one's food and smacking the lips over it, and so on. Adults who already know the rules can take these nonplayful exaggerations with the necessary grain of salt, even smile at them. For children who have not yet internalized the rules, however, this "puffery" is just as much a part of the curriculum available to them as the catechism, the Scout Oath, and the pledge of allegiance.

The "Beat the Time" sequences on "Sesame Street" teach the children to "read" television's game shows. The featured stars teach the children to recognize not only names and faces, but also show-business categories, such as lead, supporting cast, and extras. The sequences featuring Batman and Robin, Superman, and the rest of television's syndicated heroes, are appreciation courses for beginning watchers of the original programs available on almost every local station in incessant reruns. In addition, they teach the children to "read" the action-adventure and crime-show formulas that advertisers use as electronic envelopes, tucking in the commercial "messages" designed to create public attitudes and consumer needs that can be linked to particular products. Indeed, the programs are themselves full-length commercials, hawking over and over again the kind of world view that is compatible with postindustrial, privatized, consumer-society, complete with "goodthink."[12]

It's all show-and-tell for the consumer society's version of "the good life"—the cars, the planes, the helicopters, the housing patterns, industrially produced foods and music, to say nothing of the electric refrigerators and blenders and mixers and household equipment, all taken as much for granted as standard props on "Sesame Street" as on any sitcom or variety show, any daytime serial or game show, any action-adventure or crime drama or even any animated series booked into the Saturday-morning children's ghetto. As the children internalize these images, they become captive consumers, wise in the lore associated with the many goods and services loaded into the glamorous showcase whose audience is now the entire globe.

What about all those commercials and the sign-off, heard and seen hundreds of times by now: " 'Sesame Street' has been brought to you through the courtesy of the letter *L,* the letter *U,* and the numbers *4* and *5* "? This is a very obvious part of the hidden curriculum; it legitimizes a commercial system of broadcasting that depends for support on purchases of human attention by self-interested people manning institutions with funds enough to afford the expenditure. Practices such as these now determine the culture of childhood to such an extent that when those who are now children reach adulthood, the "normalcy" of this system will be taken for granted. Under such conditions, any future challenge to existing policy is heavily handicapped.

CULTURAL NEUTRALITY

The creators of "Sesame Street" are as aware as anyone else of the hidden curriculum in all educational materials, their own included. Indeed, they had originally turned to television precisely because they were sensitive to the medium's broadly general and pervasively encompassing power. Equally sensitive to the many cultural differences in the backgrounds of the millions of children who make up their target audience, CTW has tried hard to maintain "cultural neutrality" in the programs. Even so, exceptions abound. For example, "Sesame Street" does not hesitate to indoctrinate children about appropriate male sex roles,

"in order to upgrade the black male," explains Joan Ganz Coo-
ley. She goes on to explain further why Children's Television
Workshop decided to indoctrinate them about appropriate occupations for women, too:

> "Our society doesn't need more babies, we need more doctors."
> So she pushed for Susan, who is portrayed as also married but
> childless, to get a job outside the home . . . "The reason we chose
> public-health nurse," said Mrs. Cooney, "was that the medical
> services in this country are going to need more and more people.
> Then, too, we wanted a job with a uniform that little girls could
> identify." Mrs. Cooney likewise remarked in the same interview,
> "We talked about making her a doctor, but it didn't seem real,
> with them living where they live."[13]

In a universe that boasts no perspective-free point, cultural
neutrality is a patent impossibility. One can scarcely show and
tell something without showing it from a particular angle of
vision, telling it in a specific idiom. On the simplest level, all
these programs are show-and-tell for family structure and family relations, food and table habits, household arrangements,
occupational roles, age- and sex-roles, rural and urban behavior
patterns, economic pursuits such as buying and selling and
going to work, ecological policy, fashions in vehicles and dress
and hair styles, health practices, and . . . well, just about everything. It is a contradiction in terms to assert that these repeated
images of culture and social interactions can be divested of cultural content, and the claim that they can be has been challenged by many critics.[14]

The program's hidden curriculum teaches subtler lessons as
well. Show-and-tell depends heavily on the language of time and
space, and CTW productions are outstanding examples of creative use of movement, rhythm, and pacing. This is a language
that communicates a world of significance, especially, perhaps,
to preschool children who are still more fluent in body language

than in verbal language. One set of spatial relations mutely signals importance or intimacy or consent; another indicates that the relationship is distant or consent is to be withheld, or that the goings-on are unimportant, peripheral to the main event. Children must learn the spatial codes for their own culture and subcultures. Play-acting—their own and dramatizations they watch—is essential to this learning.

Nor is the time-sense that we take so for granted inborn in our young. Children in our culture—at least those raised by educators and television executives—must learn to pace their internal rhythms to mealtimes, playtimes, quiet times, nap times, and bedtimes. Children from every stratum in all social systems must grasp what their culture and subcultures mean by long and short duration, proper synchronization of one's reaction time to others, margins of permissible promptness and tardiness under different conditions—all learned. Music and chants, among other rhythms, help synchronize these cultural rhythms and internalize them.[15] This is only one way in which music is no more culturally neutral than any other kind of language.

In consideration of the Puerto Rican and Chicano children in its target audience, "Sesame Street" delivers many musical spots in Latin American style. Guitars are frequently seen and heard; so are *marracas, guiros,* castanets. *Tango, rhumba, mambo, samba, bolero, merengue, danza* rhythms, and so on are frequently heard. American jazz, folk tunes, country-and-western, and rock rhythms and themes are likewise featured, perhaps just a bit more. The ABCs are often sung to the tune of the alphabet melody from Haydn's Variations on an Original Theme of Mozart ("The Alphabet Symphony"). Since no sequence on the show lasts longer than two minutes, the structure simply does not permit introduction of anything more than snatches of music. Thus, the children are never given a chance to see operas or hear operatic music (although sequences may caricature opera), or to be introduced to symphonic music or chamber music or choral music or, indeed, any of the music that up to now has helped to nourish imaginations and set the beat of Western culture.[16] The structure is hospitable, however, to mass-produced and mass-distributed music of the type discussed in chapter 9.

The standard measurements of time that we take so for granted—a twenty-four-hour day, a sixty-minute hour, a sixty-second minute—are socially defined and change from culture to culture, from one historic period to another. In the present historic moment, television is introducing massive changes in the way this whole country—especially children—experiences time, even though they are so ever present and widespread that most people hardly have a chance to notice how these rhythms are changing. "Sesame Street" teaches children the fragmented hour and the fifty-four-minute hour. In this it joins with the rest of American television that fractures time and teaches the fifty-and-a-half-minute hour in prime time, the forty-four-minute hour during most of the day.* It joins, too, in teaching the sixty-second commercial, even the twenty- and thirty-second commercial as entrenched rhythms and rhythm markers. In that twenty- or thirty-second interval, marked by the new, universal metronome, information and images are so tightly packed that we pay only glancing attention to any specific element, "reading" the whole simultaneously in a single, seemingly timeless instant; and as we do, we scarcely notice the absence of opportunity to reflect and consider intellectually what we have taken in emotionally.

In sum, then, along with letters and numbers and relational concepts, the "Sesame Street" curriculum is teaching the culture of the midway impressed into the service of selling products and

---

*In my town, Ithaca, some of the schools now pace the periods in the lower grades in such a way that a twenty-minute lesson period is interrupted by a ten-minute break. This rhythm, reminiscent of the television half-hour, continues throughout the day.

ideas. It is a curriculum that has nothing to do with books or with the culture of books and reading. Not one program, not one sequence in any cycle of "Sesame Street" shown in the United States or overseas, has ever starred a book! The daily dramas on the street have never featured anyone absorbed in a book, laughing or crying over a book, or so gripped by a book that he cannot bring himself to set it aside. No sequence has ever shown a child pleading to stay up a little longer to finish a book, or sneaking a flashlight under the covers to keep on reading after lights-out. People caring enough about a book to risk prison for possessing it or to face death for writing it, even for reading a forbidden book—never! The incessant "commercials" sing the praises of the letters and numbers, but never of books and reading. The set itself, the familiar scene on the street, doesn't even give the children a chance to see books. They never appear among the merchandise in Mr. Hooper's store.

Given the stated intentions of "Sesame Street" to push literacy, its failure to push books may seem contradictory. And yet, is it really so paradoxical? All teachers teach who they are, how they think, much more than what they know.[17] It is only natural for show business wedded to advertising and sales to teach the culture of the spectacle.[18]

In a democratic society, literacy is not a legitimate goal in and of itself. There is, after all, more than one kind of literacy. The literacy that goes with books and literature can free the mind, stretch the imagination, liberate the reader from his bondage to the present, linking him back to all of human history, all of human culture, all of human experience. (That's why we still say "*liberal* education," meaning education that liberates.) But there is another kind of literacy that does not have much use for books. A workforce must read to be able to operate equipment in a modern factory. Consumers must read to decipher the instructions on a package of cake mix. The citizenry must read to be able to fill out income-tax forms and use an automated post office. Automobile drivers must read to find the right exits off the throughway. Even a nation of television watchers must be able to read the listings in the local equivalent of *TV Guide* and to follow all the puffery about the stars, to say nothing of deciphering the streamer across the bottom of the screen announcing, "Mature subject matter. Parental guidance suggested."

20

The Marketing
of Auras

Children are charmed by CTW's programs. They approach the screen, try to pat the cheeks of the characters and caress those delightful muppets. The natural warmth and affection they direct toward the cast, the muppets, the animations, the songs, the music, envelop them all in an aura so real it's almost tangible: tangible enough, in any case, to be packaged and sold by CTW to companies producing a variety of products for sale to the children and their parents.

CTW follows the lead of other television production companies, linking their programs into a total support system of income-producing franchises. Their CTW Products Group licenses over a hundred items for production and sale. This is really small-time, compared with the big operators in the franchising end of the television business; and the CTW Products Group is continually reaching out for more customers;[1] "behind a mask of fun . . . the media is [*sic*] different, the message is the same."[2]

Companies producing CTW tie-in products include massive conglomerates encompassing commercial broadcasting companies, among other subsidiaries, as well as some of television's biggest advertisers. An abbreviated list would feature Random House (a subsidiary of RCA, the parent company of all the NBC interests), Columbia Records (a subsidiary of CBS, Inc.), the Fisher Price Company (a subsidiary of Quaker Oats), the Milton Bradley Company, Ideal Toys, J. C. Penney, Burlington Industries, the Lilly Company, and the Elgin Watch Company.

And it's a two-way street. CTW, in its turn, has made a deal with Marvel Comics, publishers of *Spider-man* (among other comic books) to use that copyrighted character as a CTW regular on "Electric Company," their remedial-reading television show. They use him, as well, in comic-book form, *Spidey Super Stories,* published by Marvel. In both roles, "Spidey" softens up the children not only to "buy" the letters and numbers CTW is selling, but also to buy the original Spiderman series sold by Marvel, as well as the many products licensed by them to use the Spider-man image and logo. These include chewy multiple vitamins produced by the Hudson Pharmaceutical Corporation (owned by Marvel's parent company),[3] which compete for sales against vitamins represented by other television salesmen such as the Flintstones and Bugs Bunny (for Miles Laboratories) and Monster vitamins (for Bristol-Myers).

The stars themselves try to cash in on that CTW aura and sell it to their own advantage. Bill Cosby describes how he makes commercials for Jell-O. "They get about 500 kids in a room before I even get into the building . . . show them me in 'Electric Company' tapes and they watch . . . for the five kids who are most turned on . . . and they grab them and give them to me for the ad. The rest is easy . . ."[4] Morgan Freeman, who portrays "Easy Reader" and other characters on CTW's "Electric Company,"

has played the supporting role in a commercial that gave the lead
to Procter & Gamble's deodorant, Sure. He has also appeared in
a John Hancock Insurance spot singing, "We put our John Hancock on a John Hancock for our family." Harold Miller, who
plays Gordon, has done a commercial for Bristol-Myers' Exce-
drin; Rita Moreno, a regular playing assorted roles, has done a
commercial for Gabrielle Wigs.[5]

Companies that have bought the Sesame Street franchise produce products ranging from toys and games to children's clothes
and bedclothes: books, too, of course—even though many of the
Sesame Street books are not exactly proper books but pop-ups,
comic books, magazines complete with centerfold, and a
"scratch and sniff fragrance book."[6] The companies producing
them can and do take advantage of the export market that overseas sales of CTW programs open up for them, although the
franchising system metastasizes overseas, as well. South American, West German, Brazilian, and French companies are offered
the same opportunity to divert the aura their children invest the
program with, and reattach it to their own products. In Colombia, for example, Sesame Street books are published by
Norma (stationery supplies and publishing). In Mexico it's Dem-
pla and Editorial Navarro (comic books). In West Germany it's
Grunner and Jahr and Inter Valag, subpublishers also for our
own Western Publishing Company products. In France, similar
publishing and franchising deals are sought.[7]

The CTW Products Group cashes in on an aura that becomes
discernible whenever symbols are widely recognized and socially
shared. The franchising arrangements they contract were developed to a fine point in Hollywood's heyday. Walt Disney Productions, creators of Mickey Mouse and friends, did not invent the
system; but they applied Hollywood's technique for mass production and total merchandising of auras to the symbols of childhood. The Sesame Street contribution joins a long parade of
licensed images that now inundate the pool of symbols that

nourish children's imaginations all over the world—a parade led
by Mickey Mouse and his retinue. These charming and amusing
figures and their characteristic ways of behaving and relating to
each other, are, by now, mythic images in the culture of childhood, more powerful and more pervasive even than Mother
Goose, Little Red Riding Hood, Snow White, and the Three
Little Pigs—all taken over by the Disney enterprises and punch-
ing time clocks at the Disney studios.

THE TALE OF THE MOUSE[8]

The year 1928 is a good starting point; in 1928 the Disney studios
began to produce the earliest versions of Mickey and his friends.
Going to the movies was already the nation's most popular lei-
sure-time activity. Movie houses, looking for short subjects to
serve as curtain raisers, immediately bought the earliest Disney
cartoons. The cartoons not only gave latecomers a chance to find
seats before the feature started; as an extra added attraction, they
were popular in their own right.

Walt Disney Productions made sure that any warmth of feeling Mickey and his friends generated in moviegoers would not
cool off by forming a character-merchandising division to keep
those fires stoked. This division sold to manufacturers the right
to stamp the various kinds of commodities they produced and
marketed with images the Disney studios' "imagineers" had
created and worldwide exposure made famous. (The term *imagineers* was invented by Disney, to describe the engineers of imagination on his studio payroll.)[9]

Even as far back as 1941, the aura that surrounded the Disney
images was so powerful that the U.S. State Department did not
hesitate to use it to promote American business interests in Latin
America, underwriting the costs of two full-length Disney films,
Saludos Amigos and *The Three Caballeros,* for that explicit purpose.[10]

As of this writing, the Character Merchandise Division of Walt Disney Productions sells licenses to about a thousand companies. It embraces nine subsidiaries: the Wonderful World of Disney Television Program, Disneyland, Retail Promotions, Consumer Promotions, Disney Motion Pictures, Disney Music, America on Parade, Publications, and the Mickey Mouse Club Television Series.[11]

By the time television opened its first "season" in 1953, raising to a power the number of people in any single audience, Walt Disney Productions was ready to cash in on the bonanza. "Davy Crockett" was the studio's first television series, and the promotions and tie-in sales of Disney's Character Merchandise Division coiffed the nation's children in coonskin caps. International distribution of the motion-picture version, backed up by the division's international arm, ensured that children in other countries would buy the same hats just as they had bought the accoutrements of El Raton Miguelito (Spain, Latin America, and the Caribbean), of Miki Kuchi (Japan), of Topolino (Italy), and so on.

THE TALE OF THE MOUSE CLUB

"The Mickey Mouse Club" has the dubious honor of being one of the first, if not *the* first television program to herd "kiddies" into "markets" through clever programing bulwarked by a merchandising and promotion system. The series, which turned out to be what the television business admiringly calls "a phenomena," opened on October 3, 1955. Prior to that year the commercial television networks had viewed the cultivation of child audiences as an unprofitable investment that could not return major revenue. Programs that attracted children were booked as if they were charitable enterprises. The Disney experience, however, "completely changed the perception of the children's market to one of substantial profit for producers, networks, stations, advertisers, advertisers of children's products and even others with less direct economic interests in children's television."[12] Pressures the FCC might have been expected to exercise to oblige license-holders to transmit to children programs that would do more than turn them into potential consumers certainly never materialized and within a short time, the marketing of children became the accepted rationale behind programing targeted to them.

By February 1956, "The Mickey Mouse Club" had achieved virtual saturation coverage in U.S. television homes. Although only forty million were penetrated by television at that time, the Disney promotional, advertising, and merchandising network guaranteed that a clubhouse with all the trimmings would find a permanent place in every child's neighborhood, whether or not the television set brought the club into each individual child's living room. For example, within just four months after the show opened, thirty-eight companies were already manufacturing, promoting, and selling the "character merchandise" that went with the show—the hats, T-shirts, records, record players, games and board games, balloons, and even "mouseguitars." "The Studio gave the merchandisers as great promotional support as they gave their own publications and recordings. Posters, streamers, banners, logos, insignia, emblems, etc. . . . were distributed and used quite freely by participating companies. Special stationary [sic] for the Mouseketeers was designed." Roy Williams and Mickey Mouse went to the manufacturers' annual Toy Fair, "where Mickey Mouse Club merchandise rated first or second in 67 of 82 general markets."[13]

As sales mushroomed, more and more manufacturers bought the rights to attach to their merchandise a bit of the aura of the Mouse Club symbols—an aura that the love and trust of so many children had endowed them with.

Department stores were the natural habitat of Mickey and the gang. Many set up mock-ups of the Mouse Club stage set as backdrops for store dummies in the likenesses of Mickey, his friends, and the Mouse Club cast. When Mickey Mouse or the Mouse Club cast appeared "in person" at these promotions, so many children flocked to the stores to be near those well-beloved characters, and to buy the merchandise they endorsed, that some were unable to handle the traffic.

The usual intimacy between department stores and the local press helped promote the club, the merchandise, and the values they stood for. Newspapers ran Mouseketeer puzzles and contests, offering trips to Disneyland and Mouseketeer outfits as prizes, arranging "tie-ins" with the production company on the one hand, the stores on the other. At the same time, their news pages bore stories about contestants, winners, and companion events going on in the stores. The stores, in their turn, again, bought advertising space publicizing the characters, the merchandise, and, of course, the newspaper contests. In the trade press, too, news coverage and paid advertising space went hand in hand[14]— a practice known in the newspaper business as a BOM, "business office must."

When the program was revived in January 1975, the press was no less reluctant to act as conduit for the Disney releases. My informant at SFM—the media-buying service placing the revived "Mickey Mouse Club" programs—told me how delighted his company was at the press's red-carpet treatment. "They're besieging us for stories," he said. "It figures. After all, many of those reporters were probably Mouseketeers themselves in the fifties and sixties." And then he added, "That's the whole idea."

The Disney enterprises rely on a system of financing which absolves them of most of the obligation to invest company money on their many ventures. Instead, they turn to other sources which underwrite the major costs. The ABC network was a prominent underwriter of production costs for the original "Mickey Mouse Club," just as, a few years before, ABC had helped underwrite the costs of Disneyland.[15] Trans World Airlines provided transportation, flying the Disney promotional staff on tour around the country in return for credits and plugs on the shows.[16] Talent hunts were combined with promotional tours, and department stores "delivered the children."

Trade and lobbying organizations "joined the jamboree." One series in the original show—nine episodes entitled "Adventures in Dairy Land"—took two of the show's most popular children on a visit to a model farm. Millions of children in the audience accompanied Annette and Sammy in imagination, receiving with them instruction in the fine points of managing a dairy farm, including, as an example of the ultimate in efficient farming methods, demonstrations of cropdusting by chemical pesticides sprayed from planes.

The American Dairy Association liked that series well enough to turn it into a promotional booklet distributed free and widely publicized.[17] Whether the association had any role in planning and designing the original shows is not available to the public record. However, the Carnation Company, one of the largest dairy conglomerates and a member in good standing of the American Dairy Association, was one of the original sponsors of the Mouse Club's first cycle. The Armour Company was another agribusiness conglomerate that used the syndicated show as a package for its commercials.[18]

The first cycle of "Mickey Mouse Club" shows ran every weekday for four years, first as an hour-long program (1955–57) then as a half-hour program (1957–59). It was retired briefly, but reappeared in 1962 when the syndicating arm of Walt Disney Productions began to peddle it here and abroad. An enterprising booker who runs SFM[19] must have noticed the show's staying power (in Australia it had held on for fourteen years).[20] In any case, Stanley Moger of SFM was convinced that the old line of goods was still salable. Although the Disney enterprises include their own syndicating division, The Buena Vista Company, Mr. Moger was able to persuade the Disney people to subcontract booking rights to his agency. They set the date for the return engagement of "The Mickey Mouse Club" as January 20, 1975.

SFM advertised the program's availability well in advance, assuring potential customers that it would be a sure-fire success in "delivering a brand new audience." The original generation of Mouseketeers* were now young adults—"family formation agents." They would, said SFM's ad, "deliver . . . 40 million uninitiated Mouse Club members [who] can come along and sing the song like the original Mouseketeers." The potential purchaser, the advertisement continued, would get more for his money than just the children. "An additional 14 million original members won't be able to resist sneaking a second peek . . . So don't wait. Lead the club into your market . . ."[21]

By the time the program opened on the scheduled date, more than a hundred stations coast to coast had agreed to exhibit it in their areas. By September 1975, SFM reported that the series had been adopted by about 135 television stations, many of them in major markets, with the result that "The Mickey Mouse Club" was being targeted to about 95 percent of all television homes in the country, "equivalent to network saturation of all markets."[22]

The arrangement is profitable to all parties concerned. The film goes free to all stations agreeing to unreel it. Each program runs for twenty-four minutes. SFM reserves two minutes of the film for splicing in their clients' commercials and is paid for this service. Since four minutes are left blank on the film, the local station is at liberty to sell the use of this time to their own advertisers, pocketing the full amount of whatever they collect, plus fees for "intro" and "outro" commercials. And as if this were not yet enough, the station even gets brownie points for scheduling a wholesome children's program rather than a rerun

---

*The program features on-camera children as the regular cast of club members. The host invites children in the audience to join the club. All club members are called "Mouseketeers," and entitled to buy and wear the club's insignia—a pair of Mouseketeer ears.

of "Ironside" or "Mod Squad" or "Mission: Impossible" or any of the crime shows available in syndication, going clear back to "Dragnet."* The national advertisers are happy, too: "The Mickey Mouse Club" becomes a nationwide envelope they can tuck their commercials into, at rates substantially less than they would pay for equivalent network exposure.

This system, widely used in television, is referred to as a barter system. Many game shows are distributed in this manner; as are many so called "access programs" (programs filling the 7–8 P.M. hour Eastern time, closed to network entertainment programs, except on Sundays). Some of these programs are beginning to follow Disney's practice of including the name of the principal in the title, as in "Mutual of Omaha's Wild Kingdom."

The old "Mickey Mouse Club" programs have been culled and edited for this revival, so that as of this writing there are 390 properly cropped half-hours—a very respectable chunk of merchandise, enough programing to keep those "kiddies" with their heads turned toward the screen for a long time to come.

Not just "kiddies" either. SFM's advertisement in *Variety* was quite right about the program's appeal to young adults raised on it. "The demos are terrific," I was told. And I learned the success story of Station WAVE-TV, Louisville, which had scheduled "The Mickey Mouse Club" at five-thirty, as lead-in to their local six-o'clock news. It replaced their former lead-in, which was the last half-hour of one of those old movies local stations are so dedicated to. Quite a daring thing for WAVE-TV to do really, since stations schedule programs that will channel adults, not children, to the evening news. ("The Mickey Mouse Club" is defined, of course, as a children's program.) WAVE's gamble paid off: their ratings showed that the number of young women tuning in to that half-hour just before the news had

---

*Such gems can be saved for the 7–8 spot following network news and preceding network sitcoms.

doubled. The last half-hour of the rerun movie had racked up a twelve rating (12 percent of available sets tuned in). Now it was racking up a twenty-four rating. A real killing, since the television business sees women eighteen to forty-nine years old as their most profitable product. My informant put it this way. "That mouse lead-in delivered a tremendous, high quality audience to the local news!"

With 390 programs in cans, uninterrupted exposure is virtually guaranteed to 1977, at which point a new version of "The Mickey Mouse Club" is scheduled for national and international release, spiked with recycled clips from films stored in the Disney warehouse. Animated sequences and Disney Music's songs, dating back to the studio's earliest productions, will again have a chance to be showcased in these new programs.

The new production updates themes and costumes, vocabulary and speech mannerisms that lend the early, resuscitated series the character of anthropological documentaries. Dress and styles of grooming that were modish in the fifties, turn out to be period costuming in the seventies. Speech mannerisms and idioms, even body movements so natural in their day that they passed unnoticed, now stand out clearly as quaintly dated.

That's the way it is with old films; they make visible what in their day was invisible; and "The Mickey Mouse Club" programs are no exceptions. When "Adventures in Dairy Land" taught the children of the fifties about the benefits chemical pesticides sprayed from planes brought to farming, nobody in the production end of the show considered it important to introduce into the program any doubts about the practice. Nor did any eyebrows go up at the unquestioned acceptance of a farm policy that directly converts grain into milk and meat, feeding it to cattle, not to starving people.

The refurbished series, however, includes the same episodes that will exhibit the same farming practices to the new crop of the nation's children, endorsing them a second time around.

While it is likely that the ideological bias will be visible to more critical viewers today than in the fifties, the three-to-eleven-year-olds to whom the programs are targeted are not likely to be heavily represented in the ranks of the critical.

The show's casting policy makes visible another custom widely practiced at the time but in its day considered unworthy of notice by producers and broadcasters, as well as by agencies responsible for keeping broadcasters honest. The original "Mickey Mouse Club" features an all-white cast. Until the Civil Rights Act of 1964 named it an offense to federal law and to the spirit of the Constitution, this lily-white casting policy prevailed in a business charged by law and by public trust to further the public interest, convenience, and necessity. Only after 1964 did the television business begin to alter its unwritten rules for the show-and-tell that daily validated race prejudice and discrimination before the eyes of the watching nation. But even now this long-standing policy of excluding minorities from view is never mentioned or examined; it is simply expunged from the record exposed to public sharing, quite as if the whole sordid affair had never occurred. This new silence again helps the citizenry avoid confronting the way our most respected institutions nourish the terrain within which race prejudice flourishes. Without such awareness, of course, education in any profound sense about the sources of the insane emotions racial tensions still evoke, is severely handicapped. Here the new "Mickey Mouse Club" follows the lead of the rest of television, quietly "correcting" this troublesome matter of color and mutely claiming no harm done. Just as black-and-white film used in the original cycles gives way to color in the new ones, the all-white cast of the originals gives way to a mixed cast. The new cycle shows the nation and its children what the producers in their wisdom consider "a proper balance" of Blacks, Orientals, and Latins; no more, no less, and no real emotional change.

THE IDEOLOGY OF THE MIDWAY

Using a medium of mass entertainment as a conduit to transmit
to the public a trade association's view of the universe; accepting
the policy implications in what seem to be purely technical
procedures; exposing only white children to public view and
suppressing images of children from all other races—none of
these practices was unique to "The Mickey Mouse Club" or to
television. All existed elsewhere in American society but were
not necessarily accepted by a hundred percent of the citizenry.
Television's complacent acceptance of them, however, is a nice
example of what the Nixon White House called "ideological
plugola,"[23] and what Marx and Engels named "ideological
hegemony."[24] Both terms call attention to the power to distort
culture that goes hand in hand with the power to expose a point
of view to widespread public sharing or relegate it to oblivion.
The points of view of those who provide major financial support
to the channels of public information are in a particularly advan-
tageous position. The BOM practice in the newspaper business
confers that advantage by a deliberate and conscious act. It is far
outweighed by advantages conferred, often unthinkingly, often
unintentionally, by media decision makers who, sharing the sociological position of business executives and public officials, tend
also to share their social practices and viewpoints, to shave the
points of moral scorekeeping in the same, consistent direction.

The system that leads newspaper editors to accept the BOM
leads station managers and producers to accept the hidden commercial. Yet print is print and dramatized appeals are dramatized appeals. Broadcasts do what broadsheets have always done,
but the nature of the newer medium transforms the act. The
hidden commercial's[25] line of descent is more clearly traceable to
the barker and the pitchman than to the newsroom. All advertising has a certain affinity with these hustlers of the midway but
the broadcaster's affinity is especially close. Like them, his prin-

cipal acknowledged function is to collect "the rubes" into a crowd and pass them on to whatever is to be sold—the merchandise, the spectacle, or both.

To an untutored eye, it still seems as if television's official barkers are the commercials; just as barkers used to be stationed outside the tent on the local fairgrounds, commercials still seem to be marked off from the rest of the show by noticeable breaks. But the form evolves as time moves. On television, coattails, fly-by's, and plugola, all surreptitiously slip the barker inside the tent. Game shows do it openly, mixing the merchandise and the commercials together in a single promiscuous spectacle in which the show is the barker and the barker is the show.[26] The franchising system the Disney enterprises perfected, which all of television now follows, completes the cycle. Now the whole show becomes a commercial for itself, its stars, even its own props. It's the spectacle of the pitchman working the most glamorous midway of all times, coast to coast and worldwide.

THE SALE OF THE MOUSE

The success of "The Mickey Mouse Club" revivals is measured in Nielsen ratings which report daily coverage nationwide, and in Arbitron ratings which report coverage in thirty-three metropolitan areas. To these, the SFM people have added their own informal rating system. "We have all those Nielsens and Arbitrons and the demos and all that, but the best evidence of the program's success is the sale of Mouseketeer ears. We call them our 'earbitrons.' "[27] Before the show hit the television screens in January 1975, a Long Island company, which had bought the license to produce Mousketeer ears, was turning out about forty thousand pairs of ears a week. As soon as the show opened, production began to zoom and within two months the company was producing three hundred and sixty thousand pairs of ears— a projected yearly rate of more than eighteen million pairs of

Mouseketeer ears produced by that single company.

Not only sales of ears increased, but sales of other franchised products increased as well: books, comic books, songs and records, modeling dough, bubble toys, jump ropes, stuffed characters, plastic novelties, home entertainment films, card games, board games, musical instruments (including the "mouseguitar"), jigsaw puzzles, gumball banks, dolls, school supplies, lunch boxes, party goods, gift wrappings, sportswear, T-shirts, nursery equipment, furniture, bedclothes, wall clocks,[28] and an updated version of the Mickey Mouse watch.[29] This is a partial list. The same rights are bought and sold internationally, as well.

SFM's hunch that indicators such as "earbitrons" provide more sensitive measures than official ratings is right on the mark. Rating systems make it possible to price audiences, informing the market that advertisers shop in. Measures of merchandise tie-in sales, however, could show the country a sort of barometric reading on what is happening to its patrimony of symbols. They could show the movements of these symbols from the public domain into the domain of self-interested enterprises that preempt them and then sell them back to the public at a price. Readings such as these, which could perform a service informing public policy, are not available; they remain "proprietary information" of the marketers.[30]

Even without the neatly calibrated measures, however, the extent of saturation of the public habitat is unmistakably observable. Almost all producers turning out television programs package and sell the aura that recognition, enjoyment, and widespread sharing create around them. Producers of programs for attracting children take the lead. Hanna-Barbera Productions, whose studios mass-produce most of the animated cartoons booked into American television as of this writing, claim "the largest merchandising operation of its kind in the world. More than 1500 licensed manufacturers turn out some 4500 different products ranging from Flintstones window shades to Banana

Splits bubble bath." They produce cartoons featuring Huckle-
berry Hound, Yogi Bear, and other well-known talking animals
from the casts of television shows which children watch, then sell
the rights to manufacture products in their images.[31]

DePatie-Freleng Enterprises, Inc., a competing studio, sub-
contracts the franchising end of their business. The subcontractor for an ABC series they produce, "The Oddball Couple,"
advertised available licensing opportunities awaiting "manufacturers of quality products and/or their advertising agencies interested in attracting the greatest number of children and teenagers
to their merchandise." The advertisement urges them to buy the
license and "to use the names and likenesses of The Oddball
Couple Stars in their advertising, on their products and in their
promotion . . . For information regarding a Meaningful and
Profitable Merchandising License," they need only contact Sam
Clark Ziv International, Inc. A footnote to the ad announces,
"Please Note: 'The Oddball Couple' stars are available for TV
and Radio Commercials."[32]

"Star Trek,"* "Planet of the Apes," "Pink Panther," the puppets produced by Sid & Marty Krofft Productions, "Bugs
Bunny," "Roadrunner," "The Addams Family"—all join in
franchising deals that go clear back to "The Lone Ranger,"
"Superman," and even "The Howdy Doody Show."[33] Regardless
of which logo they use, the franchised items are virtually identical. Plastic models for the dolls and equipment can be used
interchangeably. Leftover equipment can be repainted and renamed to conform to whatever series is currently eliciting the
heaviest demand.[34]

One of the earliest and perhaps the largest concern that does

---

*"Star Trek" fans have a nationwide organization. The "Trekkies" (as they call them-
selves) hold conventions, get together, and exchange memorabilia and mementos about
these old programs. In this way, organized like movie fans into fan clubs, they become
an even more concentrated available market for still more memorabilia and mementos.

nothing but sell rights to use the aura surrounding symbols is the Licensing Corporation of America. Its chief executive estimated the total take from such sales as over four hundred million dollars—and that was back in 1966. In that single year, the Licensing Corporation grossed at least one hundred and fifty million dollars, selling the aura surrounding Batman and the props associated with him. Other characters and shows whose auras are peddled by this firm include Superman, "Star Trek," Aquaman, and James Bond.[35] A companion licensing firm, Columbia Pictures Licensing, places ads signed by "Not Needy, Just Greedy! Honest Ed Justin."[36]

Up to now, licensing companies have acted mainly as middlemen and brokers, arranging to unite salable auras with salable commodities. The next step is already visible—creating commodities for the purpose of taking advantage of the existence of those salable auras! This turn of the screw is credited to a man who used to run an ordinary licensing business like Honest Ed Justin's. Mr. Stan Weston had the foresight to see the opportunity, and forthwith established a new firm, Leisure Concepts, "which develops new products designed to take advantage of well-known names . . . he now works with many of the licensing companies that were once his competitors."[37]

Children all over the world can watch the new, improved version of "The Mickey Mouse Club," just as their parents watched the old. They can watch "Sesame Street," just as they watch the rest of this country's television exports—"Bonanza" and "Gunsmoke" and "The Lone Ranger," "Batman" and "Gilligan's Island," "The Carol Burnett Show," "The Mary Tyler Moore Show," and several generations of "Lucy" shows; "The FBI", "Mission: Impossible," "Mod Squad," "Dragnet," "The Untouchables," "Dr. Kildare," "Medical Center," "Marcus Welby, M.D."—the list is almost endless. They can watch "Kojak" and "S.W.A.T." and "The Flintstones" and "Planet of the Apes" and "The Oddball Couple" and all the other spinoffs of spinoffs. When they turn off the set they can buy dolls, games, and toys made in the likenesses of the shows and the stars. Kenner sells dolls in the likeness of the Six Million Dollar Man and his consort, the Bionic Woman, along with replicas of Donny and Marie Osmond and the entire cast of "Star Trek," plus their gear. Mattel sells replicas of the entire "S.W.A.T." cast plus *their* gear. Mego pours its polyvinyl chloride polymers into molds which shape dolls in the image of Sonny and Cher Bono, and promotes them along with the appropriate costumes and "play environments" to fit them in. Ideal buys the right to call its baby doll Joey Stivic and advertise it as Archie Bunker's grandson. Hasbro specializes in paint-by-number sets that reproduce scenes from "Star Trek," "The Flintstones," "Superfriends," "Batman," "Casper," and "Scooby Doo."

Franchise buyers urge upon children scores of games that engrave these programs, characters, and scenarios indelibly in their minds. The Addams Family ("If you win, you lose"); Fat Albert and the Cosby Kids (Object: to be the first to get the gang together); The Flintstones (Object: first to get home from a vacation wins; turn the disc and draw the Flintstone Family with "Rotadraw, winner of the educational toy of the year award"). They can play Kojak in The Stakeout Detective Game (Object: players, attempting to pinpoint the culprit's whereabouts, dispatch prowl cars, stake out buildings, obtain tips from informers). They can play Six Million Dollar Man (Object: your job is to prove you are Six Million Dollar Man. The computer-spinner reads out your moves and gives you the power to handle assignments for NASA, Interpol, and the CIA).

When they are not buying replicas of the shows and stars, they can buy replicas symbolizing the companies that purchase the audiences assembled by the shows and stars—replicas of McDonald's fast-food stands, of Kentucky Fried Chicken, Pizza Hut, Holiday Inn; of trucks and service stations bearing insignias of Gulf and Exxon and Shell; and they can even buy a King Oil game that sends them off in imagination to search for oil to augment the holdings of one or another of the international energy conglomerates that are among television's major advertisers.

Television's sophisticated versions of games children and young people used to play spontaneously are now mass produced and mass marketed. Concentration is in its eighteenth edition, Password in its fifteenth, Jeopardy in its eleventh. Beat the Clock and Musical Chairs and Twenty Questions—all games created and developed by the folk culture, have been preempted, industrially produced, and sold back to their own creators. Turning play over to the industrial process in this fashion has enriched, among others, the Fisher Price division of Quaker Oats; Kenner Products and Parker Brothers, both subsidiaries of the General Mills; The Aurora Corporation, a toy company that is a subsidiary of Nabisco; Wilson Sporting Goods, owned by Pepsico; Creative Playthings, owned by CBS; and the Elmex Company, owned by W. R. Grace.

When the children are not watching the shows, studying the stars, or playing with these dolls and games, they can sleep on sheets stamped with the same symbols. They can wear them as signs upon the bosoms of their T-shirts, bind them as time pieces on their arms. The songs they sing, the music they dance to, the rhymes they chant, the games and toys and puppets and dolls they play with, the foods they eat, the fragrances they sniff, their vitamins and medicines, candy and chewing gum, clothes and furniture and coloring books—all, all, all, all act like sausage casings which do not themselves nourish, but concentrate and bind together the stuff that does. All these commodities, now, collect and concentrate the auras that surround symbols, and feed to children the very stuff that nourishes their minds.

THE MOUSE CLUB HYMN

The SFM advertisement announcing the return of "The Mickey Mouse Club" reminded potential customers that the new crop of children waiting to be developed into a market would "come along and sing the song like the original Mouseketeers." The legally copyrighted title of the song the advertisement refers to is "The Mickey Mouse March." It is a catchy tune, so widely known that Army recruits who learned it when they were children during the program's first cycles, sing it as they march, keeping step to its rhythm. With the revival, the song has turned into more than a marching song. Reporters and columnists publicizing the show's reopening often referred to it as "The Mickey Mouse Hymn;" and one of the *Washington Post*'s syndicated columnists nostalgically reminded ex-Mouseketeers that Mickey Mouse "asked for our allegiance, our devotion, our reverential love—and he got it."[38]

To generations socialized in a different era, the comment seems nothing more than an amusing turn of phrase. But time still moves. Reverence and veneration must always be generated anew in the newly born. They come into being through some mysterious interaction that takes place when as yet unformed generations repeatedly bask in auras emanating from ever present, widely shared, socially validated symbols.

Art, drama, music, stories, play, and games are symbolic environments for imaginations to wander in, with no coordinates in physical space. Television has taken over these invisible, ephemeral, intangible environments of enchantment, entering its own versions electronically into every neighborhood, every home. A total support system makes these symbols palpable through a process reminiscent of the spells in fairy tales. The victims of enchantment yearn for whatever object the eye first lights upon. The instantaneous marketing system television has brought into being makes the object so easy to acquire that virtually no one can avoid the temptation. It is the victims, in fact, who fill their own surroundings with talismans bearing the images of the sorcerers who have cast the very spells which hold them in thrall.

So thoroughly has television saturated the environment we make and share with one another, that nearly every child born in this country is inescapably immersed in its symbols during the most formative years of infancy and childhood. What will happen to the body movements and body rhythms of these children, their facial expressions and their emotive use of language, their dreams and their fancies and their fantasies? Will all converge toward some Universal Mean? What are the symbols that will then call forth their "allegiance, devotion, and reverential love?"

Nobody knows the answer to such questions. Still, it does not take much wisdom to see that what is going on right now is a kind of cultural imprinting that was science fiction when Huxley wrote *Brave New World*[39] two generations ago. Was his insight actually foresight?

The answer is not determined. Human social development is not fixed, not immutable, not beyond human control. Still, for any society, any culture, there is a point of no return. The "imagineers" have already dominated the thought environment of the country's first television generation. No society based on reason and democratic forms of control is likely to survive equivalent domination a second time around.

21

Command/Obey.
Thought/Imagination.
Ford/Disney.

This whole book about American television has scarcely mentioned television journalism. Television's coverage of news and public affairs, even its reporting of the key democratic process, the orderly change of government through elections, has been passed over. This is not to deny that television has played a major role in the political and civic life of the nation. Quite the contrary, it has already brought about perhaps irreversible changes in this country's political coloration. But the major changes begin with standardizing the terrain of imagination. Compared to this, whatever shifts in civic life, politics, and government may have been occasioned directly by broadcasts labeled "political," "informational," "news," "public affairs," or "documentaries," have been less clear-cut and more transitory.

No independent reporter accompanies the spaceship *Enterprise* as it tootles along the galaxy colonizing planets or leaving them alone according to the whims of Captain James Kirk. Not a word gets back to earth about these exploits except what the captain and a few chosen members of his crew see fit to pronounce—a state of affairs the program takes for granted. The millions of children who watch these dramatized tales over and over observe the consistent exercise of military power that goes on unchecked by the protests of any opposition. The lesson they learn here can constitute as grave an injury to love and respect for a free press and an open society as did the Crown's laws against seditious libel, in whose name John Peter Zenger was thrown into a colonial jail in 1734.

COMMAND/OBEY

Governments can govern only if people are governable. What makes them so is a state of mind. Access routes to minds go through the pathways of imagination, terrain in which ideas, images, and symbols dwell. In this country, the access routes are congested by now with ideas, images, and symbols that have come to us through the television screen. They govern us more than we know.

In the institutions we call *government,* power-wielders sit in visible seats of command. They expect to be obeyed. It is willing obedience they wish for, since their right to wield the power they exercise over others rests—they are deeply convinced—on proper legal, moral, and ethical rules of conduct rooted in community traditions and shared by all right-thinking people. When the populace feels the same way, willing obedience follows and the social order is stable. When such claims to legitimacy are widely and publicly questioned, challenged, denied, the established social order loses stability. Violent controls replace social controls. *Government by tyranny,* we say, *government by terror,* as if all that were involved were a simple substitution, harsher forms of control replacing gentler ones. Whenever sheer might unseats moral authority as the basis of power, however, a whole new social equation emerges and terms like *oppressors* and *op-pressed*, rather than *governors* and *governed* are more apt.[1]

Social life is riddled by innumerable command-obey relation-ships and our lives are governed by more than the institutions we call government. No matter where the command posts are set up, the same kind of dialogue goes on between the powers that shape our lives and the rest of us whose lives are shaped. When we feel that it is all in the name of law, order, morality, tradition, right, justice—when we feel this way in our bones—everything seems right and natural. Commands are virtually unnecessary—just a few reminders do the job.

In an orderly social system, command over most governed aspects of our lives rests on the sort of legitimacy that is so widely acknowledged, so taken for granted, that compliance seems natu-ral. Willing obedience is easy to come by when people have the idea that most of the rules they live by are either expressions of their own will or the will of nature rather than those of manmade laws and social conventions—or, at any rate, that they dovetail with them. Under such conditions, it's easy to lose sight of the many command-obey relationships that govern behavior; their dominion goes unnoticed. Nevertheless, they are still there, ready to be called to consciousness. What philosophers have called "the social contract" is one aspect of this.

The upshot of it all is that something seemingly as tenuous and ephemeral as ideas that get inside our heads and feelings that get inside our bones turn out to be the ultimate locus of social order and social control.

THOUGHT/IMAGINATION

Imagination and thought are inseparable. There is no way to think without calling up imagination. No idea, no opinion, no conclusion, political or otherwise, is self-evident. To arrive at enlightened and responsible judgments a person needs to *take thought* about his lot. Taking thought, we actually take our thoughts in imagination from one part of the world to another, from the present to the future, then back into the past. We try out conflicting views, alternative outcomes: "What if it were like this instead of like that?" To say, "I have this opinion," or even, "This I know," is to say, "My wanderings have come to rest." Let something happen to send my thoughts on new excursions, and my opinions can change. Even what I call *knowledge* can demand revision. These excursions in imagination are the source of what Kant called "an enlarged mentality," essential, he said, to political thinking; for without it no one can truly get to know his own interests, no one can make responsible choices.

Political thought, no less than any other kind, takes place in imagination. In imagination we move around the social system so that we can peer at social reality first from this vantage point, then from that one, each time taking our bearings from the different slant. In this way we manage to close in on social reality even though, in fact, it is always moving and refuses to be pinned down.

Political thought is representative: it is in imagination that the representation occurs. I form an opinion as I consider something from many vantage points, not just my own. I make present to my mind the standpoints of those who are absent. In this sense, I *represent* them in imagination. The absent ones include even unborn generations who will harvest tomorrow whatever grows from seeds I and my cohort on earth's surface sow today. It is a harvest I can only imagine.

This representative and discursive quality of thought is what Kant's term, *enlarged mentality,* referred to. It is quite different from the unconsidered opinings we often pronounce without having reflected on other points of view—for example, when a public-opinion pollster comes to the door.

Only where the citizenry has had ample opportunity to develop an enlarged mentality can representative democracy exist.

Without it, the vote is a ritual. Without it, we yield up our uniquely human prerogative of freely and consciously making the history that makes us. Yet, the essential conditions for developing it are not easy to come by. I live my life, not yours. My place in the social system is here, not there. How can I get a squint at social reality as you see it so that I can consider your view as I evaluate my own?

Moving from one corner of the social system to another does it in part—and to that degree, social mobility enlarges mentality, in the Kantian sense. Some shifts of social place occur automatically in almost every social system: the social terrain a child lives in is different from the one grownups live in. Since all of us move from childhood to adulthood, just plain maturing shifts our viewpoints accordingly. In this country, occupational shifts, regional shifts, shifts in economic well-being—all these kinds of social mobility give us a chance to learn at first hand what life looks like, indeed, what it *feels* like, in yet another neighborhood of the social system.

It is, however, beyond human capacity to visit certain neighborhoods of the social system in the flesh. John Howard Griffin managed to change the color of his skin from white to black; in this way he learned at first hand what it feels like to live on the wrong side of our social system's color barrier and what our neighbors over there see as they look across it.[2] Robert Cowell even made a transexual shift, moving from husband and father to Roberta Cowell, single woman.[3] These sorts of wide swoops around the social system, however, are beyond the reach of most of us. Yet, even though we cannot do what John Howard Griffin and Roberta Cowell did, we can and do observe other social fates through the lives of people we know: our family members, friends, associates, neighbors. Still, however well we may get to know their lot, we cannot live their lives—except in imagination. It is in imagination that we can look at social reality as they do, feel what it would have been like had their social fates been our own. For most of us, this does not effectively enlarge our mentalities by very much. Most of the people we get to know well tend to be those whose social fates are close to our own. Most of the time, our spheres of circulation are quite limited. Then, too, since we usually feel more comfortable in the company of the like-minded, it suits our taste to gravitate toward them.

There are even further limits to the social terrains we have a chance to get to know at first hand. Neighborhoods in social space, no less than those in physical space, change through time. If John Howard Griffin were to repeat in the seventies the exploration of race barriers he undertook in 1959, historical changes would cause him to regard things from a somewhat different angle of vision; he would surely have different social experiences and different ideas and feelings about them. Since things change, understanding a social situation always requires some kind of historic backdrop, a context broader than just the momentary present to which we are always confined. There is only one place we can make history present to our minds: in imagination.

These imaginary travels through the social terrain are not idle wanderings. They are highly political. To be politically conscious, I must be conscious of my own social condition; but this can occur only if I have the opportunity to survey and resurvey a good part of the social terrain beyond my own little corner. I become aware that I am hungry by the peristaltic action of my stomach; but that my life is poverty-stricken I can know only by being able to cast up my lot against the lives of others. A young wife grieves when her husband dies of black-lung disease; but unless she becomes aware that other men who live and work in different social conditions enjoy longer and healthier lives, how can she even begin to think about the social injustice her husband's death represents? Just *suffering* hunger, just *suffering* the ravages of the miner's disease—that's very poignant, but there is no way to make a reasoned judgment about either until the raw materials of the sheer happenings are transformed into some kind of social equation. Their social meanings emerge as we imagine the situation as it could *otherwise* have been. We can imagine that *otherwise* only by learning how our own fates compare with the fates of others whose lives *are* otherwise. It is this contrast that gives us our bearings in social space. The *otherwise,* being contrary to fact, can exist only in imagination. Representing in imagination the conditions that govern other people's lives, turns out to be the only way we can become aware of the conditions that govern our own.

Thus, there is nothing more political than the opportunities a social system holds out to its members, permitting and encouraging them to live in imagination the lives of others whose fates in the social system are otherwise. Literature and art, drama and music, song and story, ballads and rhymes and chants, tales and play and games, myth and history help us do this. When they are authentic, they help us see and feel the many human conditions that make up the human condition, and thus to realize our own. When they are inauthentic, they muddle thought, drop a veil between us and our fellow human beings, disguise our own social realities.

THOUGHT IS SOCIAL

Thought is social. It takes place in imagination; art and music, literature, drama, and history are essential to it. They are politically important. These claims are quite contrary to today's conventional wisdom. We like to think that we deliberate over our decisions in the privacy of our minds and that our behavior is a consequence of such calculation. The world out there is a huge data bank; we scan it for relevant factual information, process the pros and cons of perceived alternatives, then come to a conclusion that leads to voluntary action. Some of us know a lot and do this skillfully; others know less and are less skillful; but the data and our modes of processing them are essentially the same.

If that were the whole story, then, to realize our own social condition, we would need principally factual data and a computer-like intelligence. The baldest facts about the distribution of wealth would let me know that I am poor; the most unadorned morbidity and mortality statistics would let the miner's wife realize that her dead husband has been robbed of years of life.

This model of what thinking is lies at the root of the ideal we call *objective news.* We count on it to feed to us stay-at-homes the relevant facts that let us know what life is like throughout the social terrain, especially the parts we and those we know never get to in the flesh. The press's job is to survey and resurvey this terrain on our behalf and enter the factual data to be observed there into society's public journal. *Mass media,* we say. The term makes it easy to forget that what today we call *mass media,* we used to call *the press,* and that *the press* includes much more than what literal presses turn out to be read. It includes as well everything the figurative presses of radio and television turn out. *Journalism,* we say; and to journalism we assign the task of making public—*publishing*— the daily journal of purely factual truth about the many realities that together make up the human condition. There is the data bank, we say. Each individual scans and analyzes it according to his own needs, interests, and capacities, and in this way comes to know social reality. Objective journalism refurbishes the data bank as needed, providing it with the factual information which it is up to the rest of us to retrieve as we can and as we will.

The model is spurious. Even if journalism were diligently and accurately to make public all the relevant vital statistics, not many miners' wives are equipped to discern in the raw data their significance for widowhood. This is not unique to miners' wives, nor does it reflect a deficiency of brain power. Such discernment requires study, and most people—those who make it a point to follow the news regularly in newspapers, radio, and television, as well as those who do so casually—seldom devote serious *study* to the factual data these sources report. We scan our newspapers, we skip a lot, we misread. Radio and television news get only our divided attention. The sources, themselves, are deficient, hastily put together under the pressure of deadlines. These are scarcely favorable conditions for learning social reality. It is not in this manner that realization dawns.

Certainly society needs the record of the factual data journalists do their best to report. Without even their partial truths, we should never find our bearings in a bewildering hodge-podge of happenings, some behind the scenes, some beyond our range of sight. The journalistic record is, so to speak, a first draft. History is waiting, after all, to correct it. Meanwhile, what individuals can and do learn correctly from daily journalism is what comes to us with no study at all. We learn the repeated and repetitive patterns and rhythms that hit our eyes and our ears every day. You can see the Dow-Jones stock-market index in the financial section of the daily newspaper and hear it announced on daily radio and television news broadcasts; but the value of each day's index is not likely to impress itself upon your consciousness for more than a fleeting instant. Nor are you likely to learn in that manner what the index means or how it is made or why it is drawn up or who concocts it. Without any study at all, however, we all learn the inescapable lesson of Dow-Jones; that it is always news and worthy of space in every major newspaper, just as it is worthy of time at the close of every network news broadcast.

Editors making these decisions follow a simple convention of the news business, and not a very old one, at that. It could be otherwise; news broadcasts could just as easily close some other way. If it must be with an index, it could still be otherwise—an index summarizing fluctuations in the occupational correlates of selected diseases, for example. Black-lung disease might be one of the disorders figured in the average. Why not? Epidemiological information is available and most of us get sick more often than we buy and sell stocks. The matter, however, is not problematic, so it's still the Dow-Jones every night. Familiarity and patterned regularity make it easy to take for granted that the one index is worthy of public attention while the other is not.

It is difficult to remind ourselves about such conventions, so easily do they slip away from the forefront of awareness. Anything that occurs with such frequent and patterned regularity commands but glancing attention. Surely, when the Dow-Jones first began to be published, many newspaper readers must have raised an eyebrow, wondering whether it made any sense at all. Today, after decades of its regular appearance as news, it seems right, normal, natural. If we were asked to justify the practice, I suppose many of us could probably think of three good reasons why this index merits the attention news editors invite the nation to bestow upon it. It is not at all certain that the reasons would have sprung so readily to the minds of the first Dow-Jones generation.

Thus does "objective journalistic reporting" of the Dow-Jones convey to us not so much the factual truth of each day's stock-market transactions, but rather the conventional judgments the nation's editors make that these transactions are news and that this index communicates it. It is sociology that impresses itself upon our consciousness, not econometrics.

The principles behind conventions like these do not, themselves, emerge from considered evaluation of factual data, either, but from socially determined and socially shared axioms that go unnoticed: articles of faith. Widespread social sharing disguises this at the same time that it validates and revalidates their legitimacy. Even if it should occasionally cross the minds of some—a miner's wife, for example—to wonder why editors bother to give the nation a daily report on the well-being of the stock market but not on the well-being of our fellow men, just looking around and observing everyone else seemingly accepting the rightness of it all is usually enough to get the doubter to dismiss her own doubts. This happens even though it may be contrary to her interest to continue thinking the same old way.

REFLECTIONS FROM THE EYES OF OTHERS

The long-running television series, "Mission: Impossible," exploits this insight. The good guys always manage to get the bad guys to act voluntarily against their own interests, simply by reflecting back to them a social reality that happens to be false. The movie, *The Sting,* uses the same formula. Here, again, the good guys falsely define the social reality the bad guys are plunged into. In charge of deception in *The Sting* is a pair of experts in the confidence rackets. Since time immemorial, con games have worked the victims by reflecting back a false social reality that those "in the know" only pretend to believe in. In the face of their continuing validation, the victim quiets his own doubts and voluntarily plots his course. Since, however, he can only take false bearings, he ends up behaving the way the con men wish.

In these examples, what is at fault is not the victim's processing of factual data, but erroneous social verification of his quite accurate ideas about what the factual data conventionally signify. It looks like a betting parlor, everyone in it acts as if it were a betting parlor, it conforms to his own past experience of how a betting parlor functions, everyone calls it a betting parlor, no one questions his behavior when he acts the way people usually act in a betting parlor. Why on earth, under such circumstances, should any right-thinking person bother to check whether the telephone lines actually connect to the track where the race is being run? That the victim has been deceived is clear; but has his behavior been commanded by others or by the ideas inside his own head, the feelings in his own bones?

Something similar occurs in all the command-obey relationships that riddle social life, quite without any deception or intent to deceive. We can never act by scanning *all* the facts, *all* the events, *everything*. That would add up to what sound engineers call white noise, sound and fury signifying nothing. Facts and events must be arranged selectively for us or we see only chaos. Human perception can pick out only patterns; it is the patterns that convey information, never "pure" factual data unarranged. Most of the time, when we see familiar patterns, we take it for granted that the information they convey is the same information they have always conveyed, and we act as we have always acted. As long as others around us seem to see the same familiar pattern, acting as if they, too, take it for granted, we feel no need to seek further verification. Most of the time we gauge social reality by seeing our own ideas of it verified in reflections that come back to us from the eyes of others.

We "take an idea into our heads." We "feel in our bones" that something is real. But our ideas about reality have their existence just as much outside us, in society, as inside us, in our heads and in our bones. It is their reflection and refraction back and forth between ourselves and others, the continuing social validation each provides for the other, the familiarity of patterns we recognize and everyone else does, too, that lend the social reality we know its taken-for-granted quality. In making social patterns recognizable and familiar to most of us, artistic and symbolic sources command a good measure of power over us—over our heads and our bones.

Television now holds a virtual monopoly on whatever artistic and symbolic forms have a chance to be widely shared throughout the society. All the images, all the tales and ballads and chants and songs and stories that come through that screen, show-and-tell aspects of social reality that then become familiar to all. The show-and-tell machine does this job in ways that everyone can effortlessly grasp. The same images and symbols are always there, beckoning and signaling invitations that are inescapable to slip over to the corners of the social terrain *it* selects, to look at the social reality *its* angles of vision reveal. It is in this way that television comes to dominate social thought; less because its journalistic efforts provide a data bank of what we take to be the factual truths about government and politics and civic life, and more because its total efforts monopolize the socially shared lines of sight for surveying social reality and making things familiar.

MEANING IS INVESTED; IT STARTS EARLY

Scanning a data bank "out there," processing the facts, calculating alternative outcomes, reasoning things through to a conclusion—such a model of how thinking occurs assumes training, skill, knowledge, intellect, caution, reflection, control. They are qualities which cannot come into play until human beings reach a certain level of maturity; nor do all human beings possess them to the same degree. Yet, to say we do no thinking unless and until they are present on the scene is contrary to lived experience; and to say that those who rate an A for these traits feel and act with greater wisdom than those who merit lower grades, is contrary not only to lived experience, but also to history, conscience, and the principles of democracy.

Human beings get ideas, take thought about them, and act thoughtfully upon them, beginning with the earliest glimmerings of consciousness. From the moment of birth, we are bombarded by signals in the social environment that suggest to us the reference points by which significant forms and lines, behaviors and feelings, can be recognized, their patterns picked out of randomness. These signals suggest the very categories that enable us to think at all. From the moment we begin to receive these signals, they enable us to make distinctions: making distinctions, selecting the meaningful categories, is the first step in thinking. Grasping the categories and thinking are not two separate events; they are aspects of the same thing as two sides of a coin are aspects of the same coin.

Most of these signals are caught rather than taught. They come to us unwittingly. Regardless of anyone's intent, without any effort, they lodge themselves in our minds.

Minds, not brains. Everyone is born with a brain; ours is not much different, after all, from the brains of our closest evolutionary ancestors. But the organ of thinking we call *mind* begins to develop the moment these signals from the social environment start to break through to us. They begin with symbols and lines and forms and sounds and rhythms that have been organized into patterns which members of our particular human group consider meaningful.[4] These symbolic arrangements of reality are always present in all human environments, they register themselves throughout the span of a human life. They speak to all human imaginations in some kind of primal way. We respond to them in the manner appropriate to whatever level of intellectual and emotional development we have reached. There is always something here for the best of us and the worst of us, the most mature and the most infantile, the brilliant and the dull, the young and the old.

It is always true of the human condition that whoever shows what is, shows an image; and whoever tells what is, tells a story.

Television, the ubiquitous show-and-tell machine, saturates the thought-environment with images and stories it selects, and wigwags their significance to so many of us at once, that the meanings coming through its screen become known to all. They install themselves in the places where human beings store their imagery: in imaginations. There they reside as models forming the categories of thought that make thinking possible. It is minds they make—and minds are always in the making.

FORD/DISNEY

INFANT NURSERIES. NEO-PAVLOVIAN CONDITIONING ROOMS, announced the notice board.

The director opened a door. They were in a large bare room, very bright and sunny; for the whole of the southern wall was a single window. Half a dozen nurses, trousered and jacketed in the regulation white viscose-linen uniform, their hair aseptically hidden under white caps, were engaged in setting out bowls of roses in a long row across the floor. Big bowls, packed tight with blossom. Thousands of petals, ripe-blown and silkily smooth, like the cheeks of innumerable little cherubs, but of cherubs, in that bright light, not exclusively pink and Aryan, but also luminously Chinese, also Mexican, also apoplectic with too much blowing of celestial trumpets, also pale as death, pale with the posthumous whiteness of marble.

The nurses stiffened to attention as the D.H.C. [Director of Hatcheries and Conditioning] came in.

"Set out the books," he said curtly.

In silence the nurses obeyed his command. Between the rose bowls, the books were duly set out—a row of nursery quartos opened invitingly each at some gaily-coloured image of beast or fish or bird.

"Now bring in the children."

They hurried out of the room and returned in a minute or two, each pushing a kind of tall dumb-waiter laden, on all its four wire-netted shelves, with eight-month-old babies, all exactly alike . . . and all (since their caste was Delta) dressed in khaki.

"Put them down on the floor."

The infants were unloaded.

"Now turn them so they can see the flowers and books."

Turned, the babies at once fell silent, then began to crawl towards those clusters of sleek colours, those shapes so gay and brilliant on the white pages. As they approached, the sun came out of a momentary eclipse behind a cloud. The roses flamed up as though with a sudden passion from within; a new and profound significance seemed to suffuse the shining pages of the books. From the ranks of the crawling babies came little squeals of excitement, gurgles, and twitterings of pleasure.

The Director rubbed his hands. "Excellent!" he said. "It might almost have been done on purpose."

The swiftest crawlers were already at their goal. Small hands reached out uncertainly, touched, grasped, unpetalling the transfigured roses, crumpling the illuminated pages of the books. The Director waited until all were happily busy. Then, "Watch carefully," he said. And, lifting his hand, he gave the signal.

The Head Nurse, who was standing by a switchboard at the other end of the room, pressed down a little lever.

There was a violent explosion. Shriller and ever shriller, a siren shrieked. Alarm bells maddeningly sounded.

The children started, screamed; their faces were distorted with terror.

"And now," the Director shouted (for the noise was deafening), "now we proceed to rub in the lesson with a mild electric shock."

He waved his hand again, and the Head Nurse pressed a second lever. The screaming of the babies suddenly changed its tone. There was something desperate, almost insane, about the sharp spasmodic yelps to which they now gave utterance. Their little bodies twitched and stiffened; their limbs moved jerkily as if to the tug of unseen wires.

"We can electrify that whole strip of floor," bawled the Director in explanation. "But that's enough," he signalled to the nurse.

The explosions ceased, the bells stopped ringing, the shriek of the siren died down from tone to tone into silence. The stiffly twitching bodies relaxed, and what had become the sob and yelp of infant maniacs broadened out once more into a normal howl of ordinary terror.

"Offer them the flowers and the books again."

The nurses obeyed; but at the approach of the roses, at the mere sight of those gaily-coloured images of pussy and cock-a-doodle-doo and baa-baa black sheep, the infants shrank away in horror; the volume of their howling suddenly increased.

"Observe," said the Director triumphantly, "observe."

Books and loud noises, flowers and electric shocks—already in the infant mind, these couples were compromisingly linked; and after two hundred repetitions of the same or a similar lesson would be wedded indissolubly. What man has joined nature is powerless to put asunder.

". . . Reflexes unalterably conditioned. They'll be safe from books and botany all their lives." The Director turned to his nurses. "Take them away again."[4]

This is a writer's vision of how minds were to be formed in the technocratic, scientistic, authoritarian society whose shadowy outlines Huxley thought were on the horizon when he wrote *Brave New World* half a century ago. He called it the "final and most searching revolution" in human history, the "revolutionary revolution" to be achieved "not in the external world but in the souls and flesh of human beings."[5] The babies described in this scene had been produced by industrial processes; union of two private human beings had nothing to do with it. Their genetic endowment had been predetermined according to criteria considered objective and scientific, according to principles of industrial efficiency. Before these babies were decanted from the bottles that served as their prenatal environments no beating human heart, no ebb and surge of human body rhythms, no glow of human warmth had ever reached them. The sounds accompanying their gestation were the whirring and buzzing machinery activating an assembly line that moved the rows of bottles from stage to stage. No wonder the God they worshiped was Henry Ford!

But even this revolution in the way human flesh had come to be formed was not enough. The brave new world had to accomplish the truly "revolutionary revolution" by introducing equally drastic changes in ways of forming the human soul, the psyche.

It began with the treatment the infants in the conditioning room were subjected to. Ideas and feelings selected by the Ten World Controllers were "wedded indissolubly" together in the babies' minds by directly conditioning each separate physiological and psychological system. The aim was to imprint the association by reducing it to the level of a biological reflex requiring no more thought, subject to no more autonomous control, than an eye-blink.

Handling the babies in small batches by the rackful, processing each one two hundred times in the manner Huxley described, is a craft process, scarcely appropriate to the brave new world he envisioned where inefficiency was the only cardinal sin. The Ten World Controllers that ran things there could have accomplished the same end using the advanced industrial process to which commercial television has accustomed this whole country. It would have been more efficient and at least as reliable. If only they had known that images and symbols form human minds more than electric shocks and sirens condition them! If only they had realized that in their hagiography Walt Disney deserved a celestial seat at the right hand of Henry Ford!

APPENDIX
to Chapter 1

**The Power of
Patterned Images
to Change Attitudes
and Feelings**

Since so much of human thinking is analogical and associative, it is relatively easy to alter attitudes, opinions and affect by controlling visual materials and discourse in the social environment. The literature documenting this claim is too extensive to be listed here in full. A good grasp of the state of the art can be obtained from the following volumes:

Berkowitz, Leonard. *Advances in Experimental Social Psychology.* New York: Academic Press, 1965.

Brewster-Smith, Jerome M.; Bruner, S.; and White, Robert W. *Opinions and Personality.* New York: John Wiley and Sons, 1956.

Steiner, Ivan D., and Fishbein, Martin. *Current Studies in Social Psychology.* New York: Holt, Rinehart and Winston, 1965.

Snadowsky, Alvan M. *Social Psychology Research: Laboratory Field Relationships.* New York: The Free Press, 1962.

It is to be expected that children, especially, can be emotionally "deconditioned" easily, and research results bear out that hunch. Children can be "cured" even of their terrors upon watching the briefest dramatizations. In one study, youngsters three to five years old were "cured" of an initial fear of dogs immediately after viewing a short film showing someone playing with dogs and having a good time doing it. After they saw the film, most of the children played happily with the very dog that had terrified them before they saw the film.[1]

For further studies reporting how easy it is to touch the emotions of little children, and through them "recondition" them, see:

Bandura, Albert, Ross, Dorothea; and Ross, Sheila A. "Imitation of Film Mediated Aggressive Models." *Journal of Abnormal and Social Psychology* 67 (1963): 527–35.

Bandura, Albert. "Transmission of Aggression Through Imitation of Aggressive Models." *Journal of Abnormal and Social Psychology* 63 (1961): 575–82.

Hartmann, Donald P. "The Influence of Symbolically Modelled Instrumental Aggression and Pain Cues on the Discrimination of Aggressive Behavior." Ph.D. dissertation, Stanford University, 1965.

Lovaas, O. Ivar. "Effect of Exposure to Symbolic Aggression on Aggressive Behavior." *Child Development* 32 (1961): 37–44.

Mussen, Paul H., and Rutherford, Eldred. "Effects of Aggressive Cartoons on Children's Aggressive Play." *Journal of Abnormal and Social Psychology* 62 (1961): 461–64.

Siegel, Alberta Engval. "Film Mediated Fantasy Aggression and Strength of Aggression Drive." *Child Development* 27 (1956): 365–78.

Walters, Richard H.; Llewellyn-Thomas, Edward; and Acker, C. William. "Enhancement of Punitive Behavior by Audio Visual Display." *Science* 136 (1962): 872–73.

Patterned images and sound have the power to form consciousness even of the tiniest infants. This has not escaped the notice of the U.S. Government's Department of Health, Education, and Welfare. A 1971 report, commissioned for the President's Domestic Council, and submitted to HEW by its Office of Telecommunications Policy,[2] outlines the ways in which existing communications technology could be im-

---

1. Albert Bandura and F. L. Menlove, "Factors Determining Vicarious Extinction of Avoidance Behavior Through Symbolic Modelling," *Journal of Personality and Social Psychology* 8, 2 (1968), 99–108.

2. *Communications for Social Needs: Educational/Cultural.* A study for the President's Domestic Council. Draft/Outline, August 7, 1971, Administratively Confidential.

pressed into service to expand "educational opportunities" throughout the country. The draft memorandum suggests that television programs be prepared to "condition" infants in the cradle. This could be accomplished with but slight modifications in existing technology, allowing images to be beamed to the ceiling rather than straight ahead. Infants not yet able to sit upright, then, could be exposed to the television "stimuli" for indicated periods of time. (The matter of sound, of course, is not problematic.)

That even the tiniest infants respond to organized patterns of light and sound in characteristic ways, and that they develop preferences for some over others, has been well documented. In infants four to six weeks of age, capacity to control bodily movements other than sucking is highly limited. Yet, even at that early age, infants rapidly learn to use sucking to control the appearance of motion pictures and bring them into focus, watching what they seem to like and shifting the images at will. The experiments are conducted by wiring the nipples of their feeding bottles to the controls of a film projector. Such studies have been conducted under the supervision of Jerome S. Bruner at Harvard's Center for Cognitive Studies. Other experiments indicate that infants from ten days to five months of age, presented with vivid visual objects appearing in regular succession now in one window before them, now in another, soon learn to look where the action is. They fasten their gaze undeviatingly upon each object when it appears, shifting their gaze when it disappears to fasten it on the other window. They rapidly learn even to fixate on the observed object while monitoring the second locus with quick eye movements to see whether anything interesting is going on.[3]

Infants' responsiveness to sound and their capacity to adjust their own movements to it is documented by William S. Condon and Louis W. Sander, who report that neonates adjust their own body movements to synchronize with the sound and rhythm of voices in their environ-

---

3. See A. C. Mundy-Castle and J. Anglin, "The Development of Looking in Infancy," presented at Biennial Conference of the Society for Research in Child Development, Santa Monica, California, April 1969. See also J. S. Bruner, "Processes of Growth in Infancy," in *Stimulation in Early Infancy,* ed. A. Ambrose (London: Academic Press 1969).

ment, and that the body movements of babies raised in an English-language environment differ from those of babies raised in, for example, a Chinese-language environment.[4]

For those who are impressed mainly when some sort of physiological accompaniments of emotional arousal are readable on a dial or noted on a computer printout, there's the 1973 study by Victor B. Cline and associates.[5] Children who were heavy television users and children who were light television users were shown film clips of boxers violently pummeling each other. All the while, the children were wired up to gadgets that measured their blood volume, pulse amplitude, and skin conductance. As they watched, the group of heavy users was much less likely than the group of light users to show the measurable physiological correlates of emotional arousal the gadgetry recorded.

Laboratory tests claiming to register emotional arousal in such a "more objective way" (oh, that dangling comparative!) are finding their way into the literature. Malcolm Carruthers and Peter Taggart report measures taken by way of catheters and needles they insert in the veins of human "subjects."[6] It's their way of recording vagotonicity and changes in blood chemistry as these people watch film and television "stimuli." Simultaneously, EEGs measure cardiac rhythms. The "stimuli" were films showing human beings engaged in violent aggression against each other—for example, *Clockwork Orange.* The findings: at first "the subjects" registered the same reactions that are triggered among many students of medicine as they watch their first operations; they turned pallid and began to sweat profusely. But then other internal systems took over and suppressants calmed perturbations almost immediately. Only after analyzing these findings in tedious detail do the authors of this article feel free to abandon the laboratory talk of their

4. William S. Condon and Louis W. Sander, "Neonate Movement is Synchronized with Adult Speech: Interactional Participation and Language Acquisition," *Science* 183, 4120 (1974), 99–101.

5. Victor B. Cline; Roger G. Croft; and Steven Courrier, "Desensitization of Children to Television Violence," *Journal of Personality and Social Psychology* 27, 3 (1973), 360–65.

6. Malcolm Carruthers and Peter Taggart, "Vagotonicity of Violence: Biochemical and Cardiac Responses to Violent Films and Television Programs." *British Medical Journal* 3 (1973): 384–89.

own field—chemical pathology—and name the process: emotional desensitization.

The authors cite another study by P. A. Obrist. The correlate of emotional arousal this investigator chose was pulse and heart rate measured as people watched a film showing a dentist working on a patient. Similar evidence of desensitization of human emotions is reported as these people watched. Moreover, this audience watching the film reacted quite differently from a control group of people actually experiencing the dental work—who consistently evidenced sustained emotional arousal, no desensitization at all.[7] It all goes to show that feeling pain is not the same as watching images of someone else feeling pain; that getting used to someone else's suffering comes easier to us than getting used to our own.

It is worth noting that, in the quoted studies, nobody thought it necessary to measure anything at all on the part of the inserters of catheters, the boxers, or the dentists, whose emotional desensitization is not considered at all problematic. As neophytes, they are trained to lull their emotions. Watching arrived professionals inflict pain, those on the receiving end suffer it, is an important part of the lesson; the almost daily observation sessions routinize what would otherwise occasion unbearable emotional arousal—a calculated policy of desensitization presumably for their own good as well as for the public's good. Operationally, however, it's not much different from the way television's reiterated formulas routinize human pain and suffering for television watchers repeatedly observing it.

---

7. P. A. Obrist, *Psychosomatic Medicine* 25, 450 (1963).

APPENDIX
to Chapter 2

**Daytime Serials
and Family
Relationships**

Daytime Serials Scheduled by ABC, CBS, and NBC

END OF MAY 1975

	ABC	CBS	NBC
11:30–12:00	Game show	*Love of Life* Premiere 9/24/51. Produced by American Home Products.	Game show
12:00–12:30	Game show	*The Young and the Restless* Premiere 3/26/73. Produced by Screen Gems.	Game show

	A B C	C B S	N B C
12:30–1:00	Game show	*Search for Tomorrow* Premiere 9/3/51. Produced by Procter & Gamble.	Game show
1:00–1:30	*All My Children* Premiere 1973. Produced by Agnes Nixon.	Local	Local
1:30–2:00	Game show	*As the World Turns* Premiere 4/2/56. Produced by Procter & Gamble.	*Days of Our Lives* Premiere 11/19/65. Produced by Corday Productions in association with Columbia Pictures Television. Extended to an hour 4/21/75.
2:00–2:30	Game show	*Guiding Light* Premiere 6/30/52. Produced by Procter & Gamble.	"

	ABC	CBS	NBC
2:30–3:00	Game show	*Edge of Night* Premiere 4/2/56. Produced by Procter & Gamble. Moved from CBS to ABC 12/1/75.	*The Doctors* Premiere 4/1/63. Produced by Colgate Palmolive.
3:00–3:30	*General Hospital* Premiere 4/1/63. Produced by Procter & Gamble.	Game show	*Another World* Premiere 1/5/70. Produced by Procter & Gamble. Extended to an hour 1/9/75.
3:30–4:00	*One Life to Live* Premiere 7/15/68. Produced by Agnes Nixon.	Game show	*Another World*
4:00–4:30	Local	Local	*Somerset* Premiere 3/30/70. Produced by Young & Rubicam.

OCTOBER 1976

	A B C	C B S	N B C
11:00–11:30	*Edge of Night*	Game show	Game show
11:30–12:00	*Happy Days*	*Love of Life*	Game show
12:00–12:30	Game show	*The Young and the Restless*	Local
12:30–1:00	*All My Children*	*Search for Tomorrow*	Game show
1:00–1:30	*Ryan's Hope* Premiere 7/75. Produced by Labine Mayer.	Local	*Somerset*
1:30–2:00	Game show	*As the World Turns* Extended to an hour 12/1/75.	*Days of Our Lives*
2:00–2:30	Game show	"	"
2:30–3:00	*One Life to Live* Extended to 45 minutes 7/26/76.	*Guiding Light*	*The Doctors*
3:00–3:15	"	*All in the Family*	*Another World*
3:15–3:30	*General Hospital* Extended to 45 minutes 7/26/76.	"	"
3:30–4:00	"	Game show	"

Family Relationships in Daytime Serials

FIRST HALF 1975

Abbreviations: AMC, All My Children; AW, Another World; AWT, As the World Turns; DOL, Days of Our Lives; DRS., The Doctors; EON, Edge of Night; GH, General Hospital; GL, Guiding Light; HSM, How to Survive a Marriage; LOL, Love of Life; OLTL, One Life to Live; SFT, Search for Tomorrow; SOM, Somerset; Y&R, The Young and the Restless.

PREGNANCIES—THREATENING PATERNITY—
CONFUSED

Addie Williams gives birth to baby Hope Williams and dies, not of the terminal cancer from which she was suffering, but because of a car accident. OLTL

Augusta McCloud is pregnant by Dr. Peter Taylor. Augusta had hoped that when Dr. Taylor separated from his wife, Diana, he would legalize her situation. It didn't pan out—Dr. Taylor returned to Diana, leaving Augusta vacillating between single motherhood and an abortion. GH

Cathy Craig, unmarried mother, unexpectedly goes into labor in a snowstorm and delivers without medical assistance. For a while it's nip and tuck for her and the baby. The child, prematurely born, survives. The father is Joe Riley, married to another. OLTL

Diana Lamont, foster grandmother, is pregnant by Jamie Rollins, with whom she has been living pending her divorce, now final. His divorce is still pending. LOL

Erica Brent married Phillip Tyler, who did the right thing by her when he learned she was pregnant with his child. She miscarries, becomes mentally disturbed as a result, develops hysterical pregnancy, and must be committed. AMC

Holly Norris Bauer is pregnant with a child sired by Roger Thorpe. She is married to Ed Bauer. GL

Jennifer Pace is in jail. She tells Scott Phillip that she is pregnant with his child. He divorces his second wife in order to do right by Jennifer, who subsequently miscarries after running into a plate-glass window in a moment of despondency and hallucination. SFT

Jill Foster says she is pregnant with Phillip Chancellor's child. He is married to wife, Kay, who refuses to give him up. The divorce finally comes through, however, just in time for Phillip to marry Jill on his deathbed. He has been injured in a car accident his ex-wife is responsible for. The deathbed marriage is for the purpose of legitimizing Jill's child. Y&R

Joan Willis suddenly hemorrhages. It looks as if it may be difficult to save both her and the child who is born two months early and weighs in at 3 lbs. 4 oz. HSM

Julie Anderson is about to divorce Bob Anderson to marry Doug Williams, whom she loves. She finds out, however, that she is pregnant with Bob's child. As a result, she decides to stick with the old marriage after all, but plans an abortion. DOL

Pam Chandler, single mother, is pregnant by boyfriend, David. Her pregnancy has been complicated by her own rare kidney disease as a result of which she suffers toxemia. Doctors tell her it could even result in fulminating eclampsia, an ailment which surely ten to twenty million daytime-serial watchers must know could be fatal. She bravely refuses to allow the doctors to take the baby or perform a Caesarian because she wants to give the child the best possible chance of survival, carrying it as long as she can manage. The child is born prematurely, and it's fifty-fifty whether baby Samantha will survive. GL

MARRIAGES: THE TIE THAT BINDS, BUT NOT VERY MUCH

Carol Hughes to Jay Stallings. Her second. AWT

Chris Kirby to Larry Kirby. Remarriage for both after divorcing each other. HSM

Heather Lawrence to Jerry Kane. SOM

Jennifer Pace to Scott Phillips. His third, her first. SFT

Jill Foster to Phillip Chancellor. His second, her first. Y&R

Kate Swanson to Dr. Ted Chandler. LOL

Kitty Shea to Linc Tyler. Her third, his first. AMC

Lisa Miller Hughes Eldrich Shea to Grant Coleman. Her fourth. AWT

Rachel Davis Matthews Clark Frame to Matt Corey. Her fourth, his second. AW

Dr. Terry Martin to Stan Kurtz. SOM

Tiffany Whitney to Noel Douglas. Her second. EON

Wanda Webb to Winnie Wolek. OLTL

Granpa Hughes to Mrs. Kopeke. At least second time around for both. AWT

BIGAMOUS MARRIAGES

Betsy Crawford to Ben Harper. LOL

Tony Power to Dr. Allan Stewart. DRS

DIVORCES

Anne Davis Martin from Paul Martin. AMC

Carol Hughes from Tom Hughes. AWT

Chris Kirby from Larry Kirby. HSM

Diana Lamont from Charles Lamont. LOL

Joyce Coleman from Grant Coleman. AWT

Kathy Phillips from Scott Phillips. SFT

Kay Chancellor from Phillip Chancellor. Y&R

Peggy Fletcher from Johnny Fletcher. GL

SEPARATIONS, DIVORCE DECREE NOT YET FINAL

Claudette Montgomery from her husband. AMC
Lenore Curtin Delaney from Robert Delaney. AW
Phoebe Tyler from Charles Tyler. AMC
Rachel Davis Matthews Clark Frame Corey from Mac Corey. AW

DIVORCES PLANNED, UNDER CONSIDERATION AND DISCUSSION

Kim Dixon from John Dixon. AWT
Janet Norris from Ken Norris. GL
Jennifer Brooks from Stuart Brooks. Y&R
Jo Vincent from Dr. Tony Vincent. SFT
Julie Anderson from Bob Anderson. DOL
Sally Bridgeman from Jamie Rollins. LOL

DIVORCES SUGGESTED, INTIMATED, DAYDREAMED

Kate Thompson from Julian Cannell. SOM
The Peter Terrels. DRS

LIVING TOGETHER OR SLEEPING TOGETHER

Amanda Howard, Neil Curtis. DOL
Ann Martin, Nick Davis. AMC
Brooke Hamilton, David Banning. DOL
Cal Aleata, David Hart. LOL
Carol Lamont, Robert Delaney. AW
Chris Kirby, Dr. Max Cooper. HSM
Diana Lamont, Jamie Rollins. LOL
Eve Lawrence, Ned Paisley. SOM
Heather Lawrence, Jerry Kane. SOM
Jill Foster, Phillip Chancellor. Y&R
Jill Foster, Brock Reynolds. Y&R
Joan Willis, Dr. Max Cooper. HSM

Dr. Leslie Williams, Dr. Joel Stratton. GH
Liza Walton, Steve Kaslo. SFT
Monica Cortland, Robert Munday. HSM
Peggy Fletcher, Roger Thorpe. GL
Sandra Henderson, Larry Kirby. HSM
Sheila Rafferty, Timmy Siegal. OLTL
Stephanie Wilkins, Clay Collins. SFT
Stephanie Wilkins, Dr. Tony Vincent. SFT
Trish Clayton, Michael Horton. DOL

CHILDREN ARE IN PRETTY BAD SHAPE—AND ON STAGE BRIEFLY, IF AT ALL

Billy lives with mother, Peggy Fletcher. She is a nurse. Her husband is missing. Billy has not been sired by Peggy's missing husband. GL

Bruce Carson, orphaned when both parents die, is the ward of Joanne Tate Vincent and Dr. Tony Vincent. SFT

Chuckie is the illegitimate child of Sally McGuire and Snapper Foster. His legal surname is Roland since mother married Pierre Roland, deceased shortly thereafter; her aim: to give the child a name. Y&R

Danny Wolek is the son of Dr. Larry Wolek and Meredith Lord Wolek. Meredith died (July 1973) as a result of complications in carrying Danny. Danny, now around six, lives with his dad at Jim and Anna Craig's house. OLTL

Dennis Carrington is the child of Iris Carrington, divorced from husband, Elliott. As a child, Dennis was an invalid (bad heart). Now, at age fourteen, he seems to have recovered. AW

Emily Norris is daughter of separated parents, Jane and Ken Norris. GL

Emily Stewart is daughter of divorced parents, Dan and Susan Stewart. Dan has custody. The child—about four or five—was seriously ill of bacterial meningitis, but recovered. Mom is a drunk. AWT

Eric Phillips is the son of Scott Phillips's first wife. Eric has been living with Scott and second wife, Kathy, whom Scott has just divorced to do right by pregnant third wife, Jennifer. SFT

Erich Warner is the ward of Carolee Aldrich and husband, Steve. Erich's real mother, Dr. Karen Warner, forgot all about him when she was suffering from amnesia. The trauma producing the ailment occurred in an airplane crash that nearly killed them both. At the time of the crash, she was in the process of kidnapping him from his father. She later recovered, remembered Erich, and sued for his custody. Erich seems to be about seven or eight. DRS

Franny (Little Franny, they call her) is the daughter of Jennifer Hughes by an earlier marriage. Little Franny lives with Jennifer and mother's present husband, Bob Hughes. AWT

Freddie Bauer is the son of Leslie and Ed Bauer. Leslie has remarried Ed's brother, Mike Bauer; so Freddie's stepfather is also his uncle, and there's no need to change his last name. Freddie suffers amnesia while lost on a canoe trip, but later recovers. GL

Greta Powers is the daughter of Maggie Powers and deceased Kurt Van Allen, victim of a murder. Greta lives with Dr. Matt Powers and mother, Maggie. Greta is obsessed with the idea that her stepbrother, Mike, is still alive. Everyone else thinks he's dead. Greta seems to be about thirteen. DRS

Hope Williams is the infant daughter of Doug Williams and Addie Horton Williams. Addie, a terminal cancer patient, risked her life to bear Hope. She just made it—done in finally by an automobile accident. OLTL

Jamie Coles, a battered child, is the two-year-old son of socialite Stacy Coles. Mother brings him to a child-abuse center and Ann Martin kidnaps the child to protect him from further harm. AMC

Jamie Matthews is the illegitimately conceived son of Rachel Matthews and Stephen Frame (who allegedly died in a helicopter crash). Jamie lives with Rachel and her fourth husband, Matt Corey, from whom she subsequently separates. The boy seems to be about thirteen or fourteen. AW

Joanne Dawson is the daughter of divorced parents, Jane and Howie Dawson. Kidney and heart complications from a strep infection do her in. GH

Jennifer is the three-year-old adopted child of Bill and Martha Marceau. EON

Johnny Prentiss is the eight-year-old grandson of Diana and Charles Lamont. His father was Bill Prentiss, who died of leukocytemia—a rare blood disorder. His mother, Tess, has left Johnny with his grandparents to be raised. They are about to divorce, since Diana moved out to live with her young lover, Jamie, by whom she is pregnant. LOL

Joshua Hall is the foster son of Carla and Ed Hall. Ed is a cop who found this ghetto child selling dope and pushing pills. That's all over now, though. OLTL

Joyelle Willis is the infant daughter of Joan and Peter Willis. Joyelle was born prematurely and it looked as if she might not survive (another infant weighing in at 3 lbs. 4 oz.). Mother, Joan, hemorrhaged badly during the birth, and it was nip and tuck for her, too. HSM

Lori Kirby lives with Chris and Larry Kirby, recently divorced, then remarried to each other. Lori was the one who convinced them to make it legal instead of following their initial plan to live together. HSM

Martha Taylor is the illegitimately conceived daughter of Diana Taylor and Phil Brewer. Diana is married to Dr. Peter Taylor. When Martha was born (some eleven or so years previous), Diana had forced the birth by inflicting wounds on herself to induce labor. The result was a hysterectomy—no more children for Diana. Diana has spent some years in prison, leaving her sister, Beth Maynor, to take care of the child. Released from prison, Diana returns home, presumably to resume care of the child. GH

Megan is the illegitimate daughter of unmarried Cathy Craig, ex–dope addict. Megan was born prematurely. She suffers from a congenital heart defect. When she's old enough, they'll operate. Joe Riley, the father, suffers from a genetic defect that presumably prevents him from siring healthy children. OLTL

Michael Paul Stewart is son of Tony Stewart and Dr. Michael Powers. Tony is now married to Dr. Alan Stewart, since Michael has been reported dead. He returns, however, to demand custody of the child. Tony nearly died during her labor. Toxemia. DRS

Nancy McGowan is the baby daughter of Ada and Gil McGowan. Ada was in her fifties when Nancy was born. Nancy is sister to Rachel Davis Matthews Clark Frame Corey. AW

No Name. A battered child brought to the child-abuse clinic dies as a result of injuries inflicted by the parent or parents. AMC

No Name. An abandoned three-year-old in Hong Kong, in whom Nurse Dawn Wittington has taken an interest. DRS

Phillip Tyler is the son of Tara Tyler and Big Phillip, cousin to Tara's husband. When Little Phillip falls from a tree and undergoes a spleenectomy, he needs a transfusion. The real father's identity emerges as blood types are checked. AMC

Sally Spencer is recently orphaned as a result of an automobile accident. Alice and Stephen Frame plan to adopt the eight-year-old. The plan is aborted when Stephen is said to have been killed in a helicopter accident. AW

Samantha is the illegitimate daughter of Pam Chandler and boyfriend, David. She has congenital lung disease (hyalene membrane disease). Samantha is delivered by emergency surgery since mother, Pam, suffers from a form of toxemic edema. Both survive their respective crises. GL

Skipper is the ten-year-old, motherless son of Scott McKenzie. Skipper has a heart condition that keeps him sedentary. He can engage in no sports or active play. SOM

Stephanie Aldrich is the daughter of Dr. Stephen Aldrich and Carolee Simpson Aldrich. Her mother, Carolee, had been engaged to marry Dr. Dan Allison, who was dying of a heart condition. Dan dispatched himself, but he made it look as if he'd been murdered, and as if Steve were the man who'd done it. Steve was arrested and tried. Carolee, at great peril to her pregnancy with Stephanie, brought in an old diary of Dan's to clear up the mystery. The baby was born okay though, and Steve and Carolee married. DRS

T. J. has been abandoned by his parents. He suffers from severe emotional upsets, ulcerated legs, and acute malnutrition. He turns up at the hospital for treatment. The plan is to place him in a foster home, but T. J. is worried about it and runs away. Police bring him back with a hurt arm and other injuries suffered as a result of beatings by older children. Drs. Sara McIntyre and Joe Werner clear up his wounds and become his foster parents. T. J. seems to be about ten. GL

Timmy Faraday is the son of Mark and Serena Faraday, now divorced. Mom has custody but Dad wants the boy. Timmy seems to be around eight. EON

Tommy is the illegitimate son of Audrey Hobart and Dr. Tom Baldwin, conceived as the result of a rape. Tommy lives with mom and stepfather, Dr. Jim Hobart, who is abusive when drunk. Tommy's real father kidnaps him just before Tommy is about to undergo essential heart surgery. GH

Walter Curtin, Jr., is the eight-year-old son of Lenore Curtin and Walter Curtin, Sr., now deceased. Mom is married to Robert Delaney, but they have recently separated. AW

Wendy Wilkins is the daughter of divorced parents, Dave and Stephanie Wilkins. Stephanie had tried to enlist Dave's help in a plan to palm off Wendy as having been sired by Tony Vincent, whom mother, Stephanie, wishes to marry. SFT

APPENDIX
to Chapter 3

Prime-Time Series
Booked into 1974–75
Television Year
Classified According to
Type of Family and
Principal Emotional
Ties Featured

Children Are Raised by Both Parents

HISTORICAL SETTINGS

> The Waltons
> Happy Days
> Little House on the Prairie
> The New Land

CONTEMPORARY SETTINGS

> Apple's Way
> Good Times
> We'll Get By

Children of Divorce, Death, Desertion

> Paper Moon
> Sons and Daughters

Sunshine
Texas Wheelers

No Children

CHILDLESS COUPLES

Born Free
Bob Newhart Show
McMillan and Wife
Petrocelli

ADULT OFFSPRING LIVING WITH PARENTS

With Both Parents:
All in the Family
The Jeffersons
With a Single Parent
Khan!
Maude
Sanford and Son
That's My Mama
Rockford Files

Shows Starring Men Who Live Without Commitment to a Female Mate

Archer
Baretta
Barnaby Jones
Cannon
Caribe
Chico and the Man
Dan August
FBI
Gunsmoke
Harry O
Hawaii Five-O

Hec Ramsey
Hot l Baltimore
Ironside
Khan!
Kodiak
Kojak
Kolchak, The Night Stalker
Kung Fu
Lucas Tanner
Manhunter
Marcus Welby, M.D.
McCloud
Medical Center
Movin' On
Nakia
Odd Couple
Paul Sand in Friends and Lovers
Police Woman
Sanford and Son
Streets of San Francisco
Sunshine
Texas Wheelers
Rockford Files
Six Million Dollar Man

Shows Featuring Women Who Live Without Commitment to a Male Mate

Amy Prentiss
Get Christie Love
Police Woman
Mary Tyler Moore Show
That's My Mama

Shows Featuring Barracks Life as Principal Setting

> M*A*S*H
> Barney Miller
> Emergency
> The Rookies
> Sierra
> S.W.A.T.

On-the-Job Families

> Barney Miller
> Bob Crane Show
> Bob Newhart Show
> Emergency
> Ironside
> Mary Tyler Moore Show
> Sierra
> The Rookies

Male Couples

> Adam 12
> Caribe
> Chico and the Man
> FBI
> Hawaii Five-O
> Marcus Welby, M.D.
> Movin' On
> Odd Couple
> Planet of the Apes
> Streets of San Francisco

Male Swingers

> Baretta
> Chico and the Man
> Dan August

Harry O
Mannix
M*A*S*H
Paul Sand in Friends and Lovers

Female Swingers

Get Christie Love
Karen
Police Woman

Swingers in Supporting Cast

Mary Tyler Moore Show
Bob Newhart Show
The Jeffersons
That's My Mama

Other

Paper Moon (*grown man with almost nubile child*)
Hot l Baltimore (*hotel setting replaces barracks setting*)
Police Story (characters change each week)

Comedy Variety Shows

Carol Burnett Show
Cher (*reopened 1976 as* Sonny and Cher Show)
Dean Martin Roast (once a month)
Mac Davis Show
Sonny Comedy Revue
Smothers Brothers
Tony Orlando and Dawn

Family Life as a Favored Setting For Comedy Shows

PRIME-TIME SITUATION COMEDIES, 1974–75
SEASON

Situation Comedies Centered in Family Setting	*Situation Comedies Centered in Nonfamily Settings*
All in the Family	Barney Miller
Good Times	Bob Crane Show*
Happy Days	Bob Newhart Show*
Jeffersons	Chico and the Man
Maude	Hot l Baltimore
Rhoda	Karen
Sanford and Son	M*A*S*H
Sons and Daughters	Mary Tyler Moore Show
Texas Wheelers	Odd Couple
That's My Mama	Paul Sand in Friends and Lovers

*These shows might well have been classified in column I, since family scenes are often written into the script and played for laughs.

APPENDIX
to Chapter 4 & 5

Programs Booked to Attract Children

*1. Principal Social Units Featured in 34 Television Series
Directed to Children, Saturday and Sunday Mornings*

NETWORK SHOWS 1974–75

INTACT FAMILIES—CONTEMPORARY

Contemporary family	
(mother, father, children)	*None*
Monster family	The Addams Family

INTACT FAMILY—EXHIBITS

In the Stone Age	Valley of the Dinosaurs
	Korg
In the world of the future	The Jetsons

BROKEN FAMILY

No mother or no father

The Partridge Family
These Are the Days
Land of the Lost

No parents

My Favorite Martian
Bailey's Comets
The Hudson Brothers
Devlin

NO FAMILY UNIT AT ALL

Teenage gang

Yogi and His Gang
Superfriends
Scooby Doo
Speed Buggy
Fat Albert and the Cosby Kids
Wheelie and the Chopper Bunch
Sigmund and the Sea Monsters
U.S. of Archie
Pink Panther
Lassie's Rescue Rangers

Adult gang

Gilligan's Island

*Military, paramilitary,
     teams*

Star Trek
Emergency Plus Four
Harlem Globetrotters Razzle
     Dazzle Popcorn Machine

Superman formula

Superfriends
Shazam!
Hong Kong Phooey

Teenage pairs

Jeannie
Goober and the Ghost Chasers

Other   Run Joe Run
                                  Go
                                  Make a Wish
                                  Bugs Bunny

2. *Programs Aimed at the Children's Market*

NETWORK BOOKINGS 1970–76, SATURDAY
AND SUNDAY MORNINGS*

                                  LIVE ON FILM,
                                  PUPPETS, OR
ANIMATIONS   COMBINATIONS

Fall 1976

Bugs Bunny/Road Runner   Ark II
  (1 hour)   Big John, Little John
Clue Club   Far Out Space Nuts
Fat Albert and the Cosby   Hudson Brothers Razzle
  Kids   Dazzle Comedy Show
Jabberjaw   Junior Almost Anything
                                    Goes
New Adventures of Gilligan   Kids from C.A.P.E.R.
Oddball Couple   Krofft Supershow (1 1/2
Pink Panther Show (1 1/2   hours)
  hours   McDuff
Scooby Doo/Dynomutt   Monster Squad
  Hour (1 hour)   Land of the Lost (1 hour)
Sylvester and Tweety   Muggsy
Tom and Jerry/Great Ape
  Mumbly Show (1 hour)
Woody Woodpecker (1 hour)

---

*Unless otherwise indicated, these shows are scheduled for half-hour slots.

Fall 1975

Adventures of Gilligan

Bugs Bunny/Roadrunner (1 hour)

Devlin

Emergency Plus Four

Fat Albert and the Cosby Kids

Hong Kong Phooey

Josie and the Pussycats

Oddball Couple

Pebbles and Bamm Bamm

Pink Panther

Return to the Planet of the Apes

Scooby Doo, Where Are You

Speed Buggy

These Are the Days

Tom and Jerry and the Grape Ape (1 hour)

Uncle Croc's Block (1 hour)

U.S. of Archie

Valley of the Dinosaurs

Waldo Kitty

Far Out Space Nuts

The Ghost Busters

Go USA

Harlem Globetrotters Popcorn Machine

Land of the Lost

Lost Saucer

Make a Wish

Run Joe Run

Shazam/Isis Hour (1 hour)

Sigmund and the Sea Monsters

Westwind

Fall 1974

Addams Family

Bailey's Comets

Bugs Bunny

Devlin

Emergency Plus Four

Fat Albert and the Cosby Kids

Go, USA

Harlem Globetrotters Popcorn Machine

Hudson Brothers Razzle Dazzle Comedy Show

Korg, 70,000 B.C.

Land of the Lost

Goober and the Ghost
   Chasers
Hong Kong Phooey
Jeannie
The Jetsons
Lassie's Rescue Rangers
My Favorite Martian
New Adventures of Gilligan
Partridge Family, 2200 A.D.
Pink Panther Show
Scooby Doo, Where Are
   You
Speed Buggy
Star Trek
Superfriends (1 hour)
These Are the Days
Valley of the Dinosaurs
Yogi and His Friends

The Show and Tell Machine
Make a Wish
Run, Joe, Run
Shazam!
Sigmund and the Sea
   Monsters

Fall 1973

Addams Family
Amazing Chan and the
   Chan Clan
Brady Kids
Butch Cassidy
Bugs Bunny
Emergency Plus Four
Everything's Archie
Fat Albert and the Cosby
   Kids
Flintstones
Goober and the Ghost
   Chasers
Jeannie
Jetsons
Hair Bear Bunch

Go
H. R. Puf'n'stuf
Lidsville (1 hour)
Make a Wish
Sigmund and the Sea
   Monsters

Inch-high Private Eye
Josie and the Pussycats
Kid Power
Lassie's Rescue Rangers
Mission Magic
My Favorite Martian
The Osmonds
Pink Panther
Scooby Doo
Speedbuggy
Star Trek
Superfriends (1 hour)
Superstar Movie (1 hour)
Yogi's Gang

Fall 1972

Amazing Chan and the
 Chan Clan
Archie's TV Funnies
Archie's Funhouse
Around the World in 80
 Days
The Barkleys
The Brady Kids
Bugs Bunny
Bullwinkle
Fat Albert and the Cosby
 Kids
Flintstones Comedy Hour (1
 hour)
Funky Phantom (1 hour)
Harlem Globetrotters
Houndcats
Jackson Five
Kidpower

Bewitched
H. R. Puf'n'stuff
Make a Wish
Runaround
Talking with a Giant

Josie and the Pussycats in
  Outer Space
New Scooby Doo Comedy
  Movies (1 hour)
The Osmonds
Roman Holidays
Sabrina, the Teenage Witch
Sealab 2020
Superstar Movie (1 hour)
Underdog

Fall 1971

Archie's TV Funnies
Bugs Bunny
Bullwinkle
Deputy Dawg
Funky Phantom
Harlem Globetrotters
Help, It's the Hair Bear
  Bunch
Here Come the
  Doubledeckers
Jackson Five
Jerry Lewis
The Jetsons
Jonny Quest
Josie and the Pussycats
Lancelot Link, Secret Chimp
Pebbles and Bamm Bamm
Pink Panther
Reluctant Dragon and Mr.
  Toad
Roadrunner
Sabrina, the Teenage Witch
Scooby Doo, Where Are
  You
Woody Woodpecker

Barrier Reef
Bewitched
The Bugaloos
Curiosity Shop (1 hour)
Lidsville
Make a Wish
The Monkees
Take a Giant Step (1 hour)
Mr. Wizard

Fall 1970

Archie's Funhouse (1 hour)
Bugs Bunny, Roadrunner
  (1 hour)
Bullwinkle
Catanooga Cats
Dastardly and Muttley in
  Their Flying Machines
Further Adventures of Dr.
  Doolittle
Hardy Boys
Harlem Globetrotters
Heckel and Jeckle
Here Comes the Grump
Hot Wheels
The Jetsons
Jerry Lewis Show
Johnnie Quest
Josie and the Pussycats
Lancelot Link, Secret
  Chimp
Motor Mouse
Pink Panther
Reluctant Dragon and Mr.
  Toad
Sabrina and the Groovy
  Ghoolies
Scooby Doo, Where Are
  You
Scooper and the Double
  Deckers
Sky Hawks
Smokey Bear
Tomfoolery Show
Woody Woodpecker Show

The Bugaloos
H. R. Puf'n'stuf
Hot Dog
Jambo
The Monkees

APPENDIX
to Chapter 9

CORPORATE HOLDINGS, ABC, CBS AND RCA

All three networks are engaged in other enterprises which are not, strictly speaking, in the broadcasting business, but are intimately linked with it. NBC's parent company, the RCA Corporation, is one of the twenty largest, most powerful corporations in the world. It is a leader in global communications, color television receivers, consumer electronics and defense electronics. RCA's consumer electronics division makes color television sets, black-and-white sets, records, and stereo tapes. In the electronic components field, RCA manufactures color television picture tubes, discrete semiconductors, and integrated circuits as well as braodcasting and communications equipment. A variety of electronic equipment and systems is made for military and space programs under U. S. Government contracts. RCA's Global Communications Division is an international communications common-carrier operating system of satellite, cable, and radio channels. Its

Alaskan and American units are linked into this system.

RCA owns and operates the world's leading vehicle-renting and leasing corporation, Hertz. Its publishing interests include Random House and all its subsidiaries. Its food interests include Banquet Foods (frozen and prepared items) and Oriel Foods (food distribution). It owns a carpet company, Coronet Industries. RCA has begun to produce, distribute and promote video games and as of September 1977 plans to market a home video cassette recorder-player.

CBS Inc. (formerly the Columbia Broadcasting System) is also engaged in consumer activities, publishing, record, and music businesses. Columbia House also produces handcraft kits, hobby craft tools (X-Acto) and other craft products, as well as Columbia Record and Tape Clubs. The Musical Instruments Division manufactures and markets Steinway pianos as well as the instruments mentioned in the text. The Retail Stores Division sells stereo components and phonograph records and tapes through retail outlets. The Toys Division includes Wonder Products and Creative Playthings, manufacturing and retail outlets. CBS's publishing interests include the publishing company of Holt, Rinehart and Winston and its subsidiaries, as well as BFA Educational Media (audiovisual and print materials for elementary and high school markets). It also owns Fawcett Publications, Inc., which publishes *Woman's Day, Mechanix Illustrated,* and more than thirty special interests magazines, as well as Crest and Gold Medal paperback books. CBS also owns the Popular Library line of mass-market paperbacks. W. B. Saunders, publisher of books in health and sciences, is owned by CBS along with five proprietary schools catering to students preparing for paramedical careers.

ABC (formerly American Broadcasting-Paramount Theatres) has maintained its interests in motion picture enterprises, operating about a hundred movie screens in theaters and drive-ins throughout the country. ABC is engaged in producing and distributing phonograph records; ABC Records, its wholly owned subsidiary, produces records under several dozen different labels, some of which have been mentioned in the text. ABC's publishing division includes W. Schwann, Inc., *High Fidelity, Modern Photography,* and numerous satellite publications, as well as farm journals, specialty magazines, and religious works. ABC owns the Wallace-Homestead Book Publishing Company. Other enterprises include theme parks and "scenic attractions," such as the Historic Towne of Smithville near Atlantic City, Silver Springs and Weeki Wachee Spring, near Ocala and Tampa, Florida. Having moved ahead of the other two networks for the first time in 1977, the accompanying increase in revenues this corporation is considering further acquistions. (Sources: *Annual Reports* 1976.)

APPENDIX
to Chapter 13

Some Major Rating Systems

---

1. ARB, BAR, TvQ

ARBITRON

Just as the Nielsen ratings are the Bible for network salesmen, Arbitron "sweeps" are the Bible for individual stations. Issued by the American Research Bureau and sold to subscribers, Arbitron reports rely on methods similar to those the Nielsen people use—mainly surveys of a metered sample's viewing choices, supplemented by diaries.

Arbitron compiles data for 208 markets individually, based on 250 to 1,500 diaries in each market, the number determined according to population. Random samples are drawn each week for the ratings. Samples range from 2,400 to 2,600 homes in the New York area, to 200 in less densely populated areas like Helena, Montana.[1]

---

1. Martin Mayer, in *About Television* (New York: Harper & Row, 1972), gives a complete description of the ARB rating system. He explains, for example, how national advertisers use the per market data reported in *ARB Network Television Program Analysis* (a sum-

ARB sends out about 800,000 diaries by mail to homes that have been previously contacted by more than 3,000 interviewers. The return rate is said to be about 53 percent. With the diary information in hand, the company publishes its audience ratings, broken down by sex and age, in 210 books that cover markets from New York to Pippa Passes, Kentucky. The "national sweep" reports are published four times a year.

BAR

BAR reports are published by the Bureau of Advertising Research. Its rating service depends on tape recorders placed in sampled homes around the country. Participating television watchers record the sound of programs they tune in to and mail the tapes to BAR headquarters. The information is coded there and sold to networks, stations, and advertisers subscribing to the service.[2]

In 1971, stations paid up to $4,000 a year for monthly reports provided by BAR, while advertising agencies paid on a scale that topped $52,000 a year.[2]

TVQ

Marketing Evaluations, Inc., produces a rating guide called *TvQ*, which measures "qualitative degree of familiarity with particular shows" and the favorite shows of people participating in their samples. *TvQ* measures "likability of 557 performers and personalities." Samples cover ages six and up. A yearly report is issued, entitled *The 1975 Performer Popularity Poll* (or whatever year is appropriate). Ratings are available separately for the usual demographic subgroups. Networks, stations, advertising agencies, production and syndication companies, and movie companies subscribe to the service.

---

mary volume ARB issues to subscribers). A show that appeals to rural audiences, such as "Hee Haw," say, might have a New York index in that volume of 35 and a Nashville index of 145. An advertiser, by looking up these two indexes in the summary volume, could easily calculate that in New York the show was drawing 65 percent less than the national average while in Nashville it was pulling 45 percent more.

2. Martin Mayer, op. cit., p. 67.

A year's subscription to *TvQ* costs about $5,000. *Performer Q* comes to about $3,025 a year.[3]

I note in passing that in 1972 Lucille Ball's name was recognized by 99 percent of the samples polled. Stars recognized by 95 percent or more included, that year, Johnny Cash (97%), Glen Campbell (95%), Flip Wilson (95%), and Bob Hope (95%)—proportions matched only by the name of the president of the United States as recognized by those over six years of age.[4]

---

3. See Edwin Diamond, "The Mysterious Q: TV's Secret Casting Weapon," *New York Magazine*, May 26, 1975; and also Rowland Barber, "Just a Little List," *TV Guide*, August 10, 1975.

4. *Variety*, September 13, 1972.

2. Examples of Nielsen Market Section Audience Reports (Demos)

TOP OCCUPATION, INCOME, EDUCATION
RATINGS FOR CONTINUING NETWORK TV
NIGHTTIME SERIES

(See following five tables.)

BY TOTAL HOUSEHOLD INCOME

PROGRAM	$5,000–$9,999		$10,000–$14,999*		$15,000 & up	
	Rank	Rating	Rank	Rating	Rank	Rating
All in the Family (CBS)	3	28.9	1	54.4	1	33.1
NFL Football (ABC)	—	—	2	30.4	2	32.1
Friday Movies (CBS)	5	25.1	3	29.2	3	29.5
M*A*S*H (CBS)	6	23.7	4	28.2	4	27.6
Waltons (CBS)	2	29.3	5	27.9	5	26.2
Sunday Mystery Movie (NBC)	8	22.7	7	25.8	6	26.0
Sanford and Son (NBC)	1	30.5	—	(24.3)	7	25.5
Mary Tyler Moore (CBS)	—	—	6	26.3	8	25.3
Maude (CBS)	9	22.3	9	25.2	9	24.8
Kojak (CBS)	—	—	—	(24.0)	10	24.6
Disney (CBS)	4	25.2	8	25.4	—	(24.5)
Bob Newhart (CBS)	—	—	10	24.6	—	—
Gunsmoke (CBS)	7	23.3	—	—	—	—
Monday Movie (NBC)	9	22.3	—	—	—	—
Hawaii Five-O (CBS)	—	—	—	—	—	—
Adam-12 (NBC)	—	—	—	—	—	—

*Homes headed by "professional, owner, manager."

BY EDUCATION OF HOUSEHOLD HEAD

PROGRAM	Grade School		High School		College, one year & up	
	Rank	Rating	Rank	Rating	Rank	Rating
All in the Family (CBS)	2	32.1	2	29.5	1	33.0
NFL Football (ABC)	—	—	8	24.8	2	31.3
Waltons (CBS)	4	30.4	3	28.7	3	25.7
Friday Movies (CBS)	8	23.1	4	28.6	3	25.7
M*A*S*H (CBS)	7	23.6	6	25.1	3	25.7
Sanford and Son (NBC)	1	32.6	1	29.6	6	24.9
Maude (CBS)	6	24.4	6	25.1	7	24.8
Sunday Mystery Movie (NBC)	—	—	9	24.5	8	24.5
Mary Tyler Moore (CBS)	—	—	—	—	9	24.3
Bob Newhart (CBS)	—	—	—	—	10	23.1
Disney (NBC)	5	24.7	5	25.5	—	—
Hawaii Five-O (CBS)	9	22.6	9	24.5	—	—
Gunsmoke (CBS)	3	30.7	—	—	—	—
Adam-12 (NBC)	10	21.9	—	—	—	—

BY AGE OF LADY OF HOUSE

PROGRAM	Under 35		35-49		50+		Working All Ages	
	Rank	Rating	Rank	Rating	Rank	Rating	Rank	Rating
All in the Family (CBS)	7	25.7	1	34.9	1	36.4	1	30.0
Sanford and Son (NBC)	—	23.5	4	32.0	2	35.2	2	28.6
Friday Movies (CBS)	1	33.1	2	34.6	—	—	3	27.9
Disney (NBC)	4	27.8	7	27.4	—	—	4	25.4
Waltons (CBS)	2	30.4	3	33.0	5	26.9	5	25.3
Maude (CBS)	—	23.8	8	26.8	6	26.5	6	24.7
M*A*S*H (CBS)	—	21.9	5	29.1	4	27.8	7	23.8
Hawaii Five-O (CBS)	—	20.8	6	27.7	7	25.0	7	23.8
Sunday Movie (ABC)	—	23.8	—	—	—	—	9	23.1
Monday Movie (NBC)	9	24.9	—	—	—	—	10	22.7
Tuesday Movie of Week (ABC)	3	28.4	—	—	—	—	—	—
Sunday Mystery Movie (ABC)	5	27.0	—	—	—	—	—	—
Thursday Movie (CBS)	6	26.9	—	—	—	—	—	—
NFL Football (ABC)	8	25.5	—	—	—	—	—	—
Marcus Welby (ABC)	10	24.3	—	—	—	—	—	—
Sonny & Cher (CBS)	—	22.8	9	26.3	—	—	—	—
Mary Tyler Moore (CBS)	—	20.8	10	26.2	8	24.5	—	—
Gunsmoke (CBS)	—	—	—	—	3	28.0	—	—
Adam-12 (NBC)	—	—	—	—	9	23.5	—	—
Bob Newhart (CBS)	—	—	—	—	10	23.3	—	—

#Employed outside home at least 30 hours weekly.

BY OCCUPATION OF HOUSEHOLD HEAD

PROGRAM	Professional/ White Collar		Blue Collar/Skilled		Not in labor force	
	Rank	Rating	Rank	Rating	Rank	Rating
All in the Family (CBS)	1	31.4	2	33.1	1	34.3
NFL Football (ABC)	2	28.4	1	33.7	—	—
Friday Movies (CBS)	3	27.5	3	31.8	2	33.7
Sanford and Son (NBC)	4	27.0	5	30.6	3	28.0
Waltons (CBS)	4	27.0	7	26.6	6	24.6
M*A*S*H (CBS)	6	26.4	6	27.9	—	—
Sunday Mystery Movie (NBC)	7	25.1	—	—	—	—
Maude (CBS)	8	25.0	—	—	4	26.9
Mary Tyler Moore (CBS)	9	23.7	—	—	6	24.6
Disney (NBC)	10	23.4	4	31.6	—	—
Kung Fu (ABC)	—	—	9	25.8	—	—
Thursday Movie (CBS)	—	—	8	25.9	—	—
Monday Movie (NBC)	—	—	9	25.8	—	—
Gunsmoke (CBS)	—	—	—	—	5	26.5
Hawaii Five-O (CBS)	—	—	—	—	8	24.0
Bob Newhart (CBS)	—	—	—	—	9	23.8
Adam-12 (NBC)	—	—	—	—	10	23.0

Total People (3,031)

1. All in the Family (CBS) . . 46,440
2. Walt Disney (NBC). 37,180
3. Sanford and Son (NBC) . . 35,920
4. ABC Sun. Mystery Movie . 32,390
5. Hawaii Five-O (CBS). . . . 31,400
6. Maude (CBS) 31,290
7. Flip Wilson (NBC) 31,250
8. Gunsmoke (CBS) 30,680
9. Mary Tyler Moore (CBS) . 30,450
10. Adam-12 (NBC). 30,250

Men 18–49 (624)

1. All in the Family (CBS) . . . 8,470
2. ABC NFL Football (ABC) . 8,080
3. ABC Sun. Night Movie . . . 8,030
4. NBC Sun. Mystery Movie . . 7,690
5. Walt Disney (NBC). 6,750
6. Kung Fu-Thur. 9:00 (ABC) . 6,390
7. Sanford and Son (NBC) . . . 6,370
8. Hawaii Five-O (CBS). . . . 6,210
9. NBC Sat. Night Movies . . . 6,190
10. Tues. Movie of Week (ABC) 6,110

Men 18–34 (351)

1. ABC NFL Football. 4,880
2. All in the Family (CBS) . . . 4,720
3. ABC Sun. Night Movie . . . 4,570
4. NBC Sun. Mystery Movie . . 4,370
5. Kung Fu-Thur. 9:00 (ABC) . 4,260
6. Walt Disney (NBC). 3,790
7. Tues. Movie of Week (ABC) 3,630
8. Marcus Welby (ABC) 3,520
9. Adam-12 (NBC). 3,500
9. NBC Wed. Mystery Movie. . 3,470
10. Hawaii Five-O (CBS). . . . 3,470

Men 25–49 (465)

1. All in the Family (CBS) . . . 6,400
2. ABC NFL Football. 6,300
3. NBC Sun. Mystery Movie . . 6,250

4. ABC Sun. Night Movie . . . 6,150
5. Walt Disney (NBC). 5,360
6. Hawaii Five-O (CBS). 4,990
7. Sanford and Son (NBC) . . . 4,950
8. NBC Sat. Night Movies . . . 4,900
9. NBC Wed. Mystery Movie. . 4,770
10. Tues. Movie of Week (ABC) 4,730

Men 50+ (357)

1. All in the Family (CBS) . . . 6,520
2. Sanford and Son (NBC) . . . 6,060
3. Gunsmoke (CBS) 5,710
4. Ironside (NBC) 4,870
5. Maude (CBS) 4,690
6. Flip Wilson (NBC) 4,560
7. Hawaii Five-O (CBS). 4,480
8. Adam-12 (NBC). 4,160
8. F.B.I. (ABC) 4,160
9. Walt Disney (NBC). 4,090
9. Here's Lucy (CBS) 4,090

Total Men (981)

1. All in the Family (CBS) . . 14,990
2. Sanford and Son (NBC) . . 12,430
3. ABC NFL Football. 11,690
4. NBC Sun. Mystery Movie . 11,650
5. ABC Sun. Night Movie . . . 11,170
6. Walt Disney (NBC). 10,850
7. Hawaii Five-O (CBS). . . . 10,700
8. Ironside (NBC) 10,120
9. Flip Wilson (NBC) 10,060
10. Gunsmoke (CBS) 9,880

Women 18–49 (692)

1. All in the Family (CBS) . . 10,620
2. Marcus Welby (ABC) 9,960
3. Tues. Movie of Week (ABC) 8,660
4. NBC Sun. Mystery Movie . . 8,580
5. ABC Sun. Night Movie . . . 8,560
6. Hawaii Five-O (CBS). 7,520
7. Sanford and Son (NBC) . . . 7,510

8. Sonny & Cher: Wed.-8 (CBS) 7,410
9. Cannon (CBS). 7,330
10. Maude (CBS) 7,200

Women 18–34 (386)

1. Marcus Welby (ABC) 6,120
2. All in the Family (CBS) . . . 6,010
3. Tues. Movie of Week (ABC) 5,330
4. ABC Sun. Night Movie . . . 5,220
5. NBC Sun. Mystery Movie . . 5,150
6. Kung Fu-Thur. 9:00 (ABC) . 4,930
7. Hawaii Five-O (CBS). 4,580
8. Cannon (CBS). 4,450
9. Sonny & Cher: Wed.-8 (CBS) 4,410
10. Maude (CBS) 4,400

Women 25–49 (510)

1. All in the Family (CBS) . . . 7,890
2. Marcus Welby (ABC) 7,390
3. NBC Sun. Mystery Movie . . 6,480
4. Tues. Movie of Week (ABC) 6,350
5. ABC Sun. Night Movie . . . 6,180
6. Sanford and Son (NBC) . . . 5,770
7. Hawaii Five-O (CBS). 5,610
8. NBC Mon. Night Movies . . 5,510
9. Cannon (CBS). 5,460
10. Sonny & Cher: Wed.-8 (CBS) 5,410

Women 50+ (392)

1. All in the Family (CBS) . . . 9,360
2. Sanford and Son (NBC) . . . 8,230
3. Gunsmoke (CBS) 7,550
4. Ironside (NBC) 6,720
5. Here's Lucy (CBS) 6,650
6. Maude (CBS) 6,610
7. Flip Wilson (NBC) 6,190
8. Mary Tyler Moore (CBS) . . 5,950
9. Hawaii Five-O (CBS). 5,880
10. Little People (Brian Keith)
   (NBC) 5,570

Total Women (1,084)

1. All in the Family (CBS) . . 19,980
2. Sanford and Son (NBC) . . 15,740

3. Marcus Welby (ABC) . . . 14,960
4. Maude (CBS) 13,810
5. Ironside (NBC) 13,520
6. Hawaii Five-O (CBS). . . . 13,400
7. Gunsmoke (CBS) 13,190
8. NBC Sun. Mystery Movie . 13,080
9. Flip Wilson (NBC) 12,940
10. Mary Tyler Moore (CBS) . 12,710

Female Teens (210)

1. Partridge Family (ABC) . . . 2,560
2. Tues. Movie of Week (ABC) 2,460
3. Here's Lucy (CBS) 2,290
4. Mary Tyler Moore (CBS) . . 2,280
5. Sonny & Cher: Wed.-8 (CBS) 2,200
6. Brady Bunch (ABC) 2,180
7. All in the Family (CBS) . . . 2,130
8. Room 222 (ABC). 2,060
9. Bob Newhart Show (CBS) . . 1,970
9. Marcus Welby (ABC) 1,970

Male Teens (185)

1. Walt Disney (NBC). 2,320
2. Kung Fu-Thur. 9:00 (ABC) . 2,090
3. Tues. Movie of Week (ABC) 1,950
4. All in the Family (CBS) . . . 1,860
5. Rookies (ABC) 1,800
6. NBC Sun. Mystery Movie . . 1,790
7. ABC NFL Football. 1,740
7. NBC Sat. Night Movies . . . 1,740
7. ABC Sun. Night Movie . . . 1,740
10. Partridge Family (ABC) . . . 1,670

Children 6–11 (363)

1. Partridge Family (ABC) . . . 7,930
2. Brady Bunch (ABC). 7,500
3. Walt Disney (NBC). 6,610
4. All in the Family (CBS) . . . 5,360
5. Room 222 (ABC). 5,180
6. Emergency (NBC) 4,760
7. Mary Tyler Moore (CBS) . . 4,530
8. Sonny & Cher: Wed.-8 (CBS) 4,500

9. Odd Couple (ABC) 4,420
10. Waltons (CBS) 4,160

Total Children 2–11 (571)
1. Partridge Family (ABC) . . 11,460
2. Brady Bunch 11,000
3. Walt Disney (NBC). 10,830

4. All in the Family (CBS) . . . 7,500
5. Emergency (NBC) 7,050
6. Room 222 (ABC) 6,840
7. Sonny & Cher: Wed.-8 (CBS) 6,500
8. Waltons (CBS) 6,260
9. Adam-12 (NBC). 6,020
10. Mary Tyler Moore (CBS) . . 5,740

Note—These top tens rank the prime time regular network tv shows on the basis of their Nielsen record in reaching total people and various age and sex subdivisions for the average minute during the 1972–73 season. Only returning programs were included. The lists, covering premiere date through Feb. 25 (there are no demographic ratings for March and April), were compiled for Advertising Age by a broadcast researcher. "Kung Fu" and "Sonny & Cher" were tabulated only for their new mid-season time periods. In parentheses are the sample sizes for the Feb. 11 Nielsen report; the size of the samples varies slightly from one report to the next.

APPENDIX
to Chapter 17

**Summary of
Violence
Counts**

1954: 10 percent of dramas booked into television depend on incidents of "crime and horror." The study, funded by the Ford Foundation, was conducted under the auspices of the National Association of Educational Broadcasters. It is cited in Surgeon General's Scientific Advisory Committee on Television and Social Behavior, *Initial Operations, June—October 1969* (Washington, D.C.: National Institute of Mental Health, 1969), pp. 2–3.

1963: A threefold increase in proportion of violent television programs depending on incidents of "crime and horror." Cited in Baker, Robert K., and Ball, Sandra J., *Mass Media and Violence, Vol. IX,* A Report to the National Commission on the Causes and Prevention of Violence (Washington, D.C.: U.S. Government, November 1969), p. viii.

1967: Over half the programs the three commercial networks booked into their prime-time hours featured major characters who were violent. Twenty-four violent interactions in an average hour of cartoon programs the networks book to attract children; some violence in eight out of ten plays. Cited in Baker, Robert K., and Ball, Sandra J., "The Television World of Violence," op. cit., p. 315. The appendix tables give the breakdowns of violent acts by network (ABC programed slightly more violence than the other two networks during the period covered). More than thirty-seven pages of fine print chronicle whether the consequences of the violence were permanent or transitory, whether the perpetrator was a good guy or bad guy, the age and sex and racial background of perpetrators and victims, and so on.

1969: Saturday-morning cartoons include a violent episode at least once every two minutes; the use of weapons increased from 52 to 83 percent in cartoon episodes designed to attract children to the set. On the other hand, the body count of dead on all shows, whether designed to attract children or adults, declined to 34 percent—down 8 percent since 1969. Gerbner, George, "Violence in Television Drama: Trends and Symbolic Functions," in Surgeon General's Scientific Advisory Committee on Television and Social Behavior, *Television and Social Behavior, Reports and Papers,* Volume I, "Media Content and Control" (Washington, D.C.: U.S. Government), pp. 28–187, p. 40.

1971: "About three out of 10 story segments were 'saturated' with violence, and 71 percent had at least one instance of human violence, with or without the use of weapons. . . . Although in 52 percent of the segments violence was directed at humans, only in 4 percent did this result in death or injury. Although there is an abundance of violence of all kinds one is left with the impression that, after all, violence is harmless. . . . Over half of all programs was concerned with crime, the supernatural and struggles between characters . . ." This study was conducted by Dr. F. Earle Barcus, Communications Research Professor at Boston University, for Action for Children's Television. Findings based on analysis of just under 19 hours of Saturday network and local programs in May and June 1971 are reported in *Newsletter, Action for Children's Television* 2, 2 (Fall 1971).

The rate of violent incidents on prime-time and Saturday-morning programs is twice the British rate, even though British television is padded with American imports. James D. Halloran and Paul Cross, "Television Programs in Great Britain: Content and Control (A Pilot Study)," *Television and Social Behavior, Reports and Papers,* Volume I, op. cit., pp. 415–92.

1972:   Eight out of ten programs and nine out of ten cartoons contain violent incidents. No. change in prevalence of violence since 1967. Gerbner, George, and Gross, L., *The Violence Profile No. 5,* (Philadelphia, Pa.: The Annenberg School of Communications, 1973). "Prevalence of violence" is percentage of programs containing violent action and percentage of hours that include violent incidents. "Violence" is defined in these counts as "the overt expression of physical force, compelling action against one's will on pain of being hurt or killed or actually hurting or killing."

1974, 1975, 1976:   Violence in weekend daytime (children's) programing rose from an index of 194 in fall 1974 to 221 in fall 1975, then declined to 200 in spring 1976. George Gerbner, "The Family Hour and Beyond," *Human Behavior,* 5, 11, November 1976.

Spring 1976:   Five out of every ten family hour programs, eight out of ten late evening programs and nine out of every ten weekend children's programs contained some violence. The rate of violent incidents was three per cent before 9 P.M. eastern time, 7 per program after 9 P.M. and four per weekend children's program. A little over three out of every ten family hour characters were involved in violence, but there was very little killing. After 9 o'clock, seven out of every ten characters were involved in some violence, and over two out of ten were involved in killing. On children's weekend programs eight in every ten characters were involved in some violence, but there was practically no killing. George Gerbner, "The Family Hour and Beyond," *op. cit.*

Fall 1976:   Highest Violence Index on record. Three fourths of all
characters were involved in some violence. Nine out of every
ten programs sampled contained some violence. The number
of violent acts during weekend programs targeted to children
exceeds the corresponding number in programs delivered
during the last two network prime-time hours. George
Gerbner and others, "TV Violence Profile No. 8: The High-
lights," *Journal of Communications* 27, 2 (1977), 171–180.

APPENDIX
to Chapter 18

**Employment of
Protagonists
in Prime-Time Network
Crime and
Action-Adventure Series,
1974–75**

UNIFORMED POLICE

Adam 12
Police Story (cast changes weekly)
The Rookies
S.W.A.T.

CIVVIES: FEDERAL GOVERNMENT
EMPLOYEES

Caribe
FBI
Gunsmoke
Hec Ramsey
Kodiak
McCloud
Nakia
Sierra (U.S. Park Service)
Six Million Dollar Man

CIVVIES: STATE AND MUNICIPAL
EMPLOYEES

> Amy Prentiss
> Barney Miller*
> Baretta
> Columbo
> Hawaii Five-O
> Dan August
> Get Christie Love
> Ironside
> Kojak
> McMillan and Wife**
> Police Woman
> Streets of San Francisco

PRIVATE SECTOR

> Archer
> Barnaby Jones
> Cannon
> Khan!
> Mannix
> Harry O
> Manhunter
> Petrocelli
> Rockford Files

---

*Properly speaking, a sitcom, not a crime show.

**McMillan, as commissioner of police, is on the municipal payroll. His wife is in the private sector. The series could well have been double-counted for this tally. It didn't seem worth the trouble, though, since the wife was written out of the series within short order.

OTHER

Emergency (uniformed paramedics employed by municipal fire department)

Kung Fu (Shaolin priest wandering through the Western frontier of the 1880s)

Kolchak (a reporter who specializes in tracking down occurrences said to be occult)

Planet of the Apes (astronauts normally in the employ of the federal government, but they must wander through a world of the future and presumably collect no salary)

A P P E N D I X
to Chapter 19

Commercial Television
Enters the School
Curriculum

The idea of using commercial television programs in classroom instruction is attributed to two Philadelphia school teachers, Bernard Solomon and Michael McAndrew. Both were teaching at Philadelphia's Mastermann Elementary School in 1971, when they elaborated a technique which is now called "dual audio television." The National Science Foundation granted research funds to the Philadelphia Board of Education to evaluate the procedure, which was tested at the East Washington Rhodes Middle School in North Philadelphia in March 1973.

The technique simultaneously uses a videotape of the show, the script, and audio commentary. Copies of the script are duplicated and distributed to the students in the class. (The production companies, heartily approving of the entire procedure, now provide scripts free to the project.) The students refer to the script as they watch the show on the classroom television monitor. An "educator" prepares instructional commentary highlighting the day's lesson. His voice comes into the classroom simultaneously with the show, via FM radio or audio cassette. His comments are timed so that they do not interrupt the dialogue but are synchronized with the moments when the screen is busy with action and dramatic business and nobody is speaking. This is thought to have the advantage that the children will not lose the thread of the story as they listen to his voice.

In 1974, the Philadelphia public school system used reruns of "Gilligan's Island" in the test project. WKBS-TV, the station broadcasting the series, cooperated to the extent of allowing the "educator," Stephen Baskerville, to appear briefly before each episode to urge simultaneous tuning to "a cool new radio program" that would carry his voice explaining the lesson. The FM station, WUHY-FM, carried his commentary.[1]

"Kung Fu" was a particularly popular program for this sort of in-school classroom instruction[2] until it went off the air in September 1975. Teachers liked it because it could be used to teach almost anything: geography (Locate China and state its boundaries.); lessons in religion (What is a Shaolin priest?); lessons in history and sociology (Describe our importation of immigrant Chinese and explain how railroad tracks laid by such imported labor opened the West to expansion.). "Ironside" has also been used in similar fashion.

The shows are taped off the air complete with their spliced-in commercials.[3] Whether the commercials are also used as lesson material I have not been able to determine. I suppose some might even view them

---

1. *Variety*, April 17, 1974. See also Craig R. Waters, "Thank God Something Has Finally Reached Him," *TV Guide*, January 19, 1974. The research results were reported in Terry Borton, Leonard Belasco, and A. Rae Williams, "Dual Audio Television Goes Public," *Journal of Communications*, Summer 1975.

2. Craig R. Waters, *ibid*. The choice of "Kung Fu" to teach children is particularly interesting. The show stars Caine, half white, half Oriental, a Shaolin priest wandering through the West in the 1880s. It opened in 1972 and closed after three years of play. A cameraman working on the "Kung Fu" series explains what he calls "the cinemagraphic style" of Jerry Thorpe, the show's executive producer. "Slash! Kick! Chop! Violence galore! That's the kind of movie action contained in the original 'Kung Fu' script (advertisement for Eastman Kodak film in *Variety*, June 5, 1974). *Variety*, June 19, 1974, reported that England's Independent Broadcasting Authority prohibits the screening of this show before 7:30 P.M.—their bizarre response to complaints from school authorities and others that children are imitating the fighting style of this program's protagonist, a master of what is quaintly called "the martial arts."

3. T. Borton and others, op. cit.

as demonstrations of experimental laboratory techniques, as all those advertised products are "tested against the leading contender."

The idea has been elaborated in Jacksonville, Florida, where WJXT has cooperated in beaming a special television show to all eighteen thousand sixth and seventh graders in the Duval County Public Schools. *The Vanishing Shadow,* a 1934 Universal science fiction serial, was reedited for the purpose into twelve cliff-hanger installments, appropriate for television. Re-editing includes building in television techniques such as animation, freeze-frame, slow-motion, and a rock-music background. The same program has been used in equivalent "lessons" to public-school pupils in Mount Vernon, New York; Benton Harbor, Michigan; Greenwich, Connecticut; and Brooklyn, New York. All these stations are linked to the Post-Newsweek broadcasting chain.[4] Why these "educators" believe reading skills will survive these concerted efforts to reduce further the opportunities schoolchildren have to practice them or even see them as relevant is beyond my comprehension.

Junior high and high schools are blessed with additional sources of the same genre. The Xerox Corporation, for example, circulates a film made up of their own Xerox television commercials over the past fifteen years. It goes free to junior high schools, high schools, and colleges "for instructional purposes."[5]

NBC's "Today Show" has been entering about fifteen million homes daily for more than a decade. The show's authoritativeness is now cranked up a notch as high-school students throughout the country are asked to tune in each morning, all for the sake of sharpening their understanding of earth sciences and meteorology. They're told to slap a piece of Saran Wrap up against the screen, trace the weather map, and bring the tracings to class every day.[6] Can't be done without watching at least part of the show, of course.

An AP release datelined Los Angeles, April 20, 1975, reports that the

---

4. Release from Post-Newsweek Stations, Inc., March 31, 1975.

5. *Advertising Age.* July 14, 1975.

6. *Hollywood Reporter.* August 7, 1975, and conversation with Professor Ira W. Geer, chairman Earth Sciences Department, SUNY Brockport, October 24, 1975.

University of Southern California has hired a comedy writer to liven up lectures given by professors. They picked one of Johnny Carson's gag writers for the job.[7] (P-s-s-t. Did you hear the one about the square of the hypotenuse?) I suppose it won't be long before the teacher will tell the class to "stand by for this message," step up to the microphone, and deliver what the business calls a "host commercial."

7. *New York Times,* April 20, 1975.

NOTES

CHAPTER I

1. As of November 30, 1976, the Federal Communications Commission reported the following distribution of stations on the air:

> Commercial television 719
> VHF 513
> UHF 206
> Educational television 239
> VHF 91
> UHF 148

VHF stations broadcast on a frequency that is more widely received than UHF stations. As of this writing, VHF stations are the ones that are brought in when the dial on a television set clicks. UHF stations must be fine-tuned.

The Federal Communications Commission (FCC) classifies as "educational television" stations which devote some hours to curriculum instruction. These stations are in the Public Broadcasting System, and are often referred to as "public television." Both terms are misnomers. All television is educational just as all television is public. (Radio, too, for that matter.)

2.   The three networks own and control all TV affiliates in three metropolitan areas: New York, Los Angeles, and Chicago. These comprise 20 percent of all the nation's TV households. They likewise control an affiliate in each of six other large areas—another 13 percent of television homes—ABC in San Francisco and Detroit; CBS in Philadelphia and St. Louis; NBC in Cleveland and Washington, D.C. (See in the Matter of Prime Time Access Rule, FCC 75–67 Second Report and Order, January 17, 1975. Footnote, p. 5 of Glen O. Robinson, "Dissenting Statement.") Each network also owns and controls (among other holdings) fourteen radio stations in major markets (seven AM and seven FM). The count for affiliated stations at the close of 1976 was: NBC 212; CBS 198; ABC 190 plus 55 secondary affiliates.

3.   Many insightful writers have noted how the earliest stirrings of the industrial system we know introduced massive changes in the way people experienced time and depended upon such changes in time-sense to come into its own full existence. The following sources have in common their understanding that the power to control the way in which people experience time is a fundamental power, convertible into political and economic control and domination.

Lewis Mumford, *Technics and Human Development: The Myth of the Machine, Vol. 1.* (New York: Harcourt Brace Jovanovich, 1966) pp. 284–87; idem, *Interpretations and Forecasts: 1922–1972* (New York: Harcourt Brace Jovanovich, 1974) pp. 270–78.

Brodey, Warren J., "The Clock Manifesto," *Annals of the New York Academy of Science* 138 (February 6, 1967): 895–911, and also "Biotopology 1972," *Radical Software* No. 4 (Summer 1971): 4–7.

Herbert G. Reid, "American Social Science in the Politics of Time and the Crisis of Technocorporate Society," *Politics and Society* 3, 2 (Winter 1973): 201–44.

John R. Silver, "The Pollution of Time," *The Center Magazine* IV, 5 (September/October 1971): 2–9.

C. Wright Mills, *White Collar* (New York: Oxford University Press, 1951).

4. The decision to keep or cancel a series is made almost immediately after it opens, aided by information available through what is called the Trendex Callback System: householders in twenty-five cities are asked by telephone which shows they have watched and if they plan to watch them again.

5. The FCC is the government agency established by Congress when the Communications Act of 1934 was passed. This act, as amended (47 U.S.C. 151–609, 1964), still sets the guidelines and guideposts to which broadcasters are legally bound to adhere. The seven commissioners of the FCC are supposed to keep broadcasters honest; to make certain, that is, that franchise holders adhere to their pledge and statutory obligation to broadcast "in the public interest, convenience, and necessity," as a condition of holding and retaining the license to use the public's airwaves. The FCC, however, has consistently refrained from specifying how program content or format or programing practices or procurement practices affect the public interest, convenience, and necessity—either positively or negatively. As a result, the principal restrictions on the content or duration of any materials going over the air are those which broadcasters voluntarily agree to impose on themselves. The notable exception to this is a congressional statute which bans cigarette advertisements from the public airwaves.

The broadcasting industry's own trade and lobbying association is the National Association of Broadcasters (NAB). This association has established a Code Authority, which NAB members are invited to join. Those who do solemnly pledge to adhere to certain rules, among them to limit the amount of time dedicated to commercials.

Assuming compliance with this code, stations that voluntarily take the pledge fill 26.6 percent of daytime broadcast hours with extraneous materials, 16 percent of Saturday-morning hours and prime-time broadcast hours. A station on the air from 6 in the morning to 2 A.M. (about 70 percent of commercial stations fall in this category) would fill, at that rate, about five hours a day with such extraneous materials. This estimate does not include time devoted to eulogies and close-up shots of products embedded in shows as if they were merely part of the fun.

6.   The steps that "cure" strong feelings through imaginal desensitization are these:

   1. The person (called a "subject") views familiar images in a comfortable non-threatening situation. He is completely relaxed. No emotional arousal is noted.
   2. Certain images known to arouse emotional reactions are introduced. Relaxation ceases.
   3. Viewing is interrupted: viewer turns away. Scene shifts.
   4. Viewer is allowed a respite period (thirty to sixty seconds) during which he resumes relaxation. This may be facilitated by eating or drinking.
   5. As viewer's emotions subside, viewing of the same familiar images is resumed. Subject is again completely relaxed. No emotional arousal is noted.
   6. The cycle is repeated.

   H. R. Beech, *Changing Man's Behaviour* (Hammondsworth, Middlesex, England, 1969); and H. J. Eysenck, ed., *Behaviour Therapy and the Neuroses* (New York: Pergamon Press, 1960), provide succinct summaries of the state of the art in the field of behavior modification.

7.   The term appears in H. R. Beech, op. cit., p. 77.

8.   "Does it follow that because a patient can imagine a scene calmly, he will also be calm when he comes upon a similar scene in reality? Experience shows that answer to be in the affirmative." Joseph Wolpe, "Reciprocal Inhibition as the Main Basis of Psychotherapeutic Effects," in H. J. Eysenck, ed., op. cit., pp. 88–143, 94. The article continues with case studies to illustrate the point. Other articles in the same source document similar experiences.

9. Consistently ignoring certain ways of reacting, deleting them from the visible environment as if they did not even exist, as if they had never occurred, is a form of *negative reinforcement* that extinguishes the participant's feelings and aids emotional desensitization and reeducation.

Mentioning or showing whatever it is that usually elicits the extreme emotional reaction but simply withholding approval or disapproval of it is a form of negative reinforcement too. Another form of negative reinforcement is to treat all situations as emotionally similar, leveling them all to the same monotone, as it were.

Negative-reinforcement techniques range from those mentioned above to highly punishing ones such as painful electric shocks and noxious emetics that produce retching and vomiting. The literature on this subject includes lengthy discussions about whether negative reinforcers are really negative or, on the contrary, positive in the sense that the reinforcing association takes place when the painful stimulus is withdrawn (positive feelings evoked) rather than when the pain is being registered (negative feelings evoked).

10. I have found at least one "think piece" which suggests an improvement over present procedures, enlisting the viewer's own brain waves as the broadcaster's ally. The brain emits Alpha waves when a person is relaxed, a circumstance that permits learning to occur effortlesly in the absence of any act of conscious will. The article suggests that television programs could easily be woven around visual and aural "stimuli" known to elicit Alpha wave production by viewers. "Educational materials" simultaneously engineered into such programs would then be placidly absorbed by those watching them, thus programing "subjects" through "passive learning which is 'caught' rather than 'taught.' " (H. E. Krugman and E. L. Hartley, "Passive Learning from Television," *Public Opinion Quarterly* 34 [1970]: 184–90.) Dr. Krugman is responsible for corporate public relations and advertising research at the General Electric Company. Eugene L. Hartley is Emeritus Professor of Psychology, City College, CUNY, and Dean of the College of

Community Sciences at the University of Wisconsin, Green Bay, Wisconsin.

11. J. Wolpe, *Psychotherapy by Reciprocal Inhibition* (Stanford: Stanford University Press, 1958).

12. I find it ironically amusing that the behavior therapists who treat the human creature as if he were a white rat in a laboratory experiment, and in turn treat the white rat as if he were an inanimate mechanism activated only by external stimuli, nevertheless rely for "cure" on the very human quality they ignore and their epistemology denies: human imagination. "Therapy" sessions which rely on imagination aided by hypnosis are often no more successful than sessions in which unaided imagination is given its own free reign. "A good relaxer can do almost as well without hypnosis, just closing his eyes." Joseph Wolpe, "Reciprocal Inhibition as the Main Basis of Psychotherapeutic Effects," in H. J. Eysenck, ed., op. cit., pp. 88–143, p. 94.

13. *Plato's Republic,* Jowett translation (New York: Modern Library, no date), p. 72.

14. Martin Heidegger, *What Is Called Thinking* (New York: Harper and Row, 1954).

15. Suzanne K. Langer, *Mind: An Essay on Human Feeling* (Baltimore, Md.: Johns Hopkins University Press, Volume I, 1967, Volume II, 1972).

16. I am indebted to Dr. George Gerbner for calling this quotation to my attention. It appears in Andrew Fletcher of Saltoun, "Letter to the Marquis of Montrose," *Works,* p. 294.

17. This power was named in 1848: "ideological hegemony." See Karl Marx and Friedrich Engels, *The German Ideology, Part One,* C. J. Arthur, ed. (New York: International Publishers, 1970).

CHAPTER 2

1.   See, for example, Leo Lowenthal, *Prophets of Deceit* (New York: Harper Bros., 1949).

CHAPTER 3

1.   The Federal Communications Commission defines as prime time the period between 7 and 11 P.M. coastal times, 6 and 10 central and mountain time, seven days a week. Their "prime-time access rule" (first issued in 1970) sets a ceiling on the number of slots broadcasters may fill with materials procured through a network supplier.

      The ceiling applies to programs currently scheduled by a network, as well as those which had been scheduled by the network during the two preceding years. The ceiling is set at three hours for the usual entertainment series and movies that the networks program; but it may go to three and a half and even four hours under certain circumstances. As of this writing, the networks program three prime-time hours, except on Sundays, when they program four hours.

2.   The formula for these shows is discussed on pages 33–37. The count excludes seven variety shows. It includes each of five series which alternated with each other on NBC's Sunday Mystery Movie: "Columbo," "McMillan and Wife," "McCloud," "Hec Ramsey," and "Amy Prentiss."

      I did not count the made-for-TV movies or specials such as *The Godfather* and its numerous imitators. If I had included the made-for-TV movies (preponderantly crime shows), the proportion of prime-time programs that obliterate contemporary family images would have risen even higher. The appendix to chapter 3 (pages 310–315) lists all the shows discussed in this section, classified by type of relationship featured.

      Network parlance avoids the term "crime show" in favor of "action-adventure."

3. Conversation, February 13, 1975. In the original film on which this series was based, Moze and Addie were not father and daughter.

4. It's hard to tell whether Barnaby Jones and Betty share living quarters or just office space. The show's handler at the CBS network that booked it was unable to clear the matter up. "No information on that, sorry," he reported.

5. These shows run true to form. "McMillan and Wife" closed one season, reopened the next—sans "Wife."

6. "Khan!," the crime show, featured a broken family: the father, two adult offspring, no mother. "We'll Get By" and "The Bob Crane Show" were the only second-season bookings showing intact families; neither was rebooked.

7. The show reworks the formula of another successful prime-time show which had reworked the formula of a successful movie: *M*A*S*H*. In "M*A*S*H" an army medical unit during the Korean War is the setting for fraternity boy antics. In "Barney Miller," a precinct of the New York Police Department provides the setting for similar if not identical antics. The early episodes of "Barney Miller" showed his wife and daughter on stage with reasonable frequency. In later episodes they were written out of the show. In "M*A*S*H," all families are back in the United States while the men are at the front. (War is hell!)

8. ABC closed its network contract at the close of the 1972–73 season.

9. John J. O'Connor, *The New York Times,* September 26, 1974.

10. *Variety,* April 16, 1974.

CHAPTER 4

1. Alen Loren, "Who Loves Ya, Baby," *TV Guide,* January 3, 1976, describes with amusement how his daughter plays Kojak. Michael Arlen, "Waiting for the Storyteller," *New Yorker,* April 21, 1975,

describes—with considerably less amusement—a similar scene as his two children discuss the same character and the same series.

2. Until January 1975, the NAB Code Authority recognized only weekend time as "children's time." Beginning January 1975, a new category emerged: stations that choose to devote weekdays 4 to 6 P.M. to programs they target to children are admonished that this is "after-school time," and code standards apply. The standards are summarized below:

	January 1976	January 1975	January 1973–74	Prior to January 1973
Saturdays and Sundays 8 A.M.–2 P.M.: No. of minutes for commercials and nonprogram interruptions per hour	9 1/2 (15.9%)	10 (16.6%)	12 (20%)	16 (26.6%)
Weekdays 4–6 P.M. (If station chooses to program "after-school material")	12 (20%)	14 (23.3%)	(No such category recognized; prevailing standard was 16 minutes, 26.6%)	

3. "Only 8.8% of the viewing time of children between the ages of 2 and 11 is on Saturday mornings," John A. Scheider, president of the CBS Broadcast Group, informed an open meeting of the Hollywood Radio and Television Society during the week of June 3, 1974. The address was reported in *Advertising Age,* June 17, 1974.

4. The three commercial networks booked thirty-five separate series (thirty on Saturday, five on Sunday) that season. The appendix to chapter 3 lists shows booked into the 1974–75 season by the three networks, classified according to family type and principal social units featured.

5. Reynaldo Pareja, *Children Learn Whether or Not We Teach Them*, Master's essay, Cornell University, 1974. Pareja analyzed fifty-eight episodes of programs targeted to children Saturday mornings between June 16 and October 20, 1973, thus bridging the 1972–73 season and the 1973–74 season. Nurturing behavior is defined above. Excluded from the definition were instances of explicit didacticism such as someone giving instructions, explaining how something works, and the like.

6. Reynaldo Pareja, op. cit., p. 78.

7. Ibid., p. 70.

8. The five were: "The Jetsons," "The Flintstones," "The Barkleys," "The Brady Kids," and "The Addams Family." By the time the 1974–75 season opened, there were seven: "The Addams Family," "The Jetsons," "The Partridge Family," "Devlin," "The Hudson Brothers," "Bailey's Comets," and "Gilligan's Island." The ratio remained unchanged, however: seven out of thirty-five titles.

9. "My Favorite Martian" featured an "uncle" from Mars, living with a "nephew." "Bailey's Comets" featured a team of roller-skating kids—orphans. "The Hudson Brothers," a variety show, starred three young adults who billed themselves as brothers. No common parent was ever mentioned or appeared on the show. "Devlin" featured three orphaned teenagers whose adventures celebrated the motorcycle as an exciting vehicle.

10. The Pareja study (op. cit.) reports forty-four of fifty-eight episodes on which he had data showed mixed gangs of teenagers and children.

11. This is the title that appears in listings of *TV Guide* and in the Advance Program Schedules issued by ABC. Other sources sometimes refer to it as "Yogi and His Friends."

CHAPTER 5

1. The source of this figure as well as other similar citations in this chapter is: *Series, Serials and Packages: A TV Film/Tape Source Book (Domestic Edition),* Vol. 16, Issue 2D (New York: Broadcast Information Bureau, Inc., 1975). In certain cases information from this source has been corrected by direct inquiry made of the producers.

2. *1975 Annual Report and Operational Review,* Gulf + Western Industries, Inc.

3. Quoted in *Broadcasting,* November 20, 1972. Mr. Ducovny as of this writing is retired, but maintained on the CBS payroll as consultant.

4. Edward C. Devereux, "Some Observations on Sports, Play and Games in Childhood," address delivered at conference of the Eastern Association for Physical Education of College Women, October 21, 1972. See also Dorothy H. Cohen, "Is TV a Pied Piper?" address before the Midwest Association for the Education of Young Children, March 15, 1974, mimeographed and also Marie Winn, *The Plug-In Drug* (New York: Viking Press, 1977).

5. Programs booked into the ghetto hours like to show the children, women, and girls using magic more than men and boys. Analysis of ten shows during the 1971–72 television season quantified the degree of sex preference for magic tricks. Sixteen percent of all female characters in these shows used magic: 4 percent of the male characters did. The shows were "Pebbles and Bamm Bamm," "The Harlem Globetrotters," "Josie and the Pussycats," "Popeye," "Superman," "Bewitched," "Sabrina the Teenage Witch," "Jeannie," "Archie's TV Funnies," and "Scooby Doo." Sarah H. Sternglanz and Lisa A. Serbin, "Sex Role Stereotyping in Children's Television Programs," *Developmental Psychology* 10, no. 5 (1974): 710–15.

6. Pareja reported that over half of the episodes he examined pre-
    sented television actors or cartoon characters from other shows as
    visiting cast or guest stars. Reynaldo Pareja, op. cit., 59–60.

CHAPTER 6

1. Shows that filmed live actors included a few programs that were
    specially crafted for children ("Hot Dog," "Go," "Jambo," "Bar-
    rier Reef," "Take A Giant Step," "Curiosity Shop," and "Make
    a Wish"—to mention some). They include as well shows such as
    "Bewitched"—the original show, now sold in syndication, made
    originally for general audiences; "Runaround," a game show wor-
    thy of playing against any of the current daytime game shows;
    "The Monkees," a rock group appealing to the rock audience; and
    so on.Appendix p. 316 lists network bookings for the children's
    weekend ghetto 1970–76, indicating which were animations.

2. In 1972, a cartoon series could be produced at about $10,000 per
    half-hour—$1,666 per showing, given network practices of airing
    each episode six times. This is in contrast to $7,500 per half-hour
    it cost to produce a filmed show using live actors—$3,750 per
    showing, given network practices of airing each such episode only
    twice. William Melody, *Children's Television: Economics and Pub-
    lic Policy,* mimeographed (Philadelphia, Pa.: Annenberg School,
    University of Pennsylvania, 1972). Further syndication sales re-
    duce costs per episode yielding to the producers benefits of econ-
    omy of scale.

    Costs of producing animations have risen precipitously, so that
    filmed live actors are again competitive. As we go to press, latest
    network schedules for the Saturday-morning children's ghetto
    1976–77 list fifteen half-hours devoted to films showing people and
    monsters, the other fifteen showing the usual animations.

3. Christopher Finch, *The Art of Walt Disney: From Mickey Mouse
    to the Magic Kingdoms* (Walt Disney Productions), 152–54.

    Television technology, itself, gave an added impetus to the tend-
    ency to abandon animation as an artistic process. When anima-

tions were made mainly for a market of moviegoers and the artists' final creations recorded on film, the medium reproduced all details exactly as the artist had drawn them. On television, however, many details are lost: the cathode ray tube scatters them into a blurry mass of 2,000 dots which the viewer himself reconnects in his mind's eye. For an interesting discussion of the interaction between the techniques of production and the nature of the artwork, see Walter Benjamin, "The Work of Art in an Age of Mechanical Reproduction," in Hannah Arendt, ed., *Illuminations* (New York: Schocken Books, 1969), pp. 217–52.

4. Christopher Finch, op. cit., p. 25.

5. Australia was one such area. In the early 1960s Australian studios began reproducing cartoons for American television, beginning with short, six-minute segments such as "Beetle Bailey" and ending with feature-length animated films such as *Treasure Island*. In 1971 the Hanna-Barbera Production Company produced and directed in Australia sixteen half-hours of "Funky Phantom." The following year, Hanna-Barbera Productions Pty., Ltd., was launched at St. Leonard's, Sydney, Australia; and that's where "Valley of the Dinosaurs" was manufactured and produced.

   But time changes all things. The parity of Australian currency relative to the American dollar has altered several times—to the dollar's disadvantage. Production costs are no longer substantially lower than in the U.S.; Paul Hamlyn Pty., Ltd., acquired a 51 percent interest in Hanna-Barbera Productions Pty., Ltd., and Mr. Hanna and Mr. Barbera are back in Hollywood, converting their studios to computer-animation companies. (*Variety,* May 7, 1975)

6. A show that formerly took from four to six weeks to produce, even using limited animation, can now be turned out in half an hour; "risks are minimized, amortization schedules can be based upon more showings and there is generally a substantial market in syndication after first-run showings." William Melody, op. cit., p. 100.

7. See Christopher Finch, op. cit., 152–54. See also Stacy V. Jones in *The New York Times,* October 27, 1973.

8. *Synthavision,* promotional booklet issued by Synthavision, a subsidiary of MAGI (Mathematical Applications Group, Inc.), Elmsford, New York. Undated, unpaged.

9. Reynaldo Pareja, op. cit. The percentages are calculated from the data appearing in his appendix table, p. 142. He goes on to remark that all costuming is thoroughly standardized and characters are so rarely allowed a change of dress that civilian clothes are no less uniform than military and paramilitary dress or career apparel (pp. 95–96).

10. The term *career apparel* is being promoted by the Career Apparel Institute, a branch of the National Association of Uniform Manufacturers. The institute's aim is to promote the idea among corporations and business firms that clothing their employees in uniforms will "enhance the company's image as a closely knit corporate family." (*Advertising and Sales Promotion,* October 15, 1973.) The term *uniform,* however, smacks of regimentation rather than of the family; hence the euphemism *career apparel.*

    In an earlier day, *career apparel* was called by its right name, *livery.* Livery worn by civilians in the service of a noble household evolved into uniforms worn by military forces in the service of an army. "Drill made them act as one, discipline made them respond as one, the uniform made them look as one." Lewis Mumford, *The Pentagon of Power: The Myth of the Machine,* Vol. 2, (New York: Harcourt Brace Jovanovich, 1966), p. 150.

11. It is easy to forget that looking *at* something is only one small aspect of the gaze. Just as we may look at something without seeing it (the mind wanders), it is equally possible to see something without looking *at* it. Looking *at* involves a three degree arc; everything else is peripheral. Indeed, most of what we think of as subliminal perception is peripheral seeing. This kind of seeing can occur in an eye blink (under one tenth of a second). Paradoxically, in order *not* to see what is in our full range of sight, we must decide what *not to look at* as well as what merits attention. The excluded details are undoubtedly stored at least in short term memory, available to be switched to long term memory under certain condi-

tions. Hence, *opportunities to see are inextricably bound up with what is actually seen.*

12. The current term for the study of body language is "proxemics." See Edward T. Hall, *The Silent Language* (Garden City, N. Y.: Doubleday and Co., 1959), idem, *The Hidden Dimension* (Garden City, N. Y.: Doubleday and Co., 1966).

CHAPTER 7

1. And now there is laboratory "evidence" for this old saw. A psychologist has seen fit to compare children exposed to "some funny tapes" when they were alone, with others who listened to the same material in company. He also compared university students doing the same thing with and without a laugh track on the tape. Results turned out as expected. A smile was defined as "any spontaneous upward stretching of the mouth . . . without a vocal sound"; laughter was defined as "an inarticulate vocal sound" with a certain level of audibility. The results are summarized in *Human Behavior* 10, 3 (October 1974): 37–38, which does not comment on whether follow-up inquiry is planned to determine the validity of the companion hypothesis "Weep, and you weep alone."

2. This is the same dubbing-down process which is used to transfer music to the tapes or film.

3. "People are so conditioned to the laugh track that if they don't hear it they don't know it's a comedy show." This remark is attributed to a Hollywood producer of a situation comedy ("As We See It," *TV Guide,* November 18, 1972). Whether this is true remains to be seen, when the generation raised on laugh tracks reaches maturity. Meanwhile, however, I note Dial-A-Joke delivers its one-liners over the telephone, and the record is complete with laugh track.

4. Production of laugh tracks is described in Dick Hobson, "The Hollywood Sphinx and His Laff Box," and "Help, I'm a Prisoner

in a Laffbox!" *TV Guide,* July 2 and July 9, 1966, respectively, and also "As We See It," *TV Guide,* February 10, 1973.

5. "It's 5:30 in Studio 41 . . ." unsigned, *TV Guide,* June 15, 1974, pp. 14–15. The producer quoted was John Rich, formerly with the production company turning out "All in the Family."

CHAPTER 8

1. Quoted in *Ithaca New Times,* May 12, 1974. Mr. Clark's insight that the populace rejects images that do not corroborate familiar views of reality and pays attention to those that do is an echo of Jean Cocteau's observations in his version of the Oedipus myth. Annubis, jackal guard of Egypt and of the Sphinx, explains: "If we didn't appear to men looking the way they picture us, they wouldn't see us at all." "The Infernal Machine," in *The Infernal Machine and Other Plays by Jean Cocteau* (New York: New Directions Publishing Co., 1963), p. 35.

2. See Ernie Kreiling, "So You Need An Audience," *TV Guide,* December 2, 1972.

3. The term is just beginning to gain currency. It is interesting insofar as it acknowledges television's major function as creator of the occurrence, its relatively minor function as transmitter.

4. Rare Earth; the Eagles; Seals and Crofts; Black Oak Arkansas; Black Sabbath; Deep Purple; Earth, Wind, and Fire; and also Emerson, Lake, and Palmer.

5. The network advertisement read, "Share the excitement of the 200,000 rock fans who were there as the ABC Television Network presents history's most successful outdoor rock concert in four fantastic *In Concert* specials." *The New York Times,* May 10, 1974.

6. The term *feedback* is of relatively recent origin, coined by pioneers in radio working at the beginning of the century. It is a method

of controlling a system by reinserting into it the results of its own past performance. (Example: a dart player learns to control his performance by observing and acting upon the results of his previous throws.) *Biofeedback* refers to the same process when the information is picked up from cues internal to the biological system rather than external to it. Thus, subjects with relatively little training can learn to control their emission of alpha brainwaves when their previous emissions are read back to them; blood pressure, rate of heart beat, even temperature in the extremities can be controlled in the same manner. See O. Mayr, "The Origins of Feedback Control," *Scientific American* 223 (1970). See Marvin Karlins and Lewis M. Andrews, *Biofeedback* (Philadelphia: J. B. Lippincott Co., 1972) for a succinct summary.

7. *Variety,* June 20, 1973.

8. John Rockwell, *The New York Times,* July 26, 1974.

9. Ibid.

10. *Variety,* May 15, 1974.

11. *The New York Times,* February 5, 1975.

12. Melvin Herlitzer and Carl Heyel, *The Youth Market* (New York: Media Books, 1970), p. 181.

13. Ibid., p. 182.

14. The quotation is from Walt Whitman's *Leaves of Grass.* The lines are, "There was a child went forth every day / and the first object he looked upon and received with wonder or pity or love or dread, that object he became. / And that object became part of him for the day or a certain part of the day . . . or for many years or stretching cycles of years . . ." The poet lists the objects and concludes the section, "These became part of that child who went forth every day / and who now goes and will always go forth every day. / And these become of him or her that peruses them now."
    They Became What They Beheld is the title of a book by Ed-

mund Carpenter (New York: Outerbridge and Dientstfry, 1970), in which he makes many of the points I am raising.

CHAPTER 9

1. The syndicating company is Worldvision Enterprises, Inc., which was owned by ABC until 1971.

2. *Variety,* February 17, 1974.

3. Recently, however, even the commercials are going to animations, although rather hesitantly at first, combining animated characters with real people. I believe we can expect much more of this now that the television audience includes a whole generation of adults who have grown up with heavy doses of animated cartoons in their earliest years. These cartoons are now part of the culture of childhood and take on the rosy glow nostalgia lends.

4. *Broadcasting,* November 20, 1972.

5. *Multiplication Rock* opened January 6, 1973; *Grammar Rock,* September 8, 1974; and *America Rock,* September 7, 1974. As of this writing, they are spotted throughout the Saturday-morning ghetto hours (five spots); on Sunday, two more spots are aired.

6. John Pascal, " 'Multiplication Rock' Doing Well," *Ithaca Journal Showtime,* February 2, 1974.

7. Pareja's study reports that seven out of twenty-eight series featured a rock group; seventeen of fifty-five episodes he tabulated showed a rock group playing an entire musical number from beginning to end sometime during the course of the show. He further remarks that the rock groups always perform on the show regardless of relevance to the plot of the program. His conclusion: "The networks offer the children mainly one kind of music." Reynaldo Pareja, *Children Learn Whether or Not We Teach Them,* Master's essay, Cornell University, 1974, pp. 46–48.

8. The hearings are reported in Subcommittee of the Committee on Interstate and Foreign Commerce, House of Representatives, *Responsibilities of Broadcasting Licensees and Station Personnel,* "Payola and Other Deceptive Practices in the Broadcasting Field, Part 2," (Washington, D.C.: U.S. Government, 1960). The role of the song-plugger in the music and broadcasting business has been analyzed in print as early as 1941. See Duncan MacDougald, Jr., "The Popular Music Industry," in Paul F. Lazarsfeld and Frank Stanton, eds., *Radio Research 1941* (New York: Duell, Sloan and Pearce, 1941), pp. 65–109.

9. See Richard A. Peterson and David G. Berger, "Cycles in Symbol Production: The Case of Popular Music," *American Sociological Review* 40 (April 1975): 158–73.

10. The music director at Hanna-Barbera Productions, Inc., informed me that each year they record a new music library for each new series which would include dialogue—under music—bridges—chases—sneak-ups—suspense—etc. Most of this music is variations on the melody line used in the main title of that show. The music cutter is then responsible for fitting that music to his show. Hanna-Barbera Productions is the major supplier of animations to network buyers, and has held this lead for many years.

11. Tony Schwartz, *The Responsive Chord* (Garden City, N. Y.: Anchor Press/Doubleday, 1974).

12. AT&T is considering whether to adopt the Digital Audio System for Television (DATE) developed by the Public Broadcasting Service and the Digital Communications Corp. DATE can carry four-channel high-fidelity sound, sandwiching audio and video signals into one broad-band signal. This is called "diplexing," and it would free the telephone lines now being used to carry the audio signal, making possible stereo transmissions of sound, using that freed channel. Daniel R. Wells, Director of Engineering and Technical Operations for PBS, is on record to

the effect that all PBS stations could be outfitted with the equipment within twenty-four months. Even if AT&T decided to adopt the system, all American television stations would have to convert as well; the public would have to scrap their existing sets and ante up once again for new ones. The delay before American ears would be able to hear undistorted musical sounds through such a system would extend, therefore, well beyond the two-year reconversion period mentioned. *Access* No. 8, April 21, 1975.

13. *The New York Times,* February 28, 1973 (advertisement).

14. For some of the ideas expressed in this section, I am indebted to an article by Willie H. Ruff, Jr., which contains penetrating insights on the political role of music and the symbolic significance of the drum in Afro-American music (Willie H. Ruff, Jr., "We Had to Invent a Whole New Rhythm," *Yale Alumni Magazine* 37, 9 [June 1974]: 10–16); and to Jeff Greenfield, "They Changed Rock, Which Changed Culture, Which Changed Us," *The New York Times Magazine,* February 16, 1975.

15. The most provocative discussion of the role of music in externalizing and socializing the feelings, emotions, and imagination that distinguish *Homo sapiens* from other animals appears in the works of Suzanne K. Langer. See her *Feeling and Form* (New York: Charles Scribners & Sons, 1953), especially chapters 7 and 8. See also Theodor W. Adorno, *Introduction to the Sociology of Music* (New York: Seaburg Press, 1976).

16. On September 27, 1973, ABC ran a one-hour Dick Clark special to commemorate those rock-and-roll years. It was such a success that the network then scheduled a series of seven weekly half-hour specials beginning November 28, 1973, and running through January 1974.

17. ABC broadcast "Alice Cooper, The Nightmare," in April 1975. It was all part of a national tour arranged and designed to pro-

mote his then newest album, "Welcome to My Nightmare." Here is the way *The New York Times* television commentator John J. O'Connor reported it: "The program opens with Alice twisting and turning on an ornate bed. He is wearing rose satin pajamas, which could be one reason for his unrest, but we quickly learn that he is having a nightmare. That is the cue for a journey through his latest album, each song getting its own production complete with chains, witches, cauldrons, spiders, giant webs, disintegrating carousels, straightjackets, one-eyed monsters and a child's voice crying, 'Mommy, where's Daddy?' " The review concludes with this insightful comment: ". . . for all the straining after grotesquerie, the horror is curiously mild, a vat of fairly standard ingredients spiked with childish indulgence. Alice . . . is exploiting the surfaces of infantilism . . ." *The New York Times*, January 25, 1975.

18. Gene Simmons of Kiss (a four-member rock group dedicated to the tight black attire and white ghoulish make-up also affected by Alice Cooper).

19. *Variety*, October 23, 1974.

20. A new type of pornographic movie, called "snuff films," is gaining popularity. These films feature the murder and dismemberment of a human being (a woman, of course) as part of the sexually titillating images. Advertisements for the original film in this genre *(Snuff)* at first billed the murder as real. Later advertisements, however, claimed it had been staged. The matter has not yet been cleared up.

On October 1, 1975, the movie critic of WPIX-TV (Channel 11, New York) reviewed one of these films then being shown in a 42nd Street theater specializing in porno. The WPIX news team had been stationed outside the theater and interviewed passers-by about their reactions to such a film, asking whether they would pay to see it. The interviews were spliced into the commentary. All those whose responses were broadcast answered the question in the terms posed. None questioned the judgment of the reporter in structuring the interview as if this opinion were on a par with any other opinion about any other kind of movie, or no different from a preference for a Republican versus a Democratic mayoralty candidate. One man said he would pay to see the film if the murder were simulated, but he wasn't sure he would if it were real. Two or three others said yes, they'd pay to see it. One man said he would not—but then added he could not afford the four or five dollars it costs these days to go to the movies.

When the program was returned to the studio, anchorwoman Pat Harper looked discouraged and sick. "I don't want to believe," she said, "that they're showing this film; and I don't want to believe that these people said what they said." This is a rare occurrence on television news, and I believe it is to Mrs. Harper's credit that she let the audience see her own feelings. The more usual procedure is for the anchorman or anchorwoman, under the guise of "objectivity," to deadpan everything—as if showing no feelings in the face of this sort of horror were (through some perverse twist of logic) more "objective" than Mrs. Harper's frank revelation of her own human feelings on the subject.

On March 12, 1976, ABC's "Police Story" dedicated a fifty-minute show to the horror of "snuff films," as usual neutralizing any shock to the emotions by a liberal sprinkling of commercials for Purina Dog Chow and a kitty litter that killed ammonia odor (an "actual" sniff test was shown on camera).

21. *Variety,* May 22, 1974.

22. The idea has been cranked up another notch by a British movie company that plans to produce a new version of George du Maurier's *Trilby,* as *Svengali '76.* In this movie version, Svengali will manipulate Trilby into becoming a rock singer rather than an opera star, training her for the role by stretching her on a rack. This teaches her to scream in the proper fashion—screams that she then can incorporate into her own singing style. (Hank Grant, *Hollywood Reporter,* July 28, 1975.)

23. Two essays that have strongly influenced my thinking about factory-produced music are: Walter Benjamin, "The Work of Art in the Age of Mechanical Reproduction," in Hannah Arendt, ed., *Il-*

luminations (New York: Schocken Books, 1969), pp. 217–52; and T. W., Adorno, "The Radio Symphony, An Experiment in Theory," in Paul T. Lazarsfeld and Frank Stanton, eds., *Radio Research 1941* (New York: Duell, Sloan and Pearce, 1941) pp. 110–39.

24. His address was reported in *The Ithaca New Times*, May 12, 1974.

25. *The CBS 1974 Annual Report.*

26. *RCA Annual Report, 1974.*

27. *Billboard International Buyers Guide*, Los Angeles: Billboard Publishing Co., Inc., September 1974.

28. *ABC Annual Report, 1974* and *Billboard International Buyers Guide*, op. cit. See also The Network Project, *Directory of The Networks*, Notebook No. 2, 1974. Further information on network holdings appears in the appendix, p. 324–326.

CHAPTER 10

1. S. Hayakawa, *Advertising Age*, August 19, 1974. Dr. Hayakawa was elected to the U.S. Senate in November 1976.

2. Rollo May, "Language, Symbols and Violence," *Communication* 1 (1974): 213–22, p. 213.

3. Many tribal cultures identify the name with the self without distinction. Isak Dinesen describes an African tribesman's reaction to his name. "But as I read out his own name . . . he swiftly turned his face to me, and gave me a great, fierce, flaming glance, so exuberant with laughter that it changed the old man into a boy, into the very symbol of youth. Again as I had finished the document and was reading out his name . . . the vital glance was repeated, this time deepened and calmed, with a new dignity. Such a glance did Adam give the Lord when He formed him out of dust, and breathed into his nostrils the breath of life, and man became a living soul. I had created him and shown him himself: Jogona

Kanyagga of life everlasting. When I handed him the paper, he took it reverently and greedily folded it up in a corner of his cloak and kept his hand upon it . . . his soul was in it and it was the proof of his existence. Here was something which Jogona Kanyagga had performed, which would preserve his name forever: the flesh was made word and dwelt among us full of grace and truth." Isak Dinesen, *Out of Africa* (New York: Vintage Books, 1972), pp. 120–21.

4. Television dubbing in Spanish uses the *tu* form of address most frequently. "Plaza Sesamo," the export version of "Sesame Street," is a case in point. *Usted* is used rarely, if at all; *vos* and *che* never. The *tu* form is the intimate form of the second person singular, equivalent to the French, *tu.* It is used symmetrically among family members and other intimates, assymetrically to show that one member of the conversational pair pays the other the greater respect. *Vos* and *che* replace *tu* in Argentina, Chile, Uruguay, and parts of Colombia. They never appear in "Plaza Sesamo" or any other dubbed sound tracks, for that matter. Spanish speakers do not unquestioningly accept the deletion of *usted* (the formal address); those from Argentina, Chile, Uruguay, and parts of Colombia do not unquestioningly accept the deletion of *vos* and *che,* either. Yet the programers, presenting their own linguistic quirks as normal, natural, beyond question, put those who do not do so on the defensive, and, through such negative reinforcement, help to extinguish the minority usage.

CHAPTER II

1. *Advertising Age,* July 22, 1974.

2. The reference is to Lincoln Tyler, a fictional character in the ABC soap opera "All My Children."

3. The quoted phrase appeared in an advertisement for "School Chex," paid for by the Irving Trust Co., *The New York Times,* December 5, 1974.

4. See Enid Nemy, "Cosmetics: What Does Hypo-Allergenic Mean?" *The New York Times,* April 25, 1973.

5. See Richard Gambino, "Through the Dark, Glassily," *The New York Times,* July 29, 1974. See also Edwin Newman, *Strictly Speaking* (New York: Doubleday & Co., 1974), for additional examples.

6. Quoted by columnist Anthony Lewis in *The New York Times,* January 28, 1974.

7. The French government has taken official cognizance of the dulling of analytic thinking that goes with adulterated language. In 1966, the Haut Comité was created within the Office de Radiodiffusion-Television Française (ORTF)—the government agency charged with responsibility for French radio and television broadcasting. Its original mandate was to "watch over the quality and renown of the French language." It was staffed by eminent scholars, among them Claude Levi-Straus, the ethnologist and student of myth and language; and Roger Caillois, a sociologist, poet, and translator. Roland Godiveau, director of the secretariat at ORTF, is in charge of day-to-day operations of the committee. He is aware of "the enormous influence that TV and radio have over the language. To a large extent we're responsible for the future of the way French is spoken. A popular program on TV might be watched by some 15 million people. Many of these people won't be able to tell whether an entertainer is speaking the language properly or not. Particularly the children." The problem, as Godiveau sees it, is the constant danger that words can become so imprecise that they can no longer be used to communicate clearly.

Godiveau relies on a number of collaborators outside his office who follow all programs broadcast by the ORTF and submit lists of mistakes and doubtful usages. Periodically a special committee (made up of generally acknowledged authorities in linguistics) is convened to review current developments and to decide on preferred new usages. These are then published in *Hebdo-Langage,* a weekly information sheet produced in Godiveau's agency. (Michael Peppiatt, "The French Alert Their Broadcasters: 'En Garde!'," *The New York Times,* November 3, 1974.)

Insightful diagnosis of the problem is, of course, no guarantee that the proposed remedy is the best one, or even an effective one. A problem whose wellsprings bubble up from specific social arrangements that grant power to dominate human speech to a special group is not likely to be solved by bureaucratic arrangements setting up a committee. Still, it is worth noting that executives in French television are aware of the dangers to thinking as language is permitted to degenerate.

8. The story board was reproduced and run as an advertisement in national magazines.

9. Note that all children whose families consider the eating of meat or pig meat offensive are likewise encouraged to put some bacon in their fuel tanks.

10. Aldous Huxley, *Brave New World* (New York: Harper and Bros., 1932).

11. Advertisers often say their business is to sell. In this they are clearly mistaken. An advertiser advertises; a salesperson sells in a market transaction; an advertising salesperson sells nothing but advertising. The word *advertising* comes to us through the same Middle English and Latin roots that gave us our word *advert,* meaning to turn one's attention to something. Because widely advertised products are more frequently bought than others, those in the business often assert pridefully that their advertisements have done the selling. On the other hand, their own trade press characterizes a successful advertising campaign as one which increases "awareness level." Commercials are evaluated in terms of the number of "viewer impressions." Even the president of the ABC network pleads for increased advertising rates for television, based on his claim of the number of "viewer impressions" it provides. (Elton Rule, quoted in *Variety,* September 18, 1974.) An advertising firm that specializes in railroad ads says, "We hit them 44 times a month . . . your message in one of our trains is in front

of your audience an average of 1,540 minutes a month . . ."
(*Advertising Age*, May 19, 1975); and their four-color ad shows
people lined up as if they were targets in a shooting gallery, on
each bosom a huge bullseye. Advertising doesn't sell—it exposes the product widely in a most glamorous showcase, and
then lets nature take its course—the nature of the support
system that a consumer society provides. See also footnote 11,
Chapter 6.

12. John J. O'Connor, *The New York Times*, February 9, 1975. (Mr.
O'Connor notes that Mr. Della Femina is author of a book entitled
From Those Wonderful Folks Who Gave You Pearl Harbor.) He
is reporting a panel discussion in which Mr. Della Femina par-
ticipated, part of a series, "Assignment America." This discussion
was broadcast by WNET/13, February 4, 1975.

13. Ibid.

14. Raymond Rubicam, "Raymond Rubicam Enters Ad Hall of Fame
. . ." *Advertising Age*, July 1, 1974. The article describes Mr. Rubicam as "one of the creative greats and towering figures of the
agency business."

15. Carroll Carroll, *Variety*, January 31, 1974.

16. *The New York Times*, July 5, 1974. The columnist reporting this
adds that the Pepsi-Cola agency in 1972 had planned an advertising
campaign that would have packaged that beverage with the slogan,
"Pepsi people—the smilin' majority." Watergate, however, inter-
vened between the campaign's conception and execution and the
agency wisely scratched the idea. Public events had transferred the
initial positive charge the agency discerned in the term *smilin'
majority* into an unmistakable negative one.

17. *Advertising Age*, August 20, 1973, gives the script.

18. In a decision of May 24, 1976, the Supreme Court upheld the
claim that the First Amendment protects "commercial speech"
as long as it is not proven factually incorrect. (*Virginia State*

Board of Pharmacy, et al. v. *Virginia Citizens Consumer Council, Inc.,* et al. 74–895.) 425 U.S. 748 (May 24, 1976)

Mr. Justice Rehnquist dissents, claiming the decision erroneously "elevates commercial intercourse between a seller hawking his wares and a buyer seeking to strike a bargain, to the same plane as has been previously reserved for the free marketplace of ideas . . ." The majority opinion, written by Mr. Justice Blackmun, makes no such distinction. It assumes that advertising is "dissemination of information as to who is producing and selling what product, for what reason and at what price." I can only conclude that the good justice neither studies advertising in the slick magazines nor watches it on television.

19. The sources for most of the examples cited here are: Fred Nassif, "And Now a Word from Somebody Real," *The New York Times,* June 30, 1974; and Peter Funt, "How TV Producers Sneak in a Few Extra Commercials," *The New York Times,* August 11, 1974.

20. Eric Barnouw, *The Image Empire* (New York: Oxford University Press, 1970), p. 23. This era of sponsorship was well before the congressional statute banning cigarette ads from the airwaves.

21. The Public Health Cigarette Smoking Act of 1970 required all cigarette advertising to be removed from radio and television. Between 1970 and 1973, however, total domestic consumption of cigarettes did not fall; it rose. As any smoker well knows, this indicates in part the strongly habituating capacity of tobacco. It also is a tribute to the long-lasting impact of those original commercials that used to be aired and the many advertisements that still appear in every other organ of communication, even on children's toys.

The stubbornness with which the habit hangs on may also have something to do with the simultaneous disappearance from the airwaves of commercials urging the audience to stop smoking cigarettes. They began to appear when, in 1967, the Federal Communications Commission ruled that stations must open their airwaves to antismoking commercials if they were going to broadcast any prosmoking ones. The FCC argued that this was necessary in fairness to a public which must advert to our "free press" for intelligent discussion that would enable us to make informed personal decisions to smoke or quit smoking carcinogenic cigarettes. The assumption that television commercials could debate intelligently with each other was no more ludicrous than the FCC's solomonic declaration that a ratio of 4 to 1 would ensure fair public debate—four cigarette commercials for every antismoking commercial!

22. *Variety*, August 7, 1974. The text of the commercial is reproduced there.

23. Philip H. Dougherty, *The New York Times*, March 20, 1974.

24. Fred Nassif, op. cit.

25. Michael J. Connor, "It's Not as Cushy as it Sounds," *TV Guide*, November 24, 1973, 16–18.

26. The remark had been written on the copy which Dick Auerbach, producer of NBC football, had inadvertently included in a batch of papers handed to a newspaper reporter covering the games. Daniel Menaker, "How TV Tackles Football," *The New York Times*, November 25, 1973.

27. Michael D. Moore, "B & B's Buyer's Guide to TV Network Advertising," *Broadcasting*, April 28, 1975. The italics are mine. Edgar Lotspeich, Procter & Gamble's vice president for advertising, told the national television audience, "We're interested of course in whether we feel the program would be a proper setting for our kinds of products." (ABC News Closeup, "Primetime. The Decision Makers," September 2, 1974, p. III–5.) Procter & Gamble is television's biggest advertiser.

28. Michael J. Connor, op. cit. Apparently the efficiency level has not been impressive. A study by N. W. Ayer reported that fourteen out of every hundred spots did not run as ordered. Arthur Bellaire, "Monitoring Commercial Performance—It's Time to Take It Seriously," *Advertising Age*, December 10, 1973.

29. The monitoring process is now being transferred to computers, and companies like International Digisonics Corporation (IDC

Services, Inc.), Real Time Technology, and Identimatch are moving to take over the market. They keep track of whether the network delivers the goods as ordered. Arthur Bellaire, op. cit.

30. Newton Minow, "The Public Interest," in *Freedom and Responsibility in Broadcasting*, 15, 18 (Coons ed. 1961).

31. Mr. O'Connor's review of the program, it now turns out, had been based on a performance aired just for critics, from which commercials had been deleted. Still, he thinks it makes no difference. "I have developed an automatic on-and-off mental switch for the preservation of sanity," he explains. He assumes most people watching television do the same, and thus protect the dramatic presentation from any such alteration in meaning. There you have it—*The New York Time*'s professional critic of television has not caught on to what advertisers know about the power of positioning to change meanings—on-and-off mental switch notwithstanding. John J. O'Connor, "And Now a Few Words from Irate Viewers," *The New York Times*, January 19, 1975.

32. Mr. Murrow was addressing the Radio and Television News Directors' Association. He is quoted in Harry Skornia, *Television and Society* (New York: McGraw-Hill, 1965), p. 100. The current limits on commercial time—self-imposed by the broadcasters private agreement—appear in the notes to chapter 4.

CHAPTER 12

1. May 27, 1974, p. 50.

2. Harry Wayne McMahan, *Advertising Age*, June 11, 1973.

3. Al Ries, "The Positioning Strategy for Successful Advertising," *Broadcasting*, August 26, 1974.

4. The text of the commercial is: "Once there was a kid who had a big mouth that loved candy bars, but they didn't last very long.

Then he discovered choclatey [*sic*] caramel Milk Duds. The mouth loved the Milk Duds because they last a long time. (And then our campaign song.) When a candy bar is only a memory, you'll still be eating your Milk Duds." *Broadcasting,* August 26, 1974, op. cit.

Anthropologists of the future may view the crafting of this drama as a strange way for a grown man to spend his time; but psycholinguists of the future will note that the product receives positive charges from symbols like the child, the mouth, the candy, the song, the tale—indeed, the whole drama itself—at the same time that it diminishes positive charges possessed by competing candy bars with the claim that they do not last as long as Milk Duds. The principal point both should note, however, is that the commercial was widely circulated.

5. Eric Levin, "Take My Joke . . . Please!" *TV Guide,* August 16, 1975.

6. This is not a metaphorical statement. The body mobilizes energy to attend to what a commercial communicates, and that energy can be measured in various ways, such as noting pupil arousal, heartbeats, alpha wave emission rate, and so on. Herbert E. Krugman, in his provocative article, "Processes Underlying Exposure to Advertising" (*American Psychologist,* 23, 4, April 1958, pp. 245–253), summarizes some of the research in this genre. Krugman concludes that as people note communications in their environment, such as advertising, the processes they go through "involve a finite and measurable amount of work to be completed . . . the distribution of work among communicator and communicant can be measured . . . (so that) one can also identify the starting and finishing points of the learning or work process . . ." Krugman goes on to explain that once the work of learning the lesson of the advertisement has been concluded, then "the communique may only be ready to take its undramatic place in the environment, to be available when and if needed [as] 'reminder' advertising . . . available to repeatedly communicate its modest message over long periods of time . . ." (p. 252).

7. Philip H. Dougherty, *The New York Times,* July 19, 1973.

8. *The New York Times,* August 7, 1973.

9. *New York Review of Books* XX, 14 (September 20, 1973). Another advertisement in the same series recognizes the household-word strategy and its affinity with Coca-Cola. "What Do Xerox and Coke Have in Common?" is its headline. The text claims that a great name is only part of the answer; that the Xerox trademark should always be coupled with the name of the particular piece of equipment to which it refers such as Xerox copier, Xerox computer, Xerox textbook, and so on. The advertisement closes with the admonition that whether it's a certain soft drink or a certain copier, a customer must always be sure "it's the real thing."

10. A consent order is a legal device which permits the defendant to agree to cease and desist from the practices he has been accused of while still claiming that he is not now and never has been guilty of them. The Xerox Corporation filed a consent order before the Federal Trade Commission in November 1974; it was rejected by the commission in April 1975, accepted in August 1975. (*Wall Street Journal,* August 31, 1975.)

11. *Advertising Age,* March 18, 1974.

12. A Schaeffer commercial packaged this tune with the special appeal that associations with religious symbols lend. Rough and ready beer-truck drivers are hazing a newly hired hand. "You have to sing the Schaeffer beer commercial," they tell him. The newcomer doffs his hat and begins. "Schaeffer . . . is the . . . one beer to have when you're having more than one." The tenor is clear and pure. The rough men stand as if transfixed. There's a hush as one by one they fall back. Their erstwhile aggressiveness evaporates; not a dry eye in the place as their thoughts hark back to memories called forth by those bell-like tones, reminiscent of home and childhood and a choirboy singing a hymn.

13. "Ten Best Radio Spots of Year Sparkle with Music, Humor," *Advertising Age,* August 20, 1973.

14. Philip H. Dougherty, *The New York Times*, February 7, 1964.

15. Ibid.

16. The record, entitled "The Mood Maker," is subtitled "Created to show you how Eva-Tone Soundsheets and music can help you open people's minds to hear what you have to say." It has been issued by Eva-Tone Soundsheets, Deerfield, Illinois 60015.

17. "Our Man in Boston," RCA Victor Red Seal. The flip side of this record includes a medley incorporating commercials for Mr. Clean, Brylcreem, Chevrolet, Atlantic Gasoline, Philip Morris Cigarettes, Doublemint Gum, Rheingold Beer, Marlboro Cigarettes, Dial Soap, Pall Mall Cigarettes, and Newport Filter Cigarettes.

18. Leonard Sloan, "Advertising: Valentine Sending," *The New York Times*, February 13, 1974.

19. Tony Schwartz, *The Responsive Chord* (New York: Anchor Books, 1974), p. 154.

    Variable Speech Control, a device patented in January 1974, uses a similar principle. Words are played back at twice the rate they are delivered, without the distortion that sound engineers call "the chipmunk effect." It's done by deleting from the cassette or tape the pauses in normal speech. The same device can inflate the pauses for those who need to listen more slowly. (Stacy V. Jones, *The New York Times*, January 19, 1974.) The same principle is used visually in a device called "Retarded Live Television." It slows the action of fast-moving events such as football games to enable a viewer to see what is going on without being conscious of any delay. It clips a frame of perhaps one second, then stretches the rest of the frames to fill up the blank. "The action can be slowed by 15 or 20 percent without the viewer being conscious of any delay." (Stacy V. Jones, *The New York Times*, April 14, 1973.)

CHAPTER 13

1. See, for example, Edgar Morin and T. W. Adorno, *La Industria Cultural* (Buenos Aires: Editorial Galena, 1967).

2. The rating service began in 1937, a spinoff of the company's continuing analysis of the movement of foodstuffs and drugs from store to consumer. This service is still provided to subscribers by the A. C. Nielsen Company. The company also runs a coupon clearing service and issues a Petroleum Index—a service publishing indicators of geologic findings—bought by oil companies and other agencies engaged in prospecting for petroleum deposits or funding such prospecting. They also sell the Nielsen data system —a service that attempts to correct inaccuracies in magazine subscription lists.

3. Figures quoted by the A. C. Nielsen Company as of the close of 1975 are listed below.

	1973	1974	1975	1976
U.S. Households	68,310,000	70,520,00	71,460,000	73,100,000
TV Households	66,200,000	68,500,000	69,600,000	71,200,000

Arbitron figures for 1976 are: 73,590,000 U.S. Households, 71,556,200 TV Households.

4. Considering that on the average each television screen is watched by two to three persons, a thirty rating—twenty-one million homes —would yield a bumper crop of forty-two to sixty million people simultaneously sharing the experience.

5. Of course, there's always a bit for the gleaners to come along and pick up—a few of the active sets would have been tuned to independent stations and PBS—the Public Broadcasting Service. PBS stations do not buy and sell people directly the way commercial stations do; but they keep track of the harvest just as if they did, and consider themselves lucky to get a seven share. A ten is a bonanza.

6. Jeff Greenfield, "The Fight for $60,000 a Half Minute," *The New York Times Magazine*, September 7, 1975.

7. The remark was reported by Larry Michie, "In This Corner, In That Corner," *Variety*, January 29, 1975.

8. 1973, 1,131; 1974, 1,154; 1975, 1,162.

9. This service delivers Nielsen "fasties" or "overnights," replacing a more cumbersome system that for two decades served to measure radio and television audiences. It depended on the U.S. mails and involved a two-week delay before audience data could be compiled and returned to subscribers. Today's "overnights" are not really overnights. Monday totals are received by subscribers on Wednesday, Tuesday's totals come in on Thursday, Wednesday totals on Friday, and Thursday totals come in on Monday of the following week.

    The service includes twenty-four reports per year—"pocket pieces"—issued every two weeks. The delay in getting reports to subscribers is necessary to "clear the conflicts." That is, a single station will turn up with two different programs listed for the same slot, owing to errors, last-minute changes, and nonclearance of network shows by certain local stations who reject. Delay is also necessary to clear up bugs in procedures.

    During the four "non-report weeks" (called "black weeks," in the trade) subscribers get only fast weekly household data, yielding totals but no demos.

    Market Section Audience Reports list demos—age, sex, occupation, and income of head of household, listed separately by five different regions and by size of county. Audience composition reports are issued for eight months of the year, giving demos for all household members. They are issued as follows: eight reports from September through December (the first season), then February, April, May, and July are reported once each.

10. Number of NAC homes reported by the A. C. Nielsen Company were: 1973, 2,112; 1974, 2,147; 1975, 2,051.

11. See, for example, "Now, Deep Eyes," *Newsweek,* July 15, 1974; and also Dick Adler, "The Nielsen Ratings—and How I Penetrated Their Secret Network," *The New York Times,* September 1, 1974; and also letter to the editor by Marvin Kitman, *The New York Times,* September 15, 1974. Such stories detailing how Nielsen families rig the odds in favor of this program or against that one, surface from time to time. They do not invalidate the sampling procedure; they simply emphasize the point made in the text about the false precision in interpretation.

12. Stanford N. Sesser, "That TV Week That Is: Wasteland Blossoms In a Ratingless Week," *Wall Street Journal,* April 23, 1970.

13. Phillip H. Dougherty, *The New York Times,* December 10, 1974.

14. Agency executives say they never see a per-program rate card and do not need it for package buying; that per unit prices will eventually show up on bills as a necessary piece of information for "make-goods" (advertising jargon referring to the exchange of debits and credits that goes on when the network finds out that the number of audience bundles actually delivered was lower than the contract specified). See also Martin Mayer, *About Television* (New York: Harper & Row, 1972); and Les Brown, *Televi$ion: The Business Behind the Box* (New York: Harcourt Brace Jovanovich, 1971), for good reports on the complexities of buying, selling, and charging for audiences.

15. *Advertising Age,* July 14, 1975. The figure does not include the cost of commercials appearing on shows P & G owns and produces, six daytime serials, for example, as of this writing.

In 1975, top spenders on television advertising included:

Lever Brothers	94.8 million dollars
Procter & Gamble	93.7
Gillette	91.6
Block Drug Co. (Polident, Tegrin, etc.)	91.3
American Home Products	90.9

Warner Lambert	90.8
McDonalds	90.2
General Foods	87.0
Sterling Drugs, Inc.	85.5
General Mills	82.1
Colgate-Palmolive	81.3
TOTAL	979.2

Source: *Advertising Age,* August 23, 1976, p. 30. The same source lists the U.S. Government among top spenders for national advertising in 1975, 40th in rank order. This represents a step up compared with 1974, when it was in 45th place. (*Advertising Age,* May 12, 1975.)

16. Ibid.

17. *Broadcasting,* May 26, 1975, and *Variety,* May 14, 1975. Additional prices per minute for shows delivering quality audiences, as listed by Maureen Christopher in *Advertising Age,* July 15, 1974, were: CBS shows: "The Waltons," $122,000; "M*A*S*H," $102,000; "The Mary Tyler Moore Show," $98,000; "Hawaii Five-O," $96,-000; "Cannon," $92,000; "Kojak," $92,000. NBC prices quoted were: "Police Story," $74,000; "Chico and the Man," $74,000; "Walt Disney," $68,000; "Emergency," $66,000; "Ironside," $62,-000; "Adam 12," $60,000. ABC shows: "Monday Night Football," $100,000; "Columbo," $86,000.

18. *Broadcasting,* August 30, 1976

19. *Advertising Age,* June 24, 1974

20. The telecast of Richard Nixon's resignation from the presidency of the United States, a first in the country's history, was not rated. See *Variety,* August 8, 1974.

21. Here are some average ratings for programs booked into the 1974–75 season and subsequently canceled, compared with programs that were rebooked for 1975–76.

Retained		Canceled	
Medical Center	20.7	Paul Sand in Friends and	
That's My Mama	18.3	Lovers	20.9

Harry O	17.8	Gunsmoke	20.8
Petrocelli	17.5	Caribe	18.9
Six Million Dollar Man	17.1	Mac Davis	18.5
Movin' On	17.1	The Manhunter	17.8
Marcus Welby	16.6	Apple's Way	17.6
Baretta	15.1	Lucas Tanner	17.4
Barney Miller	14.7	We'll Get By	16.1
		Adam 12	15.9
		The Law	15.8
		Born Free	15.6
		Hot l Baltimore	14.7

Source: *Variety*, May 14, 1975.

22. The quoted remark is attributed to one of the vice presidents at ABC. Jeff Greenfield, op. cit.

23. The system penalizes these minorities yet again since these rating biases disadvantage stations wishing to carry programs appealing especially to them when it comes to charging for commercials. The case was made strongly by Roger Rice, speaking before the National Association of Television Program Executives in Los Angeles, February 18, 1974. He cited figures as follows: Greenwood, Mississippi, is 58 percent white and 42 percent black according to the 1970 census. An Arbitron sample for that area included 83 percent white and 17 percent black. *The New York Times*, February 18, 1974, and *Variety*, February 20, 1974.

   The disenfranchisement of blacks is particularly ironic since blacks typically spend more time in front of the set than others. "Although this was generally known in the television and advertising industries, there was no outcry, no move to set it right, no show of conscience that the ghetto black did not have a representative 'vote' as a member of the viewing masses." Les Brown, op. cit., p. 60. Only as blacks developed purchasing power and political clout was any attempt to correct the errors undertaken. Samples still under-represent minorities, including the aged, as of this writing.

24. Independent stations programing opposite network stations offer substantially the same fare since they buy so many network cast-

offs in syndication. Public television stations cater to special publics. Between the two, they average a split of no more than 10 percent of available prime-time audiences.

25. The LOP principle was named by Paul L. Klein, vice president in charge of network marketing and planning at NBC. It is the same principle restaurateurs follow in drawing up dinner menus for mass markets. They know that most diners are likely to reject dishes they've never tried before, considering only those that are familiar, settling finally on a familiar dish that seems least objectionable rather than insisting on finding a favorite or trying something new.

26. Terry Keegan, vice president for program development at NBC, quoted by Jeff Greenfield, op. cit.

27. Marvin Antonowsky, then NBC chief of programing, quoted by John J. O'Connor in *The New York Times,* December 12, 1975. Mr. O'Connor goes on to inquire, musingly, "What, precisely, is that 'price of failure'? Mediocrity? Hardly. Try something more pragmatic, like ratings, corporate profits, the possibility of being fired."

28. President Ford, whose relations with broadcasters remained warm during his incumbency, made no major television appearance during sweep weeks in 1975 and 1976, although his average rate of television appearances was twice a month. Les Brown, "TV Notes: How 'Sweep Weeks' Hype the Ratings," *The New York Times,* December 7, 1975.

29. Black weeks are usually the last week of April, last week of December, plus two other weeks during the summer which vary from year to year. For example, during the summer of 1972, black weeks during the summer were scrambled because of the Republican National Convention. These are the weeks the Nielsen people called "nonreport weeks" before the system was computerized.

30. The remark is attributed to Marvin Antonowsky, at that time vice president in charge of research at ABC. See Stanford N. Sesser, op. cit.

31. *The New York Times,* April 26, 1973.

32. Bernard Rosenberg, "Mass Culture Revisited," in Bernard Rosenberg and David Manning White, *Mass Culture Revisited* (New
York: Van Nostrand Reinhold Co., 1971), p. 7.

CHAPTER 14

1. This widespread misconception has been validated by authors with
good credentials, such as Herbert J. Gans, *Popular Culture and
High Culture* (New York: Basic Books, 1975), and David Manning
White in several sources such as the books he co-edited (with
Bernard Rosenberg), *Mass Culture* (Glencoe, Ill.: The Free Press,
1957), and *Mass Culture Revisited* (New York: Van Nostrand
Reinhold Co., 1971).

2. Edward Bleier, vice president of Warner Brothers Television,
quoted by Les Brown in *The New York Times,* October 17, 1974.

3. The writer, quoted by Nicholas Johnson, former FCC commissioner, asked to remain anonymous to avoid reprisals by the industry that provides his livelihood. Nicholas Johnson, *Freedom to
Create: The Implications of Anti-trust Policies for Television Programming Content,* Xerox copy, December 29, 1969, p. 80. In the
same document, Johnson exposes network policy of first acquiring
programs directly from independent producers and then eventually buying up the independent producers to bring them into the
corporate fold. He reports that as late as 1967 more than 93 percent
of all network fare was under direct network supervision from
start to finish (p. 37).

   Under such conditions, the writer is not much different from
any other white-collar employee, virtually filling in some blanks.
He is "not asked any more to write a play; he is asked to write a
vehicle for a particular kind of character who must go through
certain specified steps where the essential nature of the whole play
is laid out for him beforehand and there is little he can do except

go through the motions." (FCC, "Report and Order with Respect to Competition and Responsibility in Network Television Broadcasting," Docket 12782, May 4, 1970, p. 9.)

4. Federal Communications Commission, "Report and Order," ibid., p. 10.

5. Even the so-called "independent producers" are independent in name only. They "participate virtually as 'production agents' for network management . . . in reality there are few if any truly independent network program suppliers." (FCC, "Report and Order," ibid., footnote, Appendix II.)

    An excellent discussion of the relationship between the structure of the industry and network procurement practices appears in Roscoe L. Barrow, "The Attainment of Balanced Program Service in Television," *Virginia Law Review,* vol 52., (May 1966): 633–66.

6. *Mt. Mansfield Television Inc.* v. *NBC,* 442 F2d. 470, 1971. It was as a result of the FCC order in question that CBS divested itself of Viacom; NBC of NTA, Inc.; and ABC of Worldvision.

    The order prohibited only domestic sales and resales by the networks. They are still permitted to sell abroad the programs they make and book in the United States.

7. The suits were withdrawn upon allegation by the networks that the Nixon administration had brought the suits as part of a concerted attempt to intimidate them.

8. The concession, which would apply for a decade, indicates shrewd bargaining on NBC's part. The two-and-a-half-hour-prime-time ceiling would actually permit NBC to add to its holdings; since, as of the date of filing, it owned only one hour-long program in the category ("Little House on the Prairie"). The proposed eight-hour daytime ceiling would likewise allow the network to add to its daytime holdings, since as of the date of filing, NBC owned none of the daytime shows it was scheduling. The Department of Justice suit was brought, presumably, to keep the networks from

booking programs in which they have a financial interest. If this consent agreement sticks, it will do precisely the opposite for the RCA subsidiary.

9. See, for example, *Associated Press* v. *U.S.*, 326 U.S. 1945, 1424–1425.

10. An assistant attorney general of the U.S. has pointed out that antitrust crimes have milked the economy in general and individual consumers in particular of billions of dollars. More important, they erode public trust, the essential ingredient for a humane society in which people respect each other as well as law and order. Such crimes are called "victimless" only because society is the victim. Since 1961, only thirty-eight convicted antitrust offenders have drawn jail sentences, and the majority of these were for thirty days or less. By contrast, a higher percentage of persons convicted of violating migratory-bird laws were sentenced to prison, and for longer terms. (Donald I. Baker, "To Make the Penalty Fit the Crime, Remarks Before the Tenth New England Anti-trust Conference," Boston, Massachusetts, November 20, 1976, Department of Justice, Mimeographed, pp. 6 and 11.)

11. "Hollywood Report," *TV Guide*, September 6, 1975.

12. The financial terms for each television series are negotiated separately. Typically, the networks paid (in 1974) within a range of $230,000 to $300,000 for a one-hour filmed episode that might be developed into a series. The payment includes the license to rerun the pilot just once. In the past, the network payment usually underwrote the entire costs of producing the pilot. Inflation has produced a gap between the fees paid by the networks and claimed production costs, so that, for the past two or three years, the production companies have had to make up the difference out of their own pockets. Les Brown, *The New York Times*, October 17, 1974.

13. The cost of producing a pilot program is high but relatively trivial in comparison with the paper losses incurred if ratings fall below a standard level.

14. Edith Efron, "View from a Typewriter," *TV Guide,* August 3–9, 1974, 208, quoting Christopher Knopf, one of several writers interviewed by Miss Efron for this article. Miss Efron comments on this exchange: "But much of the time, the tests are invalid. The shows fail." (p. 6). Miss Efron is caught in a slip of the pen: what failed was not the show, but a rather complicated statistical extrapolation that claimed a certain proportion of eighteen-to-forty-nine-year-old members of the audience vis à vis the shows scheduled against it in the same time slot.

15. Merle Miller and Evan Rhodes, *Only You, Dick Daring* (New York: William Sloane Associates, 1964), pp. 346–47.

16. Edith Efron, *op. cit.,* p. 3.

17. The quotation is from the mimeographed transcript of ABC News Closeup's *Prime Time TV: The Decision Makers* (New York: American Broadcasting Companies, Inc., September 2, 1974), p. II–4. The executive quoted is Seymour Amlen, head of Audience Research.

18. Ibid., p. II–5, quoting Frederick Pierce, then a vice president of the ABC network.

19. One market researcher uses a polygraph alone in testing music. Tom Turicchi, working through two marketing firms (Research Consultants Incorporated and Entertainment Research Associates), claims to predict which pop music records are likely to turn into hits.

    His number-one assistant feels that in some areas a human observer may be more reliable and more versatile than the machine. "I like to watch the girls through the window when we test. . . . Their nipples get hard . . ." he said. This man claimed that the "acute nipple response" invariably predicted a hit. Michael Gross, "The Hits Just Keep On Coming," *New Times Magazine,* February 7, 1975.

20. Paul F. Lazarsfeld and Frank M. Stanton, eds., "Program Analyzer Tests of Two Educational Films," in *Radio Research:*

1942–1943 (New York: Duell, Sloan and Pearce, 1944), pp. 485–506.

The research arsenal is used in testing commercials as well. A new gadget, the oculometer, has been developed as an improvement over the program analyzer and sensors. It tracks a viewer's eye movements by means of a special infrared beam that locks into a viewer's eyes, translating unconscious eye movements into a dot of white light. Testers in another room watch the same commercial on their own monitor on which the white dot picks out for them precisely where the viewer's eyes are focusing at every instant. Viewers do not see the dot on their monitor, of course. In fact, they are told only that the test is designed to find out how they feel about the colors used in the commercials they are asked to watch. The testers can observe which elements of the commercial attract the viewer's eyes, and which are bypassed or ignored. With this information to guide editing, the odds are substantially increased that most people will look at precisely what the advertisers want to emphasize. (See James P. Forkan, *Advertising Age,* April 11, 1977, for an account of this use of the oculometer.)

The oculometer was originally developed in the U.S. space program to track astronauts' eye movements as they scanned banks of dials and meters in space vehicles. Now "private enterprise" cashes in on the investment, so that public tax money pays to make sure eyes focus on images of products and symbols a handful of advertisers want to make unforgettable.

The oculometer represents a technological advance over previously used methods of photographing eye movements to test commercials. A stand-mounted recorder photographs eye movements as the subject's head is clamped in a fixed position. The person is instructed to look at a six-by-eight-inch picture fixed at a distance about 18 inches from his eyes. His eye movements are recorded on film as a white dot, superimposed on motion picture film of the same picture he looks at. The researchers, observing the movements of the dot, can trace the path the subject's eyes took as he watched the test image. The gadget is described in N. H. Mackworth, "A Stand Camera for Line-Of-Sight Recording," *Perception and Psychophysics,* 2 (1967) pp. 119–127.

21. Les Brown, *Televi$ion, The Business Behind the Box* (New York: Harcourt Brace Jovanovich Inc., 1971), p. 121.

22. Indeed, "All in the Family" was itself an imitation. Norman Lear and Bud Yorkin bought the rights to the British series "Till Death Do Us Part," and rewrote the central characters, Alf Garnett and his liberal son-in-law, into Archie Bunker and Mike Stivic.

23. Melvin Helitzer and Carl Heyel, *The Youth Market: Its Dimensions, Influence and Opportunities for You* (New York: Media Books, 1970). See also Eric Barnouw, *The Image Empire* (New York: Oxford University Press, 1970), pp. 245–46.

24. Mr. Lear's earlier shows, produced in collaboration with Bud Yorkin, included "Come Blow Your Horn," "Never Too Late," and "Divorce: American Style." They wrote, directed, or produced (separately or as a team) such features as "Inspector Clouseau," "The Night They Raided Minsky's," "Start the Revolution without Me," and "Cold Turkey." Their production company was called Tandem Productions.

25. I note in passing that the decision to change the definition of homosexuality was adopted by the American Psychiatric Association in 1973. There had been no new scientific findings. The association had lived quite comfortably with its earlier definition of homosexuality as pathology. One is reminded of the changed definition of abortion—another "medical" turnabout in the light of no new "medical" or "scientific" findings. Geneticists do it, too. See Will Provine, "Geneticists and the Sociology of Race Crossing," *Science* 182, pp. 790–96. Such revolutionary redefinitions have been prefaced not by scientific breakthroughs but by political mobilization, organization, and action accompanied by access to the organs of communication (the press) with mass coverage.

26. All human beings must face their own mortality. What, then, binds us to a future we shall never see? The answer remains a great

mystery, elusive and unfathomable. Whatever it may be, certainly love of parents for their children is an important ingredient. That love develops in a family system which—granting that its form may vary widely from culture to culture and from historic period to historic period—nevertheless is always based on some long-term, committed intimacy between the sexes. It is in such relationships that human beings develop the emotions that are still *Homo sapiens's* best bet for any chance to develop a human civilization.

27. *Variety,* February 5, 1975, reports that eight ABC stations in major markets canceled the show after two weeks and many more switched the time for airing it to late-night hours.

28. Show business's tolerance for alternative life-styles and convictions that challenge conventional wisdom is, I believe, to the credit of the industry. I note in passing, however, that this tolerance is more noticeable for some convictions and life-styles than for others. Television's gatekeepers have already opened the doors to shows and documentaries that now saturate the thought-environment with the homosexual's own view of himself and his way of living. The same is true for divorce, multiple marriage, and premarital cohabitation. I have never seen a show or documentary, however, that presented homeopathic medicine, say, with similar sympathy, putting opponents of this school of thought ("Marcus Welby, M.D.," for example) on the defensive. Of the number of programs set, like "The Mary Tyler Moore Show," in a television newsroom, I have never seen one that called into question this mode of collecting the news, disseminating it, arousing interest in it, and securing financial support for the enterprise. I could make the same comment about a long list of antiestablishment viewpoints, likewise negatively reinforced in this manner by television's program policy.

29. *Wall Street Journal,* May 13, 1975.

30. "Hot 1 Baltimore" was not the only show to see that promise. "Maude" dedicated at least one episode to the subject; so did "M*A*S*H." MTM Enterprises got into the act: Rhoda dated an

attractive man who turned out to be a homosexual. That was good for a laugh in the days when she was looking desperately for a husband. A clinical approach to homosexuality furnished the subject of an episode of "Marcus Welby, M.D." In September 1975, ABC opened "On the Rocks," starring a team of prisoners, one of whom is homosexual. By now, the presentation of homosexuality as just one more perfectly normal "option" for consenting adults is a commonplace on network television.

31. The insatiable search for new markets to be created or developed knows no bounds. Advertisers wonder whether there is a sufficient number of illegal aliens in the country to warrant locating and developing the "illegal alien market," beginning with ethnic foods. See *Advertising Age,* July 14, 1975. The classic one, of course, is pornography which develops those suffering from all kinds of sexual pathologies into "a market."

32. See "Public Interest Groups Tap into Entertainment TV," *Access* 18 (1975): pp. 8–11.

CHAPTER 15

1. Jerome Ohlsten, vice president and research director of Cunningham & Walsh, cited in Val Cardinale, "The Shortage in Research, Part II: The Larger Problem," *ANNY,* December 21, 1973. *ANNY* is the weekly newsletter of the Advertising Association of New York.

2. An advertising newsletter ran a series of articles on the subject. In one of them, an imposter revealed that she had become a semi-professional respondent who, with full knowledge of the recruiting agent, pretended to possess whatever characteristics were in demand on the days she reported for work. (Karen Wantuck, "The Shortage In Research, Part 1, Paid Panels," *ANNY,* December 14, 1973.)

A spokesman for the market-research people whose practices were under fire responded, "There are cheaters in every field, and researchers have no immunity in this one area." He closed with a call for "fresh thinking" and a nostalgic wish for a return to the "old traditions" of the field. (Paul Gerhold, president of the Advertising Research Foundation, quoted in Val Cardinale, op. cit.)

3. See, for example, The Network Project, Notebook Number Five, *Cable Television,* 1972; and also Stanford Research Institute, *The Outlook for Cable Television,* 1974. See also Monroe Price and John Wicklein, *Cable Television, a Guide for Citizen Action* (Philadelphia: Pilgrim Press Books, 1972), for a summary of the development of cable television and current policy issues communities are facing. *Broadcasting,* April 22, 1974, pp. 22–30, gives a summary of current regulations for cable television.

4. The coaxial cable has the capacity of bringing in at least twenty channels. The same cable could bring in forty, sixty, eighty, even a hundred channels. It's as if a giant switchboard set up at the cable company's headquarters, with a hundred or so terminals, were to activate only twelve of them leaving the rest unconnected.

    Many cable systems put some of those inactive channels to use for their own profit and the profit of companies renting them. Home Box Office (HBO), owned by Time, Inc., is a familiar example. A cable channel is rented to this company, reserved for its coded signal. A decoder attached to the subscriber's TV set allows only paying customers to bring in the movies HBO books. It's a system of prepaid ticket sales, the house guaranteed. The same system is used for sports spectaculars such as championship heavyweight bouts.

    In many areas, business firms pay to reserve their own channels, like HBO, using them for computer services, in-house training programs, conferences among widely dispersed subsidiaries, and the like. With slight adjustments to the set, facsimile newspapers can be delivered by cable channel. Some cable companies keep a few channels for their own use, booking entertainment programs and selling comercials just as over-the-air stations do. It's scarcely odd that two-thirds of today's cable systems have been bought up by media interests, dedicated to the time-honored American way of neutralizing competitors: "If you can't lick 'em, jine 'em."

The FCC, in token recognition of the principle that the community has a right to expect some social benefits in return for this juicy handout, requires all cable systems to maintain one channel for use by the public at large, without rental payment, and to provide access to a television camera, as well.

5.   "AdTel Featuring a Unique Complete System Capability, Dual-Cable Television." Promotional booklet issued by AdTel, 1973, p. 6.

6.   Ibid. p. 6.

7.   Ibid., p. 5.

8.   Ibid., p. 6.

9.   Ibid., p. 8.

10. Ibid., p. 11.

11. Occasionally clients are treated to minor bonuses, sort of like the give-away in breakfast-food packages: "[As] a little icing on the cake we give them attitudes as they relate to sales." (John Adler, president of AdTel, quoted in Philip H. Dougherty, *The New York Times,* November 9, 1969.)

12. The market-research firm was the Center for Research in Marketing at Peekskill, New York. A spokesman for the firm told me it no longer operates the cable system. Their early clients were Du-Pont, General Mills, Bristol-Myers, Dow Chemical, and Brown and Williamson Tobacco Company. See also Richard K. Doan and Denis Govern, "How They Turned a Town into a Test Tube," *TV Guide,* December 10, 1966.

13. Jeff Greenfield, "The Fight for $60,000 a Half-Minute," *The New York Times Magazine,* September 7, 1975. The statement is attributed to Mr. William Rubens, head of research at NBC.

14. Robert Choate, *The Selling of the Child* (mimeographed: Washington, D.C., February 27, 1973). p. 32.

15. *Annual Report,* 1972, p. 1.

16. AdTel promotional booklet, *op. cit.,* p. 8.

17. Philip H. Dougherty, *The New York Times,* November 9, 1969.

18. AdTel promotional booklet, p. 37.

19. The rules are published in Federal Register, May 30, 1974. See also

20. Joel Axelrod, "Choosing the Best Advertising Alternative," (New York: Association of National Advertisers, December 1971), p. 26. He adds, "Design the test so that when the respondent is interviewed he does not know he is being interviewed about his exposure to an advertisement or commercial."

CHAPTER 16

1. The Gene Reilly Group, Inc., *The Child,* 1972, unpaged. See also their advertising brochure entitled "The Gene Reilly Group, A Qualitative Research Firm," undated.

2. The company has discontinued its syndicated offer and is selling single volumes to clients whose special interests they serve. For example, Le Sueur's Green Giant Co. has bought Volume 2; Fisher-Price Toys (a Quaker Oats subsidiary) has bought Volume 4. So did the Milton Bradley Co.

3. Personal communication. See also *The Child,* op. cit., and also Philip H. Dougherty, "Advertising, Important Kidding," *The New York Times,* September 18, 1972. A list of Mr. Reilly's clients would include the American Dairy Association; Bristol-Myers, Inc.; Dairy Development, Inc.; Fisher-Price Toys; General Foods; Hasbro Industries; Ideal Toys; Lever Bros.; Miles Laboratories; Nabisco; National Licorice Company; the Nestle Company; Rainbow Crafts; Xerox Learning Systems.

4. Child Research Service, quoted on p. 31 of Robert B. Choate, *The Selling of the Child,* mimeographed, Washington, D.C., February 27, 1973. This document was presented as testimony before The Consumer Subcommittee of the Committee on Commerce of the U.S. Senate. It contains an excellent summary based on Mr. Choate's canvass of research firms studying children. Since most of this material is not usually in the public domain, I have relied on his study for many of the examples cited in this section. The quotations appearing above are textual citations of public-relations materials issued by these companies, collected by Mr. Choate and his staff, plus interviews he conducted with the research firms' representatives.

5. Ibid., p. 29.

6. Personal communication from a special consultant to Gene Reilly. "Buying into" a poll means simply contracting with the polling firm to include in their questionnaire a series of "piggyback" questions—questions that have nothing to do with the ostensible subject of the poll but which are added only to serve the needs of special clients.

    The consultant, a professor at one of our distinguished universities, refused to send me a copy of the piggy-back questions, explaining that the information was "proprietary."

7. Robert Choate, op. cit., p. 25.

8. Ibid., p. 31.

9. Ibid., p. 42.

10. Ibid., p. 7.

11. Ibid., p. 37.

12. Ibid., p. 23.

13. The procedure was originally introduced by the researchers at Children's Television Workshop in their early attempts to be certain that the programs they were developing for the first cycle of

"Sesame Street" would indeed keep the children's heads turned toward the screen. Dr. Gerald S. Lesser is Professor at Harvard University's School of Education and chief consultant to the company that produces "Sesame Street" (Children's Television Workshop). I asked his opinion about implanting electrodes to ensure the children's attention to the lessons. His reply expressed honest indignation but mentioned no rationale for drawing the line at what he called "a lunatic possibility" as opposed to this cruder and less efficient manner of doing the same thing. Personal communication.

14. Robert Choate, op. cit., pp. 23–24.

15. Melvin Herlitzer and Carl Heyel, *The Youth Market* (New York: Media Books, 1970), p. 312.

16. Robert Choate, op. cit., p. 30.

17. Ibid., p. 26.

18. The entertainment is followed by a questionnaire session and the children are again asked to select a product from the array. Subgroups among whom the client's products have gained choices can be studied to find out what special appeals "worked" and for whom. Subgroups among whom the client's product has lost choices can be studied to find out what appeals turned those children away.

19. *The New York Times,* January 6, 1975.

20. Brochure for Audience Studies, Inc. Democratic theory in the market-research set does not entitle such children to a "vote."

21. Les Brown, *The New York Times,* April 4, 1974.

22. *The New York Times,* April 1, 1974.

23. Office of Social Research, Department of Economics and Research, CBS/Broadcast Group, mimeographed, February 1974, 77 pages.

24. Ibid.

25. The five were: "Valley of the Dinosaurs," "Shazam!," "The Harlem Globetrotters Popcorn Machine," "The Hudson Brothers Razzle Dazzle Comedy Hour," and "The U.S. of Archie."

   The practice spreads. Seven more Ph.D.s have found employment as consultants to the trade association of the advertising business, asked to validate the propriety of certain television commercials beamed at children. They are consultants to The Children's Advertising Review Unit of the National Advertising Division of the Council of Better Business Bureaus, established as an aftermath of an abortive attempt by the Federal Trade Commission to ban premiums as an advertising appeal to children. The seven consultants, named in September 1974, were: Dr. Lynette Friedrich of Pennsylvania State, Dr. Norge Jerome of the University of Kansas Medical School, Dr. Eli Rubinstein of the State University of New York (Stony Brook), Dr. Scott Ward of the Harvard Business School, Dr. Gerald S. Lesser of the Harvard School of Education, Dr. Paul H. Mussen of Berkeley, and Dr. Jerome Singer of Yale.

26. One of the most charming discussions I have found that explores the characteristics of authentic art for children and its role in their development appears in Welleran Polternees, *All Mirrors Are Magic Mirrors* (LaJolla, Cal.: Green Tiger Press, 1972). See also Bruno Bettelheim, *The Uses of Enchantment: The Meaning and Importance of Fairy Tales* (New York: Alfred A. Knopf, 1976).

CHAPTER 17

1. The term *media research* is not quite appropriate, since most of those who specialize in the field study not media but "subjects"—human beings who file in and out of social-psychological laboratories, answer endless questionnaires, fill out detailed forms and diaries, providing the business with inexhaustible information about themselves—while "the media" virtually escape scrutiny.

The aim of it all is to link the behavior of "subjects" back to their exposure to stimuli thought to be similar to the television "stimulus"—the same sort of investigations reported in previous chapters.

2. These instructions, passed on to writers for the show "Man Against Crime" (1949–54), are quoted in Eric Barnouw, *The Image Empire,* op. cit., p. 23.

3. "Consider the dimensions of this index. . . . One might wish to weigh slapstick violence less heavily than dramatic mayhem. . . . Why should a unit increase in the ratio P_V/P be worth fifty times a similar increase in the ratio R/P," and so on. Bruce M. Owen, "Measuring Violence on Television: The Gerbner Index," Staff Research Paper, Xerox copy, OTP-SP-7, Office of Telecommunication Policy, June 1972.

4. See, for example, Jack B. Haskins, "The Effects of Violence in the Printed Media," Appendix III-H in Robert K. Baker and Sandra J. Ball, *Mass Media and Violence, Vol. IX,* A Report to the National Commission on the Causes and Prevention of Violence (Washington, D.C.: U.S. Government, November 1969), pp. 493–502, for a discussion from this point of view. Professor Haskins concludes that any undesirable effect of violence in television or other mass media can be written off as a cost of doing business. "[It] is probably only operative among some small fraction of the population who have predispositions toward such violence in the first place, and even then only under restricted circumstances . . ." (p. 501). See also "Introduction," p. vii in the same volume.

5. A leading exponent of this viewpoint is Professor Seymour Feshback. See his chapter, "The Catharsis Effect," which appears as Appendix III-E in Robert K. Baker and Sandra J. Ball, op. cit., pp. 461–72. See also his *Television and Aggression* (with Robert Singer; San Francisco: Jossey Bass, Inc., 1971).

6. George Gerbner, "Scenario for Violence," *Human Behavior* 4, 10 (October 1975): 64–69.

7. The hearings of this committee appear in *Juvenile Delinquency, Television Programs,* Subcommittee to Investigate Juvenile Delinquency of the Committee of the Judiciary, U.S. Senate, June 5, October 19–20, 1954.

8. Quoted in Surgeon General's Scientific Advisory Committee on Television and Social Behavior, *Initial Operations, June—October 1969,* op. cit., pp. 2–3. The hearings of the Dodd Subcommittee appear in "Effects on Young People of Violence and Crime Portrayed on Television," in Hearings before the Subcommittee to Investigate Juvenile Delinquency of the Committee on the Judiciary of the United States Senate. June 8, 9, 13, 15, 16, and 19, July 27 and 28, 1961; January 24 and May 11 and 14, 1962; and also July 30, 1964. (Washington, D. C.: U.S. Government 1963 and also 1965).

9. Robert K. Baker and Sandra J. Ball, op. cit., p. 375. Italics in original.

10. Letter from Senator Pastore to Secretary Finch, March 5, 1969. Quoted in Surgeon General's Scientific Advisory Committee on Television and Social Behavior, *Television and Growing Up: The Impact of Televised Violence,* Report to the Surgeon General, mimeographed (Washington, D.C.: U.S. Government, January 1972), p. 21.

11. For example, only two of the so-called experiments show the "subjects" any television at all. The nonexperimental studies are mainly surveys which accept hearsay evidence at face value. The "subjects," whose behavior is to be evaluated scientifically, provide their own characterizations of their own behavior as "aggressive" or "nonaggressive." Teachers' reports on their pupils and mothers' estimations of their offspring are accepted as if they were accurate diagnoses of psychological traits; and so on.

    I have analyzed this research in detail in "Science in Wonderland," *Hearings on the Surgeon General's Report by the Scientific Advisory Committee on Television and Social Behavior,* March

21–24, 1972. Hearings before the Subcommittee on Communications of the Committee on Commerce, U.S. Senate, (Washington, D.C.: U.S. Government, 1972), pp. 81–88.

12. Surgeon General's Scientific Advisory Committee on Television and Social Behavior. *Television and Growing Up: The Impact of Televised Violence,* Report to the Surgeon General, mimeographed (Washington, D.C.: U.S. Government, 1972), pp. 18–19.

13. Ibid., p. 7.

14. Hearings before the Subcommittee on Communications of the Committee on Commerce on the Surgeon General's Report by the Scientific Advisory Committee on Television and Social Behavior (Washington, D.C.: U.S. Government, 1972).

15. Jesse Steinfeld, "TV Violence *Is* Harmful," *Reader's Digest,* May 1973, p. 38. The article appeared after Dr. Steinfeld left federal office. While he was still Surgeon General, he said, "I think the Committee report contains sufficient data to justify action . . . on the part of responsible authorities, the TV industry, the Government, the citizens." (Hearings, 1972, op. cit., pp. 27–28.)

16. George Gerbner and Larry Gross, *Violence Profile No. 6* (Philadelphia, Pa.: The Annenberg School of Communications, 1974).

17. Reported by Maureen Christopher in *Advertising Age,* April 14, 1975. Mr. Wiley confirmed his opinion in a letter to me dated January 8, 1976.

18. The details of the family-viewing-time provision appear in Federal Communications Commission, *Report on the Broadcast of Violent, Indecent, Obscene Material,* mimeographed, Washington, D.C., February 19, 1975. See especially footnote 13, p. 8. ". . . the networks have informed us that a standard based on 9:00 PM local time would require prohibitively expensive separate programs transmitted to each time zone." This "explanation" seems to have satisfied the commissioners; at least, the situation prevails as of this writing.

19. A. C. Nielsen projections of nationwide audiences for November
     1974 calculated that 2,210,000 children age two to eleven watched
     "Police Woman" each week on NBC from 10 to 11 P.M. on Fridays.
     Playing opposite this show at the time "family viewing time" was
     proposed and ratified was ABC's "Kolchak," which attracted 3,-
     310,000 children of the same age. At 8 P.M., about 18,000,000
     two-to-eleven-year-olds were watching television, some of them, of
     course, in the central and mountain time zones. Even at midnight,
     nearly a million children under high-school age customarily watch
     television. (*Variety,* April 15, 1975.) See also Jack Lyle and Heidi
     R. Hoffman, "Explorations in Patterns of Television Viewing by
     Preschool-Age Children," in *Television and Social Behavior,* Vol.
     IV, op. cit., pp. 257–73.
          A study of more than 500 slum children in the Bedford-Stuyve-
     sant area of New York found that over half the children in the
     families investigated turn on the television set themselves without
     asking permission of any adult. (John Culhane, "Report Card on
     Sesame Street," *The New York Times Magazine,* May 24, 1970.)

20. *Writers Guild* of America, West Inc. v. *FCC,* 423 F.Supp. 1064
     (November 4, 1976).

21. The networks do not hold licenses. The stations each network
     owns and operates, however, do.

22. Shortly after the research reviewed by the Surgeon General's
     Scientific Advisory Committee was published, a symposium was
     held at the University of Massachusetts on the effects of psycho-
     logical research on public and private policy. Children's television
     was chosen as the central theme. Network representatives who had
     agreed to attend withdrew the agreement. Frederic Hunter, "Vio-
     lence on TV," *Christian Science Monitor,* September 9, 1973, and
     also personal communication from Professor Daniel Anderson,
     one of the cosponsors of the conference.

23. Seymour Feshback and Robert Singer, *Television and Aggression*
     (San Francisco: Jossey Bass, Inc., 1971).

24. Robert K. Baker and Sandra J. Ball, op. cit., pp. 593–614.

25. I have analyzed some of these studies in Rose K. Goldsen, "NBC's
    Make Believe Research on Television Violence," *Trans/Action* 8,
    12 (October 1971): 28–35, and also "Why Do They Call It Media
    Research," mimeographed, Cornell University, Department of So-
    ciology, 1971.

26. "Report on the Broadcast of Violent, Indecent and Obscene Mate-
    rial," February 19, 1975, p. 2.

27. John Revett, *Advertising Age,* April 21, 1975.

28. Richard Doan, *TV Guide,* April 26, 1975.

CHAPTER 18

1. George Gerbner, "Scenario for Violence," *Human Behavior* 4, 10
    (October 1975): 64–69, p. 68.

2. Ibid., p. 69.

3. George Gerbner, *Human Behavior,* ibid., and also "Violence in
    Television Drama: Trends and Symbolic Function," Surgeon Gen-
    eral's Scientific Advisory Committee on Television and Social Be-
    havior, *Television and Social Behavior, Volume I, Media Content
    and Control* (Washington, D.C. U.S. Government, 1972), pp. 28–
    187.

4. Bill Davidson, "The 'S.W.A.T.' Shootout," *TV Guide,* June 7,
    1975.

5. On television crime shows, the cops and detectives in the employ
    of the state often behave in a manner indicating either ignorance
    of or contempt for constitutional principles protecting private citi-
    zens from unlawful entry, search, and seizure in the name of police
    power. "Today even the most blatantly illegal and unconstitu-
    tional behavior of police officers is glorified by an endless stream
    of television police dramas . . . What started off as merely fictional
    entertainment has now begun to have the political effect of 'soften-

ing up' public opinion and making it more accepting of such police conduct." Stephen Arons and Ethan Katsh, "How TV Cops Flout The Law," *Saturday Review*, May 19, 1977. The two authors, professors of legal studies at the University of Massachusetts, Amherst, monitored television crime shows from fall 1974 to spring 1976, to determine how legal and constitutional issues were treated. The article reports their findings.

CHAPTER 19

1. See Richard M. Polsky, *Getting to Sesame Street: Origins of the Children's Television Workshop* (New York: Praeger Publishers, 1974) for a summary of the origins of Children's Television Workshop.

2. "For example, even if televised aggression were found to be effective in holding children's attention, we would simply refuse to use it." Gerald S. Lesser, *Children and Television* (New York: Random House, 1974), p. 31.

3. "Sesame Street" programs are difficult to avoid. For example, during the first semester of the 1974–75 television season, public television stations in my receiving area, Ithaca, New York, scheduled the program three times on Saturdays, six times on Sundays, and four times each weekday for a total of twenty-nine hours a week. "Electric Company," CTW's companion show directed at slightly older children with reading disabilities, was programed a total of sixteen hours a week.

4. As of this writing, commercial television comedy and action-adventure crime shows are being used in school curricula in Philadelphia, Pennsylvania; Jacksonville, Florida; Mount Vernon, New York; Benton Harbor, Michigan; Greenwich, Connecticut; and Brooklyn, New York. See appendix to chapter 19, p. 344.

5. In 1975, overseas versions of "Sesame Street" in four different languages were accepted for broadcast in sixty-nine countries.

"Sesame Street" foreign-language productions follow essentially the same format described in the text. In Mexico, Brazil, and West Germany the segments on the streets were produced nationally by companies that have contracted with CTW for the coproduction rights. Other countries use the original English version with or without dubbing, either in its entirety or in half-hour versions spliced together from CTW material. See *CTW '72, A Special Report from the Children's Television Workshop,* New York, 1972. See also *Editorial Backgrounder: Sesame Street Overseas,* April 1973. Latest foreign sale of the show is to the Arabian Gulf States Joint Program Production Institution in Kuwait, which will put up $7,500,000 in return for all rights to the Arabic-language version of the first CTW series in Arabic. The Institution is funded by Gulf States to produce educational television for Bahrain, Iraq, Kuwait, Oman, Qatar, Saudi Arabia and the United Arab Emirates. Production of the Arab pilot is the first step. The first season of the Arabic version will include 130 half hours due to begin early in 1978. *Variety,* May 4, 1977.

6. "Remarks by David D. Connell and Dr. Edward L. Palmer, before the International Seminar on Broadcaster/Research Cooperation in Mass Communication Research," Xerox copy, University of Leicester, Leicester, England, December 19, 1970, p. 20.

7. Testimony of Joan Ganz Cooney, *Hearings before the Subcommittee on Communications of the Committee on Commerce,* U.S. Senate, April 30 and May 1, 1969. (Washington, D.C.: U.S. Government, 1969), p. 88.

8. See George Gerbner, "Teacher Image in Mass Culture: Symbolic Function of the 'Hidden Curriculum,' " in George Gerbner, Larry P. Gross, and William H. Melody, eds., *Communications, Technology and Social Policy* (New York: John Wiley & Sons, 1973), pp. 265–92. The article analyzes the stereotypes of teachers appearing in worldwide television. In the United States, the dominant stereotype shows teachers as weak and powerless (which includes ridiculous); a subdominant stereotype shows them as

powerful but evil. The combinations weak and evil or powerful and good rarely appear.

9. The overseas version in Spanish is sponsored by the Xerox Corporation. Each show is introduced by a hand which writes on the screen X-E-R-O-X, while a voiceover explains, "This program has been made possible by a grant from The Xerox Corporation." Throughout the hemisphere, it is often referred to as "the Xerox Program."

10. Test results showing consistent increments among U.S. children exposed to the program are summarized in Gerald Lesser, *Children and Television* (New York: Random House, 1974). A critical reexamination of U.S. test results appears in Thomas D. Cook, Hilary Appleton, Ross Conner, Ann Shaffer, Gary Tamkin, and Stephen J. Weber, *"Sesame Street" Revisited* (New York: Russell Sage Foundation, 1975).

    I have seen studies that analyzed test results compiled for overseas samples of children in Puerto Rico, Mexico, Chile, and West Germany. Only one study runs counter to the general finding that overseas children exposed to the program score higher on achievement tests than their counterparts who have not been equivalently exposed; or exceed their own scores before exposure. The maverick study is the work of Instituto Nacional de Ciencias del Comportamiento y de la Actitud Publica. A preliminary report on this research claims that rural Mexican preschool children register no discernible gains after exposure to the programs. This is in contrast to children from nonrural areas among whom gains were registered. See Rogelio Diaz Guerrero and Wayne H. Holtzman, "Learning by Televised 'Plaza Sesamo' in Mexico," *Journal of Educational Psychology* 66 (October 1974): 632–43.

11. Steve Austin is the hero of ABC's series "Six Million Dollar Man," which opened in the second semester of the 1973–74 television year. After experimenting with various camera effects to convey the notion of Steve's extraordinary speed and power, the producers hit upon the slow-motion technique as most effective.

12. George Orwell, *1984* (New York: Harcourt Brace Jovanovich, 1949). See also Herbert Schiller, *Mass Communications and American Empire* (Boston: Beacon Press, 1971).

13. John Culhane, "Report Card on Sesame Street," *The New York Times Magazine*, May 24, 1970.

14. "Sesame Street," rejected by the BBC in Britain, was bought by their commercial network, the Independent Television Authority. (By April 1975, however, the BBC was willing to buy "The Electric Company," CTW's remedial reading series.) In Peru, the Ministry of Education rejected the series. So did the Soviet Union. In each case, the rejection was based on the claim that the programs project a particular set of values appropriate to a particular set of social relations in a particular class within a particular social system.

The head of children's programing in Poland, however, is on record endorsing the programs as culturally neutral, saying the only cultural adaptations necessary are those that "give the Polish child a frame of reference which he can recognize. . . . For example, milk in Poland comes in bottles, not in cartons . . . [Still] A square is a square both in Poland and the United States and children's cognitive processes are the same the world over." (*The New York Times*, March 20, 1973.)

Critical articles about "Sesame Street" and its foreign-language spinoffs that stress the values in its hidden agenda are easy to find in foreign sources. See, for example, Armand Mattelart, "El Imperialismo en Busca de la Contrarevolucion Cultural," in *Communicacion y Cultura* No. 1 (July 1973), Buenos Aires and Santiago, pp. 146–224, as well as his *La Cultura Como Empresa Multinacional* (Mexico City: Era, 1974), pp. 84–100.

Similar critical articles are beginning to appear in U.S. sources. See, for example, "Down Sesame Street," New York: The Network Project, *Notebook Number Six*, November 1973; and also Thomas D. Cook and others, *"Sesame Street" Revisited*, op. cit.

15. See, for example, Edward T. Hall, *The Silent Language* (Greenwich, Conn.: Fawcett Publications, 1959); and idem, *The Hidden Dimension* (Garden City, New York: Anchor Books, 1966).

16. For a discussion of the role of music and musical beats in evolution, see Suzanne K. Langer, *Feeling and Form* (New York: Scribner, 1953), especially chapter 8. See also Lewis Thomas, "The Music of This Sphere," in *Lives of a Cell* (New York: Bantam Books, 1974).

17. "[What] teaching calls for is this: to let learn. The real teacher, in fact, lets nothing else be learned than—learning. His conduct, therefore, often produces the impression that we properly learn nothing from him, if by 'learning' we now suddenly understand merely the procurement of useful information. The teacher ... has to learn to let them learn. ... We must keep our eyes fixed firmly on the pure relation between the teacher and the taught." Martin Heidegger, *What Is Called Thinking?* (New York: Harper & Row, Harper Torchbooks, 1954), pp. 15–16.

18. See Norman Fruchter, "Games in the Arena: Movement Propaganda and the Culture of the Spectacle," *Liberation Magazine,* May 1971, pp. 4–16.

CHAPTER 20

1. Earnings from nonbroadcast activities in 1972–73 were twelve times higher than earnings in 1968–70. *CTW Annual Report,* 1973, p. 25.

2. CTW advertisement in *Time,* December 18, 1972. Franchised products include comic books, magazines, records, stick-ons, toys, games, puppets, and other playthings, school equipment, household objects, and many others.

3. "Try Spider-man Vitamins from Hudson and I'll send you a free Spider-man poster," says the advertisement on the back cover of a Spider-man comic book (January 1975). "Spider-man Vitamins are great! They're new! They're fun! And they're really delicious! ... No hassle with Mom and Dad either." Cadence Industries

Corp. owns both Marvel Comics, Inc., and Hudson Pharmaceutical Company.

As this book goes to press, Hudson and the Federal Trade Commission have agreed to a consent order that may restrict the practice. The FTC would prohibit Hudson from using Spider-man in television ads for vitamins aimed at the "child market"—but only during certain hours: 6:00 A.M. to 9:05 P.M. eastern time, 5:00 A.M. to 8:05 P.M. central. (FTC 523–3830, File No. 762–3054.) At all other hours, presumably it is the responsibility of the children themselves to shut their eyes and stick their fingers in their ears; or perhaps the parents are expected to whisk them away from the television set when those twenty- and thirty-second commercials, unannounced, flash on the screen. Fred Flintstone, Bugs Bunny, and The Monsters are still on the payroll at Miles and Bristol-Myers. Hudson's next step a few months later was to test a vitamin commercial whose refrain is "They look like Spider-man." *Advertising Age,* February 7, 1977.

4. *Advertising Age,* July 14, 1975.

5. *Advertising Age,* July 29, 1974.

6. The scratch-and-sniff book uses transparant microcapsules which contain microscopic droplets of fragrant oils within a polymeric shell. The encapsulated scent is applied to paper by high-speed printing equipment, where it remains as a stable, strong, colorless, and odorless coating until the capsules are broken. A light scratch releases the scent. There are enough encapsulated droplets in a small area for dozens of scratches and sniffs before the scent disappears. The process may be applied not only to paper but also to toys, games, novelties, educational materials, merchandising aids, T-shirts, pajamas, and so on. One company that specializes in the process claims that "Micro-Scent increases sales potential by combining visual display and fragrance," and refers to "this sweet smell of sell." "From pine to peppermint, raspberries to roses—this is the way to sell seasons, products, almost anything, luringly." Promotional material issued by NCR Appleton Papers Division, Capsular Products, 9095

Washington Church Road, Miamisburg, Ohio, 45342.

Our culture does not emphasize the sense of smell, rendering it the most negatively reinforced of the several senses. Still, it is not a sense to be trifled with. Children between the ages of three and six seem to have a strong drive to sniff. Parents and other people who care about them must be especially vigilant to monitor this tendency since they will sniff glue, gasoline, and other commonplace and easily available materials that have stupefying properties. Control of smell, moreover, controls associational links.

7. Source: *Sesame Street 1973, Playthings, Books and Records,* promotional material issued by Children's Television Workshop; and also personal communication with CTW Products Division sales staff.

8. See Ariel Dorfman and Armand Mattelart, *How to Read Donald Duck* (New York: International General Editions, 1975), and also Armand Mattelart, "La Industria Cultural No Es Una Industria Ligera. Hacia La Fase Superior Del Monopolismo Cultural," *Casa de Las Americas,* March–April 1973. See also Ariel Dorfman and Manuel Jofre, *Superman y Sus Amigos Del Alma* (Buenos Aires: Editorial Galerna, 1974). These sources discuss the hidden agenda in the Disney cartoons as well as other mass produced cultural materials in international syndicated sales and analyze the structure that ensures their international coverage and penetration.

9. Christopher Finch, *The Art of Walt Disney: From Mickey Mouse to the Magic Kingdoms* (Burbank, California: Walt Disney Productions, 1975), p. 152.

10. Ibid. pp. 113–114. See also Herbert Schiller, *The Mind Managers* (Boston: Beacon Press, 1973), for an analysis of the worldwide organization of the Disney Empire.

11. The division's brochure (undated) lists a number of ways a business might cash in on the Walt Disney character merchandising opportunity. The list includes Christmas merchandising programs, animated character displays, television commercials, radio

commercials, retail merchandising aids, full-color display posters, Mickey Mouse costumes (on a limited basis only), and store give-aways. The Character Merchandise Division also includes a sub-division that provides professional merchandising counsel.

12. William H. Melody, *Children's Television: Economics and Public Policy*, mimeographed (Philadelphia, Pa.: Annenberg School of Communications). "The result was some programs for children that were widely acclaimed for their value for children. But the more prevalent occurrence was that programs were blatantly con-structed to be in the sponsor's selling interests, rather than chil-dren's." (pp. 57–58.)

13. *History of the Mickey Mouse Club, (Long Form)* (Annenberg, Ca.: Walt Disney Productions, undated), pp. 13, 17. This publication will be referred to below as *History MMC.*

14. Ibid., p. 17.
    My home-town newspaper participated in the love affair be-tween "The Mickey Mouse Club" and the press. Mickey himself graced the cover of *"Leisure,"* The Ithaca Journal's insert, on February 15, 1975. Two inside pages were also devoted to the return of the club and the Mouseketeers. "Sold more wristwatches than Spiro Agnew," says one admiring comment.

15 *History MMC*, p. 4.

16. Ibid., p. 16.

17. *History MMC,* p. 15. This source cites the title as *The Dairy Story* and mentions only eight episodes. SFM provided the corrections as they appear above.

18. Other early sponsors included B & B Enterprises, Bristol Myers Company, Campbell Soup Company, the Coca-Cola Company, General Mills, Inc., S. C. Johnson (Gold Seal Wax), Lettuce, Inc., Mars, Mattell, Miles Laboratories, Nunn, M & M, Morton Salt, SOS (scouring pads), Vicks Chemicals, and Welch's Grape Juice. When the program was syndicated first time around, sponsors also

included B. F. Goodrich and the 3M Company. *History MMC,* p. 14.

19. A media-buying service such as SFM is a subcontractor for advertising agencies acting on behalf of their clients. Such a company is retained to negotiate exposure for advertisements and commercials prepared by or for the agency, under the most favorable conditions for the client. SFM includes among its clients some that covet child audiences. Among these are Crayola, Child Guidance Toys, and Hunt-Wesson Snak Paks. SFM's Mickey Mouse Club venture was so successful that less than a year later the company did the same with "The Adventures of Rin Tin Tin," distributing 164 recycled episodes of the twenty-year-old show free to all takers. The original television series, whose roots go back more than twenty years to the original *Rin Tin Tin* movies, was produced for network showings from 1954 to 1958 and repeated on network time through 1964. The resuscitated series combines new shots in color with original episodes tinted sepia in an effort to reduce the contrast. The new dog star is Rin Tin Tin VII. Les Brown, *The New York Times,* February 8, 1976.

20. Other countries that have broadcast the "Mickey Mouse Club" programs are France (9 years), Canada (8 years, 4 months), Italy (7 years), Switzerland (5 years), Mexico (4 years), Chile (3 years), and Japan (3 years). Countries that have run the programs a year or longer are: Spain, Austria, Colombia, Equador, Panama, Peru, Uruguay, Venezuela. *History MMC,* p. 3.

21. *Variety,* November 20, 1974.

22. One of SFM's executives provided me with much of the information reported in this chapter, including a press kit, letters and documents showing coverage, tie-in sales, and samples of merchandise produced by companies that had bought the Disney franchise.

23. "Remarks of Clay T. Whitehead," Sigma Delta Chi, Indianapolis, December 18, 1972. Reprinted in Marvin Barrett, ed., *The Politics*

of Broadcasting (New York: Thomas Y. Crowell Co., 1973), pp. 228–34.

24. Karl Marx and Frederick Engels, *The German Ideology, Part One,* C. J. Arthur, ed. (International Publishing Co., 1970). The applicability of the concept to other chapters in this volume should be apparent. See especially the discussion of what seem to be purely technical research procedures in chapters 15, 16, and 17.

25. One aftermath of the "payola scandals" of the 1960s was an amendment to Section 317 of the Communications Act of 1934, specifying this practice as illegal. All paid material on radio or television must be clearly identified as such.

26. Still another prototype is being tested nationally as the live stage show, *Disney on Parade,* tours the country. The producers invite advertisers to contract for "tie-ins" with the show. Those who do, buy the privilege of seeing their products named, exhibited, even worked into the show's entertainment material as part of the dramatic action and the "business." (*The New York Times,* August 15, 1973.) In short, this is a show made up of explicit plugs, fly-bys, coattails, and commercials. It does not contain plugola—it *is* plugola, ideological and otherwise. It remains to be seen how long it takes before the model is openly adopted by the rest of television, not just game shows. The idea has been developed by other agencies such as Mallory Factor Associates, whose director explains how he produces an "entertainment package" aiming to "maximize effect at point of sale" for clients such as the New York Bank for Savings, Central Federal Savings of Long Island, United Mutual, American Savings Bank, and E. F. Hutton & Co. These staid financial institutions are not above moving right smack into the midway. *Advertising Age,* July 19, 1976.

27. See appendix to chapter 13, page 327, for discussions of Arbitron rating system.

28. *History MMC,* p. 3.

29. *Ithaca Journal,* "Leisure," February 15, 1975.

30. See George Gerbner, "Technology, Society and Symbols: The Need for Cultural Indicators," paper prepared for International Symposium on Communications, University of Pennsylvania, March 23–25, 1972, for an interesting discussion of the way that keeping track of cultural indicators could serve public policy.

31. "History of Hanna-Barbera Productions," mimeographed, Hanna-Barbera Productions, Inc., Hollywood, California, undated. The vice president and general manager of Hanna-Barbera Enterprises announced that 200 new toys, dolls, and games bearing images franchised by his company are to be backed with over ten million dollars worth of television advertising. *Advertising Age,* February 16, 1976. The figure does not include television exposure of these images through routine network broadcasts of Hanna-Barbera series and on independent stations through syndicated buys.

32. *Advertising Age,* October 18, 1975.

33. "The Howdy Doody Show," a relic of radio days (1947–60), began to enjoy a revival in 1971 as Buffalo Bob Smith, its original host, made a tour of college campuses. The show was produced by NBC Enterprises, which also licenses products bearing its symbols. Companies aiming to create a market out of the original fans of the old series, now grown to adulthood, are still buying those rights. *Variety* (April 21, 1971) reported such purchases by a food service chain, companies turning out record albums, sweatshirts, T-shirts, and a special line of Howdy Doody hotpants.

　　Many shows that played on television during the early years of nationwide coverage are now enjoying a revival as syndicating companies offer them for sale to independent stations under much the same terms as "The Mickey Mouse Club." These shows include "Rin Tin Tin," "The Jack Benny Show," "The Phil Silvers Show," "Burns and Allen," "You Bet Your Life" (Groucho Marx), "The Honeymooners" (Jackie Gleason), and "Ozzie and Harriet."

34. Ron Goulart, *The Assault on Childhood* (Los Angeles: Sherbourne Press, 1969), pp. 102–3.

35. Ibid.

36. See, for example, the advertisement for "Little Rascals," in *Variety*, April 9, 1975. After twenty years of selling franchising rights for properties such as "Bewitched," "The Monkees," "The Partridge Family," and "Little Rascals"; as we go to press Hone$t Ed branches out on his own, adding to his role as licensing/merchandising representative that of literary agent. Advertisement in *Publishers Weekly*, August 2, 1976

37. *The New York Times*, June 20, 1974.

38. Tom Shales, *The Ithaca Journal*, "Leisure," February 15, 1975.

39. Aldous Huxley, *Brave New World* (New York: Harper Bros., 1932). See also E. L. Doctorow, *The Book of Daniel* (New York: Random House, 1971) especially pp. 285 ff. for an insightful discussion of Disney World from this point of view.

CHAPTER 21

1. For an interesting discussion of this theme, see Hannah Arendt's essay, "On Violence," *New York Review of Books*, February 27, 1969.

2. John Howard Griffin, *Black Like Me* (Boston: Houghton Mifflin, 1961).

3. Roberta Cowell, *Roberta Cowell's Own Story By Herself*, (London: William Heineman, Ltd., 1954).

4. So-called structuralists in biology, psychology, anthropology, and linguistics suggest that, built into the brain's very structure, there must be certain biologically determined models that are species-specific. These models help members of the species recognize cer-

tain patterns essential to species survival. Sensory stimuli hit the sense organs every which way; they must be arranged in an organized configuration in order to be perceived as information. By virtue of the built-in model, the individual is able to recognize patterns in what would otherwise be random stimuli, casting them up against the model and discerning similarities in configuration. In other words, the model acts like a biologically programed metaphor. Other models are added as a result of experiences a single individual undergoes in his lifetime: learning.

Note that according to this view, the mind may be seen as a series of overlaid models—in other words, the mind is made of metaphors. See for example: Noam Chomsky, "The Formal Nature of Language," in E. H. Lenneberg, *Biological Foundations of Language* (New York: John Wiley, 1967), and idem, *Language and Mind* (New York: Harcourt Brace and World, 1968). See especially Claude Levi-Straus, *The Savage Mind* (Chicago: University of Chicago Press, 1968), *The Raw and the Cooked* (New York: Harper Torchbooks, 1969), and *From Honey to Ashes,* (New York: Harper & Row, 1973). See also Karl Pribram, *Languages of the Brain* (New York: Prentice-Hall, 1971); Robert E. Ornstein, *The Psychology of Consciousness* (San Francisco: W. H. Freeman, 1972); Roger W. Sperry, *Problems Outstanding in the Evolution of Brain Function* (New York: American Museum of Natural History, 1964); and Anneliese Pontius, "The Face in Sacred Art of The Upper Sepik River of New Guinea," *Journal of The American Medical Women's Association,* 29, 10 (Oct 1974 435–440)

5.   Aldous Huxley, *Brave New World* (New York: Harper Bros., 1932) pp. 12–14.

INDEX